More Praise for the *Best Food*

"This is a book worth devouring." —*Sacramento Bee*

"The cream of the crop of food writing compilations."
—*Milwaukee Journal Sentinel*

"An exceptional collection worth revisiting, this will be a surefire hit with epicureans and cooks." —*Publishers Weekly*, starred review

"If you're looking to find new authors and voices about food, there's an abundance to chew on here." —*Tampa Tribune*

"Fascinating to read now, this book will also be interesting to pick up a year from now, or ten years from now." —Popmatters.com

"Some of these stories can make you burn with a need to taste what they're writing about." —*Los Angeles Times*

"The book captures the gastronomic zeitgeist in a broad range of essays." —*San Jose Mercury News*

"The next best thing to eating there is." —*New York Metro*

"Stories for connoisseurs, celebrations of the specialized, the odd, or simply the excellent." —*Entertainment Weekly*

"Spans the globe and palate." —*Houston Chronicle*

"The perfect gift for the literate food lover."
—*Pittsburgh Post-Gazette*

"With this typically delectable and eclectic collection of culinary prose, editor Holly Hughes proves her point made in the intro that the death of 68-year-old *Gourmet* magazine a year ago didn't lead to the demise of quality food journalism . . . There's a mess of vital, provocative, funny and tender stuff . . . in these pages."
—*USA Today*

best *Food*
WRITING
2012

best *Food* WRITING
2012

Edited by

HOLLY HUGHES

Da Capo
LIFE
LONG

A Member of the
Perseus Books Group

Set in 11 point Bembo by the Perseus Books Group

Cataloging-in-Publication data for this book is available from the Library of Congress.

First Da Capo Press edition 2012
ISBN 978-0-7382-1603-4

Published by Da Capo Press
A Member of the Perseus Books Group
www.dacapopress.com

Da Capo Press books are available at special discounts for bulk purchases in the United States by corporations, institutions, and other organizations. For more information, please contact the Special Markets Department at the Perseus Books Group, 2300 Chestnut Street, Suite 200, Philadelphia, PA 19103, or call (800) 255-1514, or e-mail special.markets@perseusbooks.com.

10 9 8 7 6 5 4 3 2 1

Contents

Introduction ix
By Holly Hughes

Food Fights

On Killing, From HunterAnglerGardenerCook.com 2
By Hank Shaw

The Gumbo Chronicles, From *Outside* 7
By Rowan Jacobsen

Serving Up Sustainability, From *Edible Boston* 22
By Erin Byers Murray

Kids Battle the Lure of Junk Food,
From *Pacific Northwest Magazine* 29
By Maureen O'Hagan

Pastoral Romance, From *Lapham's Quarterly* 36
By Brent Cunningham

Farm to Table

Sweet Spot, From *Alimentum* 48
By Paul Graham

Snowville Creamery Has a Modest Goal: Save the World,
From *Edible Columbus* 56
By Eric LeMay

Matters of Taste, From *Tomatoland* 62
By Barry Estabrook

Olives and Lives, From *Extra Virginity* 69
By Tom Mueller

This Little Piggy Went to Market, From *Memoir Journal* 74
By Laura R. Zandstra

HOME COOKING

How to Live Well, From *An Everlasting Meal* 82
By Tamar Adler

Still Life with Mayonnaise, From *At the Kitchen Table* 92
By Greg Atkinson

The Fried Chicken Evangelist, From Leite's Culinaria 97
By Lorraine Eaton

Lasagna Bolognese, From SmittenKitchen.com 103
By Deb Perelman

The Forager at Rest, From *Bon Appetit* 111
By Christine Muhlke

Better Cooking Through Technology, From *Technology Review* 117
By Corby Kummer

FOODWAYS

The Pastrami Dilemma, From Chow.com 128
By John Birdsall

Passover Goes Gourmet, From *Sunset* 133
By Rachel Levin

The 2011 Dyke March Wiener Taste Test, From *The Stranger* 136
By Bethany Jean Clement

The Missing Link, From *The Times-Picayune* 140
By Brett Anderson

Foraging and Fishing Through the Big Bend,
From *Desert Terroir* 149
By Gary Paul Nabhan

Italian America, From *Saveur* 162
By John Mariani

What Makes Sushi Great?, From GiltTaste.com 169
By Francis Lam

Food for Thought, From the *New York Times* 173
By Jeff Gordinier

DUDE FOOD

Learning to Barbecue Helped Make Me a Man,
From *Food & Wine* 180
By Joel Stein

Memphis in May: Pork-a-Looza, From *Garden & Gun* 185
By Wright Thompson

Truffle in Paradise, From *Gastronomica* 193
By John Gutekanst

A Slice of Family History, From *Food & Wine* 204
By Daniel Duane

Barbecue Road Trip: The Smoke Road, From *Garden & Gun* 208
By John T. Edge

THE FAMILY TABLE

The Food-Critic Father, From *The Washingtonian* 214
By Todd Kliman

The Legacy That Wasn't: Wonton Soup,
From *A Spoonful of Promises* 230
By T. Susan Chang

Curious Cookies, From *Edible Vancouver* 237
By Eagranie Yuh

Chicken Brick, From *Fire & Knives* 241
By Henrietta Clancy

Angry Breakfast Eggs, From Poor Man's Feast.com 246
By Elissa Altman

Sweet Southern Dream, From *Saveur* 250
By Ben Mims

SOMEONE'S IN THE KITCHEN

The King of Pop-Up, From GQ 258
By Brett Martin

Hot Plate, From *Minnesota Monthly* 267
By Rachel Hutton

Austria's Culinary Ambassador, From *Edible Manhattan* 276
By St. John Frizell

Remembering Savoy, From *Edible Manhattan* 289
By Rachel Wharton

Appetite for Perfection, From *Los Angeles Magazine* 298
By Ed Leibowitz

Supper Clubs in Denver, From the *Denver Post* 313
By John Broening

Why Chefs Sell Out, From Chow.com 317
By Richie Nakano

A Chef's Painful Road to Rehab, From the *Chicago Tribune* 320
By Kevin Pang

Bitter Start to a Life of Sweets, From *Sacramento Bee* 327
By Chris Macias

Personal Tastes

Kitchen Confessional: Burnin' Down Da House,
From Leite's Culinaria 336
By David Leite

Do I Dare to Eat a Peach?, From *Texas Monthly* 342
By John Spong

A Proposal for Feeding the Fat and Anxious,
From *Gastronomica* 354
By Josh Ozersky

The Bone Gatherer, From *Saveur* 359
By Mei Chin

They Don't Have Tacos in the Suck, From *Houston Press* 364
By Katharine Shilcutt

I Won't Have the Stomach for This, From the *New York Times* 374
By Anna Stoessinger

Recipe Index 379
Permissions Acknowledgments 380
About the Editor 385

Introduction

By Holly Hughes

∽

I'm easily mesmerized when it comes to food shopping—inhaling the yeasty scent of the bakery, gently plucking ripe items from the produce bins, shivering in the frosty air of the freezer section. But lately it seems that all I do in the grocery aisle is pore over package labels. Yes, I'm following Michael Pollan's sage advice in *Food Rules* (no food products with more than five ingredients, no ingredients you can't pronounce, nothing your great-grandmother wouldn't have recognized—you know the drill). But I have two other compelling reasons to vet the foods I feed my family.

Our kitchen now must be totally nut-free, after my college-age son went into anaphylactic shock from a dinner of Thai shrimp and cashews. A game-changer? Absolutely. So now I scrutinize the fine print on every package of food that enters our home. Even when the ingredient list doesn't include nuts, there's the dreaded caveat: *manufactured in a facility that also processes tree nuts.* Maybe it's a slim chance of cross-contamination, but I can't take that risk—put the Le Petit Ecolier cookies back on the shelf and choose Choco Leibnitz instead.

We'd just gotten used to that New Normal when my younger daughter threw another wrench in the works: She's decided to go vegan three days a week, filling our refrigerator with tubs of tempeh, seitan, and Tofurkey. Usually I'm wary of any dietary regimen that's so exclusionary, but I'm going along with this one, because A) this too shall pass, and B) until it passes, she's been inspired to try all sorts of healthy foods she wouldn't touch before. It's actually expanding her culinary horizons instead of narrowing them, and I'm all in favor of that. But now I have to apply a second filter when I read food labels. And lo and behold, what's the main source of protein in many vegan products? You guessed it, nuts. So my kitchen has become a bit of a battleground.

Sound familiar? When it comes to food, our entire society seems to be a battleground these days. Americans were once known as a nation of slapdash, thoughtless eaters; now it almost seems we think about nothing else. On the one hand, we obsess over food as entertainment, fetishizing "decadent" desserts and all-you-can-eat buffets and trophy high-end dining. On the other, we relentlessly worry about nutrition, health, and the environmental impact of what we eat. People feel so invested in their dietary choices that the age-old concept of sharing a common meal—breaking bread together, even if it's gluten-free—gets short shrift. It's almost impossible to throw a dinner party these days without negotiating a minefield of various guests' food demands.

Enter food writers, who every year become more and more indispensable as guides to this shifting gastronomic landscape. Since editing the first edition of *Best Food Writing* in the year 2000, I've witnessed an explosion in the number of magazines, websites, newsletters, and TV shows devoted to food; the shelves of my local culinary bookshop (New York City's esteemed Kitchen Arts & Letters) are crammed with expensively produced cookbooks, best-selling culinary memoirs, and scholarly works on all aspects of food. It's been a thrilling metamorphosis to observe firsthand.

In those years, I've watched food stories move from the "women's pages" of newspapers onto the front pages and op-ed pages. Check out the issue-oriented pieces in the opening section, Food Fights—stories like Rowan Jacobsen's venture into post-oil-spill Louisiana fishing waters (page 7), Brent Cunningham's questioning of farm-to-table as a cure-all for America's food supply (page 36), and Hank Shaw's defense of hunting (page 2). And here's another sign of the times: Many of this year's writers earned their stars as bloggers (Elissa Altman of PoorMansFeast, page 246; Smitten Kitchen's Deb Perelman, page 103; Katharine Shilcutt of EatingOurWords and SheEats, page 364), a source of food writing that was barely on anyone's radar thirteen years ago.

In a food-obsessed culture, trend-spotting is always risky. Nevertheless, when you spend months combing through bookstores and magazines and websites, as I do, every year certain themes pop out. I think of 2012 as the Year of the Three F's: fermentation, foraging, and fennel. What inspired the fermentation craze is anybody's guess, but it's a fair bet that foraging rose to the forefront thanks to Rene Redzepi's Copenhagen restaurant Noma (see Christine Muhlke's profile on page 111). The fennel? It may just be me, but ever since reading Tamar Adler's *How to Live Well* (page 82), I've noticed roast fennel and shaved raw fennel on menus everywhere.

2012 also produced a bumper crop of pieces concerned with cooking as a Guy Thing. Hence our whole new section on Dude Food, congregating a tailgate party's worth of male food writers, no less than two of whom—Joel Stein (page 180) and Daniel Duane (page 204)—have recently written entire books on the subject of Manliness.

Always looking for new frontiers, Americans have recently developed an avid curiosity about diverse food cultures. Our Foodways section examines a wide spectrum of those, from sushi (Francis Lam, page 169) to Passover seders (Rachel Levin, page 133) to red-sauce Italian-American (John Mariani, page 162). And because chefs are the new rock stars, Someone's in the Kitchen profiles all sorts of chefs—from Kevin Pang's cautionary tale of a chef on the skids (page 320) to Chris Macias' inspiring profile of one redeemed (page 327).

Some pieces in this year's *Best Food Writing* feature the very newest developments, such as pop-up restaurants (Richie Nakano, page 317, and Brett Martin, page 258) and the high-tech wonders of *Modernist Cuisine* (Corby Kummer's review, page 117). But the Old always has a place alongside the New: witness Paul Graham's lyrical essay on syrup making (page 48), Jeff Gordinier's look at eating as an act of meditation (page 173), or Mei Chin's musings on broth and bones (page 359).

Speaking of balancing the Old with the New, this year's book features a number of writers who have graced these pages often: Deans of the food writing world such as Southern food champion John T. Edge (page 208), political watchdog Barry Estabrook (page 62), locavore crusader Gary Paul Nabhan (page 149), the always witty David Leite (page 336), philosopher of home cooking Greg Atkinson (page 92), and the man whose food writing helped save New Orleans, Brett Anderson (page 140). But the robust state of food writing ensures that there are always new personalities bursting onto the scene—writers such as Vancouver chocolatier Eagranie Yuh (page 237), San Francisco's John Birdsall (page 128), New England's T. Susan Chang (page 230), Londoner Henrietta Clancy (page 241), and transplanted Southerner and sweetaholic Ben Mims (page 250).

So while fretting over package labels has become a necessity for me, I gratefully turn to food writing to remind me that food should also be a pleasure. Instead of limiting their options, I've found ways to help my kids expand their food choices—teaching my son to make a stir-fry that's better than risky takeout, surprising my daughter with a savory lentil salad full of diced raw veggies. Here's hoping that this year's *Best Food Writing* will help you too navigate the gastronomic landscape with zest and an open mind. The food scene doesn't have to be a battleground, after all—there's room enough for all of us at the table.

Food Fights

On Killing

By Hank Shaw

From *HunterAnglerGardenerCook.com*

Foraging and fishing have gained hipster cachet recently, but
hunters still are often shunned by politically correct foodies.
Hank Shaw—former line cook and commercial fisherman,
and author of *Hunt, Gather, Cook*—demands equal respect for
those food lovers who slay their meat.

I have been dealing a lot of death lately. I've hunted five of
the past eight days and have killed birds on each trip. My
larder is filling, and Holly and I are eating well. Lots of duck, some
pheasant and even a little of the venison I have left over from the
2010 season. That is the good side of all this, the side of hunting
that most people can embrace. I hunt for a lot of reasons, but for
me the endgame is always the table.

It is the journey to that table that can sometimes give people
pause. What I do to put meat in my freezer is alien to most, anath-
ema to some. In the past seven years, I can count on one hand the
times I've had to buy meat for the home. This fact alone makes me
an outlier, an anomaly. And that I am unashamed—proud, really—
of this seems to cause a lot of folks I meet to look at me funny: I
am a killer in their midst.

Not too long ago, I was at a book signing event for *Hunt,
Gather, Cook* when a young woman approached me. She was very
excited about foraging, and she had loved that section of my book.
Then her face darkened. She told me she'd also read my section on

hunting. "How can you enjoy killing so much? I just don't understand it. You seem like such a nice person, too." It took a few minutes for me to explain myself to her, and I am grateful that she listened. She left, I think, with a different opinion.

A few weeks later, I was at the University of Oregon talking about wild food to some students. When I mentioned hunting, I could feel the temperature in the room drop. It occurred to me that no one there was a hunter, nor were they close to any hunters. I called for a show of hands. One guy raised his. I asked him briefly about his hunting experience, and it was obvious that it had been traumatic for the poor kid. I let the topic slide and moved on to mushrooms.

When I was in Cambridge, Massachusetts, I spoke with more than 100 diners during my book dinner at Craigie on Main. Only four were hunters, although a few more wanted to start. Over the course of the night, I fielded weird question after weird question from diner after diner. *Have I ever shot someone? Did I actually eat what I shot? Wasn't I afraid of diseases?* It was a stark show of ignorance. Not stupidity, mind you, just an utter lack of knowledge of what hunting is all about.

To be sure, these encounters were in college towns among a certain set of people. I had some book events, notably those in Montana, Pittsburgh and Austin, where most everyone who attended either hunted or was at least familiar with it. And in most places I could be assured of a healthy smattering of fellow hook-and-bullet types or farmers, who are equally familiar with the death of animals.

But the fact remains: Most people reading this have never killed anything larger than an insect, and among those who have it's usually been a fish, or an accident—like running over someone's dog. Most people have no idea what it's like to take the life of another creature, let alone why someone would actively seek to do so. Let me try to explain to you the way I did to my young foraging friend on book tour. Let me tell you what it means to kill, at least for me.

To deal death is to experience your world exploding. It is an avalanche of emotion and thought and action.

Armed with a shotgun, it is often done without thought, on instinct alone. A flushing grouse gives you no more than a few seconds to pull the trigger before it disappears into the alders. A rabbit can leap back into the brambles in even less time. Unless you are perfect in that split second, the animal wins. And being human, we are far from perfect. Even with ducks, where you often have plenty of time to prepare for the shot, their speed and agility are more than adequate defenses. We hunters fail more than we succeed.

This is why we will often whoop it up when we finally bring a bird down: We are not being callous, rejoicing in the animal's death. It is a hard-wired reaction to succeeding at something you have been working for days, months, even years to achieve. In some corner of your brain, it means you will eat today. This reaction can look repulsive from the outside.

Should you arm yourself with a rifle, you then must wrestle your conscious mind. Buck fever is real. A huge set of antlers will hypnotize the best of us, man and woman alike. Even if the animal lacks antlers, as mine often do, you have to contend with The Twin Voices: On one shoulder sits a voice shouting, *Shoot! Shoot! You might not get another chance!* On the other shoulder sits another voice, grave and calm: *Be careful. You must not put that bullet in a place where the animal will suffer. Better to pass a shot than wound an animal.* A wise hunter does not kill lightly.

In that moment when the game shows itself and you ready yourself to shoot, all that matters is that you do your job correctly. And that job is to kill cleanly and quickly. The animal deserves it; we would want no less were the tables turned. And make no mistake: A great many hunters, myself included, do this mental table-turning with some frequency. Seeing animals die so often makes us think of our own death, and I can assure you most of us would rather die with a well-placed shot than wither in a hospital.

We also know all too well that we are fallible creatures. When we fail to kill cleanly, when we wound the animals we seek, it is our duty to end their suffering ourselves. If there is a moment in this whole process that breaks my heart, it is this one. Everything wants to live, and will try anything it can to escape you. We see ourselves in this struggle, feel tremendous empathy for the struggling bird, the fleeing deer. It is a soul-searing moment where part of you marvels at the animal's drive to live—*to escape!*—at the same time the rest of you is consumed with capturing it as fast as possible so you can end this miserable business. This internal conflict is, to me, what being human is all about. A coyote or a hawk has no remorse. We do.

I am not ashamed to tell you that I have shed a tear more than once when I've had to deliver the coup de grace to a duck. I'm not sure what it is about ducks, but they affect me more than other animals. I always apologize to it, knowing full well that this is a weak gesture designed mostly to help me feel better. But it does help me feel better. At least a little. So I keep doing it.

As the moment of killing fades, death rides home with you in the back of the truck. Once home, you must transmogrify the animal you killed into meat. The transformation is a mystical one, and every time I "dress" game—such a pleasant euphemism, that—I marvel at how fast my mind toggles from hunter to butcher to cook.

It is a necessary process, and one that is vital to why I have chosen this life, why I am a hunter.

I look down at my keyboard and see death under my fingernails. I smell the fat and gore and meat of dead ducks upon me; it's been a good week of hunting. And because I **eat everything on a duck but the quack**, I have become intimate with the insides of waterfowl. Over the years, I've gutted and taken apart so many animals that I know the roadmap blindfolded. And that road leads to meals long remembered. I reach into a deer's guts without thought: I want those kidneys, and that liver. I turn my arm upwards and wrap my fingers around its stopped heart, slick and firm. It will become **heart cutlets**, or **jaeger schnitzel**.

Once plucked and gutted, I can take apart a duck in 90 seconds. Maybe less. My fingers intuitively know which way and how hard to pluck each feather from a pheasant's carcass. I know just where to put my boning knife, sharp as lightning, to slice the tendons that hold a hog's tongue into its head. I use the same knife to caress its hind legs, separating the natural muscle groups apart along each seam. Some will become roasts, others salami. Animal becomes food. The pop of a goose's thigh bone disjointing from its body no longer sickens me; all it means is that I need to slip my knife under that bone and around the coveted "oyster," the best bite on any bird.

Wasting meat is the sin I cannot forgive. When I kill an animal, its death is on my hands, and those animals to whom I've had to deliver the coup de grace are especially close to me. There is a bond between us that requires that I do my part to ensure they did not die for nothing. This is why I spend so much time creating recipes for every part of the animal. Nature wastes nothing, and neither should I. It pains me to know that some hunters do not share this feeling, that they care only for backstraps or breasts—and while I know that coyotes and buzzards will eat what we do not, I do not hunt to feed those creatures.

You might ask me that with all this, why bother eating meat at all? Why deal with all the moral and emotional implications? In the face of such constant death, is it not better to be a vegetarian?

For me, no. It is a cold fact that no matter what your dietary choice, animals die so you can eat. Just because you choose not to eat the flesh of animals does not mean that their homes did not fall to the plow to become acres of vegetables and soybeans, wheat and corn. Habitat, more than anything, determines the health of a species. The passenger pigeon may have been snuffed out by hunting, but it was the massive destruction of virgin forest—forest cleared to grow crops—that brought the pigeon to the brink. I have nothing against vegetarians, and the vast majority I've met understand what I do and respect it. But to those few who do not, I say this: We all have blood on our hands, only I can see mine.

It all boils down to intimacy. Hunting has created an uncommon closeness between the animals I pursue, the meat I eat, and my own sense of self. There is a terrible seriousness to it all that underlies the thrill of the chase, the camaraderie of being with my fellow hunters and the deep sense of calm I feel when alone in the wild. I welcome this weight: It fuels my desire to make something magical with the mortal remains of the game I manage to bring home. It is a feeling every hunter who's ever stared into the freezer at that special strip of backstrap, or hard-won bird or beast understands.

Meat should be special. It has been for most of human existence. And no modern human understands this more than a hunter. I am at peace with killing my own meat because for me, every duck breast, every boar tongue, every deer heart is a story, not of conquest, but of communion.

THE GUMBO CHRONICLES

By Rowan Jacobsen

From *Outside*

How successful was BP's much-touted cleanup of the Gulf of
Mexico after 2010's Deepwater Horizon oil spill? Food
writer/environmentalist Rowan Jacobsen (author of *American
Terroir*) sailed out with Louisiana crabbers, oystermen, and
shrimpers to fish for the real truth.

In the predawn steam of a Louisiana night, I stood in a yard
surrounded by catfish heads. The headlights of dualies
towing fiberglass crabbing boats swept into the yard and illuminated wooden pallets stacked six feet high, holding tens of thousands of fish heads: eyes, whiskers, stringy stuff coming out the
back. Men in baseball caps stepped out of the trucks, loaded pallets
into their boats, and pulled away.

It was 4:30 A.M., and I was in the yard of Vincent Comardelle,
67, who supplies bait to the crabbers in Larose, a small Cajun town
abutting Bayou Lafourche (pronounced la-*foosh*), a 109-mile,
shellfish-heavy waterway that peels off from the Mississippi River
above New Orleans and winds through the marshes of southern
Louisiana to the Gulf of Mexico. I was waiting to meet Ryan Comardelle, Vincent's son and one of the top crabbers in the area,
who had promised to take me out on the marshes. Finally, a white
pickup pulled up. Ryan stepped out and peered at me. He was

wearing a tight red T-shirt over a massive chest and Popeye biceps. Buzz cut, goatee, merciless blue eyes.

"You bring any food?" he asked. I hadn't. He shot me an unimpressed look. "We gonna be out there all day," he said. "I don't like to share my food."

Vincent shambled into the house—he has a limp from an old boating accident that ended with an outboard propeller buried in his back—and returned with a package of peanut butter crackers. We launched Ryan's boat from a nearby dock and motored through a series of shallow, brackish marshes—crab heaven—until we reached Little Lake, which is no longer little, thanks to erosion and land subsidence. Southern Louisiana is sinking, and every year the salty Gulf of Mexico covers more of it, killing the grasses and trees that hold the land together. This is a problem for native shellfish, which rely on a delicate, finely tuned balance of fresh inland water and salty tidal flow.

A full moon hung in the west, silhouetting the rocket-ship spires of gas rigs and the bones of dead oak trees, killed by encroaching water. Ryan, who has crabbed for most of his 40 years, steered while his friend Reggie, an athletic guy sporting a Bud Light cap and a bewildered expression, handled the traps. Reggie was a little off, which Ryan kept pointing out.

"He ain't exactly stupid," Ryan said. "He just got no sense."

"Oh yeah?" Reggie said.

"Yeah."

Reggie tried to think of a comeback, failed, and went back to the traps. We could just make out ghostly foam floats bobbing on the water. Attached to the side of Ryan's boat was a metal rake, its teeth combing the surface and snatching the line dangling beneath each passing float. When the rake hooked a float, a wire trap came up, dragging near the back of the boat. Reggie opened each trap, shook the captured crabs into a plastic crate, and removed the rotting catfish heads, tossing them overboard. Then he added two new heads and dropped the trap back into the water. For eight hours this is what we did. The boat never stopped. Reggie never stopped. The crabs piled up: olive shells, turquoise legs, orange claws reaching for Reggie when he got close. Every time they pinched him, he'd yelp, "Oh mercy!"

Most traps held just two or three crabs and the occasional flounder. "I used to run 400 cages," Ryan said. "Now I'm running 700 and making less money."

"Bad season?" I asked.

Ryan glared. "Today might be my worst day ever," he said. "Normally I fill 20 pans. Last time I filled 13. I'm hoping to catch half that today. That don't even cover my expenses."

Ryan was going to give up for the year if things didn't change in a week or two, and he wasn't alone. When I was in Bayou Lafourche, in September 2011, many crabbers didn't even bother to go out. Apparently, they hadn't got the memo that everything in the Gulf was fine. A year and a half after BP's April 2010 Deepwater Horizon oil spill, virtually the entire fishery was open for business, and federal and state officials were happily trumpeting the health of the Gulf's marine life. Ryan had nothing but contempt for those officials.

"Dey tellin' everybody everything's OK," he said, in the region's ubiquitous Cajun accent, which features a lot of *dis* and *dat*. "And it's not. The crabs are not getting fat. A lot of dem are dying right when dey shed. The biologists say everything's normal. Well, shit. We out here on the water almost every day of our lives. We know what changes from one day to the next. Where the little crabs? Before BP hit, they'd be all over this boat. Where dey at? We screwed."

Ryan was much happier talking about arm wrestling. He was ranked number one in Louisiana for his weight division. "No guy around here can put my arm down. You want to see why?"

"Sure," I said.

Ryan grabbed the next float from the rake and curled it tightly against his chest as the boat churned along. The cage dragged in the water, half-submerged and spraying a wake. "That's how I won my biggest match!" Ryan said, veins popping. "Other guys use weights. I just come out here and work. Wanna try?"

I did. The cage jerked me to the back of the boat, and mercifully, the float ripped out of my hand before I was dragged overboard. Ryan smiled and went back to crabbing. We struggled to fill six crates. I counted time in catfish heads. Around noon, I broke out the crackers.

In the immediate aftermath of the Deepwater Horizon spill, many observers—myself included—anticipated an unthinkable disaster: the death of the Gulf Coast fishery and the final ruination of the Gulf's beleaguered estuary system. Nearly 206 million gallons of oil leaked from the Macondo well. More than 88,000 square miles of fishing grounds—37 percent of all federal Gulf of Mexico waters—were closed, along with most affected Louisiana waters, including Bayou Lafourche. Oil filled the estuaries and worked its way into the bayou marshes. Destruction appeared imminent.

And then the oil just seemed to fade like disappearing ink. This happened, we were told, thanks to naturally occurring hydrocarbon-eating bacteria, aided by beneficial ocean currents at the site of the leaking well. By October 2010, most Louisiana state fisheries were reopened, including Bayou Lafourche. Since then thousands of seafood samples have been tested for the carcinogens found in hydrocarbons and deemed safe. On April 12, 2011, with the one-year anniversary of the spill approaching, Eric Schwaab, assistant administrator for fisheries at the National Oceanic and Atmospheric Administration (NOAA), proudly declared that "not one piece of tainted seafood has entered the market." Meanwhile, BP has mitigated the damage to its image with a $20 billion fund to pay the claims of affected businesses, plus a slick TV ad campaign to lure tourists to the region. In January, *The New York Times* ran an editorial lauding the recovery effort as a shining example for future industrial cleanups. These days the consensus from state and local governments, BP, and pundits alike is that everything is pretty much fine. We dodged a bullet, they tell us.

All of which seemed incredible to me. I reported from the Gulf during the spill, and I watched the Vessels of Opportunity (local boats hired by BP to lay boom and corral oil) and saw how ineffective they were. I worried about what polycyclic aromatic hydrocarbons—the mutagens and carcinogens found in crude oil—might do to the generation of shrimp and crab larvae that were getting soaked in gunk. I wondered about the effects of the 1.8 million gallons of chemical dispersants that BP sprayed to prevent the oil from accumulating on the ocean's surface. And I thought about the scientists who said it would take years before we could comprehend the effect of the spill, much less make grand diagnoses about the Gulf's health.

These were guys I quoted in my 2010 book on the spill, *Shadows on the Gulf,* among them Florida State University oceanographer Ian MacDonald, who said, "I expect the hydrocarbon imprint of the BP discharge will be detectable in the marine environment for the rest of my life." And University of South Florida oceanographer John Paul, who said, "The impact on commercially important larvae that are bathed in this stuff is hard to say. We might see grouper with tumors three years from now."

I wanted to believe in the recovery—who doesn't like miracles?—but the spin was hard to cut through. So I decided to do some personal recon to see if the facts on the ground jibed with the reports being fed to the public. In my mind, there was no better way to assess the Gulf's health than by traveling around and sourcing one of my favorite meals—seafood gumbo—in the heart of bayou country.

I've written a lot about food traditions, and I've always had a thing for gumbo, a delicious stew that came about after a bunch of poor people from elsewhere were stuck in a marginal environment, handed a cooking pot, and told to fend for themselves. The poor people were Acadians, French Catholic farmers who got booted out of Nova Scotia by the British in 1755, arrived in Louisiana, looked around at the soupy, unpromising environment, and thought, How do you make dinner out of this? Not only did they succeed, but they designed a culinary miracle, a spontaneous dish born of the holy trinity of crab, shrimp, and oyster that's as American as anything we've got.

It's no exaggeration to say that Bayou Lafourche has traditionally been the finest place in the world to find ingredients for gumbo. Route 1, which hugs Lafourche, is often called "the longest Main Street in the world" because of the way one linear town eases into the next. There are few significant side streets; the only solid land is the two parallel strips of high ground built up on either side of the bayou by millennia of flood sediment. As soon as you get away from that, you sink into the marshes. Those marshes are some of the most fabled crab, shrimp, and oyster grounds on the planet. And they were directly in the crosshairs of the spill. The way I figured it, if I could still make an all-Lafourche gumbo, then America's seafood soul was intact. So I bought a plane ticket and called my buddy Jim.

Jim Gossen is the CEO of Louisiana Foods Global Seafood Service, a major Gulf Coast supplier. We first met a few years ago, at the International Boston Seafood Show, and bonded over our enthusiasm for all things oyster. Gossen, who is 64, grew up in bayou country and has been buying from its fishermen since the 1970s. Not incidentally, he has a beach house on Grand Isle, a long barrier island that sits where Bayou Lafourche meets the Gulf of Mexico. When I told him about my plan to toast the non-death of the Gulf with gumbo, he offered to guide me to local fishermen and host the celebratory cook-off. "I just need to cancel a week's worth of appointments," he said.

Gossen, who has slicked-back, thinning hair and a gourmand's earthmover-size spare tire, picked me up from the airport in his white SUV on a warm September afternoon, air conditioning blasting. We rolled down Route 1, past moored shrimp boats and ramshackle stores advertising bait and boudin, a Cajun sausage. Our destination was the house of Wilbert Collins, a legendary septuagenarian oysterman. "There's something about oysters," Gossen said. "I always loved them. My dad loved them. My grandfather loved them. We'd buy sacks in the wintertime and sit in the backyard and shuck."

Louisiana oysters tend to grow faster than other kinds, thanks to the warm waters of the lower Mississippi River and an extraordinary abundance of phytoplankton. Collins's specimens were particularly fat. I'd eaten them with Gossen before. They were too large to fit in any human mouth, which stymied me until I watched Gossen take the edge of one in his lips and slurp it like a massive linguine.

At one time, 16 family-run oyster businesses plied the waters of Lafourche Parish. Gossen used to send a tractor-trailer down Bayou Lafourche and load the entire thing with oysters. But Lafourche's marshes have been under assault for years, long before oil started fouling its beaches. Those marshes, along with the rest of the lower Mississippi, constitute the fastest-disappearing landmass on earth. There are two reasons for this: the leveeing of the Mississippi River by the Army Corps of Engineers, and the digging of canals through the marshes by the oil-and-gas industry in search of new reserves. The levees prevented natural flooding, which over time had deposited enough sediment in the marshes to compensate for natural subsidence. The new canals allowed pure saltwater to intrude inland and kill the marsh grass that held the mud in place. The result: sinking, disintegrating land as the Gulf of Mexico chewed its way farther north every year.

Oysters do best in brackish water. Fresh water kills them outright, and while they can grow just fine in salt water, the ocean brings with it numerous critters that relish young oysters, especially snails and drumfish. As the salt water has encroached, many traditional oyster reefs have succumbed to predation and hurricanes. By the early nineties, the reefs near Bayou Lafourche had declined so much that Gossen stopped sending the truck. By the time Deepwater Horizon blew, only the Collins Oyster Company was still in operation. When we arrived, we discovered that it, too, had gone under.

"Collins Oyster Co. Out of Business After 90 Yrs.," read the sign in the yard, "Because of BP's Oil & Governor Jindals Fresh Water." In May 2010, as the oil crept closer to the Louisiana wetlands, Governor Bobby Jindal and local officials tried to push it back by fully opening seven of Louisiana's floodgates on the Mississippi for the first time in history. River water poured through the brackish marshes, turning them fresh. After being threatened for years by overly salty water, most of the reefs in the Barataria and Lake Pontchartrain basins—some of the state's richest oyster grounds—were decimated.

Gossen and I stared at Collins's boat, dry-docked beside the bayou. "Whenever I drove down to my beach house," Gossen said, "I used to stop at Wilbert's and say, 'Please pick me out some good ones! A couple of sacks—make sure they're real nice.' " He shook his head. "I don't want to see this die."

Louisiana harvested some seven million pounds of oysters in 2010, down from 15 million the year before. Crabs aren't faring much better. The state's crabbers pulled in 53 million pounds of crustaceans in 2009 and 31 million in 2010, when some areas were closed because of the spill. With the fishery reopened in 2011, everyone expected a rebound, but that didn't happen. In the normally plentiful month of May, crab landings for the region that includes Bayou Lafourche were 460,068 pounds, down from 953,503 in May 2010 and 1,471,987 in May 2009. There were so many reports of crabs dying with mysterious infections that the state launched an investigation. Normally, when landings plummet, prices rise, but not when consumers suspect your product is contaminated. Prices had plunged from $1.42 per pound in 2009 to between 35 and 55 cents at the time of my visit.

Gossen and I continued down to Grand Isle. As we drove, he told me about another program he'd started at Louisiana Foods, to buy and promote forgotten fish like drum, almaco jack, and wild catfish. "The goal is to cultivate new fishermen," Gossen said. "As I get older, I've seen less and less fishermen. We losin' 'em, one by one. If there's no way for a young guy to get into it and make a living, he's going to go into gas or oil."

Luckily, we had a Plan B: farmed oysters. Last year, Gossen teamed up with an oysterman named Jules Melancon and a professor from Louisiana State University, John "Soup" Supan, to build a nursery on Grand Isle. They wanted to grow oysters in wire cages, as is done in most of the world. This had never been attempted in Louisiana, thanks to the abundance of wild reefs. But after watching saltwater-loving predators deplete Bayou Lafourche for years, Gossen decided that farming was Louisiana's future.

In June 2011, Soup seeded the waters of Barataria Bay, which borders Grand Isle, with 100 million oyster larvae and supplied 250,000 baby oysters the size of match heads to the Gossen and Melancon's project. The idea was to grow the oysters on land, in barrels of water, until they were large enough to be transferred to the bay, where they would live in submerged cages that would protect them from predators. Melancon, a fourth-generation oysterman with underwater leases in Barataria Bay, provided the real estate, the boat, and the labor. Gossen provided the startup cash. The oysters weren't very big yet, according to Gossen, but I just wanted enough to fill out our gumbo.

When we pulled up to the docks at Grand Isle, Melancon, 54, was scrubbing algae from plastic barrels filled with seawater and oysters the size of fingernails. He has huge shoulders and hands that seem to be made of petrified wood, the result of spending his teenage summers hauling 100-pound sacks of oysters from his grandfather's 400 acres of reefs, which were located in a marsh a couple of miles from where we stood. Now those reefs were entirely under saltwater, thanks to erosion, and surrounded by predators. The only option was cages.

Melancon had no oysters for us. He took us out to his leases in his 23-foot flat-bottomed boat to show us why. For an hour we motored gently through the calm, flat water, passing flocks of ibises and pelicans, until we moored the boat and Melancon winched up a cage. It surfaced dripping black slime. The oysters were coated in shiny goop. Melancon plunged his tongs into the water and pulled up a jiggling mound of black pudding.

"What the hell is that?" I asked.

Melancon scooped some up with his hand. It held like shaving cream. "I think it's oil," he said. "Look how it stains your hand. Dat's carbon." Grand Isle is the sandiest spot in Louisiana. Its reefs are normally a pleasing jumble of shell and grit. But when Melancon checked this one on August 26, two weeks before I arrived, it was buried under a foot of black gunk. "Dis land was clean," he said. "Just shells and sand. Not all dis fuckin' bullshit."

Upon discovering the gunk, Melancon called the mayor of Grand Isle. The next day, the Coast Guard and a state fisheries employee turned up to collect samples, which they delivered to the Gulf Coast Claims Facility—the organization run by "claims czar" Kenneth Feinberg that adjudicates damage payments for BP. At the time, Feinberg had distributed about $5 billion of BP's $20 billion fund to 200,000 victims of the spill, who were granted payments of twice their documented 2010 losses in exchange for waiving the right to future compensation. (The exception was oystermen, who were granted up to four times their 2010 losses.) But an estimated 100,000 claimants have refused to settle, instead filing a monstrous class action. Now BP is arguing that future payments should be curtailed, since the Gulf's tourism and fishing industries have rebounded.

Since the samples were submitted, Melancon had heard nothing. Now we scooped more samples into ziplock bags to send to an independent researcher at the University of Georgia.

According to some scientists, the presence of oil near shore is a distinct possibility, though tracing it to Deepwater Horizon could be tough. "It would not necessarily be surprising that there is some residual oil in these wetlands," said Don Boesch, professor of marine science at the University of Maryland Center for Environmental Sciences, who served on the National Commission on the BP Deepwater Horizon Oil Spill in 2010. "However, that area is one of intense development by oil-and-gas companies. After a year and a half, the natural process would change the chemical composition of the oil from Deepwater Horizon. It becomes more difficult over time to identify oil with a specific well."

Such statements are of little comfort to Melancon. He dropped the mess over the side and motored back in. We drove the samples up Route 1, looking for a place to FedEx them. As we rode, Melancon told me how, after the spill, he had worked for BP skippering a Vessel of Opportunity, hauling boom on his boat. He was paid $3,300 a day. By my calculations, he earned half a million dollars, an amount that takes some of the sting out of losing your life's work. Many other "spillionaires" on Grand Isle saw similar paydays. The island is crawling with antique roadsters. But a lot of the spillionaires, like fishermen everywhere, have only a passing familiarity with the Internal Revenue Service. They had no idea a tax bill was coming and saved no money for it.

Melancon, on the other hand, bought nothing. As a well-known boat operator with a 500-ton hauling license and no oysters to harvest, he was in high demand. As we drove, he took a call from a guy who offered him a job in Texas working as a barge captain for a chemical company. One hundred and thirty grand per year, plus benefits.

"Can't do it right now," Melancon said. "I'm tied up with Jim on dis seed business."

He hung up, and then his phone rang again. It was a state official with the test results. "Uh-huh," he said. "But it's carbon. Smear it on your finger. You can tell. It's contamination." He hung up.

"Dey say it ain't oil," he told us. "Dey say it's sludge. What's dat mean?"

"Could mean a lot of things," I said. "Maybe it's stuff that washed down the Mississippi."

"Never did before." Melancon Googled "sludge" on his phone. "Semisolid material left from industrial wastewater," he read aloud.

"Maybe somebody opened up their holding tank over your reef," Gossen offered.

"I'm worried about my gumbo," I said.

"There's a place up here called Bob's Seafood," Melancon said. "Maybe he's got oysters." He kept poking at his phone, eyebrows knit. "Sludge. Sounds like contamination to me."

Bob's shop looked pretty barren: the stainless steel oyster-shucking station was gleaming and clean, and a nearby walk-in fridge was just about empty. "Got any oysters?" Melancon asked.

"I got one half-gallon tub from Chauvin," Bob said. Chauvin had dodged both the oil and the fresh water. "Why?"

"We gonna make gumbo," Melancon said.

Bob marveled at Melancon. "Oysterman wants to buy oysters?"

It was looking like our gumbo might be skimpy on crabs and oysters, so we decided to go heavy on the shrimp. Grand Isle, after all, is America's unofficial shrimp capital, complete with its own shrimp king. Actually, *don* might be a better word.

Dean Blanchard, 53, is the only guy I know who's done time in prison for illegally transporting red snapper across state lines. He once drove to New York City's Fulton Fish Market in a Corvette and threatened a deadbeat seafood buyer with an Uzi. He fits in well on Grand Isle, a place that's proud of its pirate heritage, which dates to 1810, when the buccaneer Jean Lafitte set up camp nearby, smuggling slaves and rum into New Orleans by poling them up Bayou Lafourche.

Blanchard is the top shrimp broker in the country, single-handedly responsible for 7 percent of the shrimp bought and sold in the U.S. At least he was. Since the oil spill, Grand Isle shrimp have been few and far between. Chances are you haven't noticed. While the Gulf Coast is still America's top shellfish producer, 90 percent of the shrimp you see in stores is imported from Asian farms. Louisiana shrimpers can't compete; three-quarters of them have disappeared in the past 25 years, a result primarily of competition from the East. When the last Gulf fisherman hangs up his hip waders, Red Lobster will not be fazed. Blanchard is not only the biggest shrimp buyer in Grand Isle; he's the last.

When Gossen and I pulled up to Blanchard's house—a newly renovated, *Sopranos*-esque affair on an island of beach camps, built with internal steel beams to withstand hurricanes—there were four men, one on a forklift, polishing his massive motor home, which he had just driven to and from the Saints-Packers game in Green Bay, Wisconsin. Next to it was a Hummer with decorative Saints plates. Dean was inside watching football in his recliner, wearing shorts and a sleeveless T-shirt.

"How are your shrimp?" I asked.

"I wouldn't eat dat shit," he said, rubbing his spiky gray hair.

"Really?"

"Dat water's poison. Every day, dey haulin' dead porpoises in front of my place. Wildlife says dey was dying before the oil spill. I say, Yeah? I musta been sleepin'. Cause I ain't never seen y'all haul one in front of my place before. Now I see y'all haul a hundred of these motherfuckers!"

It should be noted that Dean is one of the claimants in the class action angling for a massive settlement with BP. He therefore may not be the most objective source. But his story more or less checks out. NOAA reported some 80 abnormal dolphin deaths between January and April 2010. Since the spill, more than 450 dead dolphins have washed up on Gulf Coast beaches. Many were newborns or stillborns, leading some biologists to hypothesize that ingested oil had contributed to a wave of miscarriages. NOAA has declared the situation an "unusual mortality event."

If none of the seafood tested by NOAA showed oil contamination, how could the Gulf's marine life be so affected? A recent paper by LSU biologist Andrew Whitehead provides a clue. Whitehead examined Gulf killifish—minnows that live in the marshes and are an important food source for many species—before, during, and after the oil hit. He found that even tiny amounts of oil caused genetic abnormalities and tissue damage in the fish, enough to impair their reproductive abilities. And you wouldn't have known this simply by testing them for contamination.

"Though the fish may be safe to eat," Whitehead said, summarizing the report, "that doesn't mean they are capable of reproducing normally." This problem may extend to other marine life. And many fishermen blame low yields on BP's dispersants, though the scientific jury is still out.

"The dispersant is biodegradable," said Ralph Portier, professor of environmental science and oceanography at LSU. "The oil is biodegradable. So we're not worried about their presence over a long period. The real issue is whether the mixture of dispersant and oil made it to the marsh and had a catastrophic effect on key organisms. There are literally hundreds of scientists working on these problems, but right now there are too many variables and not enough data."

Perched on his dock at the very edge of the Gulf, Blanchard has a unique vantage point to speculate on such things. And what he wanted to tell me was that the white shrimp season was a bust. "White shrimp are born on the beach," he said. "Dey ain't got a chance to go nowhere. Dey layin' in polluted fuckin' water. Dey dead! Unless dey like Jesus and can raise from the dead, dey ain't comin' back. Usually, I buy about 250,000 pounds opening day. This year I didn't buy one. First time in my life."

Again, Blanchard's not lying. According to Clint Guidry, president of the Louisiana Shrimp Association, the white shrimp haul was down 80 percent across Louisiana in 2011. On November 30, in the face of overwhelming evidence of the poor season, Feinberg, the claims czar, announced that commercial crab and shrimp harvesters would be entitled to four times their documented 2010 losses, instead of two times, in exchange for waiving their right to sue. This was good news for the 1,000 or so shrimpers and crabbers still holding out but an affront to the 4,000 who had already accepted a settlement and were told that there would be no retroactive payments.

I asked Blanchard whom he blamed for the disaster. "The French media came and asked me whose fault it was. I told 'em Napoleon. He should've killed all the British at Waterloo. The German media came. I told 'em Hitler. He should've bombed 'em with the fuckin' Luftwaffe. The American media came. I told 'em it was George Washington's fuckin' fault. We been fightin' the British on this island since 1673."

We decided not to buy our shrimp from Blanchard. Instead, we bought it back up the bayou, in areas less affected by oil, from an old guy on a boat called the *Tootsie*. I paid for five pounds, and he shoveled about 20 into our cooler. As he handed it over, he said, "Hey, lemme show you dis shit we found on the west side of the bayou." From the cabin of his boat he produced a tar ball and a big chunk of hard, black crude. "Never seen nothin' like this in my life," he said.

On the way back to Grand Isle, we tuned in the local talk-radio station. A caller had hijacked the show and was on a full-blown BP rant. "I blame Napoleon!" he yelled.

Making gumbo is a social affair. That's the point. People gather, work side by side, drink beer, celebrate the bounty of the sea. Against all odds, that's what we did. Word spread around Grand Isle: gumbo at Jim's house. Melancon showed up with his wife, Melanie. Vincent and Ryan Comardelle didn't make it, but a guy who ran the port commission did, having heard the news. So did "Soup" Supan from LSU. He stared in mute horror at the photos we'd taken of Melancon's reef. "Jules," he said, "get those cages out of there."

Gossen boiled the shrimp to make a stock. I peeled off the tails. Gossen made the roux—flour and oil simmered and stirred until it turns mahogany brown. Then he threw in onions, celery, and bell peppers. *Gumbo* is an African word for okra, a mucilaginous vegetable that came over with the slave trade. Around New Orleans, okra is the standard thickener for gumbo. But down in bayou country, where there were no plantations, the gumbo has always been thin, heavy on the seafood.

Melanie pulled a box of live crabs from the fridge. The chill had slowed them considerably. "We down here at the end of the world," said Melanie, who has lived on Grand Isle all of her 50 years. "Nobody knows what goes on here." Then she ripped a live crab in half. I'd never seen a woman do that before. Every now and then, a crab would warm up enough to sink a claw into her, elicit-

ing a giggle. "Oooh, he ticklin' me!" she'd say. "Stop dat, now."
Then, with a twist, she'd pop his top shell off, pull out his lungs,
snap off his mouth, wrap a meaty hand around each half of his
body, and snap it in two. That put an end to the tickling.

The crabs went into the pot, guts and all. Once the crabs and
veggies were cooked, we threw in the shrimp and oysters and
turned off the heat. I'd never made a gumbo with live crabs and
shrimp right off the boat. It was sweet as all get-out. I dipped my
spoon in and fished up some shrimp and oysters. A crab claw pro-
truded from my bowl.

"Nice job, Jim," I said, raising my beer.

His eyes got big. "I just want to see it come back!" he said.

Me, too. But I wonder. Complex systems do complicated
things. The night after Hurricane Katrina passed through southern
Louisiana, everyone breathed a sigh of relief. We dodged a bullet,
they said. And then the river came pouring through the levees.
Since the spill cleanup ended, the government, the media, and the
oil industry have been only too happy to announce that we got
lucky. Wait and see, though. You can still hustle up a meal from the
marshes of Bayou Lafourche. But a way of life is ending along the
lengths of the longest Main Street in the world.

Serving Up Sustainability

By Erin Byers Murray

From *Edible Boston*

Cold New England waters offer very different seafood
harvests, as no one knows better than Erin Byers Murray,
author of *Shucked: Life on a New England Oyster Farm*. So how
do Boston chefs and restaurateurs define sensitive issues of
seafood "sustainability"?

"Is this sustainable?"
Restaurant chefs are faced with the question regularly,
especially when it comes to seafood. But as most of them are
learning, there is no easy answer.

Depending on what's on the plate (salmon, sea bass, tuna or lobster), the answer might be yes—with the justification that it's
caught or farmed in a way that maintains healthy fish stocks; that it
keeps the ocean floor intact; and that harvesting it results in limited
bycatch. All three, if true, would be valid answers, at least on the
surface. But look deeper into any single species and the chef might
be falling into murky territory.

Take Atlantic bluefin tuna, for example. Right now, this local
species is one to "avoid" according to the Monterey Bay Aquarium's Seafood Watch list. This list uses what the aquarium calls
"science-based, peer-reviewed and ecosystem-based criteria" and
many restaurant chefs rely on it, or others like it, to determine
what to put on their menus. Bluefin has been on the list for several
years, and in November 2010 the Center for Biological Diversity, a

group that campaigns to protect endangered species, initiated a "bluefin boycott," asking chefs to pledge to avoid serving the species and diners to pledge to avoid restaurants that serve it.

But if a chef were to talk to a small day boat fisherman working out of Plymouth or New Bedford last summer, he might reconsider the boycott. Fishermen working in and around those waters found the tuna to be considerably abundant, so much so that guys were hitting their season quota in just three or four days.

Buyers were heeding the watch lists and avoiding bluefin altogether so the fishermen found that the wholesale demand had dried up. Yet the tuna fishery in Massachusetts is closely regulated so while landing a tuna might not have been considered morally correct, it was (and is) still very much legal. In light of the boycott and a dying market, would a fisherman throw the tuna back? Why, when landing a large one might bring him a large profit—a profit that would help his business, feed his family and put money into the local economy?

Looking at it that way, the chef's choice is easy: he's buying tuna from a local fisherman who caught the product legally and within regulations and in turn, he's showcasing a quality fish on his menu, which he likely got for a great deal because the market has pushed prices down. He realizes that he can turn a nice profit on the plate with that bluefin tuna—and what's more, despite the boycott, people are going to order and eat it. So what if he's going against a watch list and an industry ban: Can the chef afford not to put that bluefin on the menu?

The answer is probably no. Restaurants all over Boston, no matter the size, shape or concept of the restaurant, will tell you that they have, in fact, put bluefin and other species like it on their menu—and that customers continue to order it.

It is, undoubtedly, a complex web of issues that chefs struggle with every day. And because there are as many types of restaurants as there are fish in the sea, each chef will handle the situation differently. In the end, each chef needs to create his or her own definition of sustainability. Is it about the restaurant's bottom line? Is it about the fisherman's livelihood and buying local? Or, is it maintaining the population of a species?

It's about all of the above, and more.

The good news is that in Boston, many chefs weigh their buying decisions carefully. They study watch lists, they discuss options with their distributor, they ask questions of local fishermen. Sometimes, they make compromises. Other times, they draw a hard line and refuse to cross it. Either way, putting sustainable seafood options on their menu is a job that chefs have started taking very, very seriously.

Defining Priorities

Chef Michael Leviton, who owns Lumiere in Newton as well as the newly opened Area Four in Cambridge, is well known for focusing on sustainable practices across his menu. (This spring, he was named the director of the board of overseers at Chefs Collaborative, a nonprofit dedicated to sustainability education.) When it comes to seafood, he defines sustainability through three different domains: environmental (a species that is caught or farmed using low-impact methods but also doesn't have to travel thousands of miles); economic (micro in terms of "can he afford that fish?" and "can he put it on the plate for an amount his customers will pay?"; macro in terms of the economics of our state and regional fishing industry); and social diversity (maintaining a 400-year-old industry). He also adheres to a strictly local policy by only using seafood from waters between the Chesapeake Bay and northern Canada and prides himself on knowing the name of every boat his fish comes off of, which he gets directly from purveyors.

"I drew the line at a certain point," Leviton says about his seafood choices. He long ago cut salmon from his menu altogether due to the environmental impact of shipping fish from thousands of miles away. "So as long as there are other alternatives that are equally good I don't think it's an issue," he says. "The first rule of running a sustainable restaurant is to keep your doors open. I am no good to the sustainable agenda if I don't have my pulpit," he adds.

Leviton's practices might seem extreme but they resonate with other like-minded chefs. Steve Johnson, chef-owner of Rendezvous in Central Square, maintains a similar philosophy: Sourcing locally actually helps narrow his seafood buying decisions.

"It's made it easier for me to develop a very focused approach, which is that almost all of the species we serve are north Atlantic," he says. His priorities start with healthy fish stocks, so migratory species that are carefully regulated such as striped bass and blue fish, are served in season while a species like squid, caught off of Point Judith, Rhode Island, are on the menu year-round.

But Johnson admits that certain factors have to fall to the bottom of the hierarchy. Catch methods, for example, are less of a concern for him. While he's aware that squid and scallops caught with nets may have an impact on the ocean floor, he justifies purchasing them, saying, "I have to believe that someone is working to improve the technologies so that we can have fewer issues environmentally."

In general, small restaurants that can update their menus frequently seem to have an easier time with local options. Fish Market, a tiny sushi restaurant in Allston, forgoes exotic species from Japan in order to utilize local species. Chef and co-owner Kin Chan says about 70% to 80% of his menu is locally sourced. "There are plenty of options here: mackerel, sea bass, fluke, sea urchin," he says. "I'd rather get it here than something that's been on a ship from Japan for two weeks. It's very important to me."

On the other end of the spectrum, larger seafood restaurants like Summer Shack have as many as five locations and serve several hundred diners a day.

Summer Shack owner Jasper White says their seafood orders are tremendous. But White, who advocates strongly for the Boston harbor advocacy group Save the Harbor/Save the Bay still puts sustainability at the top of his priority list—and in his eyes, sustainability does not come down to watch lists. "I question everyone. I question the integrity of some of those groups. I don't think they have much concern for the humans involved," he says. After opening his first Summer Shack in Cambridge, he became so frustrated with the regular seafood supply chain that he launched his own wholesale company. Run by former commercial fisherman Max Harvey, Summer Shack's wholesale arm supplies all of White's restaurants along with a few other select accounts. Because of Harvey's fishing background, he chooses to get information directly from the men and women who are out on the water every day. From his vantage point, he says he's seeing good change: "There's been a lot of work done to rebuild certain stocks."

Gathering Information

Determining where to look for trustworthy information takes practice, most chefs say. While some use watch lists as a guide, others dig deeper. Leviton speaks to his distributors—Kim Marden of Captain Marden's Seafood in Wellesley and Ingrid Bengis, a seafood purveyor out of Stonington, Maine—almost daily to learn what's coming off the boats. Others go directly to the fishermen themselves.

"I get as much of my information as I can from the people who are harvesting, growing and catching the fish," says chef Jeremy Sewall, a partner in Kenmore Square's Island Creek Oyster Bar who not only works closely with oyster farmer Skip Bennett of Island Creek Oysters but also with his own cousin, Mark Sewall, a lobsterman up in Maine. Those direct relationships have given him connections to other commercial fishermen who are helping him grasp what should or should not go onto his menu. So not only is he getting information directly from the source, he's also asking questions of his purveyors and others in the industry in order to get a well-rounded look at what is happening on the water. In some cases, he finds that he's the one educating his purveyors—a role that more and more chefs find themselves in these days.

All of that information gathering gives Sewall the unique advantage of being able to read the market daily. "You're seeing different species become more popular out of necessity rather than creativity," he says. he brings up the examples of fluke and sea trout, which are both delicious fish that have been scattered on menus for a long time but have recently become more popular now that some mainstream species (Atlantic halibut, cod) are showing up on watch lists. "One fish is taking the pressure off another, which means fishermen have had to go to alternative species to fill the void of things they just can't offer like they used to," says Sewall.

In Gloucester, restaurant owner Mark McDonough is located close enough to the docks so that he can literally have conversations with fishermen every day. And he does. his restaurant Latitude 43 buys directly from the smaller, family-run day boats that come in and out of Gloucester harbor because, he says, "we believe that if we buy local, we're safe."

Chris Parsons, the chef-owner of Parsons Table in Winchester chooses to take it even one step further: he discusses many of his seafood buying decisions with two marine biologist friends from Rhode Island. "They opened my eyes to the larger story," Parsons says, explaining that they've given him in-depth background information on what goes into salmon farming. That knowledge has helped him shape a plan for buying from farms that use low-impact methods. "I'm not an expert," he admits. "I could read some articles online and base my decisions on a little bit of research but that won't give me the full picture. Working with these guys really helps me cut to the chase."

Factoring Cost

Making responsible choices is just part of the equation. Most chefs will admit that ultimately what they serve comes down to price. "There will always be critics that say farm-raised salmon is bad. And yes, I think wild king salmon is the top of the line in terms of a well-managed species but it is ungodly expensive," says Jeremy Sewall. "It's hard to put a piece of fish on the menu at $44 per plate. Your guests aren't going to feel like they can come in every day and order it." Instead, he says, the farmed salmon he uses, farmed salmon from the Faroe Islands, "has a minimal impact on the environment and they're pretty responsibly raised." And he only charges $26 for it.

For other chefs and restaurants, dollars and cents equal out to more than just the final tab. Karen Masterson, a co-owner of Nourish restaurant in Lexington, considers the cost to the fishermen themselves. This spring, she started working with Cape Ann Fresh Catch (CAFC), a community-supported fishery, on a pilot program that incorporates restaurants into the community-supported model; Cape Ann now delivers weekly shipments of fish directly from Gloucester day boats to her restaurant kitchen. (CAFC is looking to launch the program at other restaurants, including Dog Café in Gloucester, this summer.) The setup is risky in that Masterson never knows what she might get (whole yellowtail flounder one week, cod filets the next). But once she receives the shipment, her kitchen staff comes up with specials and that's what she serves through the weekend.

While it is undoubtedly more expensive than working with a traditional wholesaler, she's chosen this route because CAFC provides a direct conduit to the fishermen. So instead of spending money with a third party week after week, she's paying slightly more to receive fish directly from the boat—and her dollars are going right back to the fishermen. "It's a truer cost of our food. From my perspective, that's a more just purchase," she says.

The Hook

Even while chefs struggle with making sustainable decisions, they do it knowing their efforts are part of a larger movement. For Steve Johnson, that means keeping his dollars in the local economy. "People in our own community, in Gloucester, are suffering. In this small way, I know I can keep my money here," he says.

Michael Leviton sees a larger impact. "Part of doing what I do is the hope that there is this eventual trickle-down in sustainability," says Leviton. "That it just becomes the way we do things so that everyone can afford it."

Kids Battle the Lure of Junk Food

By Maureen O'Hagan

From *Pacific Northwest Magazine*

✆

Battling America's childhood obesity "epidemic" takes
more than preachifying, as *Seattle Times* reporter Maureen
O'Hagan examines in this award-winning three-part feature
story. This first installment profiles a pair of obese teens and
the daily minefield of temptations they navigate.

Nathan Stoltzfus has a problem.

It starts first thing in the morning, when he catches five
or 10 minutes of TV just before heading out the door to
Northshore Junior High. "There's these commercials for Cookie
Crisp cereal or Pop-Tarts," he says. "They show some really happy
kid eating them."

Over at school, he makes his way to homeroom as the smell of
French toast drifts from the cafeteria.

At lunchtime, he sees a sign over the ice cream and cookies. It
says, "Treat yourself today." He tries to focus on his veggie-filled
sandwich. But invariably, one of his buddies will jump up for another run through the lunch line. "Who wants to come with me
to get some cookies?" the kid'll ask.

To Nathan, this innocent question is a trap. As the heaviest kid
at the table, he tells himself, keep your eyes on the veggies. But he
also wants to fit in. "It's very tempting," Nathan says. "You feel like
you almost have to do it in order to be friends."

Now, Nathan's just 14, but he's no slouch. He's articulate, creative, has a good group of friends and seems to take time to think about what he's doing. He's dedicated, too, singing for years with the Northwest Boychoir.

He's also been overweight for most of his life. To him, it feels like a curse.

And the pressure never subsides. There's the school's annual pie day to celebrate "pi"; there's the group Slurpee runs after school; the torment of his skinny brother devouring Oreos; the weekend trips to the mall. "A couple weeks ago, there was like 16 of us. One of the guys said, 'Oh my gosh you have to try this ice cream,'" he recalls.

What's a kid to do?

Right now, leaders here are trying hard to help. In the past decade, local agencies have been awarded at least $53 million in grants and other funding to combat obesity—most of it in the past year. They've enlisted hundreds of partners in this effort, and they're using some of the most newfangled approaches.

Within the next year, for example, they'll have spent at least $1.8 million getting healthy produce into corner stores. In the next two years, another $276,000 will be spent on building school gardens. Money will go to rejigger P.E. curriculums, train cafeteria workers and try to get kids to walk to school.

Still, all this effort will miss one of the biggest battlegrounds of all: what's going on inside Nathan's head.

"Treat yourself today," the sign in the cafeteria commands. Just say no, Nathan tries to tell himself. Let's call this the Temptation Complication.

It's a problem for Nathan. It's a problem for tens of thousands of overweight kids in Washington. And it's a problem for all of us.

It'll take a lot more than school gardens to dig our way out of this one.

People who work on childhood obesity often talk about how different the world was a generation ago. When she was a kid, University of Washington researcher Donna Johnson told me, soda was a special treat. Now, sugar-sweetened beverages are just a few quarters away, in the school vending machine. In surveys of Washington adolescents, about 40 percent said they drank at least one soda yesterday.

When he was a kid, former FDA Commissioner David Kessler says, there weren't coffee shops on every corner selling super-duper, fat-and-sugar, grande frappa-yummies. There wasn't the cacophony of chips and cookies at every gas station.

When I was a kid, I recall, we ate pretty much what our parents ate. Now, vast product lines are designed just for youngsters: the Go-Gurts and Lunchables and drink pouches. Experts say more new food products are introduced each year for kids than for adults. And guess what: Studies show kid food has more sugar than the adult version.

And don't even get me started on the "fruit leathers" and "fruit snacks" with nary a drop of juice. "When I was a kid," snickers Margo Wootan, director of nutrition policy at the Center for Science in the Public Interest, "they were called jelly beans."

This special kid food is sold on special TV stations created just for kids by special advertising execs who study youth culture as if they were researching a doctoral thesis.

Meanwhile, kids are noshing practically nonstop. "Your product doesn't have to be for a meal anymore," says Laurie Demeritt, president of the Bellevue market-research firm the Hartman Group. "Now there are 10 different 'eating occasions' throughout the day."

What we have here is a supply problem. Food is everywhere. That means temptation is everywhere. If Nathan makes healthy choices half the time, it's probably not enough.

But the Temptation Complication has another layer, one that's older than Go-Gurt and Nickelodeon and Mountain Dew. It has to do with biology.

Patsy Treece says her daughter, Hannah, has a "face that radiates kindness." She's right. Her eyes are a beautiful brown; her smile shines. At age 13, Treece says, Hannah's the kind of kid who'll stop to help if someone gets hurt on the playground.

She also has an appetite that won't quit.

At dinner, she'll ask for seconds, even thirds. "I'm really, really hungry," she explains.

Well, maybe not hungry exactly.

"It's just that if I see something good," she sighs, "I automatically pick it up and eat it." Like a lot of us, she gets pleasure from food. But afterward, she also feels pain.

Hannah's twin brother is slim and athletic, but her mom is also overweight. Treece has tried different diets with Hannah. She's tried sports. Delay. Portion control, using 100-calorie snack packs. "She'll have a couple of them," Treece says.

Don't even mention Flamin' Hot Cheetos. "She would kill somebody to get a package of those," Treece says. "It's almost like a compulsion." No kidding. Remember the old ad campaign, "Betcha can't eat just one"? That was Lay's Potato Chips. The same company makes Hannah's Cheetos.

Some people simply *can't* stop. There's science to prove it, says former FDA Commissioner Kessler.

Here's a guy who fought Big Tobacco. He's a doctor; he knows what's healthful. Yet until recently, he could come undone over a chocolate-chip cookie. "I have suits in every size," he says ruefully.

Our desire to eat doesn't originate in the stomach, really. We're wired to crave salt, sugar and fat, Kessler says. You see it in laboratory rats, too. They'll brave the possibility of electric shocks to keep eating their junk food. Even *bacteria* swim to sugar.

There's more.

"We used to think people were lazy or it was a question of willpower," Kessler explains. "I can now show you the (brain) scans. The vast majority of people who have a hard time controlling their eating have excessive activation of the brain's emotional core."

When you eat things like cookies or Cheetos you get an immediate reward. You feel good. Your brain actually changes when you eat that stuff, Kessler explains. The neurocircuitry gets rewired. Stumble across a "food cue"—maybe an ad for cereal, or the smell of French toast—and suddenly, your brain lights up. Your thoughts slip into those newly laid tracks and can't get off, like the way your skis follow along in a cross-country trail. Your brain, Kessler says, gets "hijacked." And the new pathway is reinforced further. Scientists say it's not exactly that we're addicted to food, but it sure is an awful lot like that.

Problem is, these food cues are everywhere. "We're living in a food carnival," Kessler says.

So we're not just fighting temptation like Nathan. We're battling our very biology, that automatic response that makes Kessler crumble at the thought of cookies and Hannah unshakable in the face of orangey-red salt.

Let's call this the Cheeto Compulsion. Betcha can't eat just one.

Hilary Bromberg, strategy director at the Seattle brand/communications firm Egg, says they sometimes put clients through a little exercise: *Talk about your food history.* "They enter almost a trance state," she says. "They say, my grandmother made me this, or my mother made me this. There's this visceral attachment."

Eating, in other words, isn't some sort of clinical calculation of calories. Most people aren't thinking, *Gee, I better have carrots instead of cake because I didn't get my five servings of vegetables today.* "Food is a source of sensual pleasure," Bromberg explains. "The emotions around food are profound." She's saying this as a marketing maven. She's also saying this as someone who studied cognitive neuroscience at Harvard and MIT.

Nathan's mother, Susan Stoltzfus, knows this, too. "Food has been that comfort or that source of consolation or that sense of belonging," she says. It's immediate, too—unlike losing weight, which requires forgoing that sense of pleasure over and over and over. "How do you live for that delayed gratification?" she wonders.

Nathan and Hannah might not explain it the same way. But they understand. Food is pleasure. Food is family, culture and tradition. Food is love.

Let's call this the Comfort Connection. And I'm willing to bet it's within arm's reach right now.

Marlene Schwartz, a clinical psychologist at Yale University, suggested a little experiment. Ask a roomful of people, *Who thinks junk-food marketing works?* All the hands will go up.

Ask, *does it work on you?* The hands will vanish.

"I think people decide, once it's in their pantry, it's no longer junk food," she says. Talk about getting inside your head. These marketing guys can put an idea in there and you don't even know it.

And it's growing even more sophisticated. Food producers have long hired experts to survey thousands of consumers at once. But in the past decade or so, the behind-the-scenes work has become even more stunning in its scope and highly particular in its findings. Some of the topics food marketers have studied recently: mother/daughter baking rituals; parents' stress level on car trips; the habits of kids at sporting events; how preschoolers are using their parents' smartphones; the traits of parents who are strict versus parents who are more permissive—and what it all means for their kids' eating habits. There's an entirely new genre of marketing and advertising firms, in fact, that focus on youth culture.

Meanwhile, in the past decade or two, says Demeritt of the Bellevue market-research firm, food-marketing companies also started going directly into people's homes. Shopping with them. Asking detailed personal questions. It's called ethnographic research, and it's being done in many cases by social anthropologists. Hordes of psychologists have been enlisted, as well, to better get inside consumers' heads.

The result is that marketers know exactly how families eat, what they eat and why. They know what makes them keep coming back, even when they know it's probably less nutritious.

Take Go-Gurt, for instance. It's one of the most successful kid foods ever. Moms are doling it out for breakfast, yet it's got more sugar per ounce than Coke. Yoplait sells $129 million worth of this stuff a year. Unnatural-hued goo in a squeezable tube!

How did Go-Gurt come to be? Really good research. In phone interviews, typical consumers would say breakfast was a sit-down, family affair. But when General Mills hired an anthropologist to spend time with ordinary families, she discovered they were actually eating on the go. A niche was identified: Families could use something portable. And squeezable yogurt was born.

It appeals to a kid's taste buds for sure. But the makers of Go-Gurt aren't selling that, per se. They're selling fun, coolness. Remember Kessler and the way food activates the emotional core? Bingo.

The opportunities to hit that emotional core are greater than ever. Advertisers can reach kids on their own cable channels. They can reach them on the Internet—for a lot less money. At the same time, they'll learn even more about them. Marketers know the search terms consumers enter, the information they put on social-networking sites, the pages they view and countless other metrics. Companies are prohibited from collecting personal data on users less than 13 without parental permission, but a *Wall Street Journal* investigation found even youngsters' online activities were being tracked, and in some cases offered for sale to advertisers. "Youth in 2010 will be the first generation in the post-digital economy the retailer will know by name," one marketing report said last year.

Check it out. There are Go-Gurt pages on Facebook. Go-Gurt videos on YouTube. There's even a Go-Gurt game. Betcha can't quit at one.

Last December, Demeritt's firm conducted a nationally representative survey about weight issues. Forty-two percent of people said childhood obesity is a big problem. But among the same people, only 3 percent agreed it was a problem in *their* family. "It shows you why people don't really do anything about weight," she says.

Other studies have found that most people aren't driven by a desire to be healthy. Instead, they judge their own weight in relation to their peers. If your peers are heavy, there's less motivation to reduce. As it turns out, we have a lot of heavy peers.

And look what we're up against: the Temptation Complication, the Cheeto Compulsion, the Comfort Connection.

Then there's the sheer firepower of food producers. "I remember a honcho at the CDC looked at me and said, 'They're way smarter than we are, and they have more money,'" the UW's Johnson recalls. She spends a lot of time nowadays thinking about the food environment, how it's easier to get Cheetos than it is to get an apple. But even if apples were everywhere, I ask her, would Nathan choose them? Would Hannah forgo her Cheetos? That's a tough one, she says.

"Most of us," she says sadly, "are going to choose fat and salt and sugar over foods that don't have those things in them." It's biology. It's culture.

Then she thinks, what if apples were made to seem more appealing? "It's not like Madison Avenue is inherently evil, right?" she muses. "If we could harness that . . . oh, man . . . Think of the potential of what they could sell."

PASTORAL ROMANCE

By Brent Cunningham

From *Lapham's Quarterly*

Is back-to-the-land agrarianism the answer to American food reform, or just another salvo in the culture wars? Political journalist Brent Cunningham, who is deputy editor of the *Columbia Journalism Review*, offers some healthy skepticism, based on grassroots research in a struggling Rust Belt city.

Betty Jo Patton spent her childhood on a 240-acre farm in Mason County, West Virginia, in the 1930s. Her family raised what it ate, from tomatoes to turkeys, pears to pigs. They picked, plucked, slaughtered, butchered, cured, canned, preserved, and rendered. They drew water from a well, cooked on a wood stove, and the bathroom was an outhouse.

Phoebe Patton Randolph, Betty Jo's thirty-two-year-old granddaughter, has a dream of returning to the farm, which has been in the family since 1863 and is an hour's drive from her home in the suburbs of Huntington, a city of nearly fifty thousand people along the Ohio River. Phoebe is an architect and a mother of one (soon to be two) boys, who is deeply involved in efforts to revitalize Huntington, a moribund Rust Belt community unsure of what can replace the defunct factories that drove its economy for a hundred years. She grew up with stories of life on the farm as she watched the empty farmhouse sag into disrepair.

Recently, over lunch in Betty Jo's cozy house in a quiet Huntington neighborhood, I listened to them talk about the farm, and I eventually asked Betty Jo what she thought of her granddaughter's notion of returning to the land. Betty Jo smiled, but was blunt: "Leave it. There's nothing romantic about it."

Leave it? But isn't Green Acres the place to be? Listening to the conversation about food reform that has unspooled in this country over the last decade, it's hard to avoid the idea that in terms of food production and consumption, we once had it right—before industrialization and then globalization sullied our Eden. Nostalgia glistens on that conversation like dew on an heirloom tomato: the belief that in a not-so-distant past, families routinely sat down to happy meals whipped up from scratch by mom or grandma. That in the 1950s, housewives had to be tricked by Madison Avenue marketers into abandoning beloved family recipes in favor of new Betty Crocker cake mixes. That the family farm was at the center of an ennobling way of life.

Evidence of the nostalgia abounds. There is an endless series of books by urban food revolutionaries who flee the professional world for the simple pleasures of rural life, if only for a year or so: *Growing a Farmer: How I Learned to Live Off the Land; Coop: A Family, a Farm, and the Pursuit of One Good Egg; The Bucolic Plague: How Two Manhattanites Became Gentlemen Farmers: An Unconventional Memoir.* A new crop sprouts each year. There's Michael Pollan's admonition, in his best-selling book *Food Rules*, to not "eat anything your great-grandmother wouldn't recognize as food." And then there are countless articles about the young and educated putting off grad school to become organic farmers. A March 5 piece in the *New York Times* is typical. Under the headline, "In New Food Culture, a Young Generation of Farmers Emerges," it delivers a predictable blend: twenty-somethings who quit engineering jobs to farm in Corvallis, Oregon—microbrews, Subarus, multiple piercings, indie rock, yoga. This back-to-the-landism is of a piece with the nineteenth-century, do-it-yourself fever that has swept certain neighborhoods of Brooklyn, complete with handlebar mustaches, jodhpur boots, classic cocktails, soda shops, and restaurants with wagon wheels on the walls.

The surest sign that this nostalgia has reached a critical mass, though, is that food companies have begun to board the retro bus. PepsiCo now has throwback cans for Pepsi (the red-white-and-blue one Cindy Crawford famously guzzled in the 1990s) and Mountain Dew (featuring a cartoon hillbilly from the 1960s) in which they've replaced "bad" high-fructose corn syrup with "good" cane sugar. Frito-Lay is resurrecting a Doritos chip from the 1980s (taco-flavored, a sombrero on the package). When nostalgia is co-opted by corporate America and sold back to us, as it invariably is, the backlash can't be far behind. Consider this the opening salvo.

It's unlikely that most serious food reformers think America can or should dismantle our industrial food system and return to an agrarian way of life. But the idea that "Food used to be better" so pervades the rhetoric about what ails our modern food system that it is hard not to conclude that rolling back the clock would provide at least some of the answers. The trouble is, it wouldn't. And even if it would, the prospect of a return to Green Acres just isn't very appealing to a lot of people who know what life there is really like.

I came to Huntington last November with my wife, the food writer Jane Black, to research a book about the effort to build a healthier food culture there. This is where celebrity chef Jamie Oliver last year debuted his reality television show, *Jamie Oliver's Food Revolution*, after the Huntington metro area was labeled the nation's most unhealthy community by a 2008 Centers for Disease Control study. It is a place that has suffered the familiar litany of postindustrial woes: a decimated manufacturing base, a shrinking population, a drug problem. It is also precisely the kind of place where the food-reform movement must take hold if it is to deliver on its promise of large-scale and enduring change.

How would the messages and assumptions that have powered the movement in the elite enclaves where it took root over the last decade—like Brooklyn, where we live, Berkeley, Washington, DC, etc.—play in communities like Huntington? Places where most people don't consider Applebee's and Wal-Mart to be the enemy. Where the familiar and the consistent are valued over the new and the exotic, especially when it comes to what's for dinner. Where a significant portion of the population lives in poverty or perilously close to it.

Jane and I suspected that the environmental, social justice, it-just-tastes-better case for eating seasonally and sustainably that our foodie friends consider self-evident would be met with skepticism—or shrugs—by people who have more pressing concerns than the plight of tomato pickers in Florida or the fact that cows are meant to eat grass, not corn. Nostalgia, though, did not immediately register with us as part of the movement's message problem. Perhaps because we live in the same world as the people who write those My-Year-Doing-X books, foodie nostalgia only seemed an innocuous, if annoying, bit of yuppie indulgence.

But in Huntington we kept meeting people like Betty Jo. Alma Keeney, for instance, who also grew up on a farm, is baffled by her daughter-in-law Shelly's decision to launch a goat-cheese business. Shelly runs the fledgling Yellow Goat Farm with her friend, Dominique Wong, and together they tend their Nubian and Alpine dairy goats on a small plot in Proctorville, Ohio, just across the river from Huntington. The eighty-seven-year-old Alma, Shelly told us, prefers individually wrapped American slices of cheese, not "farm food," which brings back memories of hard times. Jane and I started thinking about the uncritical, even simplistic way that our agricultural past—and our kitchen-table past—are referenced in American society generally, and in the conversation about food reform specifically.

The farmer is among the most enduring figures in the American pantheon. "Those who labor in the earth are the chosen people of God," wrote Thomas Jefferson in *Notes on the State of Virginia*, his classic work on the promise of the American experiment. The agrarian ideal—a belief that the family farm is the soul of the nation, a pure embodiment of our democracy—is a recurring theme in the national narrative. In 1782, J. Hector St. John de Crèvecoeur, in his *Letters from an American Farmer*, celebrated the notion of independence and self-sufficiency that is central to the story: "Where is that station which can confer a more substantial system of felicity than that of an American farmer, possessing freedom of action, freedom of thoughts, ruled by a mode of government which requires but little from us?"

The exalted status of the farmer has influenced political strategy and policy decisions throughout our history: in New Deal legislation that sought to place the family farm, which struggled mightily during the Depression, on par with other industries primarily through price supports; in an amendment to the Selective Service Act of 1940, which granted deferments to young men who were "necessary to and regularly engaged in an agricultural occupation"; in the creation of the U.S. food-assistance program in 1954, which pitted the stalwart American farmer against the menace of Soviet collectivized agriculture. And it surely informs the nostalgia that shrouds today's food-reform movement. One can essentially trace a through line from Thomas Jefferson's romantic image of the farmer to a recent defense of rural America in the *Washington Post* by Tom Vilsack, the U.S. Secretary of Agriculture: "There's a value system there. Service is important for rural folks. Country is important, patriotism is important."

Today most of us are so removed from the agricultural life, and so ignorant about its realities that this wholesome and nostalgic lens is the only one we know. Research by the FrameWorks Institute, a think tank employed by nonprofits to strategically reframe public conversation about social issues, found that for Americans, "Rural Utopia" is the dominant image of life beyond the cities and suburbs: a countryside "filled with poor but noble, tough and hardworking people living healthier and fundamentally better lives than the rest of us." This despite the fact that the reality in rural America today is one of decline: unemployment, rising divorce rates, a scramble to get out. According to the Bureau of Labor Statistics, farming is the nation's fourth-most-dangerous job.

Still, nostalgia has been a useful tool for the food-reform movement. It has provided a blueprint for how to think about and act on the daunting environmental, moral, and health problems associated with our industrial food-system for people who have the resources—financial, social, and educational—that allow them to participate in the movement if they so choose, and that predispose them to be sympathetic to the cause in the first place. Whether they started raising chickens in their backyards or simply became better informed about how their food is produced, this idea that we've lost our way has helped make food *important*, and in ways that go beyond simple sustenance.

Most of these food revolutionaries won't become actual farmers, and most of those who do—including those microbrew-swilling kids in Corvallis—won't make a career of it. But the movement has, I suspect, permanently changed their attitudes toward food, and this alone is already forcing modest systemic change. Since 1994 the number of farmers' markets in the U.S. has risen from 1,700 to more than 6,000. And between 2000 and 2009, organic-food sales grew from $6 billion to nearly $25 billion—still less than 4 percent of total U.S. food sales, but it's a start. Twenty years from now, most of these young "farmers" will have rejoined the professional ranks. Like their middle-class forefathers who tuned in, turned on, and dropped out in the 1960s, the appeal of financial security and a climate-controlled office will, in most cases, win out. That said, they probably won't be regulars at McDonald's, and they'll instill these values in their own kids.

Nevertheless, a "bourgeois nostalgia" pervades the food-reform movement, as Amy Trubek, an anthropologist at the University of Vermont who studies food and culture, points out. This is a perception of our food history that is the luxury of people who have little or no experience with farming, or more generally with manual labor. A perception that appeals to those who have never had to cook from scratch, let alone milk cows, kill chickens, and bake bread, just to get food on the table every day. A perception of people for whom it makes perfect sense to redefine their *leisure* time to include things like making *guanciale* or Meyer-lemon marmalade. As such, it may not resonate with great swaths of the public who don't fit this demographic profile, and it is a perception that ignores some crucial truths about our food history.

The reality of America's food past is far more complicated, and troubling, than is suggested by the romantic image at the heart of our foodie nostalgia. In *Revolution at the Table* and its sequel, *Paradox of Plenty*, the historian Harvey Levenstein provides a more sober, and ultimately more useful, accounting of that past. Levenstein shows how, starting in the late nineteenth century and continuing through the twentieth, food preparation steadily migrated outside the home. The reason is simple: if you have no choice but to plan and prepare multiple meals every day, cooking not only isn't cool, it's tedious and damned hard work.

Jane and I experienced this firsthand in West Virginia. We both are skilled and enthusiastic cooks, and as part of the reporting for the book, we wanted to see how well, and local, we could eat, and for how much money, preparing three meals a day. But we also understood that we were the kind of people for whom cooking is a hobby. Outside our door in Brooklyn, there is a cornucopia of options for the nights when we are busy or not in the mood to cook. In Huntington, though, most of those options are missing. Three months in we began to notice, with dismay, that as soon as one meal was finished, we had to start thinking about the next. Four months in, the joy of cooking was replaced by a growing irritation, a longing to amble down the block for *banh mi* or a bowl of ramen. By mid-March, Jane wrote in her journal, "Officially sick of cooking."

Between 1880 and 1930, the fruits of industrialization—canning, bottling, the growth of food manufacturers and restaurants—enabled the outsourcing of food preparation that Levenstein describes. Improved transportation—first the railroad and then the automobile—and food-preservation processes—refrigerated rail cars, for instance—brought an end to seasonal and regional restrictions on what we ate. Soon, people in Kentucky had the same food choices as those in New York or California.

The standardization of the American diet, so bemoaned by people like me, is what many—maybe even most—people want at mealtime. It is reassuring to have what everyone else has. The desire to have the same Big Mac in Syracuse as in San Diego is a big part of why fast-food outlets became America's default dining-out option, and why suggesting that as a nation we return to a more seasonal and regional way of eating will be a tough sell.

The family farm itself was not immune to these developments. By the 1920s and '30s, the gap between city and farm diets had begun to collapse, as processed foods became high-status items in rural areas. Poor Appalachian farmers began to prefer canned hams to country hams; farm women who could afford store-bought canned vegetables and other processed food embraced this new convenience without a second thought that they were abandoning a purer, nobler way of life.

There's a reason that less than 2 percent of people in this country are engaged in farming today, and it isn't simply that they've been driven off the land by Cargill and ADM. Just like Betty Jo Patton, many of them wanted things to be easier. This revolution at the table—the one that produced the food culture that today's revolutionaries are trying to counter—was considered a tremendous leap forward. It was modern. It gave people time for things other than keeping the family fed.

There is an even more fundamental concern about our nostalgia: America's food system has always depended on the exploitation of someone, whether it was indentured servants, slaves, tenant farmers, braceros, and other guest workers, or, now, immigrants. In his ode to the American farmer, Crévecoeur made it clear that he had a little help on his farm. "My Negroes are tolerably faithful and healthy," he wrote. This is an aspect of our agricultural heritage that rarely gets mentioned in the mainstream conversation about food-system reform, and it raises thorny questions about who actually grows, harvests, processes, and prepares the food in a capitalist society. We have no history of a food system that does not depend on oppression of some sort, and it seems unlikely that we will be able to create a future system that avoids this fate. The leaders of the food revolution have, in recent years, begun to speak out on the matter of farmworker rights. But few acknowledge—at least in the public debate—that if a central goal of the movement is a more equitable food system, then the notion that we once had it right is deeply problematic.

Exploitation is as true in the kitchen as in the field. Women have always borne the burden of transforming the raw to the cooked in the American home. Interestingly, it was a confluence of these two inconvenient truths about our food past—its reliance on women and exploited labor—that helped set the stage for our national embrace of fast food.

During the Gilded Age following the end of the Civil War, and continuing into the early twentieth century, America's rapidly expanding ranks of wealthy industrialists used extravagant dinner parties, featuring French haute cuisine, as a way to showcase their status. Hosts and hostesses sought to outdo one another: chefs were imported from France; eight courses were standard, as were menu cards, elaborate centerpieces, and a labor-intensive style of service known as *Ã la Russe*, which involved a butler carving and arranging the food on plates at a sideboard, which were then delivered to guests by servants. (The traditional style had been to fill the table with platters and bowls and let the guests serve themselves.)

The fetish for French cuisine, and all the attendant showmanship, quickly trickled down, and the nation's middle-class, which also was expanding, sought pecuniary emulation of this conspicuous consumption. Competitive dinner parties became a fixture of middle-class social life. And it wasn't just at dinner; there were also multicourse luncheons and high teas to pull together. The problem, though, was that middle-class households couldn't afford the number and quality of servants necessary for this kind of entertaining. This "servant problem," as Levenstein calls it, became something of an obsession for American housewives, who saw it as the main obstacle to fulfilling society's expectations of them.

Their plight led to various time-saving experiments, including cooperative kitchens—in which meals for multiple families were prepared for pickup in a central location—and the first home-meal delivery services. The former failed because they were regarded as a violation of the "ideal of American family life," a critique that had more than a whiff of antisocialist sentiment. The latter, it turns out, was simply an idea ahead of its time. These delivery services conformed to what was then considered the standard for a "proper meal": three courses and a menu that changed daily. As such, they were too expensive to be sustainable. The inability to solve the middle-class servant problem led, eventually, to a new conception in American society of what constituted a proper meal: simpler, cheaper, and of course, faster. We know how that story turned out.

By misrepresenting—or misunderstanding—our food history, we make a realistic conversation about what to change and how to change it more difficult than it already is. America will not revert to a nation of family farms. Convenience will always be important.

Seasonal and regional limitations on what we eat can only go so far. If Americans want to cook like their grandmothers, fine, but the fact is our grandmothers, by and large, made only a handful of meals, they made them over and over again, and they used plenty of short-cuts, courtesy of the industrial age. My grandmother's cornbread, which still remains the gold standard for cornbread in my family twenty years after her death, began with a Martha White mix.

Nostalgia is part of a larger message problem that food revolutionaries face as they attempt to broaden the appeal of their cause. For example, when Wal-Mart announced earlier this year that it would, over the next five years, reduce the amount of sodium by 25 percent and added sugars by 10 percent in its house brands, and pressure other food manufacturers whose products it carries to follow suit, the overwhelming response from within the food-reform community was, "That's not good enough."

In Huntington, and in communities across the country, Wal-Mart is where a lot of people get their food. They like the way the food there tastes. If that food has less sugar and salt—incrementally less so that they will still like the way it tastes—that is an important, and realistic, step toward a healthier food culture. Wal-Mart has many bad policies, but it's shortsighted to write off every initiative just because it comes from Wal-Mart. New ideas about food need to conform to people's social and economic aspirations, and those aspirations are going to be different in 2011 than they were in 1900, and they will be different, too, in Huntington, West Virginia, than in Brooklyn, New York. Achieving fundamental and lasting change in our food system will require the efforts of those yuppie farmers in Oregon who can afford to step outside the mainstream food culture and, as they say, vote with their forks. It will also require the more hard-won, incremental reforms at the big food processors and sellers, like Wal-Mart, that feed the great mass of people who either can't or won't vote with their forks.

Somewhere in the middle of these two efforts, hopefully, we can eventually arrive at a food system that makes sense for the twenty-first century. But the process of figuring out what that will look like needs to begin with a full and honest accounting of where we've been, and what's possible given where we are.

Farm to Table

Sweet Spot

By Paul Graham

From *Alimentum*

When novelist and English professor Paul Graham drove a
tap into the one maple in his yard, he bottled more than
syrup—he captured in words the poetry of coaxing golden
elixir from a tree. His debut short story collection *Crazy
Season* was released in summer 2012.

1. Reveille

The other day, I turned a corner while walking my dog in town
and suddenly, finally, knew the *bon mot* for the taste of the late-
winter air in northern New York. It tasted *tarnished*. I'd been worrying the language for weeks, and then there the word appeared,
dull on my tongue, a little bitter. The light, the wind, the damp-
ness: these all tasted faintly oxidized, like a dented old bugle my
grandfather had played with when he was a child and one year
presented to my brother. The bugle slept in a closet until someone
impulsively decided to hold the bell to the other's face while he
lay soundly sleeping, tongue the brassy mouthpiece, tasting metal
and neglect, and explode one flatulent, croaking note. In March I
seem to hear that sound constantly—spring's pathetic reveille—as
the days lengthen but bring no other relief. The snowy silence no
longer feels refreshing, as it did early in December, when the flakes
fell big and clung to the pine-boughs. Forget my stores of books
and firewood, forget my full freezer, my loving wife and good dog.
By now the sky has reabsorbed the sand and rock salt grit, the

frozen dogshit and trash in the jagged plow-furrows, seemingly with the intention of flinging them back in my face.

I'm waiting for 40–20. Forties during the day, twenties at night. Not a big deal most places, but here, it's better news than the arrival of the first robin. Robins can lie to you like any other courier. You also can't eat them, or at least *I* haven't.

When I finally see those numbers on the nightly news around the first week of March, I look at my wife and ask, Is this guy to be trusted? How many forecasts has he blown recently?

The urge to cheat, to set the taps early, is strong. It's not bad for the tree, only your pride; you'll be the one sad fool in the county with galvanized buckets hanging from his tree while the snow swirls like sand.

I choose a weekend day to tap, so I can boil the first catch of sap that very evening. Even if the yield is only a few tablespoons, like holy water, the first run is powerful stuff. The syrup speaks of hope, and of promises kept, in the way of all seasonal foods: apples, tomatoes, berries, venison. Early in the morning I walk outside with the Makita. I bought it years ago for home improvements, knowing even then I'm not that type. I use it once a year, on average, to drill ¾" holes in a sugar maple. I can hear my furniture-maker grandfather smacking his forehead with his palm somewhere on the other side of the grave.

We have only the one tree, a haphazardly trimmed 60-footer that turns orange in October. I'd never have thought to tap it if our old neighbor, a poet who worked in an Adirondack sugarbush with several hundred trees, hadn't tapped *his* one tree. One, it turns out, can be more than enough and not nearly enough at the same time. I've tried to picture the yield from 1500 taps and can only get as far as a fleet of tanker trucks and an acre of fire.

The holes go waist-high on the western side, which receives more sun and delivers more sap. I sink two taps with a rubber mallet. I reserve a third in case one dries up. Immediately the juice starts running, dribbles to the metal lip, and trembles in the sunlight before falling into the bucket with a flat *plunk*. It seems impossible that I'll empty these buckets twenty, thirty times, but I will.

The sap, when I lift a drop to my lips, tastes of the purest, cleanest water.

2. First Haul

The first day is always a good run, the tree primed like a well-oiled pump, and when I walk outside at four o'clock, I can't believe my eyes: the buckets are half full. If I don't get started on a boil now, I'll be up all night. I pour the two buckets into one and pour that into a heavy stockpot on the strongest burner. Fire it up. Walk away.

In thirty minutes, the sap will boil. A layer of scum needs to be skimmed off the top.

In three hours, the sap reduces by half. The kitchen smells honeyed. The brew in the pot is the color of light beer.

In four hours, it needs to be transferred to a wider, shallower pot, filtered again, and re-boiled.

In five hours, the kitchen smells of vanilla. There may be almonds, honey, butter, or hazelnuts, too, depending upon the year. There's surprisingly little "maple" flavor. The poet-friend accurately compared maple syrup made from one tree to single-malt Scotch.

Then the syrup begins to foam in the pot with a tidal fizzing. I must watch it carefully now, observe how it coats a spoon. There are instruments, hydrometers and thermometers, but I don't do precision. This explains why, although I'm a good cook, I'm a miserable baker—I can't be bothered, even though I know better.

How close to disaster do I want to ride? The longer the boil, the more intense the flavors, but if I push too far, the syrup will harden when it cools. I'll have to chip the crystals out of the jar with a fork and suck on the shards.

It's late. The dog chases footballs in his sleep, his nails clicking on the floor. My wife's knitting needles tap. I'm tired, so I kill the burner and pour the syrup into a clean ramekin. There's no need to sterilize a jar. This stuff won't make it to morning.

Recipe for First-Boil Syrup

Ingredients:
As much maple syrup as you just made
A spoon
A ramekin or small bowl
A partner, if you're the generous type, in which case you'll
    need two spoons and ramekins

In the steamed-over windows and soft light, pour the limpid syrup into the ramekin and eat it still warm. Close your eyes. Marvel at the power of nature, wonder at the Indians who were first bored or desperate or clever enough to boil down tree-water for a whole day *just to see what happened*. Who the hell *does* that? You're in their debt. Taste honey, vanilla, floral notes. Feel the back of your throat burn with the sweetness of winter's end.

Go ahead, make yourself sick. Pancakes? Overrated and too much trouble.

If you have an embarrassment of riches, pour the warm syrup over vanilla ice cream. But just how much syrup would that *be*, though?

And look—it's already gone.

3. Doubters

Even up here, in the heart of the country, they exist. Like this one: sixty-something, windbreaker, her pant cuffs stained by puddle-splash. Dogless. I've never seen this snow troll before, and I wonder what thawed snowbank she's crawled out of. She looks at me kind of walleyed as I'm at the end of my driveway collecting sap one week into the season.

"You're not boiling that *inside your house*, are you?"

"Why?"

"It'll take your wallpaper right off. It'll turn your walls yellow."

We've been home-making maple syrup for three years now, and we have had zero wall-issues. But we don't have wallpaper. After stripping nearly all that came with our house, we have unflattering things to say about people who do have wallpaper. Charlotte

Perkins-Gilman nailed it. I once called the stuff The Official Dec-
orating Choice of Hell. After fifty-some boils, my kitchen walls are
still white. True, the exhaust fan over the stove burned up in the
middle of last season, but that could have been anything—a faulty
part, spiders in the wiring, or, most likely my aggressiveness in general as a cook. I love heat. *Sear* is one of my favorite verbs, *smoke
point* one of my favorite temperatures. I revel in culinary acceler-
ants: brandy, amaretto, oil, chili paste. There is often fire—inten-
tionally. The hiss of deglazing makes me hoot. I've been meaning
to replace that exhaust hood, but electrical wiring is not my forte,
and what are windows for? It's 44 degrees already, after all.

I pity this woman and all of her kind. She appears unaware that
nothing great ever gets made the easy way.

4. Regarding the Holes in the Tree

They cannot be plugged up. Not with old wine corks, not with
DAP, not with cement, rubber or real. Once I've drilled them, the
sap won't stop flowing for a month. I won't stop boiling until the
yield is so low that it's no longer worth the trouble. Unless I'm using all of those hours while the stove steams to build a time machine that will enable me to go back two weeks *and not pick up that
drill*, I'm in it for the duration.

I know this in theory, but on days when I have other things to
do, because I'm running a typical household, not a sugarbush, it
will seem as if that maple tree is cranking out liquid just to spite
me. On a good day the buckets fill several times, and I pour them
into a 5 gallon water cooler barrel. One barrel is about eight
hours' boiling with all the burners running, meaning that night
dinner will be Thai takeout, or Mexican, or cheese and fruit, but
never out at a restaurant, because only a fool would walk away
from a kitchen with that much fire pouring out of it. I'd like to ex-
pedite the process, but that seems begging for trouble.

Just yesterday I heard about someone on the other side of town
who burned his garage down while trying to do a boil in—of all
things—a turkey fryer. He had too much sap and he needed to
raise the temperature *fast*, apparently.

These are my people. Sort of.

5. A Steep and Slippery Slope

Meaning both downward and upward. Downward in the sense that after only *one* season, let alone several, you can never go back. Log Cabin, Aunt Jemima, Mrs. Butterworth, anything that comes in a plastic jar or, Godhelpus, a tiny rectangular pack from Kraft with a peel-away top—it's criminal. I'll pay extra for a vial of the real stuff if I have to, though in northern New York we have syrup like the Gulf has shrimp, so it often comes for free. A year we lived in western Pennsylvania stands out as one of the darkest in my life for many reasons, not the least of which is the crap they expected you to dump on your pancakes.

And upward, in the sense that someone always seems to have a better setup. Like a friend who taps his maples *and* his black walnut tree. One year I finally got my hands on a jar of his black walnut syrup, trading it, I'm sad to say, for some amateurish bottles of homebrewed beer I'd made. Not even the guilt of sticking it to him could keep my brain from lighting up in neon—black walnut syrup is earthy, sweet, nutty-green, with the texture of molasses. I took a walk through our tiny village lot after pouring the syrup on oatcakes as he'd recommended, hoping to find that I'd mistaken a walnut tree for a scrub pine. Thwarted, I surveyed the treeline for anything else that could be tapped. *What about that tree over there? Or that one? Arborvitae sap? Yellow birch? Why not?* People have gotten themselves killed this way, I'm certain.

6. Potential

March is the time of the year for maple festivals, where you can watch what the big boys do and sample all sorts of maple products. We've never been. We have our own maple festival nonstop for several weeks, and we seem to invent a new product every day. Of course there are the usual suspects: pancakes, waffles, French toast, regular toast with a small beaded drizzle in the butter; but we also pour the syrup over ice cream, into ice cream, and can make sorbets and gelatos; use it in place of sugar in breads, cakes, and cookies; in homemade barbeque sauce, salad dressing, and mayonnaise; as a background to sauteed Thai chiles, pad Thai, and other stir fries; with fruit, yogurt, Kefir; alone, out of the jar, like a shot of whiskey on a rough day; shot *with* whiskey, like a sweet boiler-maker, on a rougher day; as a glaze for chicken, salmon, pork, and shrimp; over oatmeal, with cinnamon and nutmeg; in a pan sauce, like Madeira; in place of honey with strong cheeses. The limits are your own apprehensions and the amount you're willing to risk wasting should the flavors fall into dissonance. The only way I *haven't* had it is as the Canadians do, dumped into a pile of clean snow on a cutting board outdoors and stirred up with a stick, then eaten, communally, with a spoon.

7. Gifts

Whether any recipient of DIY maple syrup knows it or not, the value of the gift is always high, might be called equal in dollars to the yield in ounces squared (at least), where yield is the product of a completely idiosyncratic and therefore unpredictable product of temperature, time, and sugar level. I don't know a damn thing about higher mathematics, but it seems chaos theory might be useful here.

What I do know is that most maple producers say 40 gallons of sap yields an average of 1 gallon of Grade-A syrup. Our numbers may be higher early on, lower a little later. We'll put up 1 gallon or so a year, spread across an oddball collection of jam, jelly, sauce, mason, and other jars. Some jars, the best, we'll mark with smiley faces, a special cache.

I give jars away reluctantly, and only after attempting to verify that Aunt Jemima is nowhere on the recipient's premises, the apparition of her broad-shouldered, placating form in a kitchen cabinet being, like wallpaper, deeply revealing in a number of ways.

8. Anxiety and Its Cure

You begin anticipating the temperature and then move to obsessing *over* the temperature. The end can come quickly, and not always predictably. One week the temperatures hold steady in the 40s during the day, maybe toeing 50 as if considering the idea, and then one afternoon the wind shifts and the mercury shoots into the 60s. You can recover from only one 60 degree day, but not three or four. It doesn't matter if the temperatures drop again; the syrup will be thinner, the taste not as complex, suitable for baking, perhaps, but barely. In a good year there are two or three weeks in the forties and you can see the warm-up coming. I hate to curse the spring, but I'm never ready to let go unless the season has been so good that the tree has bullied me to exhaustion. I always want just one more jar socked away for August, when the blueberries are as deep as the January snows, and for January mornings, when the snows themselves are deep and we self-medicate with elaborate breakfasts of French toast and local bacon.

But the season *does* end, of course. It must. The arrival of the bees in April tells you all you need to know. One day they just appear around the buckets, a little drunk on the sunlight, circling wildly, too drowsy to sting. The rest of the run is theirs. If you keep collecting and boiling, you're only the fox from Aesop. I grab the pliers and pull out the taps, dropping them into the bucket with a bittersweet, metallic clank. The sap begins weeping down the trunk of the tree, staining the sidewalk.

Inside, I count the final take, squirreling away jars in various cabinets and corners of the kitchen and pantry so we can forget and rediscover them one night in November. The next season seems a long way off, but now, standing in the sunlight, it's easy to idealize the winter that must come first. Spring will atone for ending the boils with wild leeks and mushrooms in May. Not too long after, there will be garlic and strawberries. Then tomatoes, and watermelons, and winter squash. You can play your favorites, and we do, but the truth is that it's never too far to the next good thing.

Snowville Creamery Has a Modest Goal: Save the World

By Eric LeMay

From *Edible Columbus*

Poet, essayist, writing teacher, webmaster Eric LeMay—author of *Immortal Milk: Adventures in Cheese*—pursues his longtime obsession with dairy products from his home in Athens, Ohio.

Pouring milk from Snowville Creamery feels blissful. When you pick up the carton, you're greeted by a lovely dairymaid who seems to embody the countryside, with its green pastures and rustic fences. She wears a white fluffy bonnet and wholesome dress. At her bosom, she cradles a pitcher, as though she were Mother Earth pouring out the milk of human kindness. Behind her, the sun rises, encircling her with its hopeful glow.

This is milk made mythic, and it's one of the reasons I wanted to meet Warren Taylor, owner of Snowville Creamery. The other is the milk itself, which is thick and frothy and delicious. The first time I tried it, I drank a quarter of a gallon, glass after glass. I thought it was a milkshake.

How, I wondered, did a small diary nooked in the hills of Southeast Ohio produce milk this good? Who was this man behind the maid?

Now, having spent some time with Warren, I see that maid differently: She's wearing a red bandana around her forehead and raising a revolutionary fist in the air. She's marching down Independence Avenue, passing out leaflets on the dangers of genetically modified foods and hydraulic fracturing. And she's smiling, because she's looking forward to a fight. She's going to take on huge corporations who want to strip our food of its nutrients and flavor. She supports our local businesses serving our local communities. She wants our kids drinking healthy milk from healthy cows raised on a healthy soil.

"Love your food," she cries. "Love each other."

She wants us to join a revolution.

"This isn't about *this*," says Warren.

We're outside, standing on the slope of a hill, looking up at what's essentially a pole barn. It's the milk plant that Warren designed from the ground up, and he's telling me how it takes advantage of gravity: Every time Snowville processes and packages milk, they have to flush the plant's metal pipes with hot water and cleaner. This happens multiple times and generates waste. Thanks to the hill, however, this waste funnels down into a huge tank on the plant's lower level. But then what? You've still got to deal with hundreds of gallons of cleaner-filled wastewater. Turns out that Warren uses cleaners that are different from those used in most dairies. His contain nitrogen and potassium hydroxide.

"And you know what those are, don't you?" he asks.

I don't. I don't know 1% of what Warren knows about dairy. Luckily, Warren gets a kick out of teaching it. He has a catchy "Isn't this so cool?" vibe about him, even when he's describing chemical cleaners.

"Fertilizer!" he booms, nodding toward a nearby field where cows graze. In the distance, an unassuming sprinkler spritzes the grass.

Gradually, I get it: That's the wastewater. "Instead of contaminating the water supply," says Warren, already moving on, "we're nourishing the soil."

I'm hustling after him, trying to keep up, as I fit this latest information into my growing picture of the plant. So far I've learned about

- The genetic makeup of the 260 cows that provide Snowville with their milk. They're Jersey, Guernsey, Brown Swiss, Milking Shorthorn, Friesian and Holstein, all intermixed by years of cross-breeding. They're heartier and give healthier milk than the huge Holsteins that are confined on most dairy farms.

- The grazing practices used to feed the herd, which rotate through many different pastures rather than remaining confined to one, so that the cows can rebuild the topsoil instead of depleting it.

- The minimal amount of processing Snowville does to its milk, which leaves the milk's nutrients and flavor intact rather than pasteurizing and homogenizing them out of existence.

- The eco-friendly and taste-preserving cartons in which Snowville packages its milk. And the delivery schedule—from cow to store in less than 48 hours—that keeps its milk so fresh.

And that's just what I've managed to scribble down, because Warren is now detailing the spatial layout of the plant. Its core, where the raw milk goes from storage tanks to finished cartons, takes up only 600 square feet, which saves space, energy and money.

"So what *is* this about?" I finally get to ask. I can't imagine putting so much care into creating a milk plant that isn't about milk.

"This," says Warren, "is about building a canoe. This is about where you go with it and what you do with it."

A canoe seems a bizarre metaphor for a milk plant, but I press on. "What do you want to do with it?"

Warren doesn't hesitate: "Save the world."

Save the world? With milk? The idea sounds absurd, the sort of thing proclaimed by a zealot or a madman. That absurdity isn't lost on Warren.

"I'm hoping to be the Che Guevara of dairy," he says.

And sure enough, on the flipside of his business card, hiding behind that milkmaid, is a smiling Che. There's also a quote: "The true revolutionary is guided by great feelings of love." Che isn't Warren's only guiding spirit; you can add John the Baptist and Neal Cassady.

"And what about that milkmaid?" I ask.

"That's not me," says Warren, throwing a friendly, quit-messing-with-me elbow into my chest. "I'm the Hunter S. Thompson of dairy."

Warren grins when he says stuff like this—it's not every dairy-man who compares himself to a Marxist revolutionary, a religious prophet, a psychedelic muse and an antiauthoritarian wild man—but his eyes have an edgy gleam. He's not joking. He's got the messianic, near-manic glow of a visionary, because he has a vision: This small milk plant in Pomeroy, Ohio, is going to spark an international movement of social justice.

But how? That's a fair question. And when you ask it, you see that Warren also possesses the keen intelligence of an engineer. He can make his case coolly and methodically, even when it comes to saving the world:

First, take a food as essential to human existence as milk. Then build a dairy plant that provides this food for people in a safe, natural and healthy state. Run that plant in an environmentally sustainable manner. Then integrate that food and that plant into the local community and economy, so that it provides both good jobs and good nourishment for the people it serves. Then make that plant a model, make its design freely available to anyone who wants it, and mentor those who want to emulate it, so that milk plants like Snowville pop up around the country and around the world.

And don't stop with dairy. Let the principles that guide Snowville—sustainability, community, harmony and love—catch on and spread. Let them inform how we grow all of our food, how we run all of our businesses. And show people that this is really possible, right now, by starting with one small milk plant in Pomeroy, Ohio. Save the world.

If that sounds like unattainable vision, so be it. Warren pursues it tirelessly. He regularly works 100-hour weeks at the plant, and when he's not dealing with broken delivery trucks or carton fillers, he's speaking at universities, community centers and city council meetings about the need for sustainability and the dangers of hydraulic fracturing. He's traveled to Italy to represent Ohio as part of the worldwide Slow Food Movement. He's testified at USDA hearings on behalf of small dairies against regulations that unfairly favor mass producers. He's started initiatives for feeding livestock with grain that isn't genetically modified and worked for more honest and clear labeling of dairy products. He's helping to create a food distribution center in Columbus, so he and other producers can pool their resources. In essence, he's working to develop an infrastructure for delivering local food to local people.

And yet, amidst all this, he can't resist riffing on the best way to eat an ice cream sandwich, or the mindset of a martial artist ("You've got to expect to get hit"), or how to domesticate a wolf.

"I wouldn't want to control Warren," says Victoria Taylor, Warren's wife and partner. Victoria is the plant's co-owner and general manager and she's equally savvy about Snowville's larger vision. She'll quietly turn from giving a group of employees shipping instructions to telling you about the omega acids in milk or the effect of herd grazing on the North American landscape. She struck me as the still point of Snowville's spinning world. After 25 years of marriage, she's come to a conclusion: "You adapt to Warren."

Sure enough, once you hear about Warren's family history, you understand that he couldn't be anyone or anyway else. Warren's brother is the president of Daisy Brand, the largest sour cream producer in the world, and his father, a renowned dairy taster, worked in the dairy industry for 35 years. Warren got his dairy tech degree from Ohio State University in 1974 and three years later he was working for Safeway, the largest milk processor in the country. He spent three decades as a dairy engineer and consultant for plants that processed up to 300,000 gallons of milk a day. (Snowville, by contrast, processes 60,000 gallons a month.) He knows every facet of the industry.

"Cut me and I bleed white," he'll say, and you get the sense that dairy and destiny fuse in Warren, that his family made him into who he is.

That's true, but not how you'd think. For me, what most revealed the man behind the milk wasn't when I heard about Warren's father the dairyman, but Warren's father the Navy pilot. During the Second World War, he led the Medical Evacuation Squadron in the Pacific. Warren told me about one of his father's rescue missions to evacuate sailors who had survived the sinking of the USS *Indianapolis*. The ship was torpedoed by a Japanese submarine after delivering the atomic bombs to an air base on Tinian island. Of the ship's 1,196 crewmen, only 316 survived. On the way to pick them up, Warren's father and the pilots of the six other planes who were flying alongside him learned they were heading into a typhoon. Four of the six turned back, but not his father. And he made it.

"I realize now, my father didn't expect to live," says Warren, his voice going quiet, "but he didn't turn back." He pauses and takes a deep breath. Then, like a bull readying for the charge, he digs at the ground with his foot. "That's what I told the USDA the last time I was in Washington: I'm not turning back."

Matters of Taste

By Barry Estabrook

From *Tomatoland*

In *Tomatoland*, Barry Estabrook exposes how agribusinesses
compromise the environment, exploit migrant workers, and
obliterate the taste of Florida tomatoes. Estabrook's inves-
tigative food journalism has appeared in *Gourmet, The Atlantic,
Gastronomica*, and on his blog politicsoftheplate.com.

In early 2010, I enjoyed a supermarket experience that I'd
never had before. I bought a pretty, stridently red winter
tomato that actually tasted like something. It was by no means a
great tomato, harboring only hints of the flavor wattage of a vine-
ripened August tomato, but it was nonetheless unmistakably a
tomato, in taste as well as appearance. As is de rigueur with so-
called premium produce nowadays, my purchase, which weighed
three-quarters of a pound and cost $3.47, versus 80 cents a pound
for its nearby commodity cousins, bore a little sticker with the
trademarked name Tasti-Lee. A few days later, I returned to the
same store hoping to replenish my tomato larder, but the Tasti-
Lees had all been sold. And I was left to ask, what made this tomato
so different? How come I had never heard of it? Why don't all supermarket tomatoes taste like it did? And where could I get more?

With those questions on my mind, I drove to the University of
Florida's Gulf Coast Research and Education Center, a curvilinear
structure faced with pinkish bricks that rises like a space station
from the endless fields of strawberries and tomatoes a half hour's

drive southeast of Tampa. There, in an office crammed with all manner of tomato kitsch—coffee mugs, antique labels for packing boxes, framed vintage magazine advertisements for Campbell's Tomato Soup, tomato piggy banks, tomato salt and pepper shakers, and teetering stacks of—who knew—*The Tomato* magazine—I met John Warner Scott, a professor of horticultural sciences. Scott, who is known far and wide in the tomato business as "Jay," is one of the most prolific breeders of new tomatoes in the state. Over his three-decade career at the university, he has developed more than thirty varieties, although he doesn't keep track. "I haven't gone back and counted in a while," he told me. Unlike seedsmen who rely on molecular biology, DNA sequencing, and in the case of some crops, genetic modification, Scott is the last of a dying line of old-fashioned plant breeders. His tools are the same ones the great nineteenth-century tomato grower Alexander Livingston used to develop the Paragon: a keen eye, a disciplined palate, and superhuman reserves of patience. Each year, Scott grows several hundred different varieties of tomatoes, called "parent lines," in test plots surrounding the Gulf Coast center. His goal is to find plants with complementary traits—one may have disease resistance but low yields, another high yields but weak immunity—and crossbreed them hoping that some of the offspring will carry the best traits of both parents. Toiling in the hot sun, Scott pulled a floppy sun hat over his close-cropped graying hair and plodded through the rows, notebook in hand, carefully examining each plant and ticking off a mental checklist: How many fruits has it set? Are they big? Do they have cracks? Are their bottoms smooth and rounded, or do they still have scar tissue where the blossoms fell off? What's the color like? "With some of them, you can just look at the plant and just throw it out," he said.

If a plant passed visual muster, Scott took out his pocket knife and, still standing in the field, lopped off a slice and tasted it. "Plant breeding is a matter of seeing what's good," he said. "But you can't make any decisions based on one season. You have to grow a variety a lot of times in a lot of environments to see if it's really good."

Tasti-Lee is not perfect. Its fruits are smaller than commercial growers like. But it is as close as Scott has ever come to finding Tomatoland's Holy Grail—a fruit thick-skinned enough to shrug off the insults of modern agribusiness, but still tender at heart and tasting like a tomato should. . . .

Developing a better tomato can take years, and even then, there is no guarantee that it will be picked up by professional growers and have a shot at commercial acceptance. Florida's multimillion-dollar tomato industry is littered with once promising but now forgotten varieties. But in early 2010, after more than a decade of painstaking growing, breeding, and crossbreeding, Tasti-Lee left the rarified confines of academic test plots and rigorously monitored consumer-tasting panels to try to make its way in the competitive hurly-burly of the produce section. If Tasti-Lee lives up to its early promise, Scott will achieve a plant breeder's version of immortality. The rest of us finally will be able to head to the local supermarket any day of the year and bring home a half-decent-tasting tomato.

But it won't be an inexpensive tomato. Scott developed the Tasti-Lee to provide farmers in his state with a crop that can be planted outside to compete with hydroponic, greenhouse-grown tomatoes, the latest competitive threat to the Florida fresh tomato industry. Beginning from almost nothing in the early 1990s, greenhouse tomatoes expanded from a tiny niche-market novelty mostly imported from Europe to a mainstream produce item. They are now in every supermarket and account for about 10 percent of fresh tomato sales. Although Florida's field-grown slicing tomatoes remain as popular as ever in the food-service industry, sales have declined sharply in supermarkets. With Tasti-Lee, Scott hopes to give growers a baseball-size tomato that packs the same flavor as the popular ping pong ball–size salad tomatoes produced in greenhouses and often sold in clusters on the vine. "It seems to me that it would be a win-win situation," said Scott. "Consumers tend to be spoiled. They go into the grocery store and they expect to see fresh tomatoes any time of year, even if they grumble about the quality. I want people to buy Tasti-Lees because they like them, not just because they are the only tomatoes there."

Like many plant varieties, Tasti-Lee owes its existence to a combination of serendipity and the time-sharpened instincts of a great plant breeder. In Florida, the summer of 1998 was a terrible season for anyone trying to grow a tasty tomato. For some unknown reason—too wet, too cloudy, too hot—Scott's tomato field tests failed to produce fruits with any sweetness. Even tried-and-true varieties that had been sweet during previous years tasted dull. But one morning after tasting fifty varieties, each more bland than the other, Scott spotted a nice-looking tomato called Florida 7907. He picked a fruit, cut off a wedge, and popped it into his mouth. "Aha!" he said.

It was sweet, but Florida had one big flaw that made the variety a nonstarter for commercial production: It was too spherical. Florida growers like their fruits to have defined shoulders and slightly flattened bottoms. And that's only one item on a list of must-haves. Because producers are paid strictly by the pound, plants first and foremost must produce high yields of large, uniform fruit. They have to be able to resist diseases and tolerate extremes of heat and cold. And their tomatoes need to have a long shelf life. Taste enters the equation, if it enters at all, only after all those conditions are met. "Sometimes I wonder why we even bother with flavor," said Scott. "There is no easy way to breed for taste. It's not like there's one genetic marker that tomatoes must have to taste good," he said.

The structure of a tomato also makes breeding for both taste and toughness a difficult balancing act. The grocery part of a tomato, called locular jelly, has most of the all-important acidity. The pericarp tissue, the walls of a tomato, give it strength and some sweetness, but no acidity. The harder a tomato is, the more bland it is likely to taste. Even if you have a perfect balance of sugars and acids, there are still many obstacles in getting decent-tasting tomatoes from field to consumers' kitchens. Most Florida tomatoes are picked at the so-called mature green stage. Under ideal circumstances, a mature green tomato, reddened by being exposed to ethylene gas, will ripen and develop a measure of taste—not great taste, but something. The problem is that short of cutting one open, there is no definite way to tell a mature green tomato from one that is simply green. Inevitably, some immature tomatoes get picked and they will never develop flavor, although the ethylene will give them the appearance of ripeness. Finally, even if all else goes according to plan, a tomato can lose its taste if exposed to cold temperatures at any time between harvest and being eaten, after which point it can never recover it. Crop specialists even have a scientific term for this process: "chilling injury." Whether it happens in a truck, warehouse, produce section, or home refrigerator, a tomato that is held at temperatures lower than 50 degrees soon becomes a tasteless tomato. For reasons unknown, chilling reduces the fragrant volatile chemicals that are all-important in giving the fruit its distinctive flavor. Unfortunately, keeping tomatoes cool extends their shelf life, too, so the temptation to refrigerate dogs tomatoes every step of their journey to the table. Years of efforts by a plant breeder can be destroyed by a few days in a refrigerator.

Scott was also developing a line of what he calls "ultrafirm" tomatoes during the same season he happened on the sweet-flavored 7907. Among those he was developing was a tomato called Florida 8059. It was hard and had the right shape. Sensing a match made in heaven, Scott crossbred the sweet but too-spherical 7907 with the firmer 8059, and in the fall of 2002 the first of what was then referred to as Florida 8153 ripened. Scott thought the new hybrid carried the best traits of both parents. At trials conducted by the university, consumers on test panels agreed. Time after time, 8153 beat out other tomatoes. Subsequent chemical analyses showed that the fruit had a desirable balance of sugars, acids, and volatiles. It also had a surprise bonus: Both of its parents possessed what plant breeders call the "crimson" gene, which was originally revealed when the pioneering tomato geneticist Charlie Rick crossed a wild *L. chilense* (a relative of the domestic tomato) with a commonly grown variety. The crimson gene gives 8153 a striking fire-engine red color and an extraordinarily high level of lycopene, a sought-after antioxidant. "It sounds like magic, doesn't it?" said Scott. "It really is, in a way."

Florida 8153 had everything going for it, except for a catchy, appetizing name. Scott christened and trademarked his new baby Tasti-Lee, Lee being the first name of his mother-in-law, a tomato lover who had encouraged and supported his research through the years. "You hear lots of stories about bad mothers-in-law, I had a great mother-in-law," Scott said, a flash of emotion overcoming his usual deadpan. "She had tasted what was then still just called Florida 8153. She really liked it and encouraged me. Sadly, she fell terminally ill. I went to visit her in the hospital. She was in a coma at that point, but I took in a tomato anyway and showed it to her and told her that I was going to name it after her. I like to think she heard me."

Four seed companies lined up to bid for rights from the university to produce and distribute Tasti-Lee seeds. The winner was Bejo Seeds, Inc. A large, family-owned, Dutch firm with offices around the world, Bejo's specialties are cabbage, carrots, and other cool-weather crops. "We felt that marketing would be a key to Tasti-Lee's success," said Scott. "It seemed like Bejo would be hungry to get into the tomato market and that they would push Tasti-Lee pretty hard."

The job of giving Tasti-Lee that push fell to Greg Styers, Bejo's sales and product development manager for the southeastern United States, who has been known to board airplanes lugging twenty-five-pound boxes of tomatoes as carry-on baggage. "We had a vision to start with a grassroots movement," said Styers. "We were going to start with roadside growers and chefs. People who were interested in good flavor and good quality. Then we were going to work our way up." It didn't turn out as planned. Styers, who was looking for a grower who shared his vision that Tasti-Lee was "born to be a premium tomato," approached Whitworth Farms, which grows vegetables on seven hundred acres near Boca Raton, making it a small player in the Florida tomato business. "Whitworth was big enough to deal with some large retailers, but small enough that they were willing to take a chance on Tasti-Lee. It was a perfect fit for us," said Styers.

One of Whitworth's customers was Whole Foods Market. Glenn Whitworth, who owns the farm along with his sister and two brothers, approached one of the company's produce buyers. Weeks went by before the buyer would even schedule a meeting with Styers and Whitworth. When they did finally get some time, Styers stopped by a Whole Foods store beforehand and bought one of every tomato on display and added a Tasti-Lee to the mix. On the basis of that impromptu conference room taste test, the buyer agreed to test-market Tasti-Lee. In February 2010, Tasti-Lees began appearing in sixteen Whole Foods stores in Florida. By late March, reorders were coming in faster than Whitworth could grow Tasti-Lees. Later that spring, Whole Foods stores as far north as Washington, DC, began to carry Tasti-Lees, and by the end of the year, other retailers and even a few restaurant chains were expressing interest. "I think the stars really lined up for Jay when he developed this variety. It truly is remarkable," Styers said.

Scott, who drawls his carefully chosen words with little inflection and almost no emotion, didn't go that far. "I stand behind it," he said. "For a full-size tomato, it's better in my opinion than what's out there. Hopefully, it goes." If it doesn't, Scott has plenty to keep him busy. He's currently developing heat-tolerant tomatoes, tomatoes with resistance to the virulent leaf-curl virus, and tomatoes that can be grown on the ground and theoretically harvested by machine. And he hasn't given up on flavor. "In some work we've done, there is this fruity-floral note that adds pique to the sweetness," he said. "We've crossed a big, crimson tomato with that trait into one of Tasti-Lee's parents. The result might have even better flavor."

OLIVES AND LIVES

By Tom Mueller

From *Extra Virginity*

∞

Living in Liguria in an ancient stone farmhouse surrounded
by olive groves, writer Tom Mueller found ready inspiration
for this groundbreaking book about the international olive oil
trade—its frauds, its failures, and the artisanal producers
striving to restore honor to the label "extra virgin."

For the De Carlo family olives mean home, not only because their family tree has intertwined with their groves
and with oil-making for the last four centuries, but literally as well;
their house is perched atop their mill like the keep of a castle. The
impression of defensiveness at casa De Carlo is accentuated by the
imposing security wall which rings the property, as well as the sur-
veillance cameras which film everyone who approaches the main
gate and project them on screens inside the house. Local producers
are periodically held up by armed oil bandits, who drive tanker
trucks with high-pressure pumps to siphon oil out of storage silos.
"After a certain hour we don't open the gates," Saverio said as we
returned to the house for lunch, after touring the De Carlo groves.
Francesco and Marina were waiting for us beside a large olive-
wood fire, Francesco resting his head in his sister's lap as they ate
pickled *cima di Mola* olives from a small porcelain bowl and tossed
the pits onto the coals. (Olive pits are an excellent fuel, and oil-
makers often sell their olive pomace—the solid residue from oil

extraction, consisting mostly of crushed pits—to electric companies and other industries, to be burned in furnaces.)

Grazia knelt on the hearth beside them, and set several pounds of suckling lamb on a grill over the coals to cook. While the meat sizzled and popped and we watched the little eruptions of flame from each drip of fat, she told a true story of poisoning, blindness, and death, and said she half wished it would happen again.

In March 1986, she said, hospitals in northwest Italy began to admit dozens of people suffering from acute nausea, lack of coordination, fainting spells, and blurred vision. Twenty-six died, and twenty more went blind. Investigators eventually discovered that each victim had recently drunk a local white wine; several producers, they found, had been raising the alcohol levels of their wines by cutting them with methanol, a highly toxic substance also called wood alcohol. The scandal, and the resulting government crackdown, devastated the Italian wine industry. Consumption plummeted, and hundreds of producers, most of them honest, went bankrupt. Ultimately, however, the crisis radically improved Italian wine-making and forced a generalized shift from quantity to quality.

"Before the methanol scandal, people around here didn't make wine like this," Grazia said, pouring glasses of Rivera Il Falcone 2004, a garnet-red wine made from a local grape varietal, *nero di Troia*, by a producer at Castel del Monte, a nearby medieval castle. "And even if they had, nobody would have bought it. Most people just bought their wine in big jugs without labels. You'd see them on tables in restaurants, where they'd been sitting open for days. Most people wouldn't dream of buying a bottle of wine with a label on it."

After the methanol crisis, consumers grew more particular, and the producers who survived the market consolidation learned to use techniques and technology pioneers by French enologists. "After the scandal, producers started creating brand names they were proud of and wanted to defend. Only after methanol did people start thinking about what they were buying and drinking, and become willing to pay for the good stuff. And only after methanol did the government get really serious about checking quality, and making sure that the bottle contained just what the label said."

During the 1990s, dozens of premier Italian wines emerged, and wine became a major export product (wine recently topped $1 billion in annual sales in Italy).

Grazia brought the wine to her lips, then stopped and put it down without tasting it. "In olive oil, we're where the wine-makers were before methanol," she said. "We're stuck in the dark ages." She shook her head disconsolately. "It would be awful to see my children's livelihood damaged, even destroyed. And I'd certainly never want to see anyone hurt. But sometimes I wish there could be a methanol scandal in olive oil, which would obliterate this corrupt industry completely, and rebuild it in a healthy way. It's been Babylon around here for far too long."

Our lunch began with a succession of seasonal vegetables, mostly from the De Carlos' own garden: *lampascioni*, a small wild hyacinth bulb marinated in oil and vinegar; meaty, densely flavored cherry tomatoes; *puntarelle*, the tender tips of a local chicory; and flat little artichokes as big around as a pound coin or a quarter, lightly fried. "*Pugliesi* eat an incredible amount of vegetables—we're like goats," said Francesco, a rangy twenty-four-year-old with a crew cut and large, dark, serious eyes that watch you unblinkingly, though their intensity is softened by a faint, unsarcastic smile that never leaves his lips. He holds a degree in food quality and a diploma in olive oil tasting from the University of Naples and recently launched a De Carlo line of vegetables in extra virgin olive oil: mushrooms, artichokes, peppers, and other produce grown on their lands, as well as green table olives of the *picholine* and *cima di Mola* cultivars. "I introduced them to broaden our product offering so that our facilities would remain active throughout the year," he explained. "But given the sorry state of oil prices nowadays, they're a much higher-margin business and help us stay profitable." His modern financial jargon was so different from his father's homespun way of talking about the oil business that I instinctively asked if he and Saverio worked well together.

Francesco didn't miss a beat. "No. We argue every day," he said. "Every single day!" And when the laughter, a shade nervous, subsided, he added, with a quick, testing look at Saverio: "Disagreeing, sharing different opinions, deciding together the best way forward—that's the best way to collaborate, no?"

For all his university training, Francesco clearly shares his father's visceral enthusiasm for olive oil. His earliest memories also concern the family mill—such as the time, as a three-year-old, when he fell asleep in a little nest between sacks of olives, and slept through the increasingly despairing cries of his family as they searched for him amid the whirring blades and grinding wheels.

"If you'd come a couple of weeks earlier, or later, you'd be eating a completely different meal," Francesco said, looping a green ribbon of Arcamone oil over a big bowl of a half-dozen different wild-looking greens, most of which I'd never seen before, and whose names he knew only in the local dialect, not in Italian: *cuolacidd, spunzál, sevón, cicuredd*. "We *pugliesi* are demanding about these things," he continued as he stirred the glistening leaves. "We try to eat only vegetables and fruits that are in season. Many Italians are the same. They prefer fresh things from local gardens to the brown, tired-looking produce in supermarkets, even when local crops cost more. So why don't they buy their oil the same way? Olives are a seasonal fruit, and olive oil is a fresh-pressed fruit juice—it's best shortly after it's made, and goes downhill from there. Why on earth do people buy expensive vegetables like these, and dress them with the cheapest oil they can find?"

De Carlo oil flowed for the rest of the meal, gushing over the *burrata*, a rich curdy cousin of mozzarella, and pooling in the little cups of the *orecchiette* pasta with *boragine*, a wild herb. At first I thought the De Carlos were showing off for me, but I soon saw that they used olive oil this way every day, choosing from the four different oils on the table the one that best fit each dish they were dressing. Saverio sloshed so much Tenuta Torre di Mossa, the family's pepperiest oil, over his grilled lamb that the others giggled and pointed. He bobbed his head and smiled happily, the first smile I'd seen from him. "I've spent my whole life making oil, but I can never eat enough of it. What other job gives you this?"

He handed me the oil, and I poured some over my lamb. As if it had catalyzed subtle chemical reactions in the meat, I tasted dense new flavors which I hadn't noticed in my previous, unoiled bites: the rosemary and *santoregia* Grazia had used to season it, the browned fat, the light charring from the olive-wood grill—each flavor had a new depth and intensity. The meat even felt different, more supple and juicy. This oil wasn't just a condiment, but had entered into the dish.

When I observed this, Francesco snorted. "Try telling that to a chef!" He explained that he'd recently given an oil-tasting course in Naples to twenty head chefs of prominent restaurants, most of whom had shown the most abject ignorance about olive oil. "Each of these guys ran a top-flight restaurant, right? Some had Michelin stars. They had highly developed palates for wine and for foods of all kinds. But every last one of them was using a refined olive oil or a cut-rate extra virgin in their kitchens, and even on their tables. They'd been using bad oils so long that they didn't even know what a good oil tasted like."

Grazia, who had been silent for some time, spoke with sudden force. "Then we've got to teach them. The road we've got to follow is *la cultura*; educating people about good oil is the only way out of this crisis. Because once someone tries a real extra virgin— an adult or a child, anybody with taste buds—they'll never go back to the fake kind. It's distinctive, complex, the freshest thing you've ever eaten. It makes you realize how rotten the other stuff is, literally *rotten*. But there has to be a first time. Somehow we have to get those first drops of real extra virgin oil into their mouths, to break them free from the habituation to bad oil, and from the brainwashing of advertising. There has to be some good oil left in the world for people to taste."

She stood and went into the kitchen to get dessert, leaving a sudden silence in the room. Everyone seemed to be thinking about what she'd said, and what she'd omitted: that if the economics of oil-making don't change soon, no one will be left to make real extra virgin oil. Not even the De Carlos.

THIS LITTLE PIGGY
WENT TO MARKET

By Laura R. Zandstra

From *Memoir Journal*

Before she became a creative nonfiction writer and oral historian, teenaged Laura Zandstra helped her Indiana farming
family sell produce at a weekly farmer's market in Chicago.
With impressionistic strokes, she evokes the market day experience as seen from behind the scales and cash register.

Chicago at four a.m. smells like two hundred years of dirt and one hundred years of oil and gasoline spilled on pavement and then congealed in the dew before daylight. About that time on Saturday mornings, our 1979 Mercedes truck pulled into the high school parking lot at 29th and King Drive, thirty miles from our Indiana fields, and eight of us would tumble out into the darkness, throw open the rear roll-up door, and set to work unloading our wares.

The cabbages were in fifty pound boxes that, try as I might, I could not heave off the back of the truck by myself. The beans were in square wooden crates, the green onions in fancy waxed cartons with pictures on them. We bought the green onions from our neighbors, the DeJong brothers. They sold us radishes, too, be-cause we didn't quite have the space or the dirt or the patience to grow them ourselves, as prone to pests and in need of constant looking after as radishes are. The tomatoes, however, were ours, and kept in cardboard that cushioned their soft red flesh. The spinach was ours, too, packed into bushel baskets with lids held in place by wooden slats secured under metal handles.

The beets, the carrots, the turnips, the corn: load by load, we paced the lot from the rear of the truck to unmarked spots on the pavement, arranging these boxes and bushels on the blacktop where their contents would be displayed once the sun was up and the community emerged. While we worked, a handful of people would stray past, illuminated beneath the streetlights the last ones to sleep and the first ones to wake. They'd wish us good morning, or stop to tilt their heads and watch our efforts.

Brother Al was one of this handful. He always appeared long before darkness had melted from the sky, with hair that looked like an old Brillo pad and gray coveralls that smelled like sweat and dust.

"You got any butta' beans, Baby?" he'd ask me.

I'd shrug. "I don't know yet."

"You don't know yet?" he'd tease with a grin and a gentle elbow jab.

"It's too early," I'd tell him with a scowl.

"Too early for what? How old a' you?"

"Eleven."

"You just a baby."

"The truck isn't all the way unloaded yet," I'd say, mad. "So it's too early for me to know if there are any lima beans today." Then defiantly under my breath: "I'm not a baby."

Our vegetable stand was the most primitive at the South Side farmer's market. My father and his brother had purchased canopies from a man with a fancy welder who lived a few towns over. The man had cut one-inch metal pipe into long pieces that served as beams and short pieces that served as rafters. These made sturdy rectangular frames once fitted into welded steel corners that looked like hollow-limbed spiders. We'd bungee gray tarps over two such frames and then erect them, three medium-length pipe legs on each long side of a rectangle.

Beneath the tarps we balanced old doors on tall, conical bushel baskets that arrived from southern states packed tight with pole beans and purple hull peas. The doors had come from deep in the junk stocks of our farm where they'd congregated for years, gathered two and three at a time from dumps and construction sites and neighbors who were remodeling. There is room on a farm for all manner of almost-garbage—car carcasses and plywood scraps and retired traffic signs—and always the sense that one day, hoarded odds and ends will fall precisely into place in the puzzling mill of farm projects.

The doors and baskets had found just such fruition, and once they were lined up in long skinny rows, we piled them with produce picked from our fields in the days before. Yellow squash next to zucchini, leaf lettuce next to green peppers, pickles next to tall stalks of dill. The melons arrived on their own flatbed truck and were too heavy to arrange on our rickety doors, so we'd line up from truck to table front, tossing Millionaires and Sangrias, Saticoys, muskmelons, and honeydew one man to the next, arranging them on the pavement until handsome foothills of fruit girded the walkway beneath our gray tarps.

To the left and around the corner from us in the line-up of vendors was Lyon's Orchards, whose apple cider is still the best I've ever had. Tom Lyon—a dashing football player of a farmer's son with wavy black hair slicked back from his forehead—enjoyed harassing me as much as Brother Al did. He'd throw rotten fruit at me from time to time just to watch me get mad, which I always did in spite of myself.

Don the flower guy was to our right. His sandy blonde hair stuck out in wings beneath his green seed company cap and hung in a thick mustache under his nose. He chain-smoked from open to close, a cigarette dangling between his lips while he handed out change or put bouquet stems in plastic bags so as not to drip mud and water onto paying customers. He gave me leftover bunches of baby's breath at the end of the day.

"Here comes trouble," he'd always say when he saw me approaching.

At the far end of the parking lot, across a wide expanse of gravel and cracked pavement, were two vegetable growers—our competition. They tried to outsell us by offering cheap produce bought in bulk from California, or so the farmer rumor went. I squinted my eyes in their general direction whenever I had a moment to spare and assumed that they squinted back.

It was my job to scout out the nature of these competitors to make sure we were on level playing fields. After setup, I'd nose around their fancy, store bought display tables and bright blue tents, memorizing the price per pound of everything I could, and then present the information, along with note of any dubious products, like red peppers in June, to Uncle Butch, my boss. He'd sigh and heave a bit, then say, "Good work, Laura. We couldn't do this without you," and send me off to sell melons.

Melon prices were always set on dollars and quarters, so one could conduct sales and dig change from the green money-apron pockets without the need for plastic bags or proper scales or speed in simple math.

"Muskmelons are two for a dollar," I'd tell those who stopped to sniff at the alligator skin of the fruit.

"Mush melons?" people would snarl in disgust.

"No, muskmelons. They're just like cantaloupe."

"Got any half-price melons?"

"Not yet, Brother Al. Come back later and I'll have some set aside for you."

"Come back later?" he'd chuckle. "You just a baby, but I'll see if I can't come back after lunch, get me some melons and butta' beans. What about okra? You got any okra today?"

"I think I saw some halfway down the table," I'd say and point timidly, knowing that if I was wrong, further harassment would ensue.

Brother Al would snort with a smile and pat my shoulder before ambling off into the crowds.

By the time I turned twelve, I had graduated from melons up to the greens table. I was shocked to learn of its existence. Unbeknownst to me, somewhere hidden deep in its flat acres, our farm produced endless bushel baskets of turnip greens, curly mustard greens, slick mustard greens, collards, and kale. Unlike the rest of the vegetables at our stand, these items had never made an appearance at our dinner table. I'd never even heard of them, and yet they were significant enough to require a sizable display and separate staffing. Fortunately, my lack of knowledge mattered little. The greens went like hot-cakes no matter who was selling them.

"Now," my uncle instructed, joining me briefly on my first day behind the greens table where two bushels of each variety were pushed up against each other in haphazard showcase, "when one basket is almost empty, you dump the last few handfuls into the other bushel of the same kind and then put a new one up on the table. Got it? I'll come and check on you in a while."

Within moments of him leaving my side, women crowded in to claim five pounds or five bushels, stuffing handfuls of leaves into plastic bags that we bought at discount because they'd been mis-printed. "Tank you!" smeared in red, four times across white bags engorged with produce. "Fred's Discont Grocer," "Mike's Meaatts Welcomes You!"

The misprints didn't matter either. The women jabbered to-gether and rolled deep laughter over their purchases as they planned for good food and family. Then, while still scrutinizing the spread as if they might have missed a perfect handful of leaves in a bushel basket not yet considered, they'd absent-mindedly hand me their bags to be weighed.

"Baby, how much I got there?"

I'd place the bag on top of the scale and then drag my finger right across the price table, which calculated from fifteen cents a pound all the way up to a dollar twenty-five.

"Four pounds at fifty cents a pound . . . " I'd figure to myself. "Two dollars."

"What d'you say, Baby?"

We had to pay for our scales to be reckoned and licensed. A man in a nice button-up shirt would come with a briefcase full of weights on the first day of market each summer and examine the front and back panel of the display windows as he gingerly placed two pounds, five pounds, ten pounds in the pan on top. Without fail, he'd renew our machines with an official sticker slapped onto the front. He'd smile, shake hands with us and take our money, gone within moments of appearing, yet the event always caused a nervous stir in my Uncle Butch, which infected me even though I knew that we would never deliberately cheat anyone. My family was raised in the tradition of John Calvin and the Heidelberg Catechism; vigorous moral standards were part and parcel to the ins and outs of days. Short-changing people on their vegetable purchases was almost as bad as rejecting the church, and this religious intentionalism was only enhanced by an existence that hinged on the wiles of the earth.

The Lord giveth and the Lord taketh away, I knew. There were floods and droughts and there were perfect warm springs and fields made rich from the old swamps of Lake Michigan. There were years with too many locusts, with lightning storms and early frosts that burnt whole fields of tomatoes, but there was always enough food to keep our family far from hunger, so we were in a position to do the giving and not the taking away.

The scales, though, were prized and pricey possessions to be handled with extreme care. Drop them once and they were ruined, rejected by the man in the button-up shirt, thrown irrevocably out of whack, the glass cracked, the mechanics jarred so that no more than half a pound could be correctly ascertained. Sometimes Uncle Butch would shove a screwdriver into the metal guts of an ailing machine, but the prognosis for such a procedure was generally grim. I was therefore not to pick up the scales when they were loaded on and off the truck, my arms too flimsy to be trusted with the weight and investment of the things.

I was allowed only to take bags from customers, place them on top of the scale, figure the weight, and then state the price. "Four pounds. Two dollars."

"Four pounds? Gimme 'notha bag. I need more than that. Got the pastor's family comin' over for dinner tomorrow after church! Phew! Pastor loves those curly mustids. You ever try those?"

"No."

"Well, why not? Here, try one. Take a bite."

I shrugged slightly at the challenge, the picture of nonchalance, then reached into a bushel basket, grabbed hold of a leaf and wiped it off on my money-apron.

"Little dirt won't hurt you none," the woman said, watching with a mischievous grin on her big, brown lips.

I nodded and bit down, grinding the green between my molars for a moment with disinterest, but when the taste spread over my tongue I didn't try to hide my shock and disgust. The woman broke into giggles and those at her elbows looked up to see what was going on.

"Curly mustid," she said by way of explanation as she nodded at me, and then everyone was chuckling.

"Got a little bite, don't it?" another one said with a knowing flop of her wrist.

"Yeah," I said, examining the curly mustard as if to gain a better understanding.

I never imagined that a frilly leaf colored such a happy shade of green could have so much heat and pepper coursing through its veins. This was almost as mean as feeding jalapeños to my younger cousins, but the ladies loved me for my innocence. I was the scrawny farm girl with glasses and freckles and a limp brownish ponytail straggling over ratty work clothes, selling greens, easily coerced into taking big bites of fire leaf. They came back every weekend for years, knowing me as I finished junior high and started high school, knowing me as the girl who sold the mustids and took the food stamps.

"How you doin', Baby?" they'd say every week. "Mm-mm-mm, look at these greens! I need six pounds. You got any butta' beans today?"

The markets stretched out across the summer, starting in mid-June when the asparagus and rhubarb and peas were just in, and ending with the last days of October. As the months passed, more and more doors were balanced on bushel baskets and covered with the burgeoning harvest until the frosts set in and the fields went brown. By then, days were so cold that I would wear four pairs of pants to work, making myself sick with all that elastic squeezing at my middle, and five layers of warmth on top so my movements were slow and padded. I despised the taste of coffee, acidic and bitter, but I started drinking it to warm my insides and keep my fingers from freezing on those mornings at the greens table, when I scooped up the leaves myself so the ladies didn't have to get their hands out of their gloves and make them wet and dirty and cold.

Home Cooking

How to Live Well

By Tamar Adler

From *An Everlasting Meal*

Tamar Adler's quirky culinary education has included working under such talented writer-chefs as Gabrielle Hamilton,
Dan Barber, and Alice Waters. In *How to Live Well*, Adler
shares recipes, kitchen tips, and a compelling philosophy of
cooking as an approach to life.

Si stava meglio quando si stava peggio.
We were better off when things were worse.
—FIFTEENTH-CENTURY TUSCAN SAYING

Beans have always been associated if not with poverty,
with the sweating classes. Fava beans, whose slightly bitter flavor is so refreshing it's common to see them being peeled
and eaten raw, were called, in ancient Rome, *faba*, a play on words
with *faber*, the Latin word for "worker." The Roman physician
Galen said of beans: "Legumes are those grains of Demeter that are
not used to make bread." He then chose them over less wholesome
wheat loaves as the staple of Roman gladiators' diets.

Most of us regard beans with suspicion, as we do stale bread and
cooking in water. Prejudices are always best dispatched, but not always unfounded. When food is boiled badly, it's fair to turn away
from it, and if stale bread isn't cooked with, or toasted, but served
dry and harsh, it's awful.

Beyond the indelible stain the poor little things will never
shake, the distaste we feel for beans is not unfounded either. Our
beans are rarely as good as they can be. They're usually so bad, in
fact, that basing an opinion of their merit on prior experience is

very much like deciding you don't like Bach after having heard the Goldberg Variations played on kazoo.

I suggest you set your doubt aside, fill a pot with cold water and two cups of dried beans, put it on your counter, and leave it there overnight. You will be on your way toward making beans that taste like that that have fed laborers and fighters for centuries.

You will also have plowed effortlessly through the hurdle of "soaking beans," a hurdle whose existence and gnarliness is a pure invention of food writers' proclivities for making cooking seem difficult.

The way to keep bean soaking from getting in the way of your cooking beans is to detach the process from today's hunger and expectations and pour dried beans into a pot and cover them with cold water whenever you think of it. Their needing to stay where they are until being cooked tomorrow won't be a problem, and you'll have soaked your beans.

A lot of bean recipes advise soaking in the refrigerator: beans are vegetables, and warmed too gently in water may think they're being asked to sprout. I soak mine wherever there's room in the kitchen, and they keep their vegetal ambitions well in check for a day.

Once the sun has set and risen, drain the beans through a colander and cover them by two inches with fresh, cold water. What gets flushed out of the beans on their overnight wallow is what inspires musicality in eaters. Feed their soaking water to your plants, who will digest it more quietly, if you like.

If you didn't put two cups of beans in a pot of cold water last night, get on the bandwagon today by putting them in a pot, covering them with five inches of water, bringing it to a boil, turning off the heat, and leaving them sitting in hot water, covered, for an hour. Then drain them and cover them with new water. This has the same effect as overnight soaking and is a good alternative.

The cooks who make the best beans are the ones who hold simplicity in high esteem. Romans and Tuscans value spare eating and living. Both of their legislative histories are peppered with sumptuary laws limiting the length and content of meals, passed whenever their citizens' affection for simple living got flabby.

Tuscans, though, make the best beans. They are known in Italy as *mangiafagioli*, or "bean eaters." Tuscans believe that frugality is next to godliness and give the humblest ingredients their finest treatment. Tuscan cooks are extravagant with good olive oil, pressed from dark trees, and with vegetable scraps and Parmesan rinds, which, along with salt and more of that fine oil, make transcendent pots of beans.

Those odds and ends are as crucial to pots of beans as fresh water. Your pot will benefit from a piece of carrot, whatever is left of a stalk of celery, half an onion or its skin, a clove of garlic, fibrous leek tops. If you must decide what to save for your chicken pot and what for stock and what for beans, save your fennel scraps with pots of beans in mind. I make notes to myself after meals, and there are enough torn pieces of paper attesting that "The best bean broth has fennel in it!" for it to have become axiomatic.

Your pot also wants parsley stems, whole sprigs of thyme, and a bay leaf. It can all be tied into a neat bundle in cheesecloth or with kitchen twine, or it can be left bobbing around, as everything in my bean pot always is.

Beans need salt. There is a myth that adding salt to beans keeps them crunchy and unlovable. Not cooking beans for long enough keeps them crunchy, and undersalting them is a leading culprit in their being unlovable. They also need an immoderate, Tuscan amount of olive oil. This is different from adding oil to a boiling pot of water for pasta. Pasta doesn't cook in its water long enough to benefit from the oil, and you use only a small amount of pasta's cooking water to help sauce and noodle get acquainted.

The liquid in a bean pot becomes broth as beans cook in it just as the water in which you boil a piece of meat does. No ounce of the water that goes into a bean pot should be discarded. Tuscan food is based as much on the broth made by the beans on which Tuscans lavish their affection as on the beans themselves. Harold McGee, who writes about the chemistry of food simply, writes that beans make their own sauce. He is right. Their sauce must be well made and it must be kept.

Cooking beans is like boiling a chicken or boiling an egg: only their water boils, and only for a brief second. The rest of their cooking is slow and steady. Light the burner under your beans, and as soon as the pot has come to a boil, turn the heat down to just below a simmer. Gray scum will rise to the top of the pot and gather around the edges. Skim it off and discard it.

The best instruction I've read for how long to cook beans comes from a collection of recipes called *The Best in American Cooking*, by Clementine Paddleford. The book instructs to simmer "until beans have gorged themselves with fat and water and swelled like the fat boy in his prime." The description is so perfectly illustrative I don't think anyone should write another word on the subject. I don't know who the fat boy is, but I feel I understand his prime perfectly, and it is what I want for my bean.

As they cook, beans should look like they're bathing. Their tops should stay under the surface of the liquid, or they will get cracked and leathery, and they shouldn't ever be in so much water that they're swimming. Taste their broth as they cook to make sure it is well seasoned. It should taste not like the pleasant seawater of the pasta pot, but like a sauce or soup.

The second good piece of advice from the same book is in one of its recipes for black beans: "Soak beans overnight; drain. Put in pot, cover with water. Add onion, celery, carrot, parsley, salt, and pepper. Simmer until bean skins burst when blown upon, about three hours." This is the only recipe I've ever read that takes the doneness of beans as seriously as it should be taken: a cooked bean is so tender that the mere flutter of your breath should disturb its skin right off.

Beans are done when they are velvety to their absolute middles. You should feel, as soon as you taste one, as though you want to eat another. The whole pot is only ready when five beans meet that description. If one doesn't, let the beans keep cooking. (My "five bean" method is good, but ever since reading Mrs. Paddleford's book, I feel like a brute when I practice it, and am quite intent, moving forward, on whistling the skin off a bean.)

Cool and store your beans in their broth. The exchange of goodness between bean and broth will continue as long as the two are left together, and the broth helps the beans stay tender through chilling, freezing, and warming up again.

Those are instructions for cooking all beans. The only exception to these instructions is lentils. On the timescale of beans, lentils are instant. They do not need to be soaked and take only a half hour to cook. It is smart to keep cans of cooked beans around, but there is no reason to buy precooked lentils. Cooking them from dried does not take any more planning than putting a pot of water on the stove, lighting a burner, and opening a plastic bag.

Other than how good they are when they're cooked well, and how many good meals you can get out of them, beans are economical because they're a cheap habit. I keep an assortment of different beans stored separately in little glass jars. I have jars of little green French flageolets, marsh-brown cranberry beans, inky black beans, turtle beans, speckled Jacob's cattle beans, and plain burnt umber kidneys.

Pots of beans have an admirable, long-term perspective on eating. It's the same to them whether you eat them tonight or in three days. Beans get better over a few days' sitting, gorged and swelled, like happy fat boy. Any longer and you should freeze them, but they'll thaw ungrudgingly when you want them back.

A bean pot has a lot of meals in it, and you've already done much of the cooking you need to for many. A bowl of *pasta e fagioli* is a pot of boiling water away. Bring a few cups of beans and broth to a simmer in a deep pan or pot along with the rind from a piece of Parmesan. Smash the beans with a spoon as they warm. Cook a short pasta like ditalini or orecchiette until it is still quite firm. When the pasta is nearly done, remove the cheese rind from the beans and scoop the pasta into the bean pot to finish cooking. Serve drizzled with olive oil, and top with freshly cracked black pepper and freshly grated Parmesan.

Simple and delicious beans and rice also only requires that you boil a pot of water and add rice. Warm your beans in their broth until they're very hot, make rice, and ladle the beans on top. Or, if it's spring, cook halved little white turnips with their long greens still attached, or English or snap peas in butter and bean broth or water, and cut little wedges of artichokes and cook them in olive oil and butter. When everything is tender, combine it in one big pan, add beans, a lot of broth, and a big handful of whatever soft herbs you have—chervil, chives, mint, fennel fronds, celery leaves—and ladle the bright, springy stew over rice. If you don't want to make rice, add a little extra butter and herbs to the vegetables and beans and serve it over toast.

A deeply comforting supper for one or two is beans and egg. Warm cooked beans in a little pan. Add sautéed kale, or roasted squash, or a little bit of roasted tomato, or add nothing at all. Crack an egg or two onto the beans, cover the pan, and cook. If you have stale bread, put a toasted piece, rubbed with garlic, in each bowl. Spoon the beans and egg over the toast, salt each egg, grind it with fresh black pepper, drizzle the beans and egg copiously with olive oil, grate them thickly with Parmesan, and dine like a Roman plebeian, or a Tuscan pauper, prince, or pope.

Cassoulet is a bean dish from southern France, where austerity is not considered next to godliness. If you can tell such things from what people eat, for Toulousians, pork, goose, and duck, all slow-cooked in fat, occupy that station.

Traditional cassoulet contains all three, plus copious quantities of fat, pork skin, and a great quantity of beans. If they were lingering, any vestigial associations between bean meals and deprivation should be erased by the very existence of cassoulet. To make an authentic one, follow any of a million good recipes. They're involved but worth the trouble.

Or make a simpler, utterly satisfying version by cooking a mixture of finely chopped onion, carrot, and celery, called mirepoix, in olive oil, browning a small, garlicky fresh sausage per person, spooning beans and mirepoix into a baking dish big enough to fit them happily, and nestling the sausages among the beans. Add bean broth to come up just halfway and put it in a 300-degree oven.

It takes about one hour for the sausages to cook through at low heat, which gives them time to get tender and for the beans to sip up some of their juices. Take the dish out when it's bubbly and the sausages are cooked, scatter the top heavily with toasted breadcrumbs, then put it under the broiler for a few minutes, until the top is crisp and brown.

There are similar dishes, made of mostly beans with some meat, in every bean-eating cuisine in the world. They range from franks and beans to black-eyed peas and ham, from chili to the majestic Brazilian *feijoada*. The principle of all is the same and the principle is good.

If there's already meat on the table, or you can go without, skip the sausages and ladle beans an inch or two deep in a small ceramic roasting pan and turn them into a rustic, herby French bean gratin. Cook mirepoix as above and mix it into the beans. Bake the gratin in the oven until it begins to bubble. Mix a big handful of any combination of chopped parsley, rosemary, and safe into toasted breadcrumbs, top the gratin thickly, and let it cook until the top is quite brown.

The world of bean soups is populous. Its population is for the most part exemplary. If you'd like to make the most straightforward one, put more broth than beans in a pot and heat it up. For the second most straightforward one, purée the mixture with a little olive oil and a squeeze of lemon.

Minestrone is much more than a bean soup; it is the complete expression of the bean's generosity, its raison d'être. Minestrone underlines all sensible cooking practices. Like the other great Tuscan soup, *ribollita*, minestrone is a beacon. If you have the ingredients to make either one of those soups, two of which are beans and their broth, it means you're cooking steadily, buying good ingredients, and saving the parts of them you don't cook immediately to cook later.

Minestrone is a precisely seasonal soup: it should reflect the season inside and outside your kitchen at all times. The beans you have cooked will always be at its center, but the rest will change throughout the year. In the winter, it will be chock-full of beans and pasta and thick enough to stand a spoon in. In spring, you will leave out the dark greens and include English peas and new onions; in summer, include the first slim green beans and basil, and little zucchini and ripe tomatoes, cut into cubes.

Minestrone is the perfect food. I advise eating it for as many meals as you can bear or that number plus one.

Minestrone

1 cup diced onion, carrot, celery, leek, fennel
3 cloves garlic, sliced
½ cup olive oil

a small pinch of chile flakes

the end of a piece of cured meat or hard salami, diced

1 cup any combination parsley, rhyme, marjoram, basil leaves

2 to 3 cups roughly chopped any combination kale, collard
    greens, Swiss chard, spinach, mustard greens, dandelion
    greens, broccoli raab, escarole, cabbage (cooked or raw),
    any stems and leaves, ribs, and cores, cooked or raw

½ cup whole tomatoes, well chopped, or drained canned
    tomatoes

optional: ½ to 1 cup chopped root vegetables (if they are there
    and need to be cooked, or cooked and need to be eaten)

6 cups cooked beans

a Parmesan rind

8 cups any combination bean broth, stock, and liquid from
    cans of tomatoes

1 cup small pasta such as orecchiette, little tubes, or small
    penne

pesto, olive tapenade, fresh ricotta, or parsley for garnish

Cook the onion, carrot, celery, leek, fennel, and garlic in
the olive oil until tender in a big pot. Add the chile flakes and
any cured meat. Stir to combine. Add the herbs, greens,
tomatoes, root vegetables, beans, and cheese rind, crushing
the tomatoes against the side of the pot. Add liquid to cover.
Simmer for 45 to 60 minutes, until everything has agreed to
become minestrone. Just before you eat the soup, cook the
pasta in a pot of salted, boiling water, only enough for the
soup you're planning to eat that week, and add it to the
week's soup. If you freeze minestrone, cook new pasta whenever you eat the minestrone you've frozen.

Garnish with pesto or olive tapenade, or a big dollop of
fresh ricotta, or simply parsley.

———

I once lived with a Tuscan in a house in San Francisco. I would
cook a pot of beans weekly, and our bean meals followed a regular
pattern. The cooked beans would sit in their broth for a half hour,
contenting themselves with their last swallows of olive oil and

herbs. When my Tuscan decided their time was up, he would stand ceremoniously, clear his throat, slice bread, open wine, and put olive oil on the table.

Then we would eat just beans and bread, and we would drink wine. I would do it all happily, he intently, glowing with genetically imprinted joy at his great fortune to be sitting there, eating beans, beans, beans.

There are a good number of bean-loving Americans who agree that cooked beans need no further fussing, and eat beans, on their own, as whole meals, as Tuscans do. In New Mexico, big pots of beans are cooked studded with pork and served for dinner. They're called *borrachos* and eaten plain and hot with an accompanying stack of warm corn tortillas and beer. In Texas, the same beans, cooked the same way, are called *frijoles* and are eaten plain and hot with plenty of corn tortillas and beer. In the South, you can still get bowls of black-eyed peas or crowder peas accompanied by chopped scallions and watermelon pickles and pepper vinegar to eat with sliced white bread and beer.

Tuscans may treat dried beans with reverence, but it is a fresh bean they worship. When you know the taste of a fresh bean, you taste in dried ones the invisible mark all true loves bear: a memory of what it was we first fell in love with. Fall in love with a fresh bean, and you will stay in love with a dried one.

Fresh beans are in season in the summer, and come in as many shapes and colors as you can imagine. To shell fresh beans, practice a technique a friend calls "the twist and tickle": twist a bean's ends, one in each direction, and then, once its seam opens, tickle its beans into a bowl. This won't work for fava beans. Their pods' insides are sticky, and if you tickle them, they tickle back.

I usually use up my bean broth in minestrone or a bowl of pasta, or warm it up and make some odd, delicious thing of stale bread and whatever else is around, and probably cook an egg on it in the end. But I've been served plain bean broth twice, and been inspired to serve it myself several times.

The first time it was served to me was at a convent in Oaxaca, Mexico. The broth was the first course of a meal so pure and simple, the air seemed to thin as we ate. The soup was smooth and golden and tasted of grass. After it there were five tiny, glossy meatballs, on a pool of serene, dark amber tomato sauce. It was a simple meal, and it was calming.

The second time was in a weathered dining room in Turin, Italy. The broth was ladled out of a ceramic jug in which beans had cooked in the fireplace. The beans themselves were served separately with torn kerchiefs of fresh pasta, but the beanless soup was hot and each spoonful told the story of the beans' slow bubbling amid herbs and garlic.

If you decide to serve bean broth, I have only the advice of a guest to whom I served it once. He thanked me for the meal after saying good evening, and suggested that the next time I might serve it hot. If you serve bean broth as a soup, do remember what I forgot and was too proud to rectify during dinner. If you are ladling it from anywhere other than an earthenware jug in a fireplace, the broth will have cooled as it sat and needs to be ladled into its own pot and heated up again before being served.

The writer Waverley Root did a thorough survey of Italian food, top to bottom, in his book *The Food of Italy*. He was deeply enamored of the noble Tuscan and insisted that the Tuscan obsession with frugality was nothing but "finesse."

I cannot associate the word *finesse* with bean cookery. It doesn't take finesse, but dried beans, good olive oil, a big pot, and time to do it well, and it takes only common sense to appreciate.

But there is great dignity in allowing oneself to keep clear about what is good, and it is what I think of when I hear the term "good taste." Whether things were ever simpler than they are now, or better if they were, we can't know. We do know that people have always found ways to eat and live well, whether on boiling water or bread or beans, and that some of our best eating hasn't been our most foreign or expensive or elaborate, but quite plain and quite familiar. And knowing that is probably the best way to cook, and certainly the best way to live.

STILL LIFE WITH MAYONNAISE

By Greg Atkinson

From *At the Kitchen Table*

Though chef-writer Greg Atkinson earned his stars in high-end restaurant kitchens, both in Europe and in the Seattle area, his meditative essays on food and cooking are less about dazzling technique than about the quiet, honest rhythms of home cooking.

"When she picked up her lunch the bag felt very light. She reached inside and there was only crumpled paper. They had taken her tomato sandwich."

—Louise Fitzhugh, from *Harriet the Spy*

Since I am both a chef and a writer, I am sometimes compelled to contemplate what cooking and writing have in common. What draws me to both pursuits is the simple joy I find in making something, and I have often said that baking a cake or writing a story satisfies the same impulse. I believe that this creative impulse is a basic human need. We all like to make things. And since I am not particularly good with power tools, I don't make houses.

But among creative outlets, cooking and writing are unique in that both endeavors produce something that ultimately becomes a part of whoever partakes in them. If I cook a meal and someone eats it, and if everything proceeds as it should, then something in that food will become a part of that person. If I read something and internalize that dialogue, then the words on the page will be incorporated into my own thoughts. Ideas expressed on the page will be reformulated in my mind into thoughts of my own.

If I write a recipe and you make it, then we are sharing both the words and the dish that results from them. Of course, you'll change the recipe. Of course, you'll hear the words differently in your head than I would in mine, but a connection is made nevertheless, and that connection is what writing recipes is all about.

When she was compiling the recipes that would eventually become *Mastering the Art of French Cooking*, Julia Child was living in France with her husband, Paul, who worked for the Office of Strategic Services (OSS), the agency that would eventually become the CIA. So it's not surprising that she maintained strict security about her recipes.

"Perhaps it was my old OSS training kicking in, or just my natural protectiveness," wrote Julia in her memoir, *My Life in France*. "But," she wrote in a letter to her sister, "the form we think is new, and certainly some of our explanations, such as that on our beloved mayonnaise, are personal discoveries." And so she sandwiched each recipe between pink sheets of paper on which she wrote "Confidential . . . to be kept under lock and key and never mentioned."

Since I learned to make mayonnaise at a very early age, I never thought of the technique as particularly secret. My mother and her seven siblings all learned it from their mother, and they in turn taught it to any members of my generation willing to learn. In our family, dishes like potato salad and Waldorf salad just had to be made with homemade mayonnaise. But some people feel just as strongly about certain brands of store-bought mayonnaise.

The novelist Tom Robbins is quite devoted to Best Foods–brand mayonnaise. "A lot of people in my hometown are loyal to Duke's," he says, "but I like Best Foods, which is the same thing as Hellmann's in the South." Robbins hails from Blowing Rock, North Carolina, and Duke's is made in Greenville, South Carolina. Hellmann's, which originated in New York City, was purchased by California-based Best Foods in 1932, and the two brands utilize the same formula and market it in similar packaging on their respective coasts.

In his 2003 novel, *Villa Incognito*, Robbins waxes poetic about mayonnaise. "Yellow as summer sunlight," he writes, "soft as young thighs, smooth as a Baptist preacher's rant, falsely innocent as a magician's handkerchief, mayonnaise will cloak a lettuce leaf, some shreds of cabbage, a few hunks of cold potato in the simplest splendor, restyling their dull character, making them lively and attractive again." The rave prompted many of his fans to start sending Robbins samples of their favorite brands of mayonnaise.

"There are some surprisingly good Mexican brands," says Robbins, "and the Japanese make extraordinary mayonnaise. I think I have about twenty-three brands in my refrigerator right now."

When Tom's wife, Alexa, invited my wife, Betsy, and me up to their place in La Conner for a private mayonnaise tasting, we hit the road with a few jars and bottles of our favorite brands. I also had, secreted away in a canvas shopping bag, a wire whisk, a deep mixing bowl, a fresh egg, a bottle of organic canola oil, some white balsamic vinegar, and a bottle of good Dijon mustard. It occurred to me that Tom and Alexa might like to learn how to make their own mayonnaise, and I wanted to see how the homemade stuff stood up in a taste test with the commercial brands, especially Robbins' beloved Best Foods.

But our evaluation of mayonnaises at Chez Robbins involved more than just the condiment itself. Mayonnaise is just one of the essential components of Robbins' favorite food, the tomato sandwich, a culinary delight he celebrated in his book of essays, *Wild Ducks Flying Backward*. In addition to various musings and critiques, the collection of stories and poems includes a piece called "Till Lunch Do Us Part," in which Robbins answers the age-old question, "What would you have for your last meal?" with an eloquent treatise on the tomato sandwich and its essential components, soft white bread and Best Foods mayonnaise. "But the mayonnaise would have to be the right mayo," Robbins reminds us. "The bread would have to be the correct bread. I don't want to leave the world on an inferior tomato sandwich."

So along with the various jars, tubes, and squeeze bottles of mayonnaise set out for our consideration, Alexa had acquired a soft and wonderful commercial white bread and several perfectly ripe red tomatoes. Then I pulled out my bag of tricks and went to work. But when I set about making a batch of homemade mayonnaise so that we could compare it to the store-bought stuff, Robbins did not appear to be interested. In fact, he seemed to deliberately avoid getting too close.

"I was occasionally watching you out of the corner of my eye," said Robbins later, "because I did find it interesting. But I didn't want to see exactly how it's made because I kind of like the idea of it being a mystery. I have been eating mayo for sixty years, and until ten years ago, I didn't even know what the ingredients are. I preferred to think of it as some kind of substance dug out of an underground cave in the French Alps.

"Socrates said, 'the unexamined life is not worth living,' but Oedipus Rex and I are not so sure. I like the mystery. I think Oedipus might have had a long and happy marriage with his mother if he hadn't found out the truth.

"I had a 1969 Mercury Montego, and in two hundred thousand miles, the head was never off the engine. I attribute that to the fact that I never once looked under the hood. I thought there was a ball of mystic light that kept the motor running.

"Beneath that silliness is a propensity for mystery. Every great work of art, whether it's a painting or a film, has an element of mystery. Mayonnaise is not a work of art, but it is the food of the gods; it is ambrosia.

"I have been quoted as saying that I don't know how to write a novel," he said, "and that was construed as a confession of incompetence. But that's not what I was saying. I'm saying I don't have a formula; I don't have a recipe for a novel." Rather, for Robbins, the creative process is something of a mystery. "I used to cook quite a bit, too," he said. "But I didn't use recipes. When I cooked, I cooked from vibration."

I like the idea of this well enough, and even though I write recipes for a living, I almost always cook without them, feeling my way from one step to the next. First this happens, then that happens. While the onions soften, I'm cutting the celery, and on a back burner, the rice is simmering away. But eventually, my left brain kicks in and I start to codify things because I want to share them. How much olive oil did I swirl into the pan? Was that a medium onion or a large one? Was it chopped or sliced? I like the geometric proof-like formula of a recipe, and I feel that if the precision of writing it down doesn't get in the way of the thing, it can be like an incantation, a magic formula for transforming a bunch of ingredients into something completely unlike its component parts. Mayonnaise is, after all, nothing like eggs and oil.

Making a recipe is not unlike making a sandwich. There is a formula, and when it is followed, real transformation occurs. That is magical.

Homemade Mayonnaise

Homemade mayonnaise is not only easy to make, it's also an exercise in practical magic. The end result is definitely greater than the sum of its parts. Many recipes, including some of mine, call for a food processor. But for a small batch of the stuff, especially someone's first batch, hand whisking is better. It helps to have a second pair of hands; one person handles the whisk and the bowl while the other person slowly dribbles in the oil. If white balsamic vinegar is not available, use white wine vinegar with a teaspoon of sugar.

Makes about 2 cups

1 egg
1 tablespoon white balsamic vinegar
1 tablespoon Dijon mustard
¾ teaspoon fine sea salt
1½ cups canola oil, preferably organic

Whisk the egg in a medium mixing bowl with the vinegar, mustard, and salt until the mixture is very smooth, almost fluffy. Whisk for at least 1 full minute before adding any oil in order to set a good foundation.

Whisk in a few drops of oil. Then, whisking all the while, build to a very slow but steady stream until all the oil is incorporated. As the sauce comes together to make a stable emulsion, the last of the oil can be added somewhat more steadily than the first few tentative dribbles.

THE FRIED CHICKEN EVANGELIST

By Lorraine Eaton

From Leite's Culinaria

∽⧼∾

Covering the local food scene for southeast Virginia's *The Virginian-Pilot* newspaper, columnist-blogger Lorraine Eaton delights in the characters and culture of Southern cooking—like Mississippi-born fried-chicken master Sydney Meers.

I was raised in the South in a home that never knew a grease-splattered stove.

My parents were displaced New Yorkers. So despite my growing up in a region where everything is fried—tomatoes, bologna, okra, pies, and, at the State Fair of Virginia, even Pepsi—I never learned the fine art of frying—especially how to make fried chicken.

Over the years, this bothered me some, sort of like a loose pot handle that was in need of fixing yet easily ignored. Now, though, my job title is Staff Epicure for Virginia's largest newspaper. Readers look to me for advice on how to dry-age steaks, open oysters, roast goose. What would they think if they knew of my fear of frying?

When I reached the half-century mark—an occasion for celebration as much as assessment—I figured the time had come to correct this culinary shortcoming. I set my sights on how to make Southern fried chicken and sought professional help from Sydney Meers, a Mississippi native who owns Stove, a quaint and quirky restaurant in Portsmouth, the Virginia town where I was raised.

Every neo-Southern meal at this 32-seater comes with a side of Syd, who intermittently cooks behind the tiled half-wall of his open kitchen and repairs to the dining room to sip whiskey, neat, alongside dinner guests.

Syd grew up in Senatobia, Mississippi. He spent many a day hanging out in the restaurant kitchen run by his Grandma Winnie Lee Johnson. There were also many mornings spent tending her half-acre garden, pulling weeds, and tamping down leaves between rows, until she'd say, "Let's go make some lunch." Then they'd cook. She shared all that she knew—all manner of pies, pork, and fried chicken—and encouraged Syd to do the same. "It's part of your heritage," she'd say. "You have to pass it on."

That notion is now a part of him. Syd is an evangelical cook, spreading the gospel of Southern fare by way of his menu and occasional cooking classes. "To say something is a secret recipe is bullshit," he once told me.

So when I called, Syd graciously agreed to bring me into the fold of folks who fry—with Grandmother Winnie Lee's recipe, no less.

Two days later, Syd hands me an apron. We're standing in front of an eight-burner gas stove in his speck of a kitchen, a honey-colored chopping block before us and pots and pans dangling above us. Metal shelving units that are stacked to the ceiling practically spill their ingredients and equipment, they're so crammed. Classical music plays from a radio that's hidden somewhere, maybe on one of those shelves.

Syd inspects the organic, free-range bird that I proffer for my lesson in fried chicken.

"Now, you've done real good, Low-raine," Syd says in a voice seasoned with the South. "This is beautiful."

Organic is fine and dandy, he explains, but that alone doesn't deem the bird worthy. It has to also be free-range and raised without hormones, just like the ones that ran around his grandmother's backyard when he was young, eating bugs and grasses, before Winnie Lee wrung their necks.

Syd makes a cut between the leg and wing with a flick of his knife. He notes that the drumette is slender, not bulging. Proof of the absence of hormones. I may not know how to fry, but I do know how to cut up a chicken. So when Syd flattens the breasts of the bird against the cutting board with his hand, I'm surprised to see that instead of slicing out the backbone, he leaves it attached to one breast.

"Sometimes grandmother would fry it up separate," he says. "Now most people just cut it out, but that's the choicest piece. The bone holds so much flavor." Huh? The things you learn.

Syd has already prepared the brine, a critical element, he says, that imparts flavor and extracts bacteria and toxins. It sits in a stockpot beside us, a simple solution of salty water with a sprinkling of crushed bay leaves and fresh rosemary sprigs from his garden.

I submerge the raw meat in the brine. Syd sets his spattered red kitchen timer for 30 minutes. We slide into his tiny eight-seat bar which he calls The Cougar Lounge. Staring down at us from the wall are mounted game—buffalo, wildebeest, and antelope—that came to him by way of a friend of a friend with an IRS problem of which Syd will say no more. He opens a split of champagne and pours us each a glass.

Syd opened his first restaurant, The Calico Cat, in Senatobia. After leaving Mississippi, he joined the Air Force and attended culinary school on the GI bill. He's owned several popular restaurants in the Tidewater region along Virginia's southern coast. His "Cowboy Syd's Sextuple Truffle Tart with Bittersweet Chocolate Whiskey Cream and Sensuously Sensational Chocolate Espresso Ice Cream" is included in the James Beard award-winning cookbook "Death by Chocolate."

Heady stuff. But sitting in the bar, waiting for the bird to brine, Syd says it all goes back to his grandmother.

As a child, he sat atop sacks of flour in her restaurant watching the line cooks while his mother waited tables. He takes a picture from the wall and hands it to me. It's a faded snapshot, circa 1955, of the diner-ish place. The sign out front says "Johnson Cafe—Bar B Q Steaks." A second sign, emblazoned with "air-conditioned," hangs over the door, a beacon to the hot and weary. A man-sized ice cream cone stands at the entrance.

"Winnie Lee," says Syd, looking at the picture. "What a girl she was."

The timer dings.

Back in the kitchen, Syd removes a hotel pan from a shelf and dumps three cups of flour and one cup of cornmeal into it. This is the start of his grandmother's dredge. Syd uses his hands to mix it up, cautioning me to rely on all-purpose flour because cake flour will absorb too much moisture and turn to clumps. His grandmother sifted her flour, but because most come pre-sifted these days there's no need to do so unless it's humid. It's always humid down South.

"We like cornmeal," he adds, "because of the crunch factor and because it helps hold the flour on the skin." He says the slightly coarse texture of stone-ground works best.

"Here's the way you've got to do the salt," Syd says. He sprinkles four pinches into flour and cornmeal and offers me a taste. The salt registers in specks on my tongue.

"Not enough?" I venture a guess.

Syd agrees. He adds two more pinches and mixes it in. I take another taste. A more uniform salt sensation spreads across my palate.

"Just right," Syd says.

The pepper that Syd sprinkles into the pan was gleaned from the bottom of the pepper grinders in the dining room. Shrewd restaurateurs don't waste a thing. I place a smidgen of the dredge on my tongue. There's just a whisper of heat. I'm surprised that Syd says the seasoning is correct given that it's much less pronounced than the salt. I voice my concern.

"Girl, that's because pepper holds up better during cooking than the salt," he says. "The salt will dissolve."

Oh.

It's time. I remove the chicken from the brine, flicking off any herbs that stick to the skin. I catch the faint aroma of rosemary and bay as I roll a drumstick in the dredge.

"No, stop doin' that," Syd says, taking over. He covers the meat with handfuls of flour, flipping and flouring and flipping and flouring the drumstick until it's completely coated. "Handle the flour, not the bird."

I can't recall what kind of oil I used during my past frying foibles, but I know it wasn't what Syd pulls out of the fridge: a clear plastic tub containing lard that's slightly off-white and as smooth as buttercream icing. At the bottom of the tub is a glistening brown gelée—drippings from braised pork bellies, a staple on Syd's dinner menu.

In this kitchen, the contents of that tub are considered gold, all but guaranteeing chicken in the same league as Winnie Lee's. Settle for nothing less, Syd says. If you don't have lard, fry up about five pounds of bacon and use the drippings. If all you have is Crisco, don't fry chicken.

Another nonnegotiable item: Syd's decades-old cast-iron skillet. Black as a cat, the pan has been wiped clean but never washed, same as Winnie Lee's. She figured the difference was her skillet, which held all the seasonings of every food she ever cooked in it. No secret. Just the soul of the pan.

Syd ignites a gas burner and adjusts the flame to medium-high. The lard melts into a pool about 1/2 inch deep. When it begins to bubble, the pitch becomes more a gurgle than a sizzle.

"They now have fancy thermometers, but this is the way you fry chicken," Syd says, noting the sound. "You've got to listen."

The throaty gurgle signals that the lard is hot enough to fry. Using tongs, we quickly nestle the chicken in the skillet, skin side up, careful to handle only the ends of the bones so we don't mar the coating or inadvertently squeeze out any moisture. The gurgling continues. Soon the meat is rimmed with a frenzy of fine bubbles, which Syd attributes to moisture from the bird. Only when these tiny globules create a goldenrod outline around each piece is it time to turn the chicken.

We take turns carefully turning the fried chicken with tongs. Grease spits and snipes at us, but Syd nixes my plea to use a spatter screen, saying it would trap moisture in the pan and turn the chicken soggy. When the pieces turn a shimmering golden brown, we tong them from the pan and set them on paper towels to rest for a spell. It's by sight, not sound, that you know when fried chicken is done.

A few long minutes later we sit in the empty bar, white linen napkins in hand, the gorgeous platter of browned chicken before us.

I bite into a thigh, piercing the perfectly crisped skin. It's juicy but not greasy. I detect a hint of herb from the brine. Syd selects a breast—the one with the backbone attached—and proclaims it just like Winnie Lee's. After we finish, he packs up the remaining thigh and breast for me and offers one last morsel of wisdom.

"You can do this, girl," he says. "The more you fail, the better you get. That's the fun of cooking."

I ask if he ever failed at channeling his grandmother's cooking. He raises an eyebrow. "Everything I've tried, I got it right the first time right on the spot," he says, without hesitation. "I think it might be a gene."

LASAGNA BOLOGNESE

By Deb Perelman

From Smitten Kitchen.com

❦

The runaway success of Deb Perelman's chatty blog Smitten Kitchen—featuring detailed photos of her cooking adventures in a tiny New York City apartment—won her every food blogger's dream: a book contract. *The Smitten Kitchen Cookbook* is due out in October 2012.

This, this is my culinary Mount Everest. This twenty-layer striation of noodles, ragu, béchamel and cheese, repeated four times and then some, took me more than five years to conquer. To be honest, six years ago I didn't know what it was. Sure, I had heard of lasagna but I wasn't terribly fond of it because I don't much care for the texture of ricotta once it has baked. (Ricotta, I'd argue, is best rich, fresh and cold on toast.) But I was galloping through a post on an Italian food blog and I stumbled upon a parenthesised side-thought that stopped me dead in my tracks. It said something along the lines of "I don't know whose idea it was to put ricotta in lasagna but . . . shudder." And I thought, but wait! *What's supposed to go in lasagna?* But there was no answer, so I set out to find one.

Lasagna alla Bolognese is an epic dish. Oh sure, it looks like an ordinary broiled mass of cheese, pasta and meaty tomato sauce but it's so much more. To make it as I dreamed from that day forward I wanted to, everything gets a lot of love and time. The ragu is cooked for hours. The béchamel (ahem, *besciamella*), although the simplest of the five "Mother Sauces," is still a set of ingredients that must be cooked separately, and in a prescribed order. The pasta doesn't have to be fresh, but I figured if I was going to do this, I was going to really, really do this, and I wanted fresh, delicious sheets of pasta to support the other cast members I'd so lovingly craft. And the cheese? There's just one, Parmesan, and it doesn't overwhelm.

So why did it take the better part of six years to conquer? First, I had to find the ragu of my dreams. I realize that most people have a bolognese they like—maybe it has milk or a mix of meats, not just beef (mine doesn't), maybe it goes easy on the wine (mine doesn't), maybe it can't be cooked for less than six hours (mine can) and maybe it just has a slip of tomatoes inside (mine doesn't). I sometimes think that there are as many interpretations of bolognese as there are people who make it; it's totally cool to use your favorite. But if you're still bolognese-hunting, oh, I do love Anne Burrell's above all else. You could forgo the pasta, the white sauce and the cheese and enjoy it straight from a bowl. But today, we won't.

Even once I found my ragu nirvana, it took a couple rounds to get the lasagna right. The first time I made the noodles, I rolled them too thin and put them on towels, where they proceeded to stick. Miserably. The dish was intended for a 2 p.m. lunch in New Jersey; at 3, Alex was running to a bodega in Manhattan to buy a box of dried pasta. On the plus side, we're still talking to each other. On the minus, we had "lunch" at almost 8 that night. I had a few other mishaps; recipes I found seemed out of balance or evasive in directions. One béchamel was too thin. And I kept ending up with too much ragu, too little white sauce, too many noodles, not enough directions, too little time. It was not until this week that I finally got the recipe exactly as I'd always dreamed of it, with I hope a level of detail that will make it replicable for anyone at home. Even if you, like me, got to the final inning and realized you were out of cheese, requiring a run to the bodega to pick up *I don't want to even talk about it* variety of so-called Parmesan. Yes, even for people like me.

Now here's the part where I know you're not going to believe me, but I implore you to consider it: This lasagna, it feels light, almost ethereal, or as close as a decidedly hearty dish can. Maybe it's the absence of ricotta and mozzarella, or the thinness of the home-made noodles but something about it feels utterly decadent, mind-bogglingly delicious, completely warming but not . . . gutting. It needn't immediately lead to a nap on the sofa. It's a miracle. A miracle in twenty parts. Let's get started.

Lasagna Bolognese

Ragu adapted from Anne Burrell, everything else from trial and error.

Serves 12 (in hearty portions) to 15 (in generous 3-inch squares). You will have double the bolognese sauce that you need because I cannot in good conscience let you spend several hours simmering a sauce that will only yield 4-ish cups of sauce. Trust me, you'll want extra.

This is a beast of a dish, and worth every second you put into it. I recommend making the meat sauce a day or longer before you need it; then, do everything else on the second day. My advice is to give yourself way more time than you could possibly need on the second day, so that you can make the dish from a place of leisure and love, and not one that is frenzied and not particularly fun. You'll be glad you did. This is a perfect project for a lazy winter weekend, something two people could then eat dreamily all week.

A note on authenticity: This is the kind of dish that gets, ahem, passionate cooks out in droves. I've been told that you cannot call it bolognese if you simmer it for less than __ hours or that it can/can't have tomato/milk/wine/only beef in it. Others will pfft over the lack of color on the crust (I had a word with my dinky oven about it). I absolutely love this about cooking—the way we care so deeply about the way our food is made, and how much I'm lucky enough to learn about the different ways people approach the same dish. But, my other favorite part about cooking is that it's just you in the kitchen and you can make your food the way you alone like it. Feel free to tweak this to your taste by replacing portions of the beef with other meats, using less tomato paste or wine if desired or replacing some wine with milk.

Bolognese sauce

1 medium onion, coarsely chopped (1-inch pieces are fine)
1 large or 2 slim carrots, coarsely chopped
2 ribs celery, coarsely chopped
3 cloves garlic, coarsely chopped
2 to 3 tablespoons olive oil
Kosher salt
Freshly ground black pepper
2 pounds ground chuck, brisket or round or combination
1 ¼ cups tomato paste (from 2 6-ounce cans)
2 cups red wine, preferably hearty but really, anything you
     like to drink
Water as needed
2 bay leaves
A few sprigs thyme, tied in a bundle

Pasta

1 ½ cups all-purpose flour
2 large eggs
½ teaspoon table salt
1 to 2 tablespoons water, if needed

Béchamel sauce

½ cup (8 tablespoons) unsalted butter
½ cup all-purpose flour
4 cups whole milk
1 teaspoon table salt
1 clove minced garlic
Freshly grated nutmeg, to taste
Freshly ground black pepper

To assemble

1 ⅔ cups grated Parmesan cheese

Day 1: Make the bolognese sauce: In a food processor, pulse onion, carrots, celery, and garlic until finely chopped. Heat a moderate-sized Dutch oven (4 to 5 quarts) over medium-high heat. Once hot, coat the bottom of the pan with two to three tablespoons of oil. Once it is hot, add the chopped vegetables and season them generously with salt and pepper. Cook the vegetables until they are evenly brown, stirring frequently, about 15 minutes.

I'm going to insert my favorite Burrell-ism here: Brown food tastes good! Don't skimp on the cooking times as this creates the big flavors that will carry right through to your plated lasagna. And now I'm going to insert my own-ism: Don't worry about sticking bits of food or uneven pieces or anything. It's all going to work out in the end.

Add the ground beef and season again with salt and pepper. Brown the beef well and again, don't rush this step. Cook for another 15 minutes. Add the tomato paste and cook for 3 to 4 minutes. Add the red wine, using it to scrape up any stuck bits in the pan. Cook the wine until it has reduced by half, about 5 more minutes. Add water to the pan until the water is about 1 inch above the meat. Toss in the bay leaves and the bundle of thyme and stir to combine everything, bringing it to a low simmer.

Here's how the next 3 to 4 hours will go: You'll keep a pitcher of water near the stove. You'll stir the sauce from time to time. As the water in the sauce cooks off, you'll want to add more but you don't want to add more than 1 to 2 cups at a time or you'll have boiled meat sauce (bleh) rather than something thick and robust with flavor. Taste it from time to time and add more seasoning if needed. Simmer for 3 to 4 hours.

You'll have about 8 to 8½ cups of sauce but will only need 4 for the lasagna. Discard the thyme and bay leaves and put half in the fridge for lasagna assembly tomorrow and the other half in the freezer for up to a couple months. Ours was still as good as day one after 6 weeks.

Day 2: Make your pasta: Combine all of the pasta ingredients in a food processor. Run the machine until the mixture begins to form a ball. You're looking for a dough that is firm but not sticky. If needed, add water a drop at a time until it comes together. Place ball of dough on a lightly floured surface and invert a bowl over it. Let it rest for an hour. (You'll have about 10 ounces or a little less than ⅔ pound of fresh pasta dough.)

Get your work area ready; I like to line a large tray with waxed paper. Dust the waxed paper with flour. Keep more waxed paper and flour nearby.

Working with a quarter of the dough at a time, run it through your pasta roller on the widest setting (usually "0"), then repeat this process with the roller set increasingly smaller (1, 2, 3) until the pasta is very thin. My Atlas machine goes to 9, but I almost always stop at 8 because this setting makes for thin, delicate pasta that's not so fragile that I'm pulling my hair out with frustration trying to move it around.

If you find your dough sticking, lightly flour it. If it gets too big to handle, cut it in half. If the piece gets too wide for the machine or becomes annoyingly irregularly shaped, I re-"fold" the dough by folding the sides of the dough into the middle, like an envelope, and press it flat. Then, run the piece back through the machine with the open sides up and down on the widest setting again (0) working your way thinner. This allows the machine to "press" any trapped air out.

Lay your pasta on the floured waxed paper in a single layer, trying to keep the pieces from touching. Flour the tops of them and place another sheet of floured wax paper on top. Repeat this process with the remaining dough and as many layers of pasta as you need.

Next, cook your pasta: Cut your pasta lengths into square-ish shapes. The fun thing about making fresh pasta for lasagna is that the shape doesn't much matter; you're going to tile together whatever you have and nobody will care if it took 9 or 16 bits to patch the layer together. Bring a large pot of water to boil. Have ready a skimmer, a large bowl of ice water and a large tray or platter that you've drizzled or spritzed with oil. Boil several squares of noodle at a time for 1 to 2 minutes each (1 minute if you, indeed, went to the thinnest setting on your machine; 2 if you, like me, stopped one shy of thinnest). Scoop them out with your skimmer, swish them in the ice water and lay them out (still wet is fine) on the oiled platter. Repeat with remaining pasta. It's okay to have your noodles touch; they shouldn't stick together in the short period of time until you begin assembling but if you're nervous, you can drizzle or spritz each layer very lightly with more oil.

Make your béchamel: Melt your butter in the bottom of a medium-to-large saucepan over medium heat. Once melted, add your flour and stir it into the butter until smooth. Cook the mixture together for a minute, stirring constantly. Pour in a small drizzle of your milk*, whisking constantly into the butter-flour mixture until smooth. Continue to drizzle a very small amount at a time, whisking constantly. Once you've added a little over half of your milk, you'll find that you have more of a thick sauce or batter, and you can start adding the milk in larger splashes, being sure to keep mixing. Once all of the milk is added, add the salt, garlic, nutmeg (if using) and few grinds of black pepper, and bring the mixture to a lower simmer and cook it, stirring frequently, for 10 minutes. Taste and adjust seasonings if needed.

At last, you may assemble your dish: Preheat oven to 400 degrees. In a 9×13-inch or equivalent rectangular baking dish, spread a generous ¼ cup of the béchamel. I mostly use this to keep the noodles from sticking. Add your first layer of cooked noodles, patching and slightly overlapping them however is needed to form a single layer. Ladle 1 cup bolognese sauce over the noodles, spreading it evenly. Drizzle ½ cup béchamel over the bolognese; don't worry about getting it perfectly smooth or even. Sprinkle the layer with ⅓ cup parmesan cheese. Repeat this process—pasta + 1 cup bolognese + ½ cup béchamel + ⅓ cup parmesan—three more times, then add one more layer of pasta. You'll use 5 layers of pasta total.

There are two ways to finish the dish. You can simply sprinkle the top layer of pasta with your remaining parmesan before baking. This makes the crunchiest lid. I like a semi-crunchy lid and first spread 1/4 cup béchamel over the top layer of pasta before sprinkling it with the remaining cheese. It still gets crunchy—and has corners that are worth fighting over—but never unpleasantly so.

---

*Yes, cold is fine. I divert from the proper béchamel method here as I've found that as long as you add your milk slowly, you do not need to heat it separately first. Hooray for fewer steps and pots!

Bake your lasagna for 30 to 45 minutes, until bubbly all over and browned on top. You should do absolutely nothing but put your feet up and drink a glass of wine while you do; you've earned it. When it comes out of the oven, I like to let it rest for 10 minutes before serving it.

Do ahead: Lasagna can be prepared right up until the baking point a day in advance, and kept wrapped in plastic in the fridge. Theoretically, you could also freeze it at this point but I haven't tried this. I'll update this to say "go for it" if many people respond in the comments that they've done so successfully. Lasagna will also reheat well for up to three days, possibly longer but in my apartment, we've never had the chance to find out.

THE FORAGER AT REST

By Christine Muhlke

From *Bon Appetit*

∽◎∾

Two of the world's hottest chefs—Noma's Rene Redzepi and
Momofuku's David Chang—meet for Sunday lunch, and
who's lucky enough to cover it? *Bon Appetit* executive editor
Christine Muhlke, who co-authored *On the Line* with another
star chef, Le Bernardin's Eric Ripert.

It's Sunday morning, and Rene Redzepi is gliding around
the kitchen in his socks while obscure Aboriginal music
drifts through his bright, cavernous, just-moved-into Copenhagen
apartment. His wife, Nadine, smiles and hands the couple's 13-
week-old daughter to her mother so she can make everyone a second cappuccino. New York chef David Chang, whose photo hangs
in the kitchen next to family portraits, is in town and has called to
say he'll be by in an hour. It's the type of scene—kind, calm, lovely
people in a spare yet creatively furnished space—that makes you
wonder why we don't all live in Scandinavia.

As the chef at Copenhagen's esteemed Noma, Redzepi has inspired cooks around the world to find their ingredients as close to
home as possible. So what does that mean when the man behind
what many consider the world's best restaurant—a place where
fried reindeer moss and coastal flowers have appeared on the
menu—is actually cooking at home?

Today's menu is, of course, seasonal and local. But it's also quick.
Nothing takes more than 90 minutes to cook. Reindeer-horn-

handled knife at the ready, Redzepi takes a parsley plant off the windowsill and cuts off a handful, leaving the stems. "There's so much flavor in the stems!" says the man who has made foraging the ultimate in locavorism. "In the winter we saute them—incredible." Next, he slices small biodynamic fennel bulbs so that the open V's resemble the slender mussels that were gathered in a fjord: "I'm imagining that if a mussel slides out of its shell, maybe it will slide in here." So this is how his restaurant dishes come to mimic nature—a gnarled breadstick mistaken for a twig, a snail replacing a nasturtium stamen.

Redzepi's talent for reconnecting natural flavors runs through the rest of the dish: The mussels will be steamed open in gooseberry juice, pressed from the sour berries that grow wild in Scandinavia. "Berries are so underestimated in savory cooking," he says. "They're so versatile, and they're not all sweet—you just associate them with pies." White wine balances the acidity. "People cook savory dishes with wine, and that's fruit juice, so what's so strange about this?"

Mussel prep finished, he starts work on the appetizer, a toast inspired by the *bo ssam* (pork shoulder served with a dozen raw oysters) served at Chang's Momofuku Ssam Bar in New York's East Village. Wild chanterelles are sauteed over high heat on the induction cooktop (below which is a clever ventilated IKEA drawer that keeps butter and other ingredients cool and close at hand; cue Scandi lifestyle envy). The mushrooms get a few tablespoons of cream, some minced shallots, parsley, and roughly chopped oysters. After several brisk shakes of the pan, the rich mixture is spooned onto sourdough toast that has practically been caramelized in butter. Translucent sheets of paper-thin Speck fat are laid atop a layer of sliced raw chanterelles just as Chang arrives.

The Momofuku chef loves the expansive, earth-forest-sea flavors of the toast, even though it's not yet breakfast time in New York, where he was just 36 hours prior. The toasts are even better with the spicy Noma beer brewed from birch sap by Skovlyst. Then the mussels are cooked for five minutes and served in mismatched bowls made by Noma's ceramist. "Samples," explains Nadine.

For the entree, there's a pot roast. But this one is celery root, not beef. At Noma, Redzepi has been treating vegetables like meat:

braising them, basting them, flavoring them with lots of herbs and butter (preferably that made from sweet, rich goat's milk). He'll even throw in a handful of coffee beans from the excellent local roaster Coffee Collective to see what happens. Earthy celery root takes extremely well to the treatment, browned and tender with herbal undertones. A quick sauce of warm buttermilk and olive oil—"basically a vinaigrette"—adds a complex tanginess. Garnished with black olives heated through in the herb butter, it's deeply, shockingly satisfying.

"This is a very good example of how we eat at home," Redzepi says: "It's vegetable based, there's a little twist to it, and it's very, very simple."

Seated at the sprawling dining table is an easy crowd. There's Alessandro Porcelli, himself an important tastemaker in the international food scene. He's a co-founder of the Cook It Raw chefs' adventure series, as well as closely involved in the inaugural MAD Foodcamp symposium, which is what has brought Chang to town. Noma sous-chef Trevor Moran, an Irishman with the most fantastic hair, is tucking into his day off. Nadine's mother holds a very sleepy infant, while toddler Arwen works on her princess drawing. And then there is the serene young Nadine, a reservationist at Noma, where the 12 tables are booked three months ahead. If people knew how beautiful she is, an Ingres portrait come to life with a smile as quietly sure, they wouldn't be upset when she tells them that the dining room is full. Possibly forever.

Maybe Nadine could send them some of her walnut cake to alleviate the sting. It's made with over a pound of nuts and a half pound of butter. "This is one of the best desserts I've had," Moran says a little sheepishly as he glances at his boss. But Redzepi isn't slighted; the British food critic Jay Rayner is coming over for dinner tomorrow, and Redzepi asks Nadine to please make another one. Everyone nods imploringly.

After coffee, Redzepi buckles Arwen into the front carriage of his dad bike and everyone walks alongside them to the King's Gardens. "This is where the king used to grow his vegetables. You can still get food here!" he says. While locals laze in the late-afternoon sun or play petanque, he heads straight for the trees. In the middle of the city—just blocks from his home—is a mulberry tree jeweled with untouched fruit. A few dish ideas are batted around by the chefs as they stare up into the leaves. "I know where we can find walnuts, too," Redzepi says and bikes ahead. Soon he and Chang are cracking open the green orbs and picking at the jellied flesh, running it between their fingers. "Trevor," he says decisively, "it's time for walnuts." Noma might be closed Sundays, but a true forager knows no bounds.

Pot-Roasted Celery Root
with Olives and Buttermilk

In this surprising main course, Redzepi pot-roasts whole celery roots. Be sure to use small celery roots; larger ones will not cook evenly. The chef also cooks small heads of cauliflower in this way.

6 servings

Ingredients
3 tablespoons plus 2 teaspoons extra-virgin olive oil plus
 more for drizzling
6 small celery roots (celeriac; each about 4 oz.), unpeeled,
 trimmed with some stem still attached
½ cup (1 stick) unsalted butter, cut into 1" cubes
Kosher salt
12 sprigs thyme
6 sprigs rosemary
6 sprigs sage
1 tablespoon coffee beans (optional)
1 cup buttermilk
½ lemon
¼ cup oil-cured black olives, pitted, quartered lengthwise

Preparation
Heat 3 Tbsp. oil in a large heavy pot over medium heat. Add celery roots and cook, turning frequently, until golden, 8–10 minutes. Add butter and a large pinch of salt. When butter begins to foam, reduce heat to medium-low. Add herb sprigs, coffee beans, if using, and 1 1/2 cups water. Cover and

gently cook, adding more water by tablespoonfuls if pan is dry, until celery roots are very tender, about 1 hour.

Remove herbs and coffee beans (if using) from pot and discard. Baste celery roots with buttery juices in pot. Remove from heat. Transfer celery roots to a cutting board, slice in half through stems, and place 2 halves on each plate.

Meanwhile, very gently warm buttermilk in a small saucepan over low heat (it will break if warmed too much). Squeeze in a few drops of lemon juice and add remaining 2 tsp. oil and a pinch of salt to make a loose sauce. Spoon sauce around celery roots on plates. Garnish with olives, drizzle with oil, and squeeze a few more drops of lemon juice over each.

Walnut Cake

Nadine Levy Redzepi created this incredibly rich, moist cake.
"Fat with fat—what could be better?" asks her husband.
Serve it for dessert or with coffee or tea for breakfast.

18–24 servings

Ingredients

1 cup (2 sticks) unsalted butter, room temperature, plus more
    for pan
6 tablespoons raw sugar, divided
7 cups walnut halves
¾ cup all-purpose flour
1 ½ cups almond flour or almond meal
¾ cup granulated sugar
6 large eggs
¾ cup heavy cream
½ cup plain whole-milk yogurt
1 teaspoon kosher salt
1 vanilla bean, split lengthwise
Whipped cream

Ingredient Info

Almond flour is available at some supermarkets and at natural
    foods stores and specialty markets.

Preparation

Preheat oven to 350°. Butter a 13x9x2" metal or glass baking dish; sprinkle bottom evenly with 3 Tbsp. raw sugar. Set aside.

Pulse walnuts in a food processor until coarsely chopped. Set 2 cups aside. Add all-purpose flour to processor and pulse until walnuts are very finely ground, 1–2 minutes. Add almond flour; pulse to blend. Set aside.

Using an electric mixer, beat 1 cup butter and granulated sugar in a large bowl until light and fluffy, 2–3 minutes. Add eggs, cream, yogurt, and salt. Scrape in seeds from vanilla bean (reserve bean for another use). Beat until well combined, 1–2 minutes. Add ground-walnut mixture and beat just to blend. Gently fold in chopped walnuts, being careful not to over-mix. Pour batter into prepared dish; smooth top. Sprinkle with remaining 3 Tbsp. raw sugar.

Bake until cooked through and a tester inserted into center comes out clean, 50–55 minutes. Let cool in pan on a wire rack. Serve with whipped cream. **DO AHEAD:** *Can be made 3 days ahead. Cover and chill. Cake is best served cold.*

BETTER COOKING
THROUGH TECHNOLOGY

By Corby Kummer

From *Technology Review*

⚬⚭⚬

Poised at the apex where gourmet cooking meets high-tech
technique, Nathan Myhrvold dazzled the food world with his
2011 multi-volume *Modernist Cuisine*. Corby Kummer, longtime senior editor for *The Atlantic*, reviewed and interviewed
Myhrvold for a tech-savvy audience.

To see *Modernist Cuisine* is to covet it. Which is why, one
day in May, the team that spent six years creating the
oversized, over-everything five-volume work came from Bellevue,
Washington, to New York City to demonstrate the wondrous object. And it is why a group of chefs, writers, and TV personalities (so
stellar that one guest remarked, "The only other event that could
bring these people together is a funeral") gathered one morning at
Jean-Georges, the flagship restaurant of Jean-Georges Vongerichten,
at the invitation of Tim and Nina Zagat. They were there to meet
Nathan Myhrvold, the mastermind and financier of a book so expensive to create that he refuses to say how much he spent (other
than to say it was more than $1 million but less than $10 million).
They wanted to try the pastrami cooked sous-vide for 72 hours, the
"tater tots" dunked in liquid nitrogen before being fried, the fruit
juices spun in a centrifuge, the mushroom omelet striped with
powdered-mushroom batter so that it looked like a piece of upholstery, with a perfectly spherical, magically just-cooked egg yolk
right in the middle. But they really wanted to see the book.

And it *is* a wondrous object. *Modernist Cuisine*'s five volumes comprise 1,522 recipes and 1,150,000 words of text on 2,438 pages, almost every one of them illustrated with color photography and charts, with dozens of gee-whiz, never-before-seen photographs of beautiful free-form color swirls that could be textile designs but turn out to be life-threatening pathogens; or sculptural objects that could be outdoor art installations but are mussels suspended in clear gelatin; or stunning anatomies of a painstakingly shelled lobster or flayed monkfish or whole chicken; or spectacular cross-section cutaways of pieces of equipment you never thought would or should be sawed in half, like ovens, woks full of hot oil, and kettle grills with white-hot smoldering coals. It weighs 40 pounds, four of them just ink. When Wayt Gibbs, the book's editor in chief, met me later that week in Cambridge, Massachusetts, at Toscanini's, an ice-cream parlor and intellectual salon heavy with MIT students and faculty, he painstakingly unwrapped the gigantic carton he had lugged on a portable dolly from Bellevue to New York and then to Boston. The café-goers grew silent and stared at the huge white volumes in their clear Lucite case, one of them later wrote me, as if they were the monolith in *2001*.

The long-awaited publication of *Modernist Cuisine*, in March, was the most significant event in the food world since . . . well, there might not be a precedent. The 6,000 copies that Myhrvold printed privately—against more conservative advice from what he describes as "cooler heads" in book publishing—immediately sold out at the introductory price of $465. "We sold 9,000 of those 6,000 copies," Myhrvold says with satisfaction. He quickly ordered 25,000 more copies to be printed.

To research the book, Myhrvold built a 4,000-square-foot laboratory–kitchen–photo studio in an 18,000-square-foot former motorcycle showroom in Bellevue, where an ever-expanding team of cooks experimented with machinery usually restricted to doctor's offices, hospitals, and commercial food processing, using powders and essences and chemicals similarly typical of the food industry.

Such experimentation had been going on for years, of course, most famously starting in the early 1990s at Ferran Adrià's El Bulli in Catalonia, Spain, and in the mid-1990s at Heston Blumenthal's

Fat Duck in Berkshire, England—the two main inspirations for Myhrvold and his team, whose lead members trained with Blumenthal. In this country, it was hard for ambitious young chefs to visit a similar nucleus of cooking research unless they could get into Grant Achatz's Alinea, in Chicago (*see "The Alchemist," January/February 2007*). Or unless they were among the favored few to be invited to one of the 30-course tasting dinners in the Bellevue lab, which were reserved mostly for cooks and industry leaders who had lent expertise or machines to the team, and for reporters like me who wanted a look at just what went into the three years of decision making, recipe testing, writing, and editing that preceded publication.

Myhrvold himself is an object of intense interest. The former chief technology officer of Microsoft and the founder of the patent investment company Intellectual Ventures, he is a genius and billionaire who still indulges his boyish enthusiasms, which include photography and dinosaurs but revolve mostly around cooking. The interest began at age nine, when he nearly set his mother's kitchen on fire in a plan to flambé everything for a Thanksgiving dinner. Myhrvold is a charming, even twinkling, spokesman for his mad invention processes—quite unlike, say, Ferran Adrià, whose trademark is a messianic intensity and utter imperviousness to anyone not as focused as he on the windstorm of creativity ever blowing round his brain. Myhrvold's voice is strong enough to come through in many sections of the book, though they're unsigned: a droll account in the third volume of traveling to Greenland and eating rotten shark, which "doesn't taste like chicken," is probably his. So is much of an excellent chapter in the fourth volume on coffee, in which he goes in search of what baristas call the "God shot" and in the process learns and shares a terrific amount of information on roasting, grinding, foaming milk, and pulling espresso shots.

Justifiable Cost

I managed to get my hands on the copy Gibbs unpacked at Toscanini's. Opening any volume brings you right to cutting-edge tech techniques that produce food unlike anything anyone has ever tasted outside El Bulli or the Fat Duck or Alinea.

But the high-tech toys and futuristic food are not why I think you should put yourself on the wait list and spend the $478 the book now costs (unless you want to spend the $800 and up being asked for "used" copies). Although some of the futuristic food is fabulous, as I learned from the 30 courses I got to try at the lab, the reason to pony up the going rate is that *Modernist Cuisine* is an incomparable introduction to many of the basic techniques of food and cooking. Within its five volumes (six, actually, including a spiral-bound book of recipes for the professional kitchen) are several long chapters that are as comprehensive and readable and valuable as any books I've seen on subjects essential for anyone interested in food.

The first volume alone contains a long, definitive introduction to food pathogens and food safety, a subject cooks ignore at their peril. The other volumes give basic information on science, ingredients, and techniques common to all cooking, not only "modernist" cuisine. And, of course, the book is a guide to the avant-garde—one far more comprehensive and usable than anything else yet written. As for the food, there are those 1,522 recipes, and if you can lay out a fairly substantial sum and clear enough counter space to start trying them—well, more on that later.

I didn't read all 1,150,000 words—no one other than Gibbs has claimed to, he told me when I spent a few days in the Bellevue kitchen. (He also admits to having tried only a few recipes, because he's not a cook.) But I'll claim a good 750,000. Watching the media appearances of the buoyant and unfailingly enthusiastic Myhrvold; visiting the book's website for cool videos of machines and pots being sawed in half or a kernel of popcorn dancing across a black screen until it explodes and soars up and off like a rocket; even eating 30 courses in Bellevue—none of it prepares you for the experience of reading *Modernist Cuisine*.

Everything about the book has been designed to keep a reader going, with bits of information in the margins and pages-long interruptions for techniques, cooking charts, and "parametric" and "example" recipes. Some sidebars go on for a few pages; they're printed in white type against black, as are most of the charts, so that the flow of text, though unusually complex, becomes intuitive. As in a magazine or textbook, captions provide complementary information and précis that make you feel you've got the gist of the main text.

The similarity to magazines and textbooks is not accidental. Myhrvold and Chris Young, a scientist and former Fat Duck chef who is listed as an author along with Maxime Bilet, another Fat Duck alumnus and the head chef of the Bellevue kitchen, were influenced by the illustrated Time-Life series of cookbooks from the late 1970s—books, like this one, assembled by veterans of the magazine and book worlds who knew how to unite text and photographs for maximal informative value. Gibbs, who's been a writer and editor at *Scientific American* and has extensive experience creating illustrated features, served as producer for a total of 44 writers, photographers, designers, researchers, and editors whose combined efforts bring life and interest to every page.

Myhrvold has been derided for producing a book, that most old-fashioned of objects, rather than a $5 app. His stock reply· a "really good" electronic version, with interactive features to scale recipes, animations for key techniques, and video clips, would be a project "bigger than the one to do this book." A book is still the best way to publish so much information, and the spiral-bound supplement, unlike an iPad, is waterproof. And with a few exceptions (including much of the fourth volume, which is devoted chiefly to thickeners, gels, emulsions, and foams—the trickiest in the new chef's bag of tricks), my interest never flagged.

Cool Tools

The book I'd make required reading for any cooking student is Volume 2, on techniques and equipment, which gives as good a description as I've seen of basic processes like baking and frying. This is also the volume that lists the toys in the toy box. Number one on the list is a sous-vide water bath—a tool that is ubiquitous in the recipes, particularly for meat. The bulk of the volume, unsurprisingly given the project's origins as an eGullet chat forum Myhrvold opened about sous-vide, is devoted to this cookery technique, which Myhrvold and many other cooks value for its precise control and predictability. Thanks to the enthusiasm of chefs like Achatz, Thomas Keller (who wrote a book on the method), and Philip Preston, of PolyScience, a manufacturer of controlled-temperature equipment who worked closely with Achatz and Myhrvold, the water bath has gone from science-lab "immersion circulator" to almost-affordable kitchen tool.

I don't have the patience for sous-vide, and I find that it produces too soft a texture in meat and fish. The piece of equipment I'd like to buy is a combination dry- and steam-heat "combi" oven, which so far hasn't found a manufacturer like Preston willing to work on one for the Williams-Sonoma crowd. There are tiny ones for $2,000, but they hold almost nothing; models not much bigger than a big microwave easily cost $12,000, and the authors say you need a couple of those. Still, the fact that the ovens thaw, steam, poach, and roast makes them as appealing to me as the microwave—which, hearteningly, the authors endorse for cooking vegetables, frying tender herbs, and turning vegetable juices into "perfect powders."

The authors do list cool tools that are within the reach of many home cooks, like digital scales and thermometers; the carbonator, for foam; a Toddy cold-brewing coffee kit, for deriving extracts of many flavorings besides coffee; and my favorite all-purpose tool, a pressure cooker, something I use nearly every night. The reason that stocks made in pressure cookers are perfectly clear, they point out, is that the water inside never boils, and the motion of boiling is what emulsifies oil and creates scum in normal stocks. They give everyday tips for ways to use the device, including making risotto (a longtime guilty secret of time-pressed Italian cooks, who will reveal it only after receiving compliments on how good their risotto is) and adding calcium chloride to the water for beans to let them soften without splitting their skins.

The tool many professional chefs may decide they need is a centrifuge, which costs $10,000 to $30,000 and can take up as much room as a washing machine. Myhrvold's team used a centrifuge to clarify juices from citrus and from sous-vide bananas, which became translucent and serum-like. Thomas Keller, chef of the French Laundry in Yountville, California, decided he needed a centrifuge after he saw the Bellevue lab use one to separate the fatty solids from peas to make "pea butter," spreadably thick and perfectly smooth.

And some chefs might sign on to the tank of liquid nitrogen that the team says is second in utility only to the sous-vide water bath. Dunking a food in liquid nitro before you fry it—"cryofrying," the lab calls it—makes the outside of, say, cubed pork or sous-vide chicken or "tater tots" hot and crisp while the interior turns out just warm and not overcooked. It also makes soft foods manageable to slice thin or to grind. Cubes of beef can be put into meat grinders, drawn out in parallel, extruded strands, and carefully rolled into plastic-wrapped cylinders. After being submerged in liquid nitro, they're cut into patties and deep-fried for hamburgers that, as Jean-Georges Vongerichten reported with wonder, are juicy and crumbly without being fatty or tough. But the grownup boy magicians on the *Modernist* team use the cooling agent, they admit, "for just about every food," because it's "just plain fun"—for instance, to "cryoshatter" olive oil for a garnish.

Possibilities

Volume 3, on animals and plants, is both an anatomy class and a guide to how proteins and fibrous plants react to heat. The section on meat includes wonderful color diagrams of muscle fibers and collagen that do more than anything else I've ever seen to explain the structure of meat and make it clear why different cuts cook differently. The section on vegetables is a good bit shorter, perhaps reflecting the cooks' degree of interest. (They seem to have been intensely interested in the heat scale of peppers, though!)

Volume 4, on ingredients and preparations, spends the most time on thickeners, this being "truly the best age ever in which to thicken a liquid." I was glad to learn about viscosity and fluid gels, and to discover that alginate, a hydrocolloid extracted from brown seaweed, is the key to the "spherification" that Adrià has made almost as popular and widespread as foams. But for anyone who doesn't plan to buy Ultra-Sperse 3 or Ultra-Tex, or N-Zorbit M or even xanthan gum—all of which are turning up in modernist-inspired kitchens, and all of which appear in dozens and dozens of recipes in the book—this will make the least absorbing reading.

I'd argue that the plated-dish recipes in Volume 5 will date the book faster than any other part. They're included to demonstrate the possibilities of all the techniques and ingredients we've learned about in other volumes, and to conclude the argument started in Volume 1 that all history builds to their inevitability. So classic recipes are updated and adapted, using a panoply of time-consuming steps few home cooks would attempt. Blanquette de veau, the classic veal stew, is liquefied to a warm cream called "veal nog" that requires a rotor-stator homogenizer and a centrifuge. Boeuf en gelée, the gel hot rather than cold, demands a homemade oxtail stock, xanthan gum, and low-acyl gellan.

Some cooks might attempt all this—perhaps ambitious professionals who haven't been able to apprentice in any of the new-wave kitchens, perhaps semi-obsessed hobbyists. But I'm not one of them, and the 30 courses at Bellevue, every one of which I tried and took notes on, didn't make me a convert. Some of the flavors and textures were revelatory: a clear, strong "beef tea" that came from a sous-vide bag; cocoa pasta, something impossible without "vital gluten" (cocoa powder has no gluten of its own), with puréed, cured sea urchin cooked sous-vide. But much of it still seems mere trickery: freeze-dried corn kernels and powders of brown butter and lime and ash in a version of the Mexican street food corn elote, the powdered fat unpleasantly greasy on the tongue; a cream of mushroom and bacon soup infused with dark miso and gelled into a too-intense foam; smoked butter made in a rotor-stator homogenizer that overwhelmed a delicate piece of fresh-caught, unfortunately brined albino salmon (cooked sous-vide, of course).

But these are matters of personal taste, and the night I visited Bellevue I was fascinated every moment. As I did at the Jean-Georges breakfast, I came away convinced that these techniques and ingredients will be essential for cooks of the future. It's too early to know how they'll be adapted, and which will be most frequently used, but my feeling when sampling the 30 courses was that as prices for homogenizers and centrifuges come down, thickening agents become easy to find, and even liquid nitrogen becomes commonplace in professional and then home kitchens, we'll make our own ketchup and many other staples, and come to cook dishes as basic as fried chicken and hamburgers in completely different ways.

Every big-name chef, however rooted in classic techniques, is already interested. A couple of hours after the Zagat breakfast, Vongerichten persuaded me to stay for lunch, to eat the tasting menu he was giving the chef Daniel Boulud as a birthday gift. He didn't send us 30 courses, but the number approached 20, and the flavors were a kind of musical composition that varied in volume and intensity but never in virtuosity. Almost none of them used any of the new techniques described in *Modernist Cuisine*; almost all of them strove to find innovative but nonrevolutionary ways to extract the maximum flavor and fragrance from the herbs, fish, and meat Vongerichten had in the kitchen.

But Vongerichten told me he's getting ready to be a not-quite-early adopter, even though "I tried meat glue, and I just don't understand—why do I need meat glue?" As we discussed the book after lunch—he had paged through it in the morning like a child with his first train set—he had a look in his eyes that was both wistful and determined. "I've got to make burgers that crumbly," he said. Another tank of liquid nitro sold.

Foodways

THE PASTRAMI DILEMMA

By John Birdsall

From Chow.com

Chow senior editor John Birdsall—a former chef who segued into food writing for the Bay Area's SF Weekly and *East Bay Express*—traces the fortunes of this Jewish deli staple, finally getting its long-overdue artisanal revival. Reuben sandwiches will never taste the same.

The joke goes: A gorilla walks into Sol's delicatessen and orders a pastrami sandwich.

"That'll be $15," says Sol, handing the gorilla a sandwich. "I gotta say, I never expected to see a gorilla in my deli."

"At $15 for a pastrami sandwich," snaps the gorilla, "you never will again."

Once, pastrami was cheap. It came from Jews on New York's Lower East Side in the 19th century, when beef was abundant. They adapted it from Romanian *pastramă,* originally made from salted and pressed geese and ducks. And since then, it's been viewed as a well-loved but lowbrow American original, like the hot dog or the hoagie. You could say it's the soul of the American deli.

But even while chefs in other parts of the restaurant industry are making their own charcuterie, pastrami has, until recently, been stuck in the deli case of the 1950s: industrialized and mass-produced.

You know all those discussions about who has the best, Stage or Katz's, Langer's or Canter's? Forget about it. Three factories make nearly all of that famous deli pastrami and distribute it around the country.

The owners of these three pastrami factories, kind of like dons in a benign pastrami mafia, each control their own turf. In Brooklyn, for example, there's Eddie Weinberg, who supplied the old 2nd Ave Deli. In Detroit, it's Sy Ginsberg, who does *Zingerman's*. Lou Sandoval of Burbank, California, supplies *Langer's*.

But finally, there's a pastrami revival going on: Artisans all over the country are starting to make pastrami the old-fashioned way. From Portland to Brooklyn to San Francisco, young chefs are opening traditional Jewish delis and bringing back the nearly extinct tradition of hand-cured, hand-smoked pastrami. But it turns out the old way is a lot harder than you'd think.

Hot Beef Injection

Picture your favorite Jewish deli: You probably have visions of a guy in a white apron slicing spicy, steaming brisket into a gorgeous tower. The truth is, that guy didn't make that brisket. Almost all pastrami in this country is made more like a Honda on an assembly line than like a craft project.

First, the meat goes into an injection machine, where it's shot up with a salty solution. Then it gets a quick brine, is coated in spices, and gets smoke flavor—either briefly, over actual smoldering wood chips, or more likely on a grill like at a backyard barbecue, where the "smoke" comes from fatty juices flaring up against hot metal. Or even in a chamber of aerosolized liquid smoke. The whole process is over in a matter of hours, after which the meat is vacuum-sealed in plastic so it can sit in a cooler for weeks before it's dumped in some deli's steamer to cook for a few hours.

And probably not surprisingly, the factory dons are vague about where they get the meat for their clients' famous pastrami. We can guess it's not grass-fed.

The truth about pastrami isn't exactly a secret. David Sax's book *Save the Deli*, published in 2009, revealed the state of industrialization of high-end deli meats. And it's not that pastrami's an unpalatable product. A pastrami sandwich from one of America's storied delis can be great. (LA food critic Jonathan Gold, for instance, thinks *Langer's* makes the best pastrami sandwich in the country.)

But handmade everything is the new ethos among a certain breed of chef. And those opening up nouveau Jewish delis think they can do better. As it turns out, though, making pastrami is a lot more challenging than making rugelach and whitefish salad.

Navel Gazing

Problem number one: To make old-timey pastrami, the way the original preindustrial New Yorkers did it, you have to use the navel: a fatty belly cut akin to bacon on a hog. It's got thick streaks of fat that ensure the meat stays moist.

At Saul's, a New York–style Jewish deli in Berkeley, California, co-owner Peter Levitt learned it's nearly impossible to use navel without going broke. Levitt, a former Chez Panisse chef, makes some essential deli products in-house: sodas, pickles, kreplach. But when it came to pastrami, the traditional ingredients were out of reach. The navel used to be a cheap cut of meat. Nowadays it's expensive, thanks to demand from Asia. (In China and South Korea, the navel is prized.) Adding to his problems was Levitt's desire to find *sustainably raised* navel—after all, Michael Pollan is a regular at Saul's.

For a few weeks, while he was trying to locate the right navel, Levitt took pastrami off the menu. A Jewish deli without pastrami? You can imagine how well that went over. For nearly two weeks, servers wore buttons on their aprons reading "Pastrami Under Construction." Some customers were pissed, and Levitt continues to get calls from people asking, with trepidation, if pastrami is still "not on the menu."

When Levitt was finally able to source sustainable navel, it was cost-prohibitive because the meat is so fatty that the usable portion from one slab of navel is very small. There's a reason why most pastrami these days is made from brisket, with a tendency toward dryness. And now Saul's is too.

Mystery Meat

Problem number two: If nobody's making "real" pastrami anymore, how are you supposed to know what it's supposed to taste like? Sort of a funny question, but that was a real conundrum for Leo Beckerman and Evan Bloom. In late 2010 when the two former college buddies started Wise Sons, a pop-up Jewish deli in San Francisco, they knew they wanted to make their own pastrami, but they had no models to follow. Nobody they knew was making honest-to-God nonfactory pastrami, so they had no one to learn from. They had to turn to the Canadians for help.

Mile End Deli in Brooklyn, opened by Canadians Noah Bernamoff and his wife, Rae Cohen, in 2009, makes its own Montreal smoked beef. (Canada never lost its tradition of delis smoking and curing their own beef the way America did.) Mile End's product was as close to traditional pastrami as Beckerman and Bloom could find. The most noticeable thing about it was the intense smokiness that most American pastrami has lost.

Using the Bernamoffs as their guide, Beckerman and Bloom began to experiment. After trial and error, they developed an authentic-tasting recipe. First the meat (they experimented with navel but soon abandoned it for brisket) gets "wet cured" in brine and pickling spices for a week. Then it sits another couple of days on a rack, coated in powdered spices, until it dries out and develops a crust (the technical term is *pellicle*). Then it smokes for six to ten hours over hickory chunks.

At the end, they get meat that's both smokier and more beefy-tasting than factory pastrami, that's chewier, and that has an almost creamy texture from fat marbling. After nearly two weeks of work, it better be good.

Is It Worth It?

Of course, not every old-fashioned process works in the modern world. Ever tried making your own salt by evaporating seawater, or not washing your hair like the Native Americans did? At Portland, Oregon, deli Kenny & Zuke's there's been some backsliding on the road to authenticity. One of the earliest pastrami revivalists, co-owner Ken Gordon started making his own while still a chef in a Portland bistro, six years ago. He used the navel. But at Kenny & Zuke's, he found the original recipe to be off-putting for many Portlanders.

"It was too fatty," he says. "My grandparents came over from Russia and Warsaw and ate serious chunks of fat and died in their 60s. These days customers want it lean."

So the deli switched to what people are used to: brisket.

Now Kenny & Zuke's pastrami has a cult following. (One reviewer described their sandwich as capable of bringing a woman to orgasm.)

And yet a week's worth of curing is a long time. Imagine you're burning through, say, 2,000 pounds of pastrami a week. How are you going to keep up? And where are you going to find the walk-in space? Such were the problems for Kenny & Zuke's. Add to that the fact that Gordon has designs on Whole Foods—he hopes eventually to get FDA approval to package his pastrami to sell to retailers.

And so, there have been some tweaks to Kenny & Zuke's traditional-ness. To shave a few days off the curing process, the meat no longer goes through the long brining. Instead, it's injected, just like the factories do it.

Berkeley's Levitt has started injecting, too. He *was* a pastrami purist, but these days he says he doesn't think the old-timey wet brine makes any difference to the taste of the meat.

And a week after opening their brick-and-mortar delicatessen, Wise Sons' Evan Bloom is already thinking about how he can speed up the curing process.

The revivalists' pastrami still tastes great, though. It still sells like crazy. And it's still handmade. After all, Gordon's and Levitt's employees are the ones holding the syringe. For now.

Somebody tell the gorilla that he can come back for a pastrami sandwich.

PASSOVER GOES GOURMET

By Rachel Levin

From *Sunset*

Once you've conquered pastrami making, why not throw a
hipster Seder for the Bay Area? Freelance travel and food
writer Rachel Levin laid to rest ghosts of Passovers past at this
pop-up event in a San Francisco warehouse.

Why was this night different from all other nights? For
starters, there was a bar. And not a bottle of sticky-
sweet Manischewitz behind it. People at this Passover Seder were
drinking. *Good* wine. *Before* the first of the traditional four glasses
was poured.

Second, people were dressed in jeans. My mother never let me
wear even my very best Jordache to any Jewish holiday. Skirts only,
and tights that would sag around my ankles. Now, three decades
later, I swapped a pair of faded cords for a stylish purple number
and heels. I hadn't felt this overdressed since I wore a bathing suit
to the Big Sur hot springs.

Third, this wasn't my grandparents' house in a manicured
Boston suburb, but a mod cafe in a former warehouse in San Francisco. My aunts and crazy cousins were clear across the country.
There were no conversations-cum-arguments about what route
everyone took to get there. Or kids' tables topped with Dixie cups
of Welch's white grape juice.

Above all, apart from my Caribbean-born gentile friend George—whom I'd dragged here while my Jewish husband was, uh, at a Black Crowes concert—this was a Seder of strangers. All different backgrounds. Fifty folks here *voluntarily,* not because their parents forced them.

The big draw? The food. Cooked, not by Grandma Hannah, but by Leo Beckerman and Evan Bloom, whose Wise Sons Jewish Delicatessen pop-up here had an instant cult following. Lines snaked down sidewalks for their hand-sliced artisanal spin on pastrami. The demand for good deli—in a city long lacking it—grew so strong that the duo recently opened a real-deal restaurant. Last April, their first-ever public Passover Seder sold out within minutes by word of mouth.

Imagine, the promise of gefilte fish *that* good.

Strangers become friends

Candles were lit. Communal tables were set. Sparely. No lacy white tablecloths or Blue Danube china. Playing silently on a screen was the '50s classic film *The Ten Commandments.* I mean, Charlton Heston's low-tech parting of the Red Sea is the kind of Seder entertainment I could've used as a kid.

I loved my grandpa Orrin, I really did. He was a kind, lanky doctor in a knit tie and corduroy blazer. But his Seders were by-the-book snooze.

Here was fresh-faced 28-year-old Leo! With waist-length dreadlocks pulled back in a ponytail, he had a cool, confident command over the room that would no doubt make his own grandfather proud. After the blessing over the wine, servers presented plates of matzo. It was blistered, cracker-thin, imperfectly shaped. And *not* from a box, but made by Bay Area local Blake Joffe of Beauty's Bagel Shop—with more than just the requisite flour and water. If all it takes is a little sea salt and olive oil to enhance matzo's typically dry-mouth taste, then I vote for a minor overhaul of tradition.

Still, this was a legit Seder. Everyone had a photocopy of a Haggadah, the book of prayers, songs, and biblical tales that recount the Israelites' exodus from Egypt and freedom from slavery.

It's a good story. But as a kid, taking turns around the table reading The. Entire. Freaking. Thing meant we didn't eat for *hours.* I'd steal sprigs of parsley from the tabletop (long after we'd dipped it in the ritual salt water)—and sit, starving and bored as hell. Grandma's dense-as-rocks matzo balls and gray, leather-tough brisket weren't any prize. But by the time dinner was actually served, I would've eaten the jar of Heinz Chili Sauce she'd "seasoned" it with.

"Tonight, we're going to move through the Passover story pretty quickly," announced Leo. "We've got eating to do!" Amen to that.

And so it began: the explanation of the Seder plate, the Four Questions (typically, the youngest person at the table is charged with tone-deaf singing this integral part of the evening, but on this night, the lone tween was too shy; instead we were treated to a woman who actually had a beautiful voice), and the Ten Plagues, detailing Old World woes. By the festive song *"Dayenu"* ("Enough"), we'd lost count of glasses of wine and were all one big, happy family—singing, clapping, exchanging smiles. George turned to me and exclaimed: "I love this! I'm with my people!"

Before we knew it, dinner was served, family-style: pickled heirloom carrots and Bull's Blood beets. "Mock liver"—a mash of organic peas and Blue Lake beans. The prettiest, most perfectly pungent, handgrated fluorescent-fuchsia horseradish I've ever had. (Note to Wise Sons: Jar that stuff!) The soup was a clean, flavorful broth buoying matzo balls as God intended them to be: featherlight and fluffy. The gefilte fish was a custom-grind of carp and whitefish in a fennel-thyme fumet—a far cry from the congealed stuff in jars you see every season at the supermarket. And the brisket: not gray! Not tough! Just fork-tender shreds of peppery sweet meat.

Three hours later, when we were down to the last sips of madeira, matched with a creamy, rich chocolate pot de crème (single-handedly bringing Passover desserts back from the dead), there was laughter; career-advice-giving; gossip about embarrassing wedding toasts and bad breakups involving people we didn't know. No barking between relatives or help-clear-the-table mandates from Mom. But hugs good-bye. And sincere cries of "Next Year—with Wise Sons!"

The 2011 Dyke March Wiener Taste Test

By Bethany Jean Clement

From *The Stranger*

The Fourth of July: The iconic American holiday, made
for parades, fireworks, and cooking hot dogs on the grill.
Seattle's wacky spin on this tradition is perfect fodder for
The Stranger managing editor Bethany Jean Clement's
subversive, droll restaurant review style.

And so we come to Independence Day, when Americans
turn to thoughts of wieners.

Fact (according to a press release received by *The Stranger* last
week about something called "Grillebration," which sounds like an
emergency room procedure): Our countrypeople will enjoy seven
billion hot dogs between Memorial Day and Labor Day. On July
4th, we will engulf more than 150 million of them. One hundred
and fifty million hot dogs: We must all do our part. So as a public
service in advance of your patriotic barbecue, we present the 2011
Dyke March Wiener Taste Test.

For the purposes of the test, three representative weenies were
selected. (We shall set aside the veggie dogs as a dangerous fringe
element.) First, the low: the bottom-shelf supermarket dog. When
I was a child, we were fed Bar-S—containing, among other things,
unspecified tidbits of pork and beef and mechanically separated
chicken, as well as corn syrup (2 percent or less of the latter, the label hastens to reassure). While among a certain set nowadays, serv-

ing kids Bar-S would get you reported to Child Protective Services, it claims to be the number-one-selling hot dog in America (with the dubious corollary claim "Only the best is branded Bar-S"). Interpreting the runes on my supermarket receipt, it appears that last Saturday, a package of Bar-S Classic Franks was on special for just one dollar. That's 12 cents per dog. TWELVE CENTS. Is this a great country or what? (Or what.)

Then there is what might arguably be called the middle way: Hebrew National, the kosher frank that brags about being all beef (unspecified "premium cuts," riiiight), with no artificial flavors or fillers (animated buns on the website wave protest-style signs about this). It's worth noting, however, that Hebrew National—just like Bar-S—contains 2-percent-or-less of four kinds of sodiums, including our friend nitrate. Furthermore, while Hebrew National touts its "humble beginnings in New York City's turn-of-the-century immigrant neighborhoods," it is now a subsidiary of food giant ConAgra, the *Wikipedia page of which*—with allegations of environmental irresponsibility, labor issues, health violations, salmonella and E. coli–related product recalls, and delicious, delicious more—truly merits all Americans' attention. The price of Hebrew National beef franks at QFC last Saturday: just about 43 cents each.

Last but not least, and just in time for the taste test, Seattle has a brand-new high-class dog: Rain Shadow Meats' house-made wieners. When I phoned the all-local-meats Capitol Hill butcher to inquire what they sold that was most like a hot dog, they reported that after extensive research and development, they'd just debuted their own—just like a regular hot dog, but made with reduced-guilt-and-ick-factor Carlton Farms pork, Painted Hills beef, "a little bit of ham," and a proprietary spice blend, all inside a lamb casing. Rain Shadow proprietor and great-name-haver Russ Flint said that while he only eats a hot dog once in a blue moon (which is really how often you should be eating a hot dog, America), the people deserve a high-quality option. Rain Shadow's wieners are peachy-colored and pornographically large in both length and girth; they're about a quarter-pound each. Uncooked, they are redolent of traditional baloney. At $6.99 a pound, each weenie will run you about $1.65.

The obvious time to conduct the taste test, as a celebration of all things U.S. of A., was during a friend's annual barbecue along the route of the Seattle Dyke March last Saturday. A gas grill was fired up on the sidewalk; the three kinds of weenies were cooked until nice and hot, with good grill-markage (except the Bar-S, which due to an unforeseen grill hot spot obtained an all-over char to which no one objected). The dogs were ensconced in cheap, squishy buns (the only proper hot-dog conveyance, no matter what Macrina Bakery may offer). The smaller dogs were cut into halves and the Rain Shadow behemoths cut into thirds, as no one in their right mind wants to eat three entire hot dogs; ketchup and yellow mustard were made available, though if utilized, had to be applied to all three samples for test consistency. The dogs were fed, unidentified, to study participants (though without actual blind-folding, as that seemed too complicated). Now: the results.

Bar-S Classic Frank: Most test subjects were administered this weenie first, and the general consensus was that, lacking any basis for comparison, it was completely adequate if "not exciting" (Ben K., attorney). One subject pronounced it "an all-American, deli-cious hot dog" (sound engineer and education coordinator Jef-fery). Small-business-owner Greg theorized that, due to its highly processed look and squishy consistency, the Bar-S sample might be a veggie dog; upon sampling, however, he said, "It tastes like it's real meat." His hypothesis briefly spread, leading Toshi (artist) to say that the dog "looked fake . . . I don't feel like it's meat." Zac (an-other artist) reported simply, "It tastes like a hot dog, straight-up." Greg, with the gimlet eye of a capitalist, offered the only real con-demnation: "If these were your hot dogs, I wouldn't invest in your business."

Hebrew National Kosher Frank: Several test subjects whose parents were less skinflinty than mine identified this as the taste of childhood. Ben K. got a bit misty-eyed, saying, "It's reminiscent of the classic hot dogs of my youth." It was judged less squishy than Bar-S, as well as saltier; "Salty-delicious," said Sara (arts administra-tor), while another subject (me, not blind, but whatever) felt it was oversalted (and I like salt). Upon visual inspection, Greg pronounced this dog to have the appearance of real meat; after tasting, it was judged to have better flavor, "a little smoky—good texture—I'm impressed." Jeffery cannily identified it as a kosher dog. "It's real good," he said succinctly.

Rain Shadow Meats' Quality Dog: Well, what do you know? This was hands down the wiener-winner. Jeffery reported (again, cannily) that it had "lots of actual flavor—less like a hot dog, more like a sausage. I feel like the pig was killed within 50 miles of here." Conjecturing about the methodology of the test, Zac said, "I feel like we're going up in quality—maybe it's psychosomatic, but I feel like we went up in meatiness." Ben B. (floor refinisher) admired both the crunch and the spice. And yet the gains in texture and taste were not at the expense of archetypal hot dog flavor; as Sara put it, "Mmmmm—hot dog." Greg liked the looks of both the size and the color, and after one bite said, "This is it. This is the shit. This is in my refrigerator. It tastes like people just cared more, whether it's quality ingredients, craftsmanship—it has more dimension. Someone cared." Informed about the added expense, he opined that if the hot dog was still only a couple bucks, it was entirely worth it—you do get what you pay for. Ben K. concurred, lauding the Rain Shadow dog's "multiple flavor notes." He then summed up the taste test thusly: "Three wieners in my mouth—what a perfect Pride weekend."

Not long after, the Dyke March went by with beating drums, aglow with the fresh legalization of gay marriage in New York and the late-evening sun. March participants wore rainbows and trilby hats and gold lamé shirts and no shirts at all, flashing peace signs and waving. The taste-testers screamed in support until all were hoarse. Is this a great country or what? (Great country!)

THE MISSING LINK

By Brett Anderson

From *The Times-Picayune*

After eleven years of covering New Orleans' food scene—most memorably through the tragedies of Hurricane Katrina and the BP oil spill—Brett Anderson recently took a year's leave from the *Times-Picayune* (in the throes of a controversial downsizing) to accept a Nieman Fellowship at Harvard.

Donald Link barely gave the chickens a chance to stop sizzling before he put his hands around them, subjecting each to a tactile examination that looked like nothing so much as a quarterback blindly feeling his way to a football's seam.

One of the chickens looked like wild game, its flesh darkened by injected Cajun spices vivified by the flames in the wood-fired oven behind it. The other, which had been brined overnight, wore the more typical mottled gold-brown armor of roasted farm-raised fowl. Both stood upright in cast-iron pans, impaled by beer cans. Link appraised them while sucking the grease off his fingers. "Turns out there are a lot of ways to cook a chicken," he said.

That statement of the obvious prompted laughter in the peanut gallery behind him, at the edge of the open kitchen inside Cochon in Lafayette.

The opening of the restaurant, a spin-off of the original Cochon in New Orleans, was still three weeks away, but on this hot August night, Link and his team had crossed the threshold where obsessive planning gives way to undressed rehearsals. Ryan Prewitt, until recently chef de cuisine at Herbsaint, Link's flagship New Orleans restaurant, explained, "We talked about (cooking chicken) for like three hours last night."

"It got pretty heated, " chuckled Stephen Stryjewski, who is, along with Link, chef and co-owner of both Cochon locations.

Cochon Lafayette has more than just a name in common with its New Orleans counterpart. The most important similarity is a concept that encapsulates Link's vision of what, to use his words, "Cajun food has become." Not since Paul Prudhomme opened K-Paul's Louisiana Kitchen more than three decades ago has New Orleans seen a new restaurant elicit such a phenomenal response from such an array of diners. That both happen to hang their hats on the food of Acadiana is a topic ripe for academic inquiry.

Evidence of Cochon's success goes beyond the crowds that regularly congest the restaurant's corner of New Orleans' Warehouse District.

Since Cochon opened in 2006, both Link and Stryjewski have won prestigious chef awards from the James Beard Foundation. In 2008, *The New York Times* ranked Cochon the third best new American restaurant outside New York. Link also won a Beard for "Real Cajun," his provocatively titled cookbook that delves deep into the pot that inspired Cochon's creation. "Gossip Girl" star Blake Lively was so besotted with the restaurant's sweet potato sauce at a recent visit that she tried to persuade staff to circumvent FDA regulations by sending her some inside a disemboweled teddy bear. (The response she received from Cochon, according to *Glamour* magazine: "We are not the drug cartel.")

Still, the new Cochon is a re-creation of the old one, not a straight replication. (An item not central to the New Orleans Cochon repertoire: roast chicken.) The fine distinction begins to explain why Link's journey back to his native Cajun country—Lafayette is its putative capital—has been filled with trepidation as well as joy.

The chef's family roots run deep in the region: He was raised in Lake Charles, on Cajun country's southwestern edge. But as much as Link identifies with the cooking of his—and perhaps as importantly, his family members'—youth, there is no erasing that he became a big shot in a city whose relationship to Cajun country has dysfunctional dimensions. As Billy Link, a Crowley soybean, rice and crawfish farmer, put it, "New Orleans is New Orleans, and there's a line between New Orleans and here. They don't mix well, in a way."

Billy Link, who is either Donald's third or fourth cousin (it depends on whom—and when—you ask), was leaning against the poured-concrete counter separating the restaurant's kitchen from one of two main dining rooms. He'd arrived with his wife, Becky, and their two young sons to feast on the dishes Cochon's chefs were fine-tuning while test-driving the new kitchen equipment.

The banquet included the two roast chickens, along with one that had been cooked in an outside smoker built by Dwane Link, another cousin; two darkly crusted pork shoulders; a whole ribeye roast cut into bite-size strips; a pan of shrimp in a butter sauce spiked with the Brazilian peppers that Donald Link grows in his Lakeview backyard; and smothered rabbit provided by yet another cousin, served with rice that Billy Link is supplying the Lafayette restaurant.

"That's the old Cajun style right here!" Billy Link proclaimed, delighted by the sight of the rabbit, which he called, in an exaggerated French-Cajun accent, *lapin*. "If they cook it like this, they'll be all right."

Billy Link has known his cousin only as a successful chef, having first met Donald at a family reunion six or seven years ago, and relishes his role as an unofficial critic of Cochon's food. He's playfully dismissive of meat smokers as an influence of the Zaunbrechers, the Cajun family on Donald Link's mother's side. ("The Link side? Non-smokers.") He wore a Cochon T-shirt but actually prefers Herbsaint, where the food reflects European traditions as much as Louisiana ones.

The preference could be a simple matter of taste. It also could have something to do with the games Cochon plays on native Cajuns' memory and sense of pride. The phenomenon might be summed up by the review Billy Link said a group of his friends gave the New Orleans restaurant after visiting: "We can cook better than that."

Donald Link responds to his family's ribbings the way he responds to irritants both mild and severe: with a crooked smile that causes him to resemble a cat that just made a snack of a pet canary. While he's no stranger to cameras or laudatory press, by the standards of a moment where chefs can become television stars without ever running a restaurant, Link counts as a throwback to the days when chefs let the food speak for itself. He insists, "I am not trying to be a celebrity chef."

The strategy has served Link well, and not just economically. Anthony Bourdain, the acerbic chef, television host and best selling author, has said of Link, "there's no one in the business with more credibility."

The challenge in Lafayette is that credibility earned for cooking Cajun food in New Orleans isn't exactly a recognized currency. In fact, it could be a liability.

"A lot of (Cajuns) know of him who haven't tried his food, but they know of him because he's up here, " Billy Link said of his cousin, raising his hand up high to illustrate the chef's exalted status. "And they're waiting for him."

One of the many ironies attending Cochon Lafayette is that its owners don't regard area Cajun restaurants to be their primary competition. Ask Link or Stryjewski what inspired them to open in Lafayette, as opposed to, say, Houston or Covington, both of which were considered, and they will invariably talk with amazement about the crowds at Pamplona Tapas Bar or the slick Japanese restaurant Tsunami in Lafayette's old downtown

"You need to check that place out on a Friday night, " Stryjewski said of Tsunami. The night-clubby restaurant is not the sort one would expect to impress Stryjewski, a tattooed, bearishly boyish man who in plain clothes often appears to have just stepped off a skateboard.

But Tsunami, like Pamplona, captured the chefs' attention because its crowd, particularly on weekends, exposes an indigenous population of young adults whose interests clearly go well beyond—and possibly don't even include—boudin and zydeco.

The opportunity Cochon's chefs see in Lafayette has as much to do with business as it does aesthetics, and it is similar to the one they road to fame and profit in New Orleans. While the level of attention Prudhomme had brought to Cajun food in the 1980s altered the way Americans eat, the Opelousas-born chef's fame was so widely felt—and his food so widely misinterpreted—that it sparked a debate over authenticity of the cuisine that has yet to quiet.

"Stir the Pot: The History of Cajun Cuisine," a definitive book on the subject, debunks the myth that Cajun food was developed in a vacuum; authors Marcelle Bienvenu, Carl A. Brasseaux and Ryan A. Brasseaux call it a "cross-cultural borrowing of the diverse ethnic and racial groups that have co-existed in the Bayou Country since the late eighteenth century."

Cochon entered into this historical fray by exposing one thing Prudhomme's revolution did not spawn: modern Cajun restaurants that uphold the highest standards of quality and service. The very fact that Link's team drew a bead on Lafayette suggests that this has been the case not just in New Orleans but in Cajun country itself, an implication that steers the age-old debate over authenticity into uncharted, potentially turbulent waters.

Link and Stryjewski are intense students of Cajun cuisine and its evolution. And the chefs' idea of "real" Cajun food around Lafayette tends to be found in the same places Cajun food purists look for it: on home cooks' stoves or in decidedly blue-collar restaurants like T-Coon's and Laura's II, both order-at-the-counter, rice-and-gravy plate lunch places that have almost nothing in common, at least atmospherically, with Cochon.

But in the crowds found at the more modern non-Cajun restaurants, Link sees "an indication of the desire of this city. If you want to feel metropolitan, if you want to go for a glass of wine and a decent meal, where do you go? It's usually fried food and beer and cocktails, and if there is wine, it's not good wine. I think there's a lot more sophistication going on in these small towns that's not being reflected in the restaurants."

Demographic evidence supports Link's hunch. The 2010 Census data puts the median household income in Lafayette Parish at $47,901. That compares to a $35,505 median household income in Orleans Parish, according to data provided by the Greater New Orleans Community Data Center.

But is it possible tonier Cajun-style restaurants are few and far between in Cajun country because Cajun diners don't trust restaurants with wine lists to properly represent a folk-art form born of subsistence living many people still remember?

Pat Mould was the chef at Charlie G's when the restaurant opened in Lafayette in 1985. He remembers raising eyebrows with the restaurant's contemporary Louisiana cooking and sleek interior, which was designed by a prominent Chicago architect.

"Because we had this perception of being a citified restaurant, we got a ton of (criticism)," Mould said. "People were suspicious. We have this jaded perspective that no one's going to cook it better than mama."

That Charlie G's remains one of the region's relatively few high-end restaurants interpreting Louisiana cuisine also points to persistent assumptions about the corrupting effects of elevated social status. In an oral history conducted for the Southern Foodways Alliance by the New Orleans historian (and Lafayette native) Rien Fertel, T-Coon's owner David Billeaud said, "I'm not a chef. I'm a cook. Cooks work hard."

In New Orleans, Cochon proves daily that questions surrounding its food's authenticity are matters of semantics and style, not substance. The food's rusticity provides cloud cover to a technical proficiency that is the mark of professionals who regard the chef title as an honor earned through labor. The results—the fried rabbit livers riding pepper jellied toasts, the hogs-head cheese shaved over fresh peas, the skillet-cooked rabbit and dumplings based on a Link relative's recipe for squirrel—are almost always prettier than anything a Cajun grandmother has ever served.

Link and Stryjewski, after all, are not Cajun grandmothers. They're chefs whose skill-sets and sensibilities were formed in restaurants as far away as northern California. But because the ingredients and recipes ground Cochon's food in Cajun country's bayous, prairies and marsh, Cochon cuts through the social baggage—name another Beard-winning restaurant offering iceberg lettuce salad, unironically—that has weighed on Cajun cuisine since its commercialization.

Diners can reasonably argue that they've never had anything like Cochon's braised pork cheeks in Abbeville, or that it is heresy to charge $8 for an oyster-meat pie, flaky as Cochon's is. But it would be impossible to conclude after eating either dish at Cochon, perhaps with a bottle of Burgundy wine alongside a free cone of fried pigs ears, that the chefs regard their source of inspiration as a backwater.

Still, theories that hold true in New Orleans are being tested all over again at Cochon Lafayette. And Link knows it.

"As a chef your (work is) always on the table. You're always up for discussion, " Link said. The difference in Lafayette, he explained, is "everybody is a food critic who could make or break you. It's a whole other level." You can't "PR your way out of" a bad night's performance when there are no waves of tourists coming in behind the diners you may have disappointed on an off night.

"I'm feeling way more pressure performance-wise, " Link added, comparing Lafayette to New Orleans, "because it's deeper."

The chef was sitting on the deck outside Cochon after dinner service on Sept. 15, the restaurant's opening night. The task of convincing Lafayette diners that the restaurant is adequately respectful of Cajun cuisine's hardscrabble roots is further complicated by its location in the city's River Ranch development, a model of mixed-use New Urbanism that architecturally looks more suburban than urban.

T-Coon's is only three miles away, but Cochon Lafayette's closest and fiercest business competition may be the Bonefish Grill. Earlier in the night, the River Ranch outpost of the Florida-based national chain hosted overflow crowds, mostly locals angling for a good view of the LSU football game. (Bonefish is also where Link's father, who lives in Lake Charles, drove to celebrate his most recent birthday.)

Cochon Lafayette won't conjure visions of the rural idylls on full-color display in Link's cookbook, but it is beautiful, particularly at night, when its lights cast a soft glow on the Vermilion River running just below the herb- and citrus-tree-lined deck and terrace. At 6,000 square feet, the restaurant seats around 250, twice as many diners as its sister location in New Orleans. It also evokes the original, with its pigmented concrete floors, blonde wood accents and open kitchen.

Beth Hebert ate her lemon-and-garlic-scented oven-baked shrimp at the restaurant's expansive bar, which overlooks the river and suggests what a fishing camp might look like if renovated by an architect specializing in urban lofts. Hebert was in Lafayette visiting relatives from her home in Los Angeles. She declared Cochon's food "not unrecognizable" from what she knew growing up. Still, she said, "I couldn't take my parents here. They're old. They'd be confused." Hebert's friends in L.A.? "They'd absolutely love this place."

If Cochon Lafayette succeeds, bridging this generational divide could be its greatest accomplishment. Cognizant of this challenge, the owners larded the opening-night staff with seasoned Link Restaurant Group operatives. Among them were Stryjewski and Prewitt, who was recently promoted to oversee all of the company's restaurants' kitchens, including Cochon Butcher, the sandwich cafe and Cajun-style butcher shop in New Orleans.

"One of the reasons we're doing this is to give our people new opportunities, provide them a career and a life," Link said. "If we didn't have the talent to open this place, we wouldn't be."

Together with Kyle Waters III, Cochon Lafayette's chef de cuisine, the restaurant's team built a menu around Cochon classics while, as Link put it, "trying not to appear like we're competing with anyone's grandma."

The smothered chicken nods to a regional mainstay, only Cochon's is smoked and gilded with pickled onions and mustard seeds. One older man told Link he enjoyed the grilled skirt steak "but didn't know what to do with" its side of collard green slaw. (Major difference between the slaw and traditional smothered collards, which are also on the menu: length of cooking.)

The fried redfish collar was certainly familiar to any Cajun fisher who has refused to waste any morsel of a day's catch—never mind that other diners may recognize the dish as a staple of Japanese cooking, too.

Cochon Lafayette's boudin is smoked, its casing charred, the space in the cavity where it's split filled with a pinch of sliced pickled chile peppers. The dish represents a reversal of Link's original vow to stay away from boudin in Lafayette for fear of becoming ensnared in the contentious regional argument over whose is best. So what if his doesn't resemble anything anyone has ever eaten in the cab of a pick-up?

"There are a lot of cultures involved in Cajun food," Link said. "No one can really lay claim to it. Why does it have to be one thing? Why can't it be different? Why can't it be in an entirely different context?"

On opening night, Cochon Lafayette was already addressing these and other questions. The restaurant's parking lot was full.

Foraging and Fishing Through the Big Bend

By Gary Paul Nabhan

From *Desert Terroir: Exploring the Unique Flavors and Sundry Places of the Borderlands*

⁂

Long before it became a foodie mantra, "eating local" was a guiding principle of Gary Paul Nabhan's pioneering work as a farmer, food writer, and conservation biologist. In *Desert Terroir*, he gives us a deeply personal look at how his life in the American Southwest forged that connection to the land.

There was a particular moment in my life when I knew I must live where I could fully taste the place in which I lived every week for the rest of my life, if not every day. I call it my Seek-No-Further moment, named for an heirloom apple that sometimes grows in old streamside orchards of the Desert Southwest. This revelatory moment did not occur exactly where I live today, but along the Big Bend of the Rio Grande, where barren rocks and towering yuccas dwarf any gardens, fields, orchards, or pastures.

It was along the Big Bend that I learned the pleasure of making a meal of foodstuffs gleaned only from the surrounding landscape. I gained the urge to make such a meal by meeting some poor Mexican families who had to eat off the land in order to survive. My time among them humbled me, for it suggested that I should never again ignore or waste the harvestable foods within reach of where I stood. To do otherwise would certainly dishonor the borderline families that so generously shared with me the little foods that they had, but it would also dishonor the plant and animal foods that emerged from some of the driest reaches of this earth.

My revelatory moment of homing took place some twenty-one years before I write this, but it has taken me all this time to fully acknowledge how that epiphany has guided my life since then. Before Big Bend, I had moved along listlessly, without much of a place or taste of my own. I meandered through life like a disengaged visitor, strolling through the garden of earthly delights merely reading the signs in front of each plant rather than reaching out to pluck the ripest among them.

And then, as I broke out of the chaos of cactus and brambles on that day of epiphany, I could at last see, as well as savor, the fruits of the tree of life growing right before me.

Ironically, my Garden of Eden was devoid of apples (no Seek-No-Furthers nor any other heirloom varieties). Instead it tasted of cornmeal-crusted catfish, wild oregano, chile pequin, and a few poisonous nightshade berries tossed into some goat's milk to make it curdle. If you can wait a little longer for me to cast the rest of this story, I think you'll understand how a catfish, some goat cheese, chiles, and oregano came to lead me home.

Oddly, I can't remember much about my life at that time. I had been living rather unhappily in the sprawling metropolis called Phoenix, working at a botanical garden filled with desert plants that seemed to be assaulted on all sides by asphalt, concrete, plywood, wallboard, and two-by-fours. Fortunately, someone suggested to me that I should study the edible flora of the Big Bend, and that I might be able to get a deal serving as a guest guide with a rafting outfit that regularly ran through the canyons there. I had never spent much time in the wilds of Texas nor in the *monte* of Coahuila, but portions of those areas had recently been conserved as biosphere reserves. I knew little about biosphere reserves except that they allowed the local, more sustainable uses of edible and medicinal plants to continue within their boundaries. I needed to get out of the city, and Big Bend was the ticket.

The Big Bend, as you may know, is a raggedy dogleg of the Rio Grande. That river—hardly more than sixty yards across and four feet deep through much of the Big Bend—briefly cuts through a series of canyons with walls four hundred feet tall. The population density of that region of the U.S./Mexico border rivals that of the bleakest reaches of North Dakota. There are more cacti than people along the Big Bend, and more emptiness than busy-ness.

Perceived by most folks as an empty, desolate, and desultory place, Big Bend has also been neglected by wild food enthusiasts, but is held in great esteem by desert rats. I myself had not thought much about nor thought much of the Tex-Mex borderlands until I was granted the chance to float and eat my way through Big Bend on a raft trip with Far-Flung Adventures in the autumn of 1988. When the proprietors of Far-Flung sent me a postcard of their six-month-old baby smiling, sitting naked in a pile of jalapeno peppers, I became intrigued.

There was a lot more than jalapenos, however, among the groceries when I and the other rafters arrived at the "put-in" site known as Solis, where we loaded the rafts with waterproof river bags, grills, canteens, and coolers with a half ton of canned food and beer. I began to wonder whether the familiar foods we'd brought along might serve as a disincentive for discerning the unique flavors of the Big Bend, but I readily accepted a cold one when someone popped open a beer and offered it to me.

Mexico's Sierra San Vicente was in sight as the trip began, and as we glanced downstream, we saw the glistening river disappear into a three-mile "tunnel" called San Vicente Canyon. Its limestone walls rose above us in subtle shades of grays, buffs, and creams; where the sun shined upon them, they were so barren and bright that we could have gone stone-blind by simply staring at them for more than a minute's time.

"This ain't Eden," I grumbled to myself, wondering how in the hell I was going to lead an "edible plant walk" later in the day when everything in sight looked as though it might bite at *me* before I could take a bite out of *it*.

If there was anything edible along that first stretch of San Vicente, it remained hidden from me. However, Marcos Paredes, our head guide, reminded me that we were visiting during the season of hunger weather, when food was hard to come by. That's why Mexican cowboys brought the cowhides they cured and *candelilla* wax they refined across the river to get cash so that they could buy canned groceries and beer. Yes, there were some desert foods out there, but they would be slow to reveal themselves. Instead, we turned our immediate attention to all the other plants that poked their thorns and spines and stickers out from the otherwise naked canyon walls.

After our first riverside lunch of cold cuts, chips, and beer in the shade of an old mesquite tree, we put the rafts in and began to float the Rio Grande in earnest. Like the Rio Colorado, the River Nile, and most other desert rivers I have floated, the Rio Grande has its banks choked by a dense thicket of shrubby tamarisks and a cane-brake of bamboo-like grass that the Mexicans call *carrizo*. As the sinuous river curved and looped back on itself like a coiled snake, grassy curls of *carrizo* offered a minimalist's hint of greenery in swirls and corkscrews and commas on the water's edge. Beyond this narrow little lip of lushness, the limestone slopes of San Vicente Canyon appeared barren, that is, unless you got down on your hands and knees beneath the creosote bushes and took a good hard look at the ground. There, hunkered down amid the dull-colored stones, were beautiful "rainbows," highly prized by cactus collectors, along with a dozen other species of cryptic cacti unique to the Chihuahuan Desert. In some places, as many as thirty-five kinds of spiny gray cacti were hiding out on each acre, some of them bearing delicious strawberry-like fruit. To recognize the cacti and to eat their succulent fruit, I first had to learn how "to get over the color green" (as Wallace Stegner once urged us to do) so as to take note of *their world*.

Down on the river, the most obvious objects other than our rafts were two-liter Coke bottles bobbing up and down, especially in the eddies just downstream from where the river bent.

"Holy *mole*!" one of my raft companions exclaimed, pointing and frowning. "The Mexican folks around here must toss all their Coke bottles into the river with no respect for the river itself."

"Well, I'm not saying they're pretty, but at least they're functional," explained Sammy, a boatman from the Far-Flung crew. Sammy was skinny, leathery, gray-haired, and goofy, and wore as few clothes as possible, rain or shine. He rowed as he spoke:

"A lot of those bottles . . . I guess they've been scavenged from our camps or rescued from the river. The Mexican folks retrofit 'em, turn 'em into floats for jug-lines to catch catfish."

"What do you mean . . . they're not all free-floating trash?"

Sammy shook his head. "No, not at all. Especially during the drought, people need to eat from the river cuz, well, they can't eat a helluva lot from the land. So they gather up four or five of those two-liter Coke bottles, put a little gravel in them, sometimes paint 'em white, caulk them closed, screw the caps back on, and they've got some pretty cheap floats for their jug-lines. Then they tie some braided twine tight around the bottlenecks. They might extend the line, oh, maybe some twenty feet or so, and start adding hooks, leaders, or sinkers, or anchor them with bricks. Or tie them to a lead line tied to a tree off the bank. Now, when a catfish hits, the bottle dips, the gravel rolls to one side, and weight shifts to the end with the cap. They come by and see the jug has shifted position, check it, and find a big ol' catfish on the hook."

"*Muy suave*. Pretty slick. Wish we could do it," I said.

"Well, hell, just keep your eye out for one of them jugs that has got loose." Sammy put one oar in his lap and pointed over toward an eddy, where the drift lines tend to get waylaid. "We like to pull in the drifters, anyway. Maybe it'll already have a fish on it, maybe it won't, but you can float it behind the raft for a while. As long as you don't let it drift loose again, and check it every half hour or so, I doubt anyone will bother you."

Late that afternoon, after we had set up camp in San Vicente Canyon, not far above the town of Ojo Caliente, I found a ghost line drifting along with a jug behind it. I pulled it in, refurbished it a little, and set it out. Within fifteen minutes of placing it in the water, I saw my Coke bottle float by, bobbing. I grabbed some gloves out of my pack, and a bucket from the cooking area, and went over to pull up my first fish of the trip.

It was most likely a Chihuahua catfish, close kin to the widespread channel cat, but a species more common on the middle and lower Rio Grande. Its tail has a shallower fork than those of both channel and headwater catfish, and the Chihuahua seldom reaches a full foot in length. Differences aside, they are all good eating, as we learned later that evening after gutting and grilling four or five more that we had caught (by rod as well as by jug).

While the Far-Flung crew reheated a pre-prepared pan of enchiladas, poured out a can of beans into a skillet to refry, and mashed some avocados into guacamole with the bottom of a beer bottle, a couple of us sat in the sand next to the grill and pan-fried our catfish. We passed around nuggets of catfish as finger food just after dark, and most everyone agreed that fresh catfish was much tastier than canned beans. The catfish was soon forgotten, however, as more beer appeared out of the coolers—Dos Equis, Tres Esquis—all the X's you could count or drink. A little beat-up guitar was passed around the group, and we tried our best to remember the words of songs by Gary P. Nunn, Doug Sahm, Steve Fromholz, Butch Hancock, and other Texas songwriters.

With the jagged lines of the canyon rim above us, I put my sleeping bag on a tarp ten feet from the river and looked up at the sky to watch for the moonrise from my sleeping bag. As usual, I faded off to sleep before the moon arrived.

In the twilight time the Mexicans call *la madrugada*, I awakened to roosters crowing not all that far away. The stars were still visible in the slot of sky framed by the canyon, but I could see from a rose-colored patch of the Sierra del Carmen in the distance that the day was coming on. I pulled on my jeans, slipped into my huaraches, put on my straw cowboy hat, grabbed my plant collection bag, and began to walk toward the sound of the roosters, where I presumed I would find the little spring-side settlement of Ojo Caliente.

The hot springs had been tapped to irrigate a few small fields, and they were in the last throes of being harvested. There were melons and squashes, corn and beans, broom sorghum, sugar cane sorghum, and pasture grass. It was hard to tell who had harvested more of the crops, the Mexicanos or the grasshoppers. Grasshoppers were everywhere, hopping around as if they had bit parts in a motion picture about biblical plagues. I wondered if these *grillos* were ever grilled and eaten when other foods were scarce. (Later in life, I carried *grillos asados* from Mexico along with me as a trail food whenever I ran rivers.)

Just as the dawn's light spilled into the canyon, I met a young Coahuiltecan woman who was going to fetch some drinking water from the springs. She carried two beat-up plastic water jugs. She had three small children in tow, and another one or two on the way, judging from her bulging shape. She was willing to talk for a while in exchange for me carrying the water back to her house. Her name was Maria de Lourdes.

When we were going back to her place, she stopped to rest in the shade of a big mesquite, so I opened the bag of plants I had been collecting and dumped them in the sand before her and the children.

"Would you mind telling me if any of these are eaten here?" I queried her.

"*Pues,*" Maria said haltingly, as she sorted through the plants freshly picked from the river's edge. "Well, you should really talk to an older, more knowledgeable woman like the *yerbera* downstream in Boquillas del Carmen."

"The *yerbera?*" I asked.

"You know, well, she's the *curandera*. Her name is Isabela. Everyone knows her in Boquillas. Even the gringos come to see her."

"Well, I'll try to find her when I get to Boquillas, but perhaps there are plants here too that you yourself use as food . . . "

"Well, yes, there are some, but most of these plants you have picked this morning are medicines, not foods. I can tell you a little about them, but Isabela knows them better."

Maria de Lourdes paused for a second to rummage through the pile, and her children crowded in around her.

"Look, you have the *gobernadora* [creosote bush]. Very good for stomachache and for kidneys. You have *calabacilla loca* [buffalo gourd]. That's not good to eat. It's good for bleaching out our bowls and towels and pots and pans. And there, you have the *hierba de la golondrina.* We give it to the babies to stop their diarrhea."

"Sounds like you have got a lot of plant medicines around here that can help you deal with stomach problems," I noted.

"What would you expect?" Maria said flatly, running her fingers back through her braided hair. Her mouth closed tightly before she began again. "*Asi es la vida.* That's how it is where you have bad well water. Here, you got river water contaminated with *mierda* from the cows. The meat and the vegetables spoil quickly in the heat if you don't have any refrigeration. On top of that, the drought all the time, too. It can keep you hungry, too."

"Well, what do you try to grow over here?" I asked.

"The *nopal* and the *tuna*—what you call the prickly pear cactus—that's the most reliable thing we got. Even in drought, we can rely on it. Not so the beans and the corn and the squash and the melons over there in the field. Even if we irrigate them, maybe we get something two, maybe three out of five years. If the heat doesn't get them then it's the grasshoppers. Or else the cattle break in. I'll show you what we grow, what we keep inside the fence around our house. . . . I can always grow some onions there. Sometimes the plants of chiles, tomatillos, and cilantro survive. You know, I just throw the dishwater on them. That's all they get."

Maria de Lourdes got up to go, motioning the kids and me to follow. I grabbed the water jugs she had filled at the springs.

"What else can you eat when the corn and beans fail?"

"You know, you have some of them here in your pile [of plants], but it takes work to pick enough of them to eat. Like this one here, the *garambullo* [hackberry]. Or that other red berry, *agrito* [wolfberry]. Sometimes, we'll even make a drink from the mesquite bean pods. Not too often anymore. Like anybody else, we'll eat the wild greens if they come up in the fields. *Qaelites. Verdolagas.* But some years, they don't even sprout—too dry here."

When we approached her little adobe house—one of only five left in the village—I was ready to drop the jugs of water from my shoulders. I looked at her, so young, pregnant for the fourth time, and wondered how she did it each day. Of course I had guessed that it wasn't easy to fill the larder from this stretch of desert, but I had never realized that a shallow well, some edible wild greens, and berries might be the only buffers against thirst and starvation.

"So how do you make it? Do the men here gain much cash from the livestock? I mean, do you gain any income from your own work—cooking, crafts, sewing?"

"With the children this age? I can't do much more than keep them fed and clean. The men proudly say they are just poor *vaqueros*. You know, they don't really keep enough *vacas* to gain much cash. If a cow gets hurt, we have to butcher it right away, no matter what the size. Butcher and jerk and dry the meat for later. My husband, he cuts *candelilla* for wax, cuts *lechuguilla* for fiber, cuts the *so-*

tol for the bootleggers, picks oregano or *chile pequins*. It's whatever people will buy. Anything so we can keep the kids fed."

"You have wild oregano and wild chiles here?"

She pointed to the backyard as I set the water jugs down for her. "We have a plant or two in our *huerta* behind the kitchen. But you'll see them down by the river, up on canyon walls, if you know how to look."

If you know how to look . . . as I had to learn to look for the ground-hugging cacti and their fruit on the canyon slopes. If you're hungry enough, you *have* to learn how and where to look for them. You would have to learn how to pick them with as much speed as you could possibly muster. You would have to learn how to dry them so that they wouldn't spoil before the buyer arrives. You would have to learn how to do all of this as efficiently as possible because your family needs food and the drink and the medicines, as well as the cash for the things you can't grow or forage. This desert is not for wimps. It exacts its price. I looked at Maria's hands: a few scars, a few burn marks, chipped fingernails . . .

"So how much might they pay you or your husband for the harvest of chile pequins?"

"Two dollars a pound," Maria whispered, as if trying to keep her neighbors from knowing what a deal she received from the buyer who came from the other side of the border.

Two dollars a pound? The same chiles retailed in stores from West Texas across New Mexico and sometimes into Arizona for *sixty dollars a pound*! The harvester—the poorest player in the entire value chain, since the chiles changed hands five or six times before reaching a kitchen table—received only one-thirtieth of the final market value. With the entire economic deck stacked against them, no wonder Maria de Lourdes and her husband could hardly keep their children fed and clothed.

"Do you have any *chile pequins* I can buy from you?"

Maria motioned for me to stay on the porch, and she went inside. She brought me back a glass Nescafe jar filled with small bright-red wild chiles, some of them round, but some of them beaked. I couldn't easily guess their weight, so I just handed her a hundred-peso bill.

"No, that's too much, and I don't have any change." She sighed, looking embarrassed. "You just take them as a gift. After all, you carried my water."

Now I was the one who was embarrassed, if not humbled. "Keep it all. Get something for the children. . . . I can eat chiles, but they need something else to eat that isn't hot."

"I know," she said, relenting. "I've had to stop eating so many chiles now that I'm pregnant since it makes the baby inside me kick. . . . Here, if you're going to give me money, why don't you take all of our chiles?"

I heard Marcos or Sammy whistling for everyone to come back into camp, get some coffee and breakfast, and pack up. "*Es la hora para embarcar*," I explained, and she nodded.

As I picked up my plants and turned to go, Maria de Lourdes put a small gunnysack of *chile pequins* in my hands. She then tucked the hundred-peso bill into her blouse and shooed me out the door. I bowed to her, departing from her ramshackle home with enough wild chiles to last me for a year.

The next village we visited, Boquillas del Carmen, was many times larger than Ojo Caliente, claiming some fifteen houses down below a mesa, another nineteen houses up on top, and five more intermingled among a few tourist stores. In Boquillas, they will try to sell you anything that can move, that has moved since the time of the dinosaurs, or that will appear to move if you ingest enough peyote to send it into flight. When I was there, I could get bootlegged sotol for five dollars a quart, and false peyote (the star cactus) for the same price. If I had persisted, I might have been able to find some real peyote for far more than that per button. I could also purchase petrified wood, ponchos, ammonites, crystals, leather purses, sombreros, leather vests, baskets, miniature *huapango* guitars, gallon jugs of cheap tequila, Christmas cacti, cheeses, tortillas, and hot sauces galore.

While my rafting companions decided whether or not to try a shot of sotol or to purchase various and sundry curios, I walked around the village until I noticed an elderly woman making something in big bowls on her porch. Thinking that she might be

Isabela the Curandera, I approached her and asked if she was an herbalist.

"No, I'm not her. But is it that you are interested in plants? I am using a little poisonous berry to make cheese right now."

"A berry? May I see what kind of berry?" I asked.

"Sure, come on up here onto the porch. I am using the berries of trompillo . . . making a batch of *queso asadero*. See, the trompillo berries are in that bowl," she said as she wiped her hands on an apron that covered her flowered cotton dress. Her gray hair was largely covered by a scarf of the same flower pattern.

I stood behind her and peeked into the bowl. There were five little golden berries of trompillo, a deadly nightshade that I guessed to be *Solanum eleaginifolium*, which is sometimes called buffalo berry in English. It is a thorny, poisonous weed that colonizes overgrazed or recently flooded areas.

"I crush two fresh berries and three old ones in a half of a cup of tepid water. See? Let them soak until the water is yellow. Like this. See? I strain out the seeds and skins of the berries," she explained. "Then I use it to congeal the curds out of the whey."

"Is the cheese made from cow milk or goat milk?"

"Our cows aren't here no more. They're being impounded on the other side. So this batch is from our goats. Bi-national goats," she said with a smile. "They browse on this side of the river, then they sneak over to that side too. They are too fast and crafty for those *Rinches de Tejas* to catch them and put them in jail. What do you call them? Texas rangers? Park rangers?" She laughed.

"Watch. I put the half cup of trompillo water in with three gallons of goat's milk. Here, I stir it for ten seconds. I'm using one-day-old *leche de agria* [sour milk] for half of the mix, and fresh *leche dulce* [sweet milk] for the other half. I can't tell you how long before the milk will have begun to curdle. If I leave this batch in the sun, it will turn to curds in three hours! Later in this afternoon, that's when I'll separate the curds from the whey. That's when I'll concentrate the whey. Make into a cream cheese we call *riquezon*."

"But why do they call what they do with the curds *queso asadero*?" I asked, having wondered why the cheese is said to be "grilled." "Do they say that the berries cook the cheese?"

"No, it's because we actually take the curds and melt them. We do that by kind of roasting or grilling them—haven't you ever seen it?—by heating them on a comal griddle over a wood fire. As they begin to melt on the griddle, we pick them up. Shape them into something like a fat tortilla, you know, a gordita. We turn them over on the griddle and leave them 'til the texture is even. Then we pick them up. We stack them, you've seen them that way, between wax paper in a pile. That's how we make the true *queso asadero*."

Milk from bi-national goats. Berries from a deadly nightshade. Cheese tortillas that are grilled as if they were hamburger patties. I had to buy them and try them for dinner.

"How much does it cost for two dozen of them?" I asked. She named her price and I complied. She went into her house and brought me out two neat stacks of *queso asadero*, wrapped them both in a paper sheet, then enveloped the piles within the paper sheet in a pale cotton cloth. She pulled the ends of the cloth over the cheese, then braided them together and tied the braids into a knot that also served as a carrying device.

"Will I get sick if you put too many trompillo berries into the milk?" I asked as I counted out my money to pay her.

"No," she said with a straight face, "you'll be dead! Why do you gringos worry so much about getting sick and dying? By the grace of God, it's to happen to all of us sooner or later. Just enjoy the few days, the ones you have left with us here in this desert," she said matter-of-factly. And then she went inside and closed her door. That was the last I saw of her. . . .

Of course, I could not undo the absurdity of floating down a river at a hundred dollars a day through a place where the few remaining residents would make only three dollars an hour for most of their lives. My catching a couple of fish did not make the loads of store-bought groceries in the eight coolers suddenly disappear. I had been floating down the River of Inequity, and all of its blatant juxtapositions were still immediately before me.

But that catfish, *queso asadero*, chile, and oregano gave me a way to be nourished by both sides of the river, and by the life of the river itself. I would no longer privilege one side over the other, nor let myself be fed by something utterly remote from where I actually stood.

The next day, as we floated out of Big Bend National Park and arrived at our "take-out" location, one kind of journey came to a close, but another one had started. My imagination and my palate had been sown with the seeds of a Seek-No-Further sensibility that would soon germinate in the desert soil of the Southwest borderlands, where wild chiles and oreganos still grew whether we noticed them or not. But I had noticed them, and I decided to put my own roots into the same soil.

Italian America

By John Mariani

From *Saveur*

John Mariani's eclectic tastes in food and wine have for years informed his reviews in *Esquire*, *Bloomberg News*, and his weekly Virtual Gourmet newsletter. In his latest book, *How Italian Food Conquered the World*, he comes home to the cuisine he grew up on: New York City Italian-American.

At my family's home in the Bronx, we ate slices of fresh, milky mozzarella with seeded bread from the Italian bakery down the block, macaroni shells stuffed with Polly-O ricotta, lasagne with little meatballs between the layers, baked rigatoni, eggplant parmigiana, chicken cacciatore, beef braciola. We drank chianti that came in a straw-covered flask and espresso from a drip pot, with a sliver of lemon peel. This was the 1950s and '60s, and though Mom was always cooking for our family and friends, Dad knew his way around the kitchen, too. He took to the stove on weekends, concentrating on a single dish: lobster fra diavolo, because my mother hated handling live lobsters.

We thought we were eating authentic Italian food, because the dishes were the same ones all the other Italian families we knew cooked and ate. But in reality, our cuisine was an American invention: an amalgam of hearty, rustic dishes brought here, primarily by southern Italian immigrants (my grandparents came from Abruzzo and Campania), then adapted and embellished upon in American kitchens. By the time I started writing about food in the mid

1970s, this homegrown cuisine had fallen out of favor as northern Italian—inspired dishes, deemed (sometimes erroneously) lighter and more authentic, became all the rage. I can't say that I didn't welcome the new trend of delicate fresh egg pasta, or celebrate the fact that grilled branzino had replaced shrimp scampi on so many Italian menus. But I will never deny my love for a supersize plate of spaghetti with homemade meatballs, or an eggplant parmesan hero, with its ample breading and sauce and molten mozzarella. There's a beauty and succor to Italian-American food, and it's for a good reason that so many chefs have been returning to those classics recently, preparing them with a newfound zeal and sense of respect.

The story of the rise and fall and rise again of Italian-American food is a fascinating one; it's an American story, its plot interwoven with the entrepreneurial drive, embrace of pop culture, proliferation of convenience foods, and creativity of home cooks that has informed our country's culinary spirit. It began authentically enough, with Italian immigrants who were skilled at making the very most from the very least. The *abbondanza* for which Italian-American cooking is known stems from the fact that these immigrant cooks, most of whom came from dire poverty, took pride in being able to feed family and friends sumptuously on the kinds of foods they couldn't afford back home. Ingredients like mozzarella and ricotta were no longer used as accents, or as meals in themselves: They were added to dishes with abandon. My father's lobster fra diavolo, which was likely inspired by tomato-based seafood stews made with small spiny or inexpensive rock lobster in Italy, was another example: When it was popularized in the 1950s in Italian-American restaurants, it became a lavish dish—far bigger in size and flavor than its predecessors—of fat New England lobsters cooked in a fiery tomato sauce. Another ingredient considered an extravagance in southern Italian cooking, veal, could be found on early Italian-American menus in myriad forms: *alla parmigiana* (breaded and covered with sauce and cheese), *alla marsala* (doused with fortified wine), and as massive one-pound veal chops, often stuffed with mozzarella and prosciutto, then smothered with tomato sauce.

Foods from the homeland became springboards for invention in the States. Take pizza, which evolved from its simple Neapolitan roots into styles unlike anything found in Italy (see *Any Way You Slice It*), with more cheese, more sauce, and more toppings. Or, tomato sauce, for that matter: When my wife and I first traveled across Italy, on our honeymoon in 1977, we saw neither marinara (that quickly cooked sauce of just tomatoes, garlic, and oil) or the long-simmered "Sunday sauce," stocked with all kinds of meats, which most families I knew while growing up served on Sunday. Of course, tomato sauce exists in Italy; the irony is that tomatoes were brought to Italy from the Americas in the 16th century and considered poisonous by all but southerners, who found them a delicious addition to their meager diet and discovered that they flourished in their sunny clime. Which explains why when more than 4 million Italians, a vast majority of them from the south, im-migrated to America between 1890 and 1910, they brought toma-toes, and tomato sauce, with them. Every cook had a version, and it became the food on which immigrant mothers staked their em-inence within their neighborhoods. Growing up, we would no more insult a friend's sauce than we would his mother or grand-mother. The sauce was sacred.

Soon enough, red sauce became emblematic of Italian food in the United States, embraced by Americans from every ethnic group and marketed by savvy restaurateurs as part and parcel of the cui-sine's abundance. My family dined out at least once a week, usually at a place called Amerigo's in the Bronx, which began as a pizza stand in the 1930s and evolved into a restaurant of extraordinary breadth, with a menu that ranged from antipasti to zabaglione, and a dining room decked out with an illuminated waterfall and a mural of the nearby Throgs Neck Bridge. It was at restaurants like Amerigo's that we feasted on the kind of fancy dishes that Mom didn't make on weeknights: I always had the gnocchi with tomato sauce and my brother, the manicotti. My father would order a mas-sive New York strip steak, introduced to the city's steakhouses by Italian-American butchers, and my mother would have filet of sole "Livornese," a dish with clams and mussels, white wine, and a mod-erate amount of garlic. Portions were huge, including the cheese-cake and cannoli for dessert. A waiter came to the table to whip zabaglione in a big copper pot.

The epitome of this style of dining was Mamma Leone's on 48th Street in Manhattan. That multistoried spectacle of Italian kitsch, with nude statuary and blocks of mozzarella and provolone cheese on every table, opened in 1906 and was operated by the same family until it was sold to a restaurant group in 1959, eventually closing in 1994. Had Verdi lived to eat there, he would have written an opera about it, and Enrico Caruso and Luisa Tetrazzini—both of whom were immortalized in pasta dishes that bore their names—would have sung the leads.

As much as Americans adored places like Mamma Leone's, Italian-American food was often referred to as grub for "greasers" and "garlic eaters." It wasn't until the arrival of first-rate Italian ingredients—many of which had been kept out of the U.S. by trade laws—in the 1970s and '80s that Italian-American cooks were able to reproduce the regional flavors that travelers to Italy complained they could never find in the States. This included prosciutto di Parma, extra-virgin olive oil from different locales, parmigiano-reggiano, arborio rice, funghi porcini, balsamic vinegar, and outstanding Italian wines from producers like Angelo Gaja and Giovanni di Piero Antinori.

By that time, many Italian-American restaurants had become tired and tiresome, and some restaurateurs tried to refine the clichés—and justify higher prices—by turning to northern Italy for inspiration. In New York there were Romeo Salta (opened in 1953), Nanni (1968), and Il Nido (1979); in Santa Monica, California, Valentino's (1972). They all downplayed the red sauce factor, substituting butter and cream sauces and adding—at $20 a plate—risotto and, of all things, polenta, a dish that had been the thrice-a-day staple of poor northern Italians who could afford to eat little else. This food was welcomed as authentic regional Italian: Lasagne with meatballs and meat sauce was dismissed in favor of *lasagne alla Bolognese*, with *besciamella* and spinach pasta. Italian-American cheesecake and cannoli were replaced by tiramisù and *panna cotta*. The old chianti bottles in straw *fiaschi* baskets were abandoned in favor of expensive barolos, barbarescos, and "super-Tuscans." Murals of Mount Vesuvio were painted over in favor of blown-up photos of Sophia Loren and Marcello Mastroianni.

Red-checkered tablecloths disappeared; now the tables were set with Frette linens.

The zeitgeist looked north for another reason: Italian fashion and design (centered in northern cities like Milan and Florence) was all the rage in the 1980s. The chicest new restaurants in the U.S. proclaimed they were Tuscan-style trattorias or grills (even if they didn't serve Tuscan food). Among the first to promote their Tuscan origins were Da Silvano, opened in 1975, and Il Cantinori (1983). Both, still operating in New York's Greenwich Village, became darlings of magazine editors, art gallery owners, and other members of the cultural elite. Before long, their menus were copied across the country, and extra-virgin olive oil became the new red sauce.

These northern Italian–inspired places adopted the tenets of the Mediterranean Diet, named for a book written in 1994 by cookbook author (and *Saveur* contributor) Nancy Harmon Jenkins. The basic argument was that what *real* Italians ate—a diet abundant in vegetables, seafood, grains, and olive oil—was far more healthful than the meaty, rich, fried, cheese-laden, red sauce–drowned food of Italian-Americans. Quick sautéed greens and *farro* were in; chicken parmesan and meatballs were out.

But who doesn't love meatballs? As influential as the Mediterranean Diet has been, the Italian food you are most likely to encounter in London, Berlin, Moscow, or Mumbai will be far closer to the old "red sauce" archetype than to regional Italian menus featuring Alba's white truffles, Sardinia's cheeses, or Venice's cuttlefish ink risotto. Even the most trailblazing purveyors of modern Italian cuisine in America, while proudly serving regional specialties, still champion the good old-fashioned Italian-American classics, even if they change the names. The addictive, confectioners' sugar-dusted fried doughballs known in the Italian-American canon as *zeppole* often show up as similar *bombolini*, and what used to be called plain macaroni is now broken down into specific subclassifications, whether it's rigatoni rigate, garganelli, or casarecci. At Osteria Morini in New York City, Michael White—born in Wisconsin and trained at San Domenico, the Michelin 3-star outside of Bologna—serves mostly Emilia-Romagna-style food, but he also offers meatballs in tomato sauce and pasta with white clams.

Moreover, traditional Italian-American restaurants are opening in higher profile, trendier spots. The 10-table, infamously hard-to-get-into Rao's in New York City opened in Vegas in 2006, serving classics like meatballs and veal chops. And, Rubirosa, owned by the same family that runs the 51-year-old Staten Island pizzeria Joe and Pat's, recently opened in downtown Manhattan, serving the kind of food I grew up on, in a dining room painstakingly designed to evoke the classic midcentury neighborhood red-sauce joint. The chef, Albert Di Meglio, and owner Angelo Pappalardo, both worked at the Manhattan restaurant Circo in the 1990s, owned by Sirio Maccioni, the man responsible for inventing pasta primavera and making it one of the most popular dishes of the 1980s at his celebrated Le Cirque. Rubirosa is returning to the Italian-American classics by serving the likes of sautéed broccoli rabe and stuffed clams.

Perhaps the place offering the most creative take on Italian-American cooking is the widely praised—"aggressively Italian-American," as Sam Sifton, former restaurant critic for *The New York Times* put it—Torrisi Italian Specialties. In a storefront on Mulberry Street, Little Italy's main drag, Mario Carbone and Rich Torrisi typically serve more than 300 Italian-American-style hero sandwiches at lunch, and at the neighborhood's annual San Gennaro festival, they set up a booth hawking mozzarella sticks. But where they really capture Italian-American food's melting pot qualities and spirit of innovation is at dinner. In a dining room decorated with a poster of Billy Joel, fifty bucks gets you five courses, which may include their inspired take on garlic bread, slathered with tomato-garlic butter; bowls of still-warm, made-to-order mozzarella; *gemelli* from Severino, a 40-year-old pasta company in New Jersey, in a hearty duck ragù; maybe tilefish with pickled green tomato relish or duck breast with broccoli rabe and mulberry mustard. The meal ends with a paper cup of Italian ice and a plate of cookies. That was last night; tonight it will all be different.

What's also different is that Carbone and Torrisi, who often incorporate Asian influences from neighboring Chinatown into their menus, use only American products. Nothing's imported, not the prosciutto, not the tomatoes, not the spaghetti, not the bread crumbs—because, what's wrong with Progresso? The message is clear: It doesn't have to be straight from Italia to be special. And if it was good enough for Italian home cooks, then it's good enough for us.

Whenever I eat at these new school, or cheffy, Italian-American restaurants, I never expect the food to taste just like my mother's. These restaurants are a testament to the fact that Italian-American food is its own living, breathing cuisine; that can evolve just like any other. What I love most about where Italian-American cooking is now is that there's an equal respect for the tried and the true, as well as the changing tastes of the day: even at home, the dishes I prepare tend to be lighter, and maybe a bit brighter with fresh herbs, than they used to be. But they still embody all that is genuine, and generously wholesome, about Italian-American food. And they're served with gusto and with just one intention: to make me and my family and friends very, very happy.

What Makes Sushi Great?

By Francis Lam

From GiltTaste.com

Francis Lam's incisive food writing for *Gourmet*, Salon, and currently Gilt Taste deconstructs the cultural value of everything from cherries Jubilee to Chinatown roast duck. You may also know Lam as a commentator for the Food Channel's *Food (ography)* and a judge on *Top Chef Masters*.

A friend of mine once met a delegation of revered Japanese chefs. There was a wizened gentleman among them who was clearly the leader. He spoke little, but the other star chefs deferred to him, paid him obvious respect. My friend finally asked, quietly, "So, what does the old guy do?" The response: "He has mastered rice."

To be honest, I don't know what that means. I mean, I know the difference between a pot of rice that I like eating and a pot that's gluey, but there aren't a whole lot of points between the two. And yet here is a man whose claim to fame among master chefs is that he makes *rice* better than the rest of them, and to accept that is to accept that there is a level of cooking that most of us will never comprehend. At some point, cooking is not a matter of skill; it's a matter of *understanding,* of learning to see the differences between one perfectly good pot of rice and another, of the minute details in something that, for most anyone else, is pure pearly blandness. Truly great cooking is, in this way, first an act of learning to see, and then a striving to do. This is why, among chefs, the truism is that simple food is hard.

Sushi, of course, is the ultimate in simple food: mostly just rice and a piece of raw fish, it would seem that anyone with a knife and one functioning hand can make it. But take an impossible eye for detail and apply it to fish—Where did it come from? How long should you age it before serving for best flavor? How long should you massage it to make it tender, but still have texture? Where should you cut a piece from, and at what angle, to highlight the flavors of different parts of the muscle? Since temperature affects aroma, how warm should you let the fish get in your hand before serving it? How hard do you press the fish into the rice to form a bite that has integrity, but is not dense?—and you begin to see where a simple food is not so simple. You don't have to buy into all the minutiae a sushi master trades in to know that the pleasures of great sushi span from the animal to the emotional and the intellectual, which is a great trick for anything to pull off, let alone a piece of raw fish on rice.

What animates a sushi master? What drives someone to be so focused, to be a god of small things?

Jiro Ono, 85 years old and counting, is a revered sushi chef who runs a restaurant inside a Tokyo subway station, and *Jiro Dreams of Sushi* is easily the best, most beautiful movie about sushi you will see this year, or, let's face it, probably any other. The film is part documentary bio-pic, part food-blogger's wet dream. (OMG, did you *see* the super-macro shot of that tuna??!? NOM NOM. Etc.) It doesn't take us into the world of technique: Jiro has mastered rice, too—his rice dealer claims that he doesn't bother to sell his best stuff to anyone else because they wouldn't know what to do with it—but while he describes how he does it, the film never shows us the whys and what-fors of his method. (Though, as Silvia Killingsworth reports for the *New Yorker*, the French-American star chef Eric Ripert describes Jiro's rice as "tasting like a cloud.")

Instead, the movie focuses on the life of a man who is utterly devoted to his craft. Jiro doesn't have a secret to why his sushi is more astonishing than anyone else's. What he says, over and over, is that great sushi—and, by extension, greatness itself—is the result of hard work, of dedication, of a commitment to excellence that, in the end, trumps everything else in life.

His search for perfection is eternal. At 85, he hasn't stopped working; he says he hates holidays because they are too long to spend away from the restaurant. Chefs, in particular, who have seen the film don't hesitate to call it "inspiring." To watch the gorgeously shot scenes of him forming pieces of sushi, jewel-like and dripping with soy sauce and life, is to wish that you might one day make so much beauty. (Indeed, a film critic friend said that her reaction to seeing this was not hunger, but to want to go home and make jewelry.)

Still, there is another side to this mastery, to this inspiring devotion. Jiro has two sons, and it's hard to tell exactly what their relationship to each other is, or to their esteemed father. The master admits to not being at home when they were young, telling a story of how one day he slept in, and his children complained to their mother that there was a strange man in the house. The younger one seemed, at first, to be the favorite, because the father helped him open his own restaurant. The older son, Yoshikazu, is still an apprentice to the father . . . at 50. But Jiro tells the camera, with a laugh, that when he helped his younger son open his restaurant, he told him, "Now, you can never come home again." As he recounts his own life, leaving his home to begin his career at nine, it's not clear that he was kidding with his kid.

With an inflection of either humble pride or resignation, Yoshikazu says that in Japan, it's the oldest son's role to take over for the father. He works dutifully; he has taken over the selection and buying of fish since Jiro had a heart attack 15 years before. He, not the acclaimed master, was the one who served the inspectors who granted Jiro three Michelin stars, the highest recognition in the restaurant world. And yet, Jiro's restlessness keeps his son forever in his shadow, unwilling to let him stand for himself.

"You must fall in love with your work," Jiro says. He refers to himself as a *shokunin,* literally an "artisan," but more accurately someone who commits the entirety of himself to his work. It's a term with gravity; you won't find *shokunin* bread in the grocery store. One of his young apprentices wells up when he tells the camera of how he finally earned the term from his master. It was after he'd worked for Jiro for 10 years. He's signed up for a life of dignity and honor and hard work. He's signed up for the life of Jiro's sons, men who may or may not have their own sons to mentor and pass their restaurants down to. He's signed up for a life given—or lost?—to the making of beautiful things.

FOOD FOR THOUGHT

By Jeff Gordinier

From the *New York Times*

❦

Bringing a cultural critic's sensibility to his food writing, Jeff
Gordinier writes often for the *New York Times* Dining section.
He has also published essays and interviews in *Esquire*, *De-
tails*, *GQ*, *Elle*, *Spin*, and *Outside*, and authored *X Saves the
World*, a manifesto for the slacker generation.

Try this: place a forkful of food in your mouth. It doesn't
matter what the food is, but make it something you
love—let's say it's that first nibble from three hot, fragrant, perfectly
cooked ravioli.

Now comes the hard part. Put the fork down. This could be a
lot more challenging than you imagine, because that first bite was
very good and another immediately beckons. You're hungry.

Today's experiment in eating, however, involves becoming
aware of that reflexive urge to plow through your meal like
Cookie Monster on a shortbread bender. Resist it. Leave the fork
on the table. Chew slowly. Stop talking. Tune in to the texture of
the pasta, the flavor of the cheese, the bright color of the sauce in
the bowl, the aroma of the rising steam.

Continue this way throughout the course of a meal, and you'll
experience the third-eye-opening pleasures and frustrations of a
practice known as mindful eating.

The concept has roots in Buddhist teachings. Just as there are
forms of meditation that involve sitting, breathing, standing and

walking, many Buddhist teachers encourage their students to meditate with food, expanding consciousness by paying close attention to the sensation and purpose of each morsel. In one common exercise, a student is given three raisins, or a tangerine, to spend 10 or 20 minutes gazing at, musing on, holding and patiently masticating.

Lately, though, such experiments of the mouth and mind have begun to seep into a secular arena, from the Harvard School of Public Health to the California campus of Google. In the eyes of some experts, what seems like the simplest of acts—eating slowly and genuinely relishing each bite—could be the remedy for a fast-paced Paula Deen Nation in which an endless parade of new diets never seems to slow a stampede toward obesity.

Mindful eating is not a diet, or about giving up anything at all. It's about experiencing food more intensely—especially the pleasure of it. You can eat a cheeseburger mindfully, if you wish. You might enjoy it a lot more. Or you might decide, halfway through, that your body has had enough. Or that it really needs some salad.

"This is anti-diet," said Dr. Jan Chozen Bays, a pediatrician and meditation teacher in Oregon and the author of "Mindful Eating: A Guide to Rediscovering a Healthy and Joyful Relationship with Food." "I think the fundamental problem is that we go unconscious when we eat."

The last few years have brought a spate of books, blogs and videos about hyper-conscious eating. A Harvard nutritionist, Dr. Lilian Cheung, has devoted herself to studying its benefits, and is passionately encouraging corporations and health care providers to try it.

At the Food and Brand Lab at Cornell University, Prof. Brian Wansink, the author of "Mindless Eating: Why We Eat More Than We Think," has conducted scores of experiments on the psychological factors that lead to our bottomless bingeing. A mindful lunch hour recently became part of the schedule at Google, and self-help gurus like Oprah Winfrey and Kathy Freston have become cheerleaders for the practice.

With the annual chow-downs of Thanksgiving, Christmas and Super Bowl Sunday behind us, and Lent coming, it's worth pondering whether mindful eating is something that the mainstream ought to be, well, more mindful of. Could a discipline pioneered by Buddhist monks and nuns help teach us how to get healthy, relieve stress and shed many of the neuroses that we've come to associate with food?

Dr. Cheung is convinced that it can. Last week, she met with team members at Harvard Pilgrim Health Care and asked them to spend quality time with a chocolate-covered almond.

"The rhythm of life is becoming faster and faster, so we really don't have the same awareness and the same ability to check into ourselves," said Dr. Cheung, who, with the Vietnamese Buddhist monk Thich Nhat Hanh, co-wrote "Savor: Mindful Eating, Mindful Life." "That's why mindful eating is becoming more important. We need to be coming back to ourselves and saying: 'Does my body need this? Why am I eating this? Is it just because I'm so sad and stressed out?'"

The topic has even found its way into culinary circles that tend to be more focused on Rabelaisian excess than monastic restraint. In January, Dr. Michael Finkelstein, a holistic physician who oversees SunRaven, a holistic-living center in Bedford, N.Y., gave a talk about mindful gardening and eating at the smorgasbord-friendly headquarters of the James Beard Foundation in New York City.

"The question isn't what are the foods to eat, in my mind," he said in an interview. "Most people have a general sense of what the healthy foods are, but they're not eating them. What's on your mind when you're eating: that's mindful eating to me."

A good place to try it is the Blue Cliff Monastery, in Pine Bush, N.Y., a Hudson Valley hamlet. At the serene refuge about 75 miles northwest of Manhattan, curious lay people can join Buddhist brothers and sisters for a free "day of mindfulness" twice a week.

At a gathering in January, visitors watched a videotaped lecture by Thich Nhat Hanh (pronounced tik-nyot-HAHN), who founded this and other monasteries around the world; they strolled methodically around the grounds as part of a walking meditation, then filed into a dining room for lunch.

No one spoke, in keeping with a key principle of mindful eating. The point is simply to eat, as opposed to eating and talking, eating and watching TV, or eating and watching TV and gossiping on the phone while Tweeting and updating one's Facebook status.

A long buffet table of food awaited, all of it vegan and mindfully prepared by two monks in the kitchen. There was plenty of rice, herbed chickpeas, a soup made with cubes of taro, a stew of fried tofu in tomato sauce.

In silence, people piled their plates with food, added a squirt or two of condiments (eating mindfully doesn't mean forsaking the hot sauce) and sat down together with eyes closed during a Buddhist prayer for gratitude and moderation.

What followed was captivating and mysterious. Surrounded by a murmur of clinking forks, spoons and chopsticks, the Blue Cliff congregation, or sangha, spent the lunch hour contemplating the enjoyment of spice, crunch, saltiness, warmth, tenderness and like-minded company.

Some were thinking, too, about the origins of the food: the thousands of farmers, truck drivers and laborers whose work had brought it here.

As their jaws moved slowly, their faces took on expressions of deep focus. Every now and then came a pause within the pause: A chime would sound, and, according to the monastery's custom, all would stop moving and chewing in order to breathe and explore an even deeper level of sensory awareness.

It looked peaceful, but inside some of those heads, a struggle was afoot.

"It's much more challenging than we would imagine," said Carolyn Cronin, 64, who lives near the monastery and regularly attends the mindfulness days. "People are used to eating so fast. This is a practice of stopping, and we don't realize how much we're not stopping."

For many people, eating fast means eating more. Mindful eating is meant to nudge us beyond what we're craving so that we wake up to why we're craving it and what factors might be stoking the habit of belly-stuffing.

"As we practice this regularly, we become aware that we don't need to eat as much," said Phap Khoi, 43, a robed monk who has been stationed at Blue Cliff since it opened in 2007. "Whereas when people just gulp down food, they can eat a lot and not feel full."

It's this byproduct of mindful eating—its potential as a psychological barrier to overeating—that has generated excitement among nutritionists like Dr. Cheung.

"Thich Nhat Hanh often talks about our craving being like a crying baby who is trying to draw our attention," she said. "When the baby cries, the mother cradles the baby to try to calm the baby right away. By acknowledging and embracing our cravings through a few breaths, we can stop our autopilot of reaching out to the pint of ice cream or the bag of chips."

The average American doesn't have the luxury of ruminating on the intense tang of sriracha sauce at a monastery. "Most of us are not going to be Buddhist monks," said Dr. Finkelstein, the holistic physician. "What I've learned is that it has to work at home."

To that end, he and others suggest that people start with a few baby steps. "Don't be too hard on yourself," Dr. Cheung said. "You're not supposed to be able to switch on your mindfulness button and be able to do it 100 percent. It's a practice you keep working toward."

Dr. Bays, the pediatrician, has recommendations that can sound like a return to the simple rhythms of Mayberry, if not "Little House on the Prairie." If it's impossible to eat mindfully every day, consider planning one special repast a week. Click off the TV. Sit at the table with loved ones.

"How about the first five minutes we eat, we just eat in silence and really enjoy our food?" she said. "It happens step by step."

Sometimes, even she is too busy to contemplate a chickpea. So there are days when Dr. Bays will take three mindful sips of tea, "and then, O.K., I've got to go do my work," she said. "Anybody can do that. Anywhere."

Even scarfing down a burrito in the car offers an opportunity for insight. "Mindful eating includes mindless eating," she said. " 'I am aware that I am eating and driving.' "

Few places in America are as frantically abuzz with activity as the Google headquarters in Mountain View, Calif., but when Thich Nhat Hanh dropped by for a day of mindfulness in September, hundreds of employees showed up.

Part of the event was devoted to eating thoughtfully in silence, and the practice was so well received that an hourlong wordless vegan lunch is now a monthly observance on the Google campus.

"Interestingly enough, a lot of the participants are the engineers, which pleases us very much," said Olivia Wu, an executive chef at the company. "I think it quiets the mind. I think there is a real sense of feeling restored so that they can go back to the crazy pace that they came from."

It's not often, after all, that those workhorse technicians get to stop and smell the pesto. "Somebody will say, 'I ate so much less,' " Ms. Wu said. "And someone else will say, 'You know, I never noticed how spicy arugula tastes.' "

And that could be the ingredient that helps mindful eating gain traction in mainstream American culture: flavor.

"So many people now have found themselves in an adversarial relationship with food, which is very tragic," Dr. Bays said. "Eating should be a pleasurable activity."

Dude Food

Learning to Barbecue Helped Make Me a Man

By Joel Stein

From *Food & Wine*

In *Man-Made: A Stupid Quest for Masculinity*, humor columnist Joel Stein—an often controversial contributor to *Time* magazine, the *Los Angeles Times*, and many other magazines—adroitly deconstructs American manhood. Here he tackles the most manly of all arts: Outdoor barbecuing.

Like most of what I do, my cooking is not manly. I fuss, apologize and occasionally—embarrassingly—look at recipes. But for the past two years, I've been trying to boost my masculinity, working on a book for which, finally, at age 39, I learn how to be a man. I've gone one round with Ultimate Fighter Randy Couture, done three days of basic training at Fort Knox, earned a badge on a Boy Scouts camping trip. But I still prepare bouillabaisse like a little girl, crying over onions and talking in French.

The manliest form of cooking that doesn't involve mounting the animal's head on a wall is barbecue; if I were really going to learn to be a man, I'd have to master it. So I went to Houston, a town that specializes in the manliest meat, beef. My plan was to eat as much barbecue as was physically possible, so I could understand life-changing 'cue. Once I knew what I was aiming for, I'd get lessons from a barbecue expert and then test my new knowledge at a barbecue contest.

I go straight from the airport to Catalan Food & Wine restaurant, where, for the moment, Chris Shepherd is chef. This fall he'll open his own restaurant, Underbelly, which will feature a full-scale butcher room (he's so manly, he calls butchering pigs his "happy place"). Shepherd is a heap of a man, incredibly friendly and passionate; the kind of guy who can get away with calling both men and women "baby." Last year, he helped create "Where the Chefs Eat" tours of Houston. And now he's going to take me on the barbecue tour, his favorite.

We head to Gatlin's Barbecue & Catering, where the pit boss's mother, Mary Gatlin, tells customers to "have a blessed day." Sitting outside at picnic tables, we eat soft, rich brisket from the pointy side of the cut, known in most places as "fatty meat." Because so much of the tip is exposed to the smoke, it has the most "bark"— the blackened, tarry bits where smoke, fat and meat mix together. To Shepherd, this is the asparagus tip of barbecue. He prizes the top, boneless cap of the sparerib for the same reason.

We eat our way around the city, making a detour to the legendary BBQ Pits by Klose, where Shepherd bought his $1,800 home pit. David Klose speaks quickly, delivering entirely unprovoked self-proclamations such as, "I'm a real quick draw." He is the most Texan person I've ever met, in his Wrangler jeans and brown camouflage cap that says "Deer Predator." Klose has made barbecue pits out of a phone booth, a mailbox and a police car. The more steel in the pit, the steadier the heat will be, and that, he insists, is the trick to good barbecue. This seems to justify why men are happy to spend thousands of dollars to cook $1.75-per-pound meat.

Our final stop is Pierson & Company Bar-B-Que, where we get a mixed trinity of brisket, ribs and sausage links that are smokier and sweeter than some we've tried elsewhere and nearly as satisfying. Texans believe that, just as you wouldn't cover Kobe beef in béarnaise, you don't smear barbecue sauce on brisket that's been cooking for 12 hours in an oven you'd need to put a down payment on. You want to taste meat, salt and spice. This is such a basic idea that I cannot believe there isn't a Doritos flavor named Meat, Salt and Spice.

The other lesson I learn is that barbecue is about timing: The brisket at Gatlin's wouldn't be nearly as delicious a few hours past its prime. Barbecue exists in time as much as it does in space. It's why so many great, small places run out of meat by 11 a.m. Why they don't get a bigger pit and buy more meat is something that leads me to many more questions about the South than I can possibly answer.

My eating tour complete, I am ready to actually try cooking. I wake up early the next day to meet curmudgeonly Robb Walsh, a recently retired restaurant critic and author of the *Legends of Texas Barbecue Cookbook*. He recently opened a Tex-Mex restaurant, El Real Tex-Mex Café, with *Food & Wine* Best New Chef 2009 Bryan Caswell right across the street from the space that will become Underbelly. And for the past year, he's been running a barbecue course out of his home. He's going to give me the simplified version. The one for Northerners.

There are three grills in Walsh's backyard. He's got a pricey off-set smoker—in which you light a wood fire in a small cylinder called the firebox, which is below and off to the side of a big grill with an exhaust pipe on top. He's got a "Mexican hibachi," an oil drum cut in half—you build a fire on one side and put the meat on the other. And he's got a gas grill, just like I do. Walsh makes it clear that I am never, ever to refer to anything I do on the gas grill as "barbecuing." Barbecuing is cooking with smoke. Grilling is what you do to your children's hamburgers.

He teaches me to put some charcoal in a starter chimney, which looks like a big metal travel mug, and light it with a burning newspaper. We drop the charcoal in the offset smoker's firebox, then add oak logs along the sides, not in a pile—exactly the opposite of the way the Boy Scouts taught me—so the fire smokes instead of roars. By controlling the amount of fuel and oxygen inside the smoker, we aim to keep the heat at around 275 degrees—a nice, slow, long cook to break down the tough, fatty cuts of meat that work best in barbecue.

Once the temperature hits 275 degrees, we place some pork ribs, brisket rubbed with just salt and pepper and a chicken marinated in Kraft Italian dressing on the grate. Walsh explains that barbecue people are "weird," spending wildly on gadgets but using inexpensive supermarket rubs and marinades. What he means is that barbecue people are men.

Unlike the brisket my Jewish family eats at Passover, this one is half fat. We set it on the grate fat side down for two hours, then flip it fat side up so it self-bastes for the next eight hours. Because we don't have to be there while all this cooking goes on, we head out on a long drive to pick up supplies and a breakfast taco.

D. W. Vasbinder's, where we stop to buy logs, looks like a junkyard, with metal sculptures of cowboys, cow skulls and a sign with wood prices that explains the honor system of payment. We pick up some oak, which Walsh says is the purist's choice, since it imparts a neutral smoky flavor. (Mesquite can be tangy and resiny, whereas pecan gives a sweet, sooty flavor that can blacken your food.) As Walsh stops a welder to ask for a piece of metal mesh for the bottom of his hibachi grill, he says, "Places like this are why you can make great barbecue in Texas. It's like car culture in L.A." I pretend I am manly enough to be part of car culture in L.A.

When we get back, we check on the meat. The chicken and ribs are done, but the brisket has stalled out at an internal temperature of 165 degrees, about 20 degrees shy of what we need. We wait another hour, during which we work hard opening and drinking local Saint Arnold beers. But the brisket is still at 165. It's a classic barbecue phenomenon—the meat gets to a point where the internal temperature just won't budge. We have a few choices: We can keep waiting and hope the problem fixes itself. We can wrap the brisket in foil, which will raise its temperature but might make it soggy. Or we can bring it inside and put it in the oven at 275 degrees, which could dry it out. I refuse to bring it inside, because inside is for womenfolk. Walsh decides to wrap the meat in foil for just 1 hour and leave it in the smoker. Which works. We lop the giant fat cap off the parts we're going to eat first, leaving the rest on to keep the meat moist.

Like most men, I feel that one day of training makes me qualified to compete, so I am headed to the World's Championship Bar-B-Que Contest, where more than 400 competitors fill the parking lot of Reliant Stadium with tents bearing giant corporate logos. I join team Drillin' & Grillin', which won for the best ribs last year. The seven-man team is run by Ernest Ramirez, a pipe fitter who has built his own enormous pit. Ramirez has a good oak fire going, but he shows me a bag of pellets made out of hickory, cherry, hard maple and apple that he sprinkles on the flames to sweeten the smoke. He hands me a syringe so I can inject chickens with marinade to keep them moist; for the same reason, we place a pan of water and chicken broth on the bottom rack. But we're mostly focused on the spareribs, which are cooking with a simple rub. There is a lot of hanging out and chatting, but we've got to pay attention: If we screw up by letting the fire get too hot, too cool or too smoky, there's no chance to recover. Because starting over takes 14 hours.

Ramirez believes ribs need a glaze to balance the sugar and saltiness, so when they're just about finished, he pats some brown sugar on top and puts them back in the pit. Then, 30 minutes later, he brushes on a glaze of brown sugar, melted butter and pepper jelly, puts the ribs in a Styrofoam container and takes them to the judges' tent.

I help slice the brisket, stealing several pieces of bark for myself. At 5 p.m., a committee member tells Ramirez that our team didn't place in the top 10 to compete for the finals. Ramirez thanks her, smiles politely and goes right back to being the caterer for his corporate sponsor's rodeo tailgate, slicing a huge brisket against the grain to keep it tender. This is what I've learned about being a man. We've come to call it repression, but it's really self-control. It's a respect not just for the contest and the people you compete with, but for yourself.

I'm going to start barbecuing at home. Not on an $1,800 pit that takes up half my yard, but on a little Weber with the wood off to the side. Mostly because nothing really tastes like smoked meat. But also because, unlike women, men need an activity as an excuse to talk. And we're not going to talk about salad.

Memphis in May: Pork-a-Looza

By Wright Thompson

From *Garden & Gun*

∽⟨&⟩∾

ESPN senior writer Wright Thompson writes mainly about
sports, though as a native of Clarksdale, Mississippi, he's
occasionally lured into food writing by his love of Southern
food. And what could be more Southern than barbecue?

Before a man with one leg got women to take their shirts
off while he poured liquor into their mouths via an ice
luge; before the wild-eyed guy who provides the pigs to the
French Laundry walked around the party slipping packages in
people's hands, which at least two of us thought were drugs but
turned out to be bacon; before Donald Link's boudin for lunch
and John Currence's andouille for happy hour and Sean Brock's
soft-shell crab for dinner; before ten-year-old Jess Edge asked his
daddy, the Southern food guru John T. Edge, "What's a Jell-O
shot?"; before we waited to hear if we'd made the finals of the
Memphis in May World Championship Barbecue Cooking Contest; before the revolutionary act of creating an all-star team that
included four James Beard Award–winning chefs, three old-school
Southern pit masters, and one boozehound writer; before any of
that, there was a pretentious but earnest idea: Could we rescue a
barbecue contest, and maybe even barbecue itself, from a crushing
sameness?

The line was drawn. On one side, us: a cooking team called the Fatback Collective, organized by barbecue industrialist Nick Pihakis, who founded the Jim 'N Nick's Bar-B-Q chain of restaurants. On the other, Memphis and its world-famous barbecue contest, entering its thirty-fourth year and drawing an estimated 100,000 fans. Now, Memphis in May is many things: a place for Parrotheads to gather between nautical-pun tours, a grown-up frat party with a hundred thousand pledges, a place where friends commune over a smoking pig, and, maybe most important, a driver of where our barbecue culture will go. Here's what it isn't: a reflection of where our barbecue has been. We wanted to turn back the clock.

Maybe that's silly. Maybe that's an idea fueled by ten cases of whiskey and two thousand Jell-O shots, but from the belly of the beast, surrounded by what many of us consider to be a threat to authentic barbecue—lean pigs, tricked out with injections, cooked not as a reflection of a family or place, not as a connection to our past, but, rather, gamed to the strange tastes of the Memphis judges—we all realized the mission of the Fatback Collective: redemption.

Redemption and about seventeen thousand calories a day, most of them liquid.

Ready, Set, Strip

It all starts with a screaming buzz saw and the smell of burning pig bone.

A hog is splayed out and gutted, with a half dozen hands reaching inside its carcass. Pat Martin, a Nashville pit master, revs the blade and digs into the backbone. Pig shrapnel flies around the tent.

When the job is done, the truly heartbreaking part begins, trimming out pounds of glorious, expensive, and carefully cultivated fat. Our team is consulting with a former grand champion, someone who is gracefully helping us understand the intractable customs of Memphis in May. He points at the thick layers of white.

The chefs look at each other, then at the pig. Reluctantly, they start stripping. Every so often, they'll make eye contact with one another and shake their heads. Someone mutters. Brock stands to the left of the pig, and Link on the right, each cutting back ribs to expose more shoulder meat. A pile of fat forms on the table.

"Too much," says Ryan Prewitt, the chef de cuisine at Herbsaint in New Orleans.

Stephen Stryjewski, the chef at Cochon who won his Beard award just four days ago, asks the expert once more if he's sure.

"They don't want marbling?" he asks.

"You don't find that in other hogs," the former grand champion says. "Technically, they don't want to see that."

"That's so 180 degrees to what I do every day," Stryjewski says.

Link, the mind behind Cochon and Herbsaint, watches in silence. This is what he's thinking: Arrrgh! There are all these Beard winners with their hands in the hog, but something is being lost in translation. A chef's job is to cook food that stays true to the essence of the ingredients. The job of a Memphis in May contestant is to deliver what the judges want, and, more important, to stay away from things they don't. Here, as best as I can tell, are some of the things the judges don't like:

1. Fat
2. Spice
3. Pork that tastes like pork, as opposed to pork that taste like it got pistol-whipped by MSG and sugar
4. Puppies

Gaming the System

The more I learn, the more I realize that winning this thing has less to do with great barbecue and more to do with anticipating the judges. They like sweet. They don't like spice. They like tenderloin. They don't like belly. On and on. So competitors study past winners, then go Mr. Wizard on the pigs. They fill the cavity with bricks of cold butter. They pack iced pillowcases around their tenderloins to stop the cooking. Some pigs are souped up with culinary nitrous oxide: liquid fat–laden injections.

This isn't happening in a vacuum. For many, these traveling cooking teams are the face of Southern barbecue. Not the guys, like the pit masters on our team, who cook pigs in the same pit three hundred days a year. The most wonderful thing about barbecue has always been its regional differences. Each pig told a story.

Rodney Scott, pit master at Scott's Bar-B-Que in Hemingway, South Carolina, uses wood he chops himself. Pat Martin was born in Mississippi but worked as a bond trader in Charlotte before realizing his calling, and his Beach Road 12 sauce, with the Carolina tang and a touch of the Memphis sweet, is a reflection of his own journey to the pit. Barbecue changes from town to town, an entire style morphing at the Tennessee River, or at the Piedmont, or when you sweep down onto Highway 61 from Memphis to Clarksdale, Mississippi. Memphis in May, the most important barbecue event in the world, rewards homogeneity. If you live in the South, maybe you've noticed how hard it's becoming to find a good, simple barbecue sandwich. Traditional barbecue is fading as competition barbecue is rewarding smoke and mirrors.

So while we do cut away some of the fat, more than the chefs would have liked, there is still plenty left on the hog. I've never seen a pig like this. It's marbled, laced with thin lines of fat. It looks like a rib eye steak. There are fewer than a thousand Mangalitsas in North America, and this is the first time, to the best of everyone's knowledge, that one has ever been barbecued. (We're putting two on the coals.) It could put a new face on barbecue or, more accurately, give barbecue its old face back. The guys shake on a rub, the extent of the doctoring, and look down at the pit-ready pig.

"I think we should do a shot of bourbon," says Drew Robinson from Jim 'N Nick's.

There are murmurs of agreement. Hell, yeah. Breakfast.

"I'll get the Pappy Van Winkle," says Brock, chef/owner of Husk in Charleston, South Carolina.

Pappy is poured into those flimsy cone-shaped water cups. I hold mine over the pig and knock it back.

"Bourbon and pigs," Link says.

The Wee Hours

Bourbon and pigs. That fairly sums up my next twenty hours. The pit doors shut and smoke rolls out. Nothing to do but wait. The chefs and pit masters hold little summits, conversations that food nerds would freak out over. There is laughter. There is boudin and soft-shell crabs and oysters and crawfish. There are trays of Jell-O shots, and big cups of bourbon, and people dance until the speakers overheat. There is some drama at the pig; the fire gets too hot, but Rodney Scott finesses the coals, brings the temperature down. There's no pit problem he can't fix. You've seen Pulp Fiction? He's the Mr. Wolfe of pork.

I fall asleep in a chair by the pit and later move to a couch. I wake up at 4:30 a.m. to find Scott and Brock still awake. Brock and I tag out, and I settle in next to Scott. He's bulletproof. I'm not. The Pappy is gone. There's a dead tall boy of Pabst and a cashed bottle of Patrón on a table, along with the empty shell casings of Jell-O shots.

"We look rough," says Sarah Johnson from Jim 'N Nick's.

"I feel rough," Brock says.

Scott puts R&B on the speakers. Al Green brings us back to life. We've been goofballs for the past two days, but when the end comes, it's all business.

"Do you feel good about this?" Nick Pihakis asks.

Brock nods.

It's time to create the Box. We've talked about the Box endlessly, lending it the importance of an advanced policy initiative, which seems slightly ridiculous, given that the Box is a Styrofoam container of cooked pig. But the Box is for the most important part of judging, the blind taste test, so there are four Beard-winning chefs on the Jim 'N Nick's mobile smoking rig. Everyone is calm, quiet, with a few jokes and short, precise comments. The Box has to go at noon. Link has a knife in his hand. Some of the Beach Road 12 sauce is in a jug; abstract ideas and theories are great, but these guys didn't become who they are by trying to lose. Some of my snark evaporates as I realize every team is doing this exact same thing.

"It's 11:50, guys," John Currence, from City Grocery in Oxford, Mississippi, says quietly.

What follows is a damn impressive ten minutes. My boys are stone cold. Nobody ever raises his voice or appears to rush, and I realize that before these guys were famous, they spent their lives in hot kitchens, cranking out dinner night after night. All thirty-four other whole hog teams are equally concerned with sticking the landing.

The Box is off, and three in-person judges are coming through. They are given the Gospel According to Fatback. Pat Martin does most of the talking. They hear about the Mangalitsas, about the pit masters and the chefs, about Martin's dream of a win at Memphis in May changing the arc of the pig industry, replacing the flavorless factory hogs with ones more like our grandparents ate. His son, he testifies, might one day enjoy the results of our work today. Finally, the last judge leaves, and Scott walks back to the pit. Sam Jones, whose joint, the Skylight Inn in Ayden, North Carolina, grew out of a family barbecue tradition that dates back two hundred years, is standing there.

"We are so full of it," Scott says.

"Full of what?" Jones asks.

"Truth," Scott says.

Fatback Glory

Pihakis is worthy of love for many reasons, for his generosity, for his terrible dancing, and for his creation of the Fatback Collective. But the moment I really want to spoon him is when he arranges for $500 worth of Gus's World Famous fried chicken to be delivered to the tent just after the judges leave. People make love to that chicken, coming up for air with faces and fingers covered in grease—"That's my last meal," Brock gushes, orbiting the tables like some sort of bird of prey—and I eat, very quickly, four chicken thighs and two pieces of Wonder bread. So, we're pigging out, and someone is telling Drew Robinson that bad news comes via a messenger on foot, but if you make it to the finals, a judge will arrive in a golf cart. At that exact moment, a golf cart pulls up.

"You mean like that?" Brock asks.

The Fatback Collective is in the final three.

The last group of judges arrive, four this time, and the show is smooth. They eat the pig and head out to make their decision. The confidence is palpable. People are flocking to the pit to pull out meat. Word has spread that the team of ringers has the greatest barbecue ever cooked. There are judges coming by just to eat. One tells me: "You've got it in the bag." A feeling arises.

"If we win this thing," Pihakis says, "people are gonna look at pork differently."

We go stand by the stage. Someone there has a pig's head on a stake, with a cigarette in its mouth, a picture of excess that defines much of Memphis in May.

"This is the old model," Edge says.

However, we are not entirely innocent. We consulted a past champion. We did a taste test on various sauces. We tried to game the judges, too, while preserving our integrity. We came here wanting to change this competition, but now, in the last moments, we want to win it. I haven't even cooked anything—my role is to be a hyper-partisan observer—and even I want to win. I've rolled my eyes for the past two days at the other teams, and now I realize my ire is misplaced. Everybody else isn't trying to educate the judges—they are trying to kick ass. And, as a look at the tense Fatback Collective confirms, so are we. Finally, the results are announced. The winner is Yazoo's Delta Q, the same team that won last year.

Fatback Collective is third.

We shuffle to the stage, trying to smile. The crowd cheers, and all our hopes of stopping the homogeneous 'cue train suddenly feel like sour grapes. We are lots of things, but we are not sore losers. Martin takes the microphone and tells the other cooks that we all respect the hell out of what they do. Those are his exact words, and after, teammates slip up to him to tell him he nailed it. We go back to the tent, and there is talk of how great it is to finish third in our first year, and hugs, and drinks, but the DJ cuts to the heart of the feelings in the tent. We are serenaded with "Auld Lang Syne."

Truth in Barbecue

After Sean Brock grew up "dirt, dirt, dirt poor," with a dream that seemed impossible from the forgotten corner of Virginia he called home; after he won his Beard medal at age thirty-two and hid with his cell phone in a Lincoln Center bathroom, weeping, calling to tell his mama, I did it; after Donald Link did for boudin what Arnold Palmer did for golf; after Sam Jones tended his pit the same way his ancestors did two hundred years ago; after Rodney Scott showed up to man the fires at midnight the night he graduated from high school; after John Currence learned to cook on a tugboat the morning after he graduated; after we traveled to Memphis to try to change the way people think about barbecue; after we succeeded, and also failed; after all that, I can't shake an image that I'll cherish long after my cardiologist buys a new ski boat with the money he'll make off the weekend: Pat Martin, our loud, opinionated mouth of the South, sitting in the corner, waiting to find out if we'd won.

He's quiet now, with his little boy on his lap. They have the same haircut. Martin gives his son a kiss and rubs his forehead. He holds him tight. Something becomes clear in this moment. The real barbecue we love, that we pretentiously and earnestly came to save, might be under siege, but it isn't dead. It lives in anyone who believes in doing things the way their grandfathers did, who believes that what we eat tells a story about who we are. It lives in anyone who cares enough to sit all night with a hog. It lives in the fading notes of "Auld Lang Syne" and in the sparks popping off the burn barrel past midnight. It lives in the way a father holds his boy when the cooking is done.

TRUFFLE IN PARADISE

By John Gutekanst

From *Gastronomica*

⬡

The proprietor of Avalanche Pizza Bakers in Athens, Ohio,
John Gutekanst has worked as everything from a pot scrubber
to a sommelier, but his great passion is pizza. His creative
pies have won numerous awards, including several in Italy,
pizza's homeland. He blogs about pizza on PizzaGoon.com.

Our car climbs the mountainous roads above the northern Italian spa town of Salsomaggiore. It is late March, and we have a job to do. I've convinced my three teammates—Tony, Bruno, and Justin—to accompany me on my quest for *tartufi bianchetti*, Italian spring truffles. The *bianchetti* aren't the hardest truffle to find in all of Italy, or the most fragrant, but they are the best at this time of year because they're fresh. By now, the white truffles have lost their intensity, and the blacks, all of their flavor. I need the *bianchetto* to make an award-winning entry for the 2008 World Pizza Championship, and these elegant truffles, paired with sweet Maine diver scallops, are perfect partners. The judges will be looking for taste, innovation, and execution. If I can find the truffle guy, I'll nail the championship.

The town of Salsomaggiore Terme, located in the Parma region of Emilia-Romagna, dates from the time the Etruscans first found mineral springs nestled in this snug valley. Today, people come for massages and bathe in the brown stink of the healing egg water, thanks to Benito Mussolini, the fortieth prime minister of Italy, who built a palatial building around the springs, called the Berzieri Spa. The waters are famed for healing.

But I am a pizza man with just one purpose: to win first place, USA, at this year's competition. Normally, I confine myself to my small pizzeria in Athens, Ohio, and suffer no illusions as to my business's place in a small college town: customers are locals and college kids; business is brisk until 4:00 A.M.; volume is high and profit is small. My customers love my products, and I'm happy but not complacent. I know the next three days won't bring me any fame, but just maybe they'll bring some validation that even a small guy can win sometimes.

The championships are held annually in a huge stadium just outside Salsomaggiore. Blooming flowers and squawking pheasants on the steep, vine-covered slope outside the building belie the intense human conflict within. This year I'm entering four pizzas: scallop and truffle pizza in the Pizza Classico category; spinach, feta, chicken, and sun-dried tomato pizza in the Pan Style category; fresh mozzarella with basil and San Marzano tomatoes in the Neapolitan category; and in Non Gluten, a new category, an onion-linguine and sweet potato orecchiette-topped pizza with dough made from rice and garbanzo-bean flour. All culinary scores are figured from 800 as perfect, with each contestant rated by cooking prowess, sanitation, presentation, taste, and knowledge of the pizza. From prior year competitions, I have also learned the unwritten rules: look Italian, cook the Italian way, make your presentation short, have confidence and a pinch of arrogance. My show of detached condescension must make the judges think I am the most knowledgeable pizza maker ever, and, as a gift, I am going to turn them on to the best pizza they've ever had. Once I get my truffles, that is.

We see the worn sign in front, Ristorante Al Tartufo, flickering across the white gravel parking lot, and we turn, circling to the back of the building. Tony Gemignani, founder and president of our American team, leans across the front seat to get a better look at the building, dark bangs falling across his forehead. He has just driven Justin Wadstein, Bruno di Fabio, and me on this four-hour expedition. He is probably weary from the winding roads and the jetlag, but Tony looks calm, as usual, and intense.

"We're here, I think." A quick smile accompanies his classically handsome Italian looks and puts us all at ease. Tony is an international legend in the pizza industry. With his brother Frank, he owns Pisano's Pizzeria in Castro Valley, California. He has won more acrobatic and culinary awards for pizza than any other person in this country and probably the world. Tony and Bruno recently opened Tony's Pizza Napoletana, a successful pizza school and pizzeria in San Francisco. Tony has already driven us around to purchase radicchio, zucchini flowers, and broccoli rabe. These truffle guys are our last stop.

"So, John," Bruno says to me. "This is the place with your amazing truffle guy, huh?" Bruno beams. He can't help himself. There on the gravel he looks like an actor about to go on stage. Both he and Tony live for strange new situations; after hearing of my last visit to the truffle guy in 2006, they had to see for themselves.

Just like last time, the quest began with creepiness, a James Bond moment by the hotel front desk when we asked for directions to the truffle guy's restaurant. Two men in pressed blue suits asked why we wanted these truffles and how we knew of the truffle guy. It seemed more like an impending drug deal than a stinky fungus inquiry. If we could get fresh truffle at the local stores, life would be simpler, but that's not how it works in Italy.

Truffle hunters gather the *bianchetto*, also known as the Tuscan truffle, from January to March, from Tuscany north to this part of Emiglia-Romagna. Its lobes, unlike the round, sandpaper-like skins of the black truffle, look like bulbous bumps on a small animal brain thrown in the dirt. It's tough to nail down the exact aroma and taste of the spring truffle: cheesy, woody, earthy, and garlicky are the usual adjectives. While not as aromatic as the white or black truffle, the *bianchetto* is particularly suited to pizza—at low, warm temperatures it gives off a mildly pungent aroma. Introducing strong flavors to a pizza can be disastrous. A great *pizzaiolo* (pizza dude) has to make sure that the competing flavors of bread, sauce, cheese, protein, and vegetable are compatible and not overpowered by another element.

Now I'm just moments away from a stash of *bianchetti*. I can almost smell them. But Justin turns and looks off into the dark green hills beyond the parking lot. "I'm not gonna get whacked for a truffle," he says. "I'm staying in the car." Justin is no coward. He's a world-class pizza-dough-tossing acrobat who once tossed three rounds of pizza dough high into the air while jumping up and down on a soccer ball. When Justin won the World Pizza Championship of 2007, the crowd jumped out of their seats, screaming in adulation and surprise.

Bruno leans in toward Justin, who's still sitting in the car. "Okay, Justin, this is the deal. If you hear some loud pops, then see me hauling ass to the van with a big bag of truffles and John's and Tony's brains splattered on my face, start the car, and we'll be gone." Bruno laughs his usual high, nasal guffaw and kicks the loose gravel. He then punches my arm and nods a "let's go" toward the back of the restaurant. We crunch our way through the parking lot. The sunlight is waning now. Clouds moving in make the mottled and muted blue sky meld with the valley below.

The restaurant's door is a huge slab of beaten, scratched wood that to my mind looks like a door to a gladiator ring. Tony, in the lead, stops to face me. "Hey, John, how do you know that this guy's your buddy? This area was a Mussolini stronghold in World War II, and there's still lots of ill will toward Americans. I've also heard of some strange deaths attributed to the truffle black market. It's a big business here, taken very seriously. Why don't you go in first and I'll back you up?"

I hesitate. Perhaps I overstated how familiar I was with the truffle guy, having met him only once, and that was two years ago. What if Justin is right and the truffle mafia decides we're interlopers?

Bruno chimes in with a chuckle. "Yeah, dude, we're right behind you. Anything happens, we'll be the first to run and get the cops or the ambulance."

I stop at the threshold and sniff the air. "Smell that?" I ask.

"Porcini, cepes. Unmistakable. Food of the gods," Tony mumbles. "You sure this is the place you visited last time?" My hands grip the near-mythical brass doorknob. I smile nervously and throw open the door.

I have indeed been here before. I'm transported back two years ago, to a late March night in the marble lobby of the Grand Hotel et de Milan in the heart of Salsomaggiore Terme. Feeling a little like Jack Nicholson at the start of *The Shining*, I had blurted out, "I need to find some truffles. Do you know where I can buy some?"

"Who wants to know?" a slender, elegant man in his mid-fifties asked. His perfectly pressed blue suit with white lapels was more suited to a movie than a hotel. He looked beyond me with such curiosity that I turned and looked myself. No one there.

"Follow me, please," he said as he clicked his way across the marble, circling behind me and out the door. The lights of downtown and the disco across the street twinkled as we walked through a black-green garden filled with huge marble statues. The fence around it reminded me of a cemetery.

"My name is Giorgio." He tapped a cigarette on his pack. "I can get you *tartufi*," he continued, his voice dropping to a whisper. "It is . . . how do you say? Not simple."

"Complicated," I said.

"Yes." Giorgio lit his cigarette and took a deep puff. He pulled out his card, wrote an address on it, and said, "Take a taxi, give him this address. When you get there, go in the back door. Ask for the owner of the restaurant and give him this card." I looked down at the cursive Italian writing. The only word I could distinguish was the last one, *tartufo*.

As I walked away, Giorgio cautioned, "Be careful, Giovanni . . . John. And keep your hands out of your pockets."

Thirty minutes later my cab reached the mountain restaurant. I walked across a parking lot under the yellow glare of its sign and opened a big wooden door—the same one I had just opened with Tony and Bruno behind me. The room was not well lit. Pale green walls showed splotches where the plaster had chipped off. Shelves all around held jars of unidentifiable brown things floating in liquid.

A dozen or so locals were bantering with their friends. Four old men at an old wooden tabletop played cards to my right. Middle-aged waitresses lounged and cackled at a small bar on the other side. I stepped into the middle of the room.

"Hi," I blurted out to no one in particular. A drop of sweat trickled down the side of my face.

Everything stopped. The abruptness was so intense that it could only have been better choreographed if someone had taken a record player and scratched the needle hard: *RRRRRRRRRIIIIIIIIP*.

I looked around, my hands and brow sweaty. Even my brain seemed to sweat. All the faces were hard and expressionless. It was one of the longest silences I've experienced in my life. I looked down. "Oh shit," I thought. There were my hands, in the pockets of my coat. The oldies at the card table had their hands under the table now. I removed my hands slowly.

"Buona sera." A man appeared from behind a patterned curtain, arms outstretched in the clothesline position. He was over six feet tall, with graying, balding hair and a bushy unibrow held up in a "what do you want" look. He cracked his neck with a snap and cocked it to one side, expressing, in timeless guy language, "Gimme what you got, punk."

"I came to get some truffles," I squeaked, cursing myself for sounding like a little girl.

"Americano?" he asked.

"Yes, er, *si*," I replied. "I need them for my pizza at the World Pizza Competition."

"Who send you?" the tall man demanded.

"Giorgio, at the hotel." I pulled out his card, trying to keep my hand steady.

A smile flashed across the guy's face. It was like someone had put the needle back on the record. All was good, all was right, just a stupid Americano.

The tall man shook my hand. From the back room he brought out a large, plastic container, covered with a cloth. He looked around again, and then summoned me with his hand. He grabbed the cloth and stared at me as though he was about to show me my future or the meaning of life. Then he lifted the lid.

The truffle fumes were overpowering. I smelled black pepper and garlic with a hint of gunpowder, cashews, and ozone. The truffle guy nodded his chin for me to take a closer whiff.

"Heaven," I muttered appreciatively.

"Tartufi bianchetti," the truffle guy said.

I paid forty dollars for three large, marble-sized truffles and a big bag of dried porcini, and I made a new friend. We completed our deal with a toast of *limoncello*, and I dashed to the waiting taxi. Considering that the porcini go for fifty dollars a pound in the

United States, I calculated I was holding over two hundred dollars' worth of great mushrooms. Not to mention the truffles.

I used the truffles to create a pizza with American bison, *fontina di Aosta*, arugula, and a béchamel sauce. I scored in the upper echelon but did not win.

Buying truffles this time around is bound to be different. I have Bruno to translate and Tony to back me up. But as I open the heavy door, I'm hit with a major déjà vu: four old men at the same table turn to stare at me. "No freakin' way. Not the same guys in the same chairs," I say to no one and everyone. I stand there with my mouth open. Tony and Bruno push me into the pale green room with the jars. Nothing has changed. We get the same silent treatment, the same record player scratch, only this time I'm armed. My weapon is Bruno di Fabio.

Bruno sidles up to a waitress at the bar. *"Buona sera."* I watch her face closely as he continues, because Bruno, besides being a consummate pizza aficionado and fluent in Italian, never hesitates to have fun at my expense. For all I know, he could be saying, "My two Hungarian friends over there are lepers. They want to know if the dishwasher found a finger in a soup bowl last night."

Bruno turns. He must have noticed me boring holes into the back of his head. "What! I just asked her where the truffle guy was."

"Those guys staring at us look harmless," Tony says, nodding toward the old guys. "Why do they all have their hands under the table?"

"They're probably holding old rusty shotguns under the table ready to blow us to smithereens," I whisper. "Didn't you ever see *Godfather II?*"

I'm interrupted by a loud *"EEEEEEEEEEAAAAAYYYYYY"* that sounds more like a shotgun blast than a greeting. Tony and I jump. It's my truffle guy, appearing from behind the curtain. *"Buona sera,* my pizza friend!" The truffle man hugs me with his lanky arms. His gray unibrow now seems welcoming. I beam. Now my buddies know who's the real pizza guy, I think. Truffle guy mutters something to the old men and they relax, but they still keep their hands under the table.

"You want *tartufi*? Porcini?" he asks as he walks to the front door, where he pokes his head out and scopes out the parking lot. Bruno takes over communications and explains what I want, accurately for once.

"Wait," the truffle guy says, disappearing behind the worn tapestry.

"I wonder what these guys would do if I grabbed this jar of porcinis and ran to the door?" Bruno asks playfully. Tony and I giggle.

"*Tartufi bianchetti,*" the truffle guy announces. He puts a two-by-one-foot plastic box on the bar, and we all crowd around. I'm surprised to see the waitress crowding too. The grand presentation begins with a *bbbllllllurrrrp* from the vacuum-sealed plastic container. Musky, pungent truffle fumes waft out. I imagine shucking an almost rotten ear of corn, popping a can of Planters nut mix, then sticking my nose next to diesel truck exhaust for half a second. I smack my tongue against my upper palate and breathe out slowly. I experience disgust and fascination, repelled and attracted in perfect, intense equilibrium.

With the pressure of the contest tomorrow, all I want is to get my truffles, nod in ignorance, drink my *limoncello* and haul ass out of there. I hold up three large truffle marbles and ask how much.

The truffle guy holds up fifteen fingers (not all at once), indicating fifteen Euro.

"Less than thirty bucks for all that?" Bruno exclaims.

"Great deal," Tony said. As a bonus, the truffle guy gives me half a bag of dried porcini that he has handpicked.

The next day, as we enter the stadium to register at the Pizza Championship, we see our competition—the world. The world sees us, too. To enter with such a pizza legend as Tony Gemignani is like being a bodyguard for the president. Heads turn to stare at him. I am proud to be on his team.

All countries are represented: Iran, Bangladesh, Ireland, Scotland, Brazil. The French show up and try to bribe the judges with some of their kick-ass Champagne. Each contender wants the title of "Best Pizza in the World." Now in its ninth year, the World

Pizza Championship makes *Iron Chef* look like a yoga class at a retirement center.

The best pizza dough I've ever tasted is from Bruno's *biga*. He's such a fanatic that he'd probably stand at the mixing bowl all night telling bedtime stories to his *biga* if he knew it would make his pizza crust better. *Biga* is pre-fermented dough, Italian style— basically, a batch of dough left at room temperature for twenty-four hours or more and added to a new batch. This approach concentrates the flavor, adds complexity, and leads to better digestibility and taste.

Bruno's goal at this year's competition is to become the "World's Fastest Pizza Maker." Five dough balls rest in a pile of fine-grained Italian flour on his table. He has to stretch them faster than all his competitors. Bruno walks three feet to the back wall, facing it as if in greeting, then pulls up his checkered cook's pants and squats, sumo style. His nose is just inches from the surface; his face is gnarled in knotted confidence as he beats his chest with closed, flour-covered fists. Puffs of flour shoot up the wall with every beat. Back at the table, he pushes each dough ball with both hands, stretching the gluten strands outward as fast and economically as possible. Bruno makes the time of 48.93 seconds, beating his close Italian friend Salvatore Salviani's 52.68-second score. When he hears the news, Bruno's primordial yell of "Yeah!" is probably audible in Bulgaria. He struts to the edge of the stage, gazes out at the crowd, and crows, "That's gold, baaaaaaby!" as only a New Yorker can.

My other USA teammate, Justin, progresses to the finals of the acrobatic championship with a great score. He places third in the world in acrobatic dough tossing.

As for me, my *biga* is ready for the fire, just twelve hours old, and incorporated into my seven-ounce dough ball that rests on the marble pizza table near the oven. Three Italian contestants burned the bottoms of their pizzas just before me. This is not promising: they are all better wood-fired pizza men than I am. The optimal temperature for baking a traditional Neapolitan pizza, 905 degrees Fahrenheit, is set by the Verace Pizza Napoletana, an organization founded to protect the way true Neapolitan pizzas are made. In this traditional method, the pizza can bake for only up to ninety seconds. But the actual temperature depends on whether the oven judges stay with an existing 900-degree temperature or whether they throw another couple of oak logs on the fire. The latter is obviously the case, as bottom bricks are burning every pie. The oven temp must be well over 1,000 degrees.

The oven judge watches as I hand stretch the *tipo 00* flour, a more refined and higher-gluten flour perfect for making high-temperature, wood-fired pizzas. I jab the tips of my fingers into the soft dough and create my eleven-inch disk, spreading Italian goat cheese from the Piedmont *(caprino di Rimella)* over it. Next, I shred fresh *asiago pressa* (un-aged, unlike the cheddar-like *asiago d'Allevo* more common in the United States) over the pizzas, followed by small squares of *mozzarella di bufala*. I add thinly sliced braised baby fennel, fresh thyme, Parmigiano-Reggiano, and my par-cooked Maine diver scallops cut in half horizontally. I sprinkle a fine chiffonade of roasted red peppers over all.

One of the pitfalls for many contestants is not making certain that the ashes are brushed out from the previous pizza or from fallout of the burning wood. Ashes ruin the bottom of a true Neapolitan pizza. Any good Italian oven judge can see the ashes, because they stick to the dough and turn the crust gray. Some oven judges see a chump coming to the final bake and "accidentally" forget to brush the oven bottom. Any contestant must remember that this guy docks points for just about anything, scratching away at his little scorecard at the tiniest screw-up. Too much flour on your dough? Scratch. Put sauce on the wrong way? Scratch. Forgot to pull the dough onto the pizza peel? Scratch. Neglect to clean your area? Scratch. Hail from Ohio? Scratch. I nod to the judge and grab the oven broom. He takes it from me and sweeps the oven himself.

I use the dome method to cook my pizza. I lift the pizza off the too-hot bottom bricks with the long pizza peel and hold it aloft into the domed upper roof of the pizza oven. This technique ensures an even bake and would have saved previous contestants from their burnt bottoms. Ninety seconds, and I withdraw my pie from the oven and place it on a plate, then pull out my truffle slicer and glide my *tartufo bianchetto* across the razor-sharp blade, depositing small, fragrant slices onto my pizza. The heat of the pizza enhances the scent. Finally, I garnish my pie with a fresh arugula and sunflower-sprout salad, and then a spritz of lemon. A great pizza, if I say so myself.

But it's Tony who wins "Best Pizza in the USA" in the Pizza Classica category, with a whopping 713 points out of 800, for his pie of white asparagus wrapped with prosciutto, Parmigiano-Reggiano, San Marzano tomato sauce, fresh *buffalo* mozzarella, and fresh basil.

Still, I end up scoring higher than any other American for all categories, having successfully completed every culinary competition at the World Pizza Championship. My pan pizza with feta, chicken, sun-dried tomato, and spinach scores a respectable 607. I place first in the USA with a 550 score for my Neapolitan pizza. Even my last place in Non-Gluten garners 438 points. The 600 for my truffle and Maine diver scallop pizza puts me in First Place USA with a total of 2,195 points.

I see my American team of Bruno, Tony, and Justin only once a year, but we always bond, despite the prickly circumstances and stress that break us down to exactly who we are inside. Our shiny varnish and outward personas vanish with the jetlag, lack of space, surly hotel kitchen chefs, hostile competitors, and the mere fact of being at the toughest pizza competition in the world. A smart guy once said, "In prosperity, our friends know us; in adversity, we know our friends."

As our last night in Italy winds down and Bruno's pathetic karaoke version of "Baby, We Can Talk All Night" wafts across the disco, I think about our *tartufo* adventure. Was there really danger or impending doom at the hands of the truffle mafia? The intrigue made the trip more exciting. Besides, I've saved the biggest truffle for myself. It's stinking up my hotel room, along with a big bag of dried porcini mushrooms. After I smuggle them home, I can tell the story of the truffle guy to my family while shaving my white beauty over freshly made risotto. Then, as we taste the memory of the World Pizza Championship, I can exclaim, "That's gold, baaaaabby!"

A Slice of Family History

By Daniel Duane

From *Food & Wine*

Hobbies have a way of turning into book subjects for San
Francisco–based novelist/lifestyle writer Daniel Duane—
surfing, rock-climbing, and now food and wine. His latest
book: 2012's *How to Cook Like a Man: A Memoir of Cookbook
Obsession.*

Several months ago, I received an unexpected UPS delivery: a cardboard box from my wife Liz's Aunt Mary in
Omaha, Nebraska. Inside, buried among the packing peanuts, I
found an old black leather knife roll—a huge one—heavily worn
and without a note. But I knew instantly what it was: the knives of
my wife's grandfather, Mary's father. And I wondered if it might
not carry a message from the past, if only I could figure out what.

I never met my wife's grandfather. He died relatively young,
back when she was in second grade. But when I first met Liz, a
picture of the man chopping vegetables hung in her kitchen, as
well as in the kitchens of all her food-besotted cousins. "Papa"—
his name was Bernard Schimmel—loomed like Moses in that family; over time, I grew more and more curious about him. A
professional chef who had trained at the world's oldest and finest
hotel school, in Lausanne, Switzerland, Bernie seems to have had
an outsize, gregarious personality, a natural party host who loved
his Scotch, his lemon drops and his three daughters, one of whom
was Liz's mother, Judy.

Bernie was also the head chef and dining consultant for the hotels that his own father had built along the rail lines south of Chicago in the mid-20th century. At one of those hotels, Omaha's Blackstone, family lore has it that Bernie invented the Reuben sandwich for one of his father's regular poker buddies, Reuben Kulakofsky. (A competing origin story credits an earlier "Reuben Special," from a New York deli, but that sandwich had neither sauerkraut nor pastrami and was not grilled.)

I'm something of a knife geek, so my first hope, as I opened Bernie's knife roll, was that I would find treasures—maybe a collection of midcentury carbon-steel Sabatiers, from Bernie's time in Switzerland. Instead, I found run-of-the-mill American stuff: stainless steel slicers for bread and big roasts; a lightweight boning knife for lamb and poultry; a long fish-filleting knife; and a bunch of accessories, like a melon baller, a butter curler, an orange peeler, an oyster-shucking knife, old salad tongs, a carving fork and a plain wooden spoon. What I found, in other words, was the functional tool kit, heavily used but well maintained, of a working Midwestern hotel chef from the 1950s.

Tools are for using, even heirloom tools, but I felt a little stumped: If I dumped all of Bernie's things into my own kitchen drawers, the collection would get lost among my many implements, fast losing their identity. If I left them all in the knife roll, they would stay there forever, unused and under-appreciated.

All this mattered to me because I never cooked before I met Liz. In fact, I never thought much about food. But after we got engaged, Liz's parents started taking us along on their competitive restaurant-going, hitting every great San Francisco spot: Zuni Café, Gary Danko, Spruce, Charles Nob Hill, Aqua. In their company and on their dime, I ate my first foie gras *torchon*, my first fresh truffles.

I knew I would never be able to afford regular Michelin-starred fabulosity on my own, so I taught myself to cook. By the time Liz and I had two daughters, cooking had become my primary pastime. I blew the first few meals I made for Liz's parents—some through poor menu selection, like serving a main course of pig's liver *caillettes* (sausage patties made from liver and spices), wrapped in lacy caul fat and baked. Other meals flopped through my sheer ineptitude, like the time I opened the oven, with dinner already an hour late, to find my chickens raw and cold. But I fought my way toward triumph, culminating in a nine-course menu from *The French Laundry Cookbook*, prepared with help from my then-seven-year-old daughter Hannah, a cheerful and brilliant assistant.

After that, Judy began to say that "Dad" would have loved knowing me, that he would've loved my fascination with the craft of cooking. I felt flattered by this, and I suspected that I would have loved knowing Bernie, too—not just the chance to learn from him, but also the chance to eat, drink and party with a man whose appetites apparently matched my own. The gift of the knives, I thought, might reflect nothing more complicated than that. They were just knives—less fancy and less materially thrilling, to be honest, than all the handmade Japanese blades I'd accumulated on my own. The talismanic power of all this stuff, if it had any, came from its integrity as a collection, and the link that it provided to Bernie himself.

For this reason, I felt grateful when Judy asked me one day to bring the knife roll to a family reunion. She was going to serve Reuben sandwiches at a picnic dinner, and she thought it would be fun to let her cousins cut those sandwiches with Bernie's big slicers. So I did, handing them over before the meal and receiving them back again afterwards. On the way home, in the car, liking how the day had felt, I thought perhaps this was the answer: As Guardian of the Knives, I would store the collection in my home as a complete entity, but I would bring it out for key family functions.

My daughter Hannah, wise beyond her years, found this ridiculous: "Daddy!" she said, exasperated. "Stuff is supposed to be used. You're not supposed to just hide it somewhere!"

I did not own a 12-inch chef's knife, so I figured I would add that one first to my regular rotation, if only for slicing big piles of leafy greens into chiffonades. Pulling that hefty knife from the roll, I noticed a few fine, bright scratches near its blade edge, as if it had been sharpened only days earlier. This caught my eye because the knife had not been touched at the luncheon. So I scraped the blade softly sideways across my forearm, a standard sharpness test: Arm hairs flicked free, effortlessly, one after another. The blade was an absolute razor, so finely honed it wouldn't have stayed that way through more than a few days' cooking.

I phoned Judy first, assuming she had paid to have the knives sharpened after her father passed away. Judy had no idea what I was talking about. So I called Mary, who laughed out loud. "Dad must have left them like that," she said, chuckling. "I haven't touched those knives since he died."

And that's how it happened—that's how I felt Bernie reaching through time, making contact with me. Every chef drags a fingertip sideways across the blade edges of his knives, testing their sharpness; Bernie's own fingers, therefore, had felt precisely the edge I was feeling.

Hannah, by this point, was poring over the contents of the knife roll, marveling at all these little tools from her great-grandfather, the legendary cook. "And what's this thing?" she asked me.

She held a battered old steel tasting spoon. It was stamped, on its face, with the names of the Schimmel hotels in curiously tiny lettering: Omaha's Blackstone, of course; but also the Cornhusker in Lincoln, Nebraska; and the Lassen in Wichita, Kansas; and the Custer in Galesburg, Illinois. Not one of these hotels remained in business, and yet this spoon had served in Bernie's most personal, intuitive act: tasting. Holding it in my hands, thinking of all the times I'd brought a sauce to my own lips, I felt a link to Bernie, and to the simple love of food he had passed along to his daughters. And, through them, to me.

Barbecue Road Trip: The Smoke Road

By John T. Edge

From *Garden & Gun*

Social historian, food writer, and tireless promoter of South-
ern culture, John T. Edge is director of the Southern Foodways
Alliance and a columnist for *The New York Times*, *Garden &
Gun*, and *The Oxford American*. His most recent book, *The Truck
Food Cookbook*, was released in May 2012.

Jess shook his head, tapped his nose, and mouthed the
words No smoke. But I insisted. How often do we get to
Covington, Tennessee? I thought, as we pondered our third barbecue pit stop of the day. We might as well give their sandwich a
shot.

My boy remained dubious. He stepped to the counter and
asked the gentleman in charge how they cook their pigs. "With
charcoal," the fellow said. "Gets it tender, and the sauce does the
rest." Jess looked up at me with all the world-weariness a ten-year-
old with a shock of blond hair and a snaggletoothed grin can
muster. He didn't have to say a word.

As we drove away, bound for the last stop on our semiannual
road trip through rural western Tennessee—a region I've come to
think of as a Land of the Lost for hickory-cooked pork barbecue
believers, where roadside purveyors still fuel masonry pits with
hickory and oak logs and undiscovered treasures always seem to
lurk around the bend—I caught his eye in the rearview mirror. Jess
smiled, shook his head, and tapped his nose again.

Jess knows barbecue. He ate his first solid food, a shoulder sandwich with slaw and sweet red sauce, in the parking lot of Spruce's Bar-B-Q in Griffin, Georgia. Through the years, on family trips to Alabama, where my wife grew up, and Georgia, where I was born and raised, he's learned to case a joint. In addition to working his nose, he knows how to survey the woodpile, ferret out freezer case menu conceits, and spot steam table pork at twenty paces.

A couple of years back, Jess and I began to take just-the-guys jaunts north, from our home in Oxford, Mississippi, through the small Tennessee towns that sprawl between Jackson and Memphis. Jess discovered how to scan for armadas of martin houses, made from whitewashed gourds. He wondered, rightly, what really goes on inside tanning salons, twirling academies, and taxidermy studios. And he learned to eat, with discernment, intelligence, and gusto.

On one of those trips, I tried to get Jess to read the text of a historical marker, erected in tribute to some long-forgotten graybeard statesman. He feigned interest, as any dutiful son would. Five minutes later, he recovered his gumption. "What if I could play laser tag and you could get a really good barbecue sandwich in one place?" he asked. "That's what we really want, right?"

Over time, Jess and I have learned each other's palates. I'm a thin vinegar sauce guy. Jess likes molasses and ketchup-thickened concoctions. I prefer whole hog, pulled into long strands. Jess likes shoulder meat, hacked into shards and piled high on a white-bread bun.

More important, we have developed a shared love of western Tennessee barbecue and the people who cook it. As he grows from a goofball boy, who sings in the shower and hugs me good night, to a querulous teenager, who questions my authority and demands the keys to the family sedan, I hope we're also honing an enduring friendship that won't depend solely on blood and genes.

On our most recent expedition, Jess and I hit two stellar spots before that misstep in Covington. (We also did a drive-by of the Mindfield, a skyscraping folk art environment on the edge of downtown Brownsville, and made a quick tour of the Alex Haley Museum, an homage to the author of *Roots* tucked in a modest neighborhood in nearby Henning.)

Helen's Bar-B-Q in Brownsville came first. Set in a metal hutch, on a hard curve north of the courthouse square, the six-seat café sits next to a retailer of discount jewelry and hair extensions. Across the street is a derelict tourist-court-style motel. Inside, Helen Turner, one of the few female pit masters in the South, stokes the fire and works the sandwich board. She's a dervish. Behind the café, in a screened pit room, she burns hickory and oak down into coals between two sheets of corrugated tin. With a long-handled shovel, she slides those coals into a concrete block berth. After they spend ten to twelve hours in a swirl of smoke, she pulls pork shoulders from that pit, chops them with a cleaver, piles the meat high on buns, and douses all with a red sauce that straddles the line between ketchup and vinegar, between sweet and hot.

Jess ate his sandwich in four greedy bites. He moaned as he ate. Literally. But he also kept glancing up at Ms. Turner, who was wearing a blue floral-print hairnet and pink hospital scrubs. As she loped about the pit room, Jess watched. As he chewed through smoke-blackened hunks of pork flesh, his eyes tracked her movements. And his mind engaged.

When we drove away, Jess was cradling a pickle jar of Helen's sauce and plotting the many ways he could employ it when we got back home. His eyes were wide. And so was his smile. He got it, I told myself. I didn't have to make some fatherly point about how women can do anything men can do. About how women work as hard as men. Ms. Turner had made those points for me. And she had dished a stupendously great sandwich, too.

Sam's Bar-B-Q in Humboldt was next. When Jess spied the woodpile, just south of downtown, he yelled for me to brake. A jumble of hickory trunks and oak stumps—delivered by friends and neighbors as they cleaned up from last spring's tornadoes—that wood served as a kind of free-form art installation and a de facto advertisement that announced HONEST BARBECUE COOKED OVER WOOD HERE.

The building is made of white block, patined with soot. The pit, set in an adjacent building, is an iron-lung-shaped double-decker, with wood burning down to coals on the bottom and shoulders smoking on racks up top. It's a feat of country-boy engineering, designed by the founder, Sam Donald, and now manned by his son-in-law John Ivory. The efficacy of that design gets proved every time customers heft a sandwich to their maw.

And that's just what Jess and I did. We hefted two beautiful sandwiches and a slice of chocolate chess pie, still hot from the oven. And we listened as locals came streaming in. "Now, you're the baby girl, aren't you?" Mr. Ivory asked a woman who ordered a barbecue bologna sandwich. "Give me a sandwich with fatty meat and slaw," said a fireman with soot on his hands.

We could have stayed all afternoon, rubbing our bellies and listening to the dulcet tones of happy eaters. But we motored on, bound for Covington. Two stops don't make a barbecue road trip, I told Jess. Three is the minimum. Everybody knows that.

By the time we left Covington, we didn't need another sandwich. We had eaten well and often. But we pushed on. That's what you do on a barbecue road trip. You push on, no matter how full you might be, goaded by the promise that the next experience might prove to be the best.

As rain began to splatter the windshield and night began to fall, we pulled into Millington, Tennessee. Our goal was Woodstock Store N' Deli, a cinderblock rectangle where Anthony Bledsoe serves a green-hickory-smoked shoulder sandwich, piled perilously high and capped with slaw. He calls it the Sleeper.

The source of the moniker became clear when Jess and I stepped back into the gloom and spread paper towels on the hood of our station wagon. Our sandwich was an overstuffed behemoth. Fatter than fat. Stacked like a napoleon of meat, slaw, and sauce. Wretched and lovely excess. Enough to put any eater to sleep.

As we picked at stray bits of meat that had fallen from the sandwich and worked up the courage to take yet another bite, a woman approached us. She was stooped. And slight. She carried a ragged umbrella. Her hand was out. She said her belly was empty. She looked directly at Jess. I reached into my pocket for some cash. Jess folded the sandwich back into its tinfoil pouch and asked if she would accept it. She did. And then she was gone.

Five miles from home, I asked Jess what he learned on our barbecue road trip. "Respect what you have while you have it," he said. That insight applies to issues of hunger and poverty. And to the barbecue traditions of the South. Not to mention father-son relations.

Though our barbecue buzz had faded by the time we rolled back into Oxford, my road-trip-fueled appreciation for Jess had grown, as had my conviction that we needed to plot another expedition. Before his hunger fades. Before he grows up.

The Family Table

The Food-Critic Father

By Todd Kliman

From *The Washingtonian*

Every new parent knows how a new baby upends family life.
But what if you're a restaurant reviewer, obligated to dine out
several nights a week? Todd Kliman, award-winning dining
critic for the monthly *Washingtonian* magazine, chronicles his
heroic efforts to accommodate the new addition.

"Welcome to my world," my friend Laura said when I
called to tell her my wife and I were having a baby.
"You mean the world of early-morning feedings and interrupted sleep?"

"I mean," she said, "the world of chicken tenders. You're in for a
rude awakening, my food-critic friend."

There are things every parent-to-be fears. The grand, existential
worries: Let him be breathing, I said to myself at the moment of
delivery. Let there not be a cord wrapped around his neck. Let him
be normal. Then there are the little, quotidian matters, the myriad
concerns of getting along with what is, let's face it, a new housemate. A wailing, demanding housemate. A housemate who makes
the slob you once roomed with—the one who raided the fridge
and lounged on the couch in his underwear—look not half bad by
comparison.

In the months preceding our son's arrival, I kept hearing that
life was about to change, that being a parent would alter my reality

in ways big and small. But it wasn't until Laura framed the terms of my soon-to-be life that the existential abstraction—change—became quotidian and concrete.

I thought I had prepared myself. Long before our son was ever a notion in our heads, my wife and I sat down one night and figured it all out—discussing, with the certainty of people for whom nothing is at stake, how we'd raise our Hypothetical Kid. We'd never buy a minivan, we wouldn't build our existence around our Hypothetical Kid's world. Hypothetical Kid would enter ours.

But what was this world I'd created? As a food critic, I ate dinner out every night—often following a long lunch. Sometimes I went out to two dinners in a single night, and the wine sometimes meant that those nights stretched into the morning.

I understood when I accepted this job that I was to think of myself as a kind of public functionary—a Designated Eater. I endured the caloric overload and the punishments to the body so readers could spend their time and money more sensibly. Not that I ever complained. This was the other thing I accepted—griping was bad form when you were eating out nightly on someone else's dime.

If it wasn't all Champagne and truffles, the fact remained that every meal was a restaurant meal. I lived a fantasy life, and I nurtured one, too. As much as I existed to feed my readers tips, I existed to feed their fantasy of the bon vivant. Some bon vivant I was about to be, I thought, spooning strained carrots and mashed peas to a newborn.

"You have to sacrifice certain things now," an obstetrician said, preparing us for our new life.

But there were sacrifices I wasn't sure I was prepared to make.

In the beginning, things were a relative breeze. In their first few months, most babies sleep 18 hours a day or more. The car seat was an ungainly purse we carted everywhere, leaving it on a chair beside us or on the floor next to our table. Jesse slept in his protective pod or stared blankly and drooled. Half the time we brought him with us to restaurants, I didn't even notice he was there until it was time to leave.

"Wait," my wife said. "It gets harder."

We hit more than 100 eateries in those first three or four months—white-tablecloth spots, dives, and everything in between. By our son's first birthday, he had been to more than 250—a fact I shared with the friends and family who gathered at our house to eat cake and watch Jesse open presents.

"You're kidding," someone said.

"Nope."

"Two hundred fifty," she said. "You're keeping a total?"

"Actually, 272," I said. "But who's counting?"

She shook her head. "You're such a guy."

In a sense, we entered a new phase when Jesse graduated from the car seat, where he mostly slept, to a high chair, where he mostly didn't. But it was the night I took my one-year-old son out for barbecue for the first time that we truly entered a new stage of parenthood.

Barbecue has always held a certain primacy for me among all the foods I cook and crave, and I wanted it to be special the first time my son dug into a pile of smoky 'cue.

It was a long drive. My wife had expressed doubts about chancing a place this far from home in rush hour, and now as we hit a patch of traffic on the Beltway, she worried we'd be getting home too late. Jesse wailed and wailed. I told her we could bail at the next exit. "Stick to the plan," she said, slipping Jesse animal crackers.

I suspected she encouraged me to keep going only so she'd have the ideal incriminating illustration to use against me the next time I suggested we venture out too late for a restaurant.

Traffic eased up. We managed to be only 40 minutes late. Fortunately, the food—ribs, pulled pork, beans, cornbread, coleslaw—came quickly. Jesse, despite the in-car appetizer, was ravenous. He attacked his plate, shoving bits of spare rib into his mouth as if satisfying some deep need. I'd never seen him go at any food like this. But I'd never turned him loose on barbecue. He's got it in his genes, I thought, marveling at his sauce-smeared face. I took pictures.

We drove home in one of those warm, expansive moods when your earlier fears have been exposed as premature and overstated and life feels loose and easy. We laughed and celebrated his initiation into the culture of barbecue and the world of adult eating.

And then at 3 in the morning, my son, snugly sleeping between Mommy and Daddy, spewed the contents of his stomach all over himself, our bed, and us. Even after we changed the sheets, the smell of wood smoke and stomach acid was unmistakable.

Yay, solid foods!

My wife laid down certain rules after that: In a high chair by 6 at the latest. If traffic is bad and we have to bail, so be it.

Dinner became something to prepare for twice. There were the preparations I needed to make for him and the preparations I needed to make for me, to ensure that my stealth mission—my anonymous visit to a restaurant as a critic—came off without a hitch.

Afternoons usually went like this: Make a reservation under an assumed name—my nom de mange, I like to call it. E-mail my wife to be ready to leave the house at the appointed time. Choose all of the dishes we'd order. E-mail our guests the "rules" for the night: what can and can't be talked about at the table, when and how to pass plates so that I'm able to sample each dish, how to quiz the waitstaff about the Syrah and the veal without lapsing into an SS-style interrogation.

At the same time: Load his bag with necessities—change of clothes, diapers, sippy cup. Choose an assortment of books along with crayons and paper. Fill and pack Tupperware containers with Cheez-Its, Cheerios, and animal crackers while relishing the irony of sneaking cheap processed food into a restaurant that charges $16 for a glass of wine.

Sometimes I prepared in vain. One night as we were nearing the restaurant, I glanced into the rearview mirror. There he was, a limp pile of limbs. "What should we do now?" I asked.

The look on my wife's face said: Tell me that's a rhetorical question.

We'd already taken him out three nights in a row. If it were just any restaurant, I said, I'd understand. But this was Important Restaurant X. I'd been waiting five weeks to get in. I proposed we give it 15 minutes, that maybe he'd wake up then and we could have our meal. I drove around the block three times.

He did not wake up.

Five more minutes, I said.

"No," she said, peeved that I'd thought to push through.

My son, if he'd known I had put my needs as a critic above his, would probably have been peeved, too.

The hostess professed understanding when I called to cancel five minutes after we were supposed to be there, but her blithe, sing-songy tone oozed the opposite. It was all peeve. As for me, I had left peeved and was approaching pissed. Dinner at Important Restaurant X turned out to be takeout pizza from Chain Restaurant Y. It was cold by the time we got it home.

It was rare that we missed a meal. But there were many I wished we had. One night when Jesse was almost two, we were at an Italian restaurant in Alexandria. The waitress was excellent, and we put in orders for drinks and appetizers. All was well until my son dropped his fork.

He was inconsolable.

"It's okay," I said, "they'll get you a new one."

You would have thought a stranger had snatched his Elmo doll. Tears streamed down his pinched red face.

I handed him my fork.

No. He wanted his fork.

How did he know this wasn't his fork? He just knew.

The stares were coming from every corner of the restaurant as he wailed. It dawned on me: I've become the diner I used to despise. I once shot dirty looks at tables with kids who wouldn't pipe down. I never thought twice about asking to be moved to another table, away from the offending baby. Now I always found myself scanning the room for tables with small children, curious to know how their dinner was going. Reading online reviews, with their frequent, raging criticism of parents who brought young children to restaurants, made me cringe. "Who do these arrogant, entitled yuppie assholes think they are?" went a typical review on Yelp. "What makes them think their oh-so-precious princes and princesses are welcome at every goddamn restaurant in the city?"

My wife, at the limit of her frustration, gathered Jesse up and took him outside. Ten minutes later, he returned . . . and remembered why he'd been so upset.

"My fork!" he cried.

He and my wife spent the remainder of the meal outside while I ate parts of two appetizers, three entrées, and two salads.

In American culture, there are restaurants for adults and there are restaurants for kids, and the two are not expected to mix. It's different at Latin and Asian restaurants, where no such divide seems to exist.

The first time I took Jesse to a roadside joint in Bladensburg's Little Mexico—he was probably six months old—the waitress fussed over him for a minute or two before extending her arms like a forgotten aunt. The expression on my wife's face was priceless: diplomacy vying with primal anxiety. You want me to hand over my baby? But she relented. The waitress scooped him up, cuddled him, cooed over him—and whisked him out of the dining room.

Now my wife's alarm was palpable.

We found our waitress in the kitchen, parading Jesse around as the cooks entertained him with their shiny tools.

Even better was the restaurant in Annandale's Koreatown where the co-owner descended on our table as if she were his bub-bub and hadn't seen him in weeks. She took him to a nearby table where her staff was chopping vegetables. For the next 20 minutes, she bounced him on her knee and dangled scallions in front of him as if they were car keys, entreating us to seize the chance to eat in quiet, just the two of us.

These were among the most extraordinary restaurant experiences I've ever had. Not only was our son showered with affection, but we were made to feel like part of an extended family. We were being embraced, too.

By contrast, whenever I walked into an American restaurant with him in those first two years, there was seldom a smile, much less an embrace. My son was a problem to be solved. "You can't bring that in here," the general manager of a popular restaurant commanded us one afternoon.

We think he was referring to the stroller.

Around the time Jesse turned two, my wife made a decision. Her decisions are never the result of minor epiphanies. They never involve switching cell-phone providers or choosing a new doctor. When she says, "I've made a decision," I brace myself.

"It's too hard taking us along," she said. "And I don't enjoy it if he doesn't enjoy it, and who can tell if he's going to? There are just so many things that can happen."

The precipitating event had occurred a few nights earlier at a restaurant in DC's Palisades I was reevaluating. She was feeding Jesse a hunk of bread and butter, and he began to choke and then cry. Every head turned. My wife quieted him after several moments, enabling us to hear all the disparaging things everyone around us was saying—condemnations of our parenting style, of our effrontery in taking him out to eat at a place like this. (Never mind that the restaurant had a high chair!) We spent the late-summer night taking turns with him out on the sidewalk, one of us holding down the table, the other walking him back and forth on the pavement, all three of us bitten by mosquitoes. At least somebody ate.

"You've got a job to do, and you're trying to make everybody happy and making nobody happy," my wife said. "So just forget it."

"What about one of the noisy places?" I suggested.

I'd come to love the noisy places, those casual midlevel restaurants with exposed ceilings and cement floors that had been popping up in DC. Young people loved them, finding in their cool industrial aesthetic a validation of their decision to live in the expensive but bustling big city; older people hated them, despairing of ever having a normal conversation. As a food critic, I saw the merits of both arguments. But as a new parent, I was a fierce partisan. I loved the protective cover they offered. My son could screech like an electrocuted cat, as he did one night at a clattering bistro, and no one would glance up from the scallop crudo. If only every new restaurant that opened had decibel levels akin to that of a construction site, I sometimes thought.

"No," my wife said, "not even the noisy places." The only exception she'd make was for a Latin or Asian restaurant.

"How about we revisit this again in a few months?" I said.

She didn't agree; she didn't disagree. "Look, we're learning," she said. "He's going through phases, but we're going through them, too. This isn't forever. And that doesn't mean you can't go out with him, just the two of you. It'll be good for you to have that time to-gether. Daddy-and-Jesse time."

Things were harder without my wife there—like being-denied-the-use-of-my-limbs harder. I hadn't realized just how smooth and skilled she was until I was forced to handle it all myself. How did she do it? How did she attend to all his needs—cutting his food into small bites, reading him a story, swabbing him down whenever his face became one big schmutz—while also serving as a sound-ing board for my impressions and ideas?

It took all of half a meal for me to realize that being a daddy and being a food critic were incompatible, like pairing foie gras with ice cream. I couldn't make mental notes about the red wine that was served too warm, the sauce that hadn't been properly re-duced, the waitress who neglected to fill the water glasses . . . and also read him a story, color with him, and cut his food into 47 pieces.

Restaurant visit number 466: I ducked into the bathroom to make notes. I figured the sanctuary of the stall would reduce the static in my head. I began pecking out letters on my iPhone: "Scal-lops = slight translucence in center, dark crusting on top. Micro-greens, dabs of corn sauce. Gazpacho blended smooth, a thickness there—bread or bread crumbs?" But I still had my son with me.

"Daddy, whatcha doin'?"

"Making notes," I said.

I heard someone enter the bathroom. "Making notes," Jesse sing-songed as the door to the next stall slammed shut. "Daddy's making notes."

My son the mole.

My stall-mate could have been a manager, a waiter. I imagined walking back to my table to the stares of the staff as the news made the rounds: critic in the house.

Among the first laws of being a food critic is not to take things personally. Our recourse is our column. A bad night is writing ma-terial. But my dinners out with Jesse several nights a week were an exercise in double consciousness. I was both the discerning critic and the anxious father. The critic in me focused on the server's knowledge of the menu and of food generally, his ability to keep

the flow of the meal smooth and steady. The father in me was fix-
ated on the waiter's regard for the little person at the table. Servers
were either with you, I was learning, or they were against you.
There was rarely an in-between.

One night a waiter set down a giant steak knife in front of my
son. Servers routinely gave him stemware. A few brought him apple juice or milk in a wine goblet.

I'll never forget restaurant visit number 684 and the cast-iron
skillet of mushrooms and polenta. "Hot—careful," the waiter
warned. He walked away, leaving the scalding handle much too
near my son's face. Jesse's little fingers drifted toward it. I grabbed
his forearm and squeezed hard. He began to cry at the pain I'd
caused—a pain to forestall a nastier, more lasting one.

Hoping to avert disaster, I created it: I knocked over a glass,
spilling water all over. The waiter materialized with napkins and
stood watching as I blotted while the spill, moving as inexorably as
floodwaters, dripped onto Jesse's lap. The manager swung by, and
the men stood watching. Doing nothing. Like men do.

The male staff at restaurants were, almost without exception,
awful. That's not to say all the waitresses were superior at their
jobs, just that the women were more inclined to understand that
having a toddler at the table meant taking care of things other than
drink requests and asking if everything was seasoned properly.
More inclined to improvise entertainments to distract Jesse—
spoons and straws to play with, pen and paper for drawing, even a
cookie fetched from the petit four plate. Some people prefer a female doctor—believing, rightly or wrongly, that a woman will be
more sensitive to their needs. I had never understood that position
until now. I didn't ask to be taken care of by a waitress and not a
waiter when my son was with me, but the father in me pleaded
silently to be given a waitress.

It was hard with him. It was hard without him. The nights that
neither he nor she came with me felt strange, as if I had one life
and they had another. I sometimes felt like a traveling salesman.

The texts my wife liked to send me while I was out at dinner
were meant to impart a sense of closeness but only reinforced this
feeling of being alone on the road. Restaurant-going had been a

huge part of our dating life. Our first dinner date had been at Red Sea, the now-defunct Ethiopian place on 18th Street in DC's Adams Morgan. Nothing fancy. I'd wanted to see whether she was my kind of woman—a real eater, up for an adventure—or a princess in need of pampering.

"How's dinner?" she would text me. If the food was good, I downplayed it. If it was mediocre, I made her think I had spared her from something awful. I declined to give dish descriptions, rendering my meal in single-word summations: chicken, polenta, sorbet.

"I made Jesse some mashed yams with cinnamon, which he seemed to love," she texted one night. "I had the rest of the chicken from Friday plus heated up some ramen." Ramen! The last resort of the penny-pinching college student. I felt a stab in my stomach.

I often brought home leftovers, which my wife dug into the next day at lunch, or sometimes in the middle of the night. Whether veal cheeks over polenta from a French restaurant or pollo a la brasa from a carryout rotisserie, it didn't matter. All distinctions were erased by refrigeration. Everything tasted like fast food. "I guess you had to be there," she'd say.

Still, I persisted: "Let me bring you something."

"Whatever you want. Enjoy yourself. I love you."

"Tell him Daddy loves him and misses him. And I love you, too."

Thinking I might persuade my wife to relax the rules, I told her one night about a new non-Asian, non-Latin place that advertised itself as kid-friendly. I had already done my homework, calling ahead to ask the manager about the menu (hot dogs and chicken tenders) and the provided-for distractions (a coloring book and crayons). What a parent is paying for in patronizing a kid-friendly restaurant is immunity from the dirty looks of other diners. Nobody who comes to a place with coloring books and crayons ought to complain about a kid acting up at the next table—or so my wife contended. "If they have a high chair," she said, "they've made the decision that kids are welcome."

Not that she trusted restaurants to understand that that's what they'd decided. My wife no longer took restaurants at their word when it came to children. "What makes this place kid-friendly?" she wanted to know, pouncing on the phrase like a prosecutor.

"Besides the menu, I don't know. A high chair? Coloring books?"

"Just because they have a high chair," she said, "doesn't mean they're going to be competent."

My God, I thought. It's happened: My wife has become a mother.

I knew the moment she pushed him out into the world that her life had changed and that ours, together, had changed along with it. But for some reason it wasn't emotionally real to me until now. This fierce protective instinct—where had it been hiding all these years? She'd always been willing to give things a try, always relished the opportunity to turn a bad situation into something good. I was under no illusion that she believed it was her job in life to make me happy, but if there was anyone, before, whom she sought to comfort or appease or please, it was me.

We never did visit that "kid-friendly" place.

The line between discernment and snobbery can seem razor-thin in the world of food. I've never wanted to be the kind of critic concerned chiefly with handing out demerits and judging dishes according to some Olympian notion of correctness. I've never wanted readers to feel that I equate a discriminating palate with a sense of my own superiority.

In my reviews, I've always strived to remember I'm writing for all sorts of readers and that my goal in critiquing a restaurant is to craft an interesting piece that diners who might never get to the restaurant would want to read. It hasn't always been easy, because to talk with any degree of specificity about food is to lapse necessarily into a kind of inside baseball. And to engage professionally in any form of artistic criticism is to choose a life in which you're constantly working out your theories and ideas—intellectualizing experiences that most people never bother to analyze.

I felt a version of this tension playing out in me as Jesse racked up the restaurant visits—not as many as in his first year but still two, three, even four times a week.

"Your son's going to be such a foodie!" people would say when they learned what sorts of foods he considered normal.

I would cringe.

Some years ago for this magazine, I edited a story about prepubescent food snobs—kids who sneered at fish sticks and pined for bacalao and who knew to order off the secret menu. My Hypothetical Kid would never be like those kids, I remember vowing. He'd eat widely and learn to love food and gain exposure to all the cultures and cuisines of the globe. He wasn't going to be one of those children whose sophistication comes across as a party trick. I wasn't going to let him become an adult in kiddie clothing.

It was, of course, premature to tell what sort of kid he would become—he was three.

A parents' group met in our neighborhood once a month, with mothers, fathers, and children coming together for a couple of hours at a playground or someone's home. Inevitably, talk of sleeping routines gave way to talk of food. Emma was a very good eater and had recently discovered broccoli, which of course she adored, while Sebastian not only ate hummus but actually liked to eat the chickpeas themselves, and Gabriella, who had only recently weaned herself from the bottle, had developed an inexplicable taste for pickles. Can you imagine? I preferred to downplay Jesse's catholicism in these sorts of conversations. I was leery of characterizing him as a precocious toddler foodie.

There was another reason I kept quiet: I feared exposing myself as the food-world equivalent of the arrogant Little League coach. I liked to joke to my wife that, eating out as often as he did and being exposed to such an astonishing array of cuisines, Jesse had already surpassed his peers who were blissfully munching away on McNuggets, ignorant of what they were doing to their bodies and (of greater concern to me) their taste buds.

But all humor conceals a darker truth.

I was proud.

In his three years on this earth, Jesse had pretty much devoured it. Thai, Indian, Salvadoran, Vietnamese, Afghan, Cuban, Greek, Turkish, Ethiopian, French, Brazilian, Portuguese, Japanese, Chinese, Armenian, Peruvian, Bolivian, Kazakhstani, Bosnian—there was nothing he hadn't tried. The list of foods he loved and asked for was long: edamame and mango lassi and chicken tikka and char siu bao and grilled stuffed grape leaves and kanom jeeb and chicken curry puffs.

He made the other kids from the parents' group look like pikers. He made me look like a piker. I had been writing professionally about food for a decade but had never tasted many of these things until I was in my mid-twenties.

Was there a correlation between trying so many kinds of foods at such a tender age and becoming a richer, more broad-minded person? I liked to think so. Jesse wasn't being dragged out to dinner night after night at Daddy's whim, I told my wife; he was getting an education. And what an education it was. You couldn't buy an education like this.

As I made this point one night in the car after restaurant visit number 872—the third night in a row I had kept him out two hours past bedtime as I worked feverishly to finish my work for a dining guide—Jesse, giddy with tiredness, was belting out songs in the back as if he'd just discovered Ethel Merman on YouTube.

"Daddy? Sing?"

"You like to think you're the guide, in control," a friend with two kids in their twenties told me. "But you're not. All you can do is direct them a little. You're not the bike. You're more like the training wheels. And what you have to remember is eventually the training wheels come off."

We were on our way to restaurant visit 924 when my son pointed out the pair of golden arches looming ahead. This is what's commonly referred to as a teachable moment, a chance to put forward a philosophy of food and, in this way, install a belief system that will last a lifetime. "McDonald's," I said, "is yucky."

"It's not yucky," my son replied.

"Ick," I said. "Ugh." I shuddered.

Jesse became agitated, thrashing against the constraints of his car seat. He was crying. "It's not yucky," he said and then, gathering himself, uttered the words with an almost sinister deliberation, driving the dagger in more deeply: "McDonald's is delicious."

It required every ounce of concentration on my part not to hit the car in front of me.

It required every ounce of concentration on my wife's part not to burst out laughing.

"How'd this happen?" I demanded. "Did someone take him to a McDonald's? One of the babysitters?"

Silence. A guilty silence.

"I mean," my wife said cautiously, "he's had fries a couple of times."

"You've taken him for fries?"

"A couple times."

"A couple—"

"Okay, a few. Maybe a burger once or twice." She winced, cutely.

"How could you?"

Number 1,000 loomed, a figure I'd been pointing to for nearly a year. But it seemed ridiculous now, all that number-keeping. All that striving.

"He's three, you know," my wife said.

"I know."

"Do you?"

"What are you saying?"

"He just enjoys being with you."

My son had had a rough week: two doctors' visits, an upset stomach, and—either because he'd just turned three or because the gods had decided to complicate our life even more—a growth spurt that made him cranky. I hadn't been around much, having been cramming in final visits to several restaurants before an upcoming family trip. That Saturday, I decided, would be Daddy-and-Jesse day.

"Aww," my wife said. "He really could use some Daddy time. What's the plan?"

I told her.

"You mean," she said, "you plan to take him to work with you."

"No. To dim sum."

"You're sure about that."

"He loves dim sum."

"I meant you're sure this isn't work? This isn't a place you're reviewing, or checking up on? What's the restaurant?"

I told her.

"I've never heard of it."

"It's new."

"Uh-huh," she said. That tone again. "Just try to have a good time, okay?"

It was noon when we arrived for restaurant visit 1,027. The place was a scene of happy chaos. Extended families huddled around big circular tables with lazy Susans, servers dashed through the room like rush-hour commuters in pursuit of a departing subway train, the hawkers with their metal carts circled in search of a sale, lifting lids and sending up little clouds of steam.

Our table was a scene of happy chaos, too. Steamed pork buns and roast pork buns. Shrimp dumplings and shrimp balls. Rice-noodle crepes stuffed with shrimp and stuffed with ground pork. Tiny custard pies and pineapple buns for dessert. I don't think I had ever seen Jesse eat so much at any one meal. For a feeder descended from a long line of feeders, there's nothing quite as gratifying as seeing someone you love eat with gusto.

Somewhere between the shrimp balls and the shrimp noodle crepes, my wife texted me: "How's it going?"

"He's loving it," I wrote back. "He looks relaxed and happy, and he's eating like someone who hasn't seen food in a week."

"I'm glad he's getting his fill. He loves being with his daddy."

A triumph.

Back home, I couldn't help myself. Before I had unstrapped the diaper bag from my shoulder, before I had helped him out of his shoes, before I had even stepped ten feet into the house, I began exulting. I was dangerously skirting the line of gloating. There were, I said, all sorts of ways to have a good time and all sorts of venues. It didn't always have to be a zoo, a park, a playground. He could come into our world, I said; we didn't have to go into his.

"I'm glad it went so well," my wife said, walking into the living room only to be crushed by my son's running, lunging hug.

"Amazingly well," I corrected.

"Jesse, did you have a good time with Daddy?"

For the next ten minutes, as my wife helped him into a new set of clothes and then all three of us went into the playroom, I listened to my son tell the story of the day. It came in bursts, a little at a time, and what he said wasn't as interesting as what he didn't say.

The afternoon, according to Jesse, amounted to the following: Sitting next to Daddy. Eating with Daddy. Blowing bubbles in the water glass with Daddy. Laughing at the waiter with the funny glasses with Daddy. Making the bunched-up straw wrapper into a snake with Daddy.

He didn't mention a single dish. He didn't mention any food at all.

My son is up to something like 1,300 visits by now.

I don't know how many exactly.

My wife and I just had another child, a son, and life is busier than ever.

In any case, I've stopped counting.

The Legacy That Wasn't: Wonton Soup

By T. Susan Chang

From *A Spoonful of Promises*

Cookbook reviewer, blogger, and essayist T. Susan Chang
looks through a prism of food memories to meditate on her
many families—the emigrated Chinese clan she grew up with,
the young singles tribe of her 20s, and the nuclear family she
and her husband have begun.

The secret of the wontons, I think, was always in the smell. It was only ground pork, with maybe some shrimp, and it was seasoned with all the usual suspects—dry sherry, soy sauce, scallions, a little ginger, a little sesame oil. But when you finally had it just right, you'd know it instantly, because it didn't smell like raw meat any more. It smelled different—fresh, sweet, and good.

My mother learned to make wontons from her mother. It's possible her mother learned it from hers. It's possible that there, beneath the misted camel-hump caves of Guizhou, generations of women related to me made wontons just like my mom's. I really can't say. What I do know is that nobody has to learn to eat a wonton. That just sort of takes care of itself.

The wonton wrappers came from the Chinese grocery store, and since this was the '70s, that meant an excursion to Chinatown, in the city. My mom would park our ugly-yet-iconic beige Plymouth Volaré station wagon and stroll from store to store, returning only to check in on me and feed the meter. I would lie in back, trying to make sense of *David Copperfield* while slowly being imprinted with the vinyl pattern of the seat. It never struck me as odd that I could better comprehend the idiom spoken in a nineteenth-century London factory than the sidewalk Cantonese being shouted just outside the window. My sister, incidentally, had named the station wagon Ouagoudougou, after the capital of then–Upper Volta (Burkina Faso now), and that seemed pretty normal too.

My mom made the filling at home. How, I couldn't tell you. I was probably busy reading the essay on Indo-European roots in the back of the dictionary, another favorite pastime. In any case, as I lolled bookishly under the bed, the smell of wontons would travel down the hallway to my room, followed with momlike efficacy by an exhortation to come to the kitchen, where the bowl of filling waited.

Then, as in Chinese families everywhere, everyone would sit around the table and wrap wontons. Even my dad sometimes helped. We'd talk about violin and piano practice, about the books my dad's company was publishing, about who was doing well in school. It was sort of like a shareholders' meeting, but with better food.

What we didn't talk about so much was the past that brought us here. Or rather, that brought our grandparents here—in a hurry, and for good.

Between 1938 and 1949, the Chang family and the Pu family, like so many other families, were on the move. My dad's dad was a financier, antiques dealer, millionaire, governor, mobster (probably), and, for less than a year, the Chinese premier. He even had a mobster nickname—the "Reclining Cicada." My mom's dad came to study English literature in Michigan, where he came by his own nickname: "Mr. Pu from Kalamazoo." My dad's family brought precious antiques, and a brilliant, perilous political past. My mom's family came with hardly anything but its resilience, and its considerable wits.

I wish I could say that the wonton soup recipe was a tangible inheritance, that it arrived on the plane in New York in the suitcases of my fleeing family (for the Reclining Cicada, it wasn't so much flight as "strategic relocation," I like to think). Maybe in my grandfather's steamer trunk, which was stamped "CKC" in gold.

But no, there was no physical recipe to puzzle over, divine, and interpret, and in any case, the wonton soup didn't come from my dad's family at all. It came from my mom's, and somehow or other, it got here safely, as did my mom's mom, my Po Po. She made wonton soup for her children, and she made it for an increasing array of grandchildren—two, five, eight, ten, finally thirteen in all. Then she started in on her great-grandchildren. Their hair might have been a little lighter colored, the eyes a little more Caucasian, but for fifty years the scene remained pretty much the same: a little head bent over a steaming bowl, focused on a small regiment of wontons staring back up from the spoon with wrinkly, Shar-Pei-like faces. An indelicate slurping provided the soundtrack. Unlike my grandfather's antiques, Po Po's wonton soup was typically gone within ten minutes of being served. But it was not hard to interpret.

It's the nature of inheritance to stick close in some places and fall free in others. As our family propagated and throve in its new home, bits of our cultural heritage dropped away. Gradually, we lost our panic, our notoriety, our accent. Our names commingled with a United Nations of new names: Yudkovsky, Fasquelle, Eramian, Barnum, McLean, te Velde. Two generations after Ellis Island, our family's China stories are evolving into myths—the last stop of a memory before it vanishes for good.

For me, the greatest loss was language. My parents spoke different dialects, and when they spoke Chinese, it was a secret language, for keeping things from the kids. By the time I tried to learn it at school, I couldn't pick it up easily. What I learned, I was too shy to practice, and therefore quickly lost.

Some of my cousins did better, becoming fluent in Chinese. To learn a language, you have to be willing to make mistakes—big, loud ones sometimes. Being a shy perfectionist with a taste for Dickens is a recipe for learning a lot of one language; it's not a recipe for learning a second or a third. So Po Po and I sat at the table smiling at each other and eating wonton soup in more or less silence, divided by language. I could taste the plain fact of my grandmother's affection, which didn't require translation into English. But I could no more ask the questions that would help me learn how to make it—however much I might wish to—than I could question the affection itself. Even a simple question like "Should you use shrimp in the wontons?" was out of the question, especially the "should" part.

Learning to make wontons didn't seem to matter much when I was studying ancient Greek at eighteen, or learning the saxophone at twenty-two, or salsa dancing at twenty-six. But when my own children were born, I began to lecture myself: Surely, I thought, your family didn't come all this way only for the wonton soup to be forgotten in two generations. And so, setting aside the problems of language for the time being, I began.

I started with a Joyce Chen recipe (written in English), dutifully measuring a teaspoon of this, a teaspoon of that. But then, after a while, I ditched the teaspoons and just sniffed and splashed my way back to what I remembered.

The smell of wonton filling evolves as you make it. First it just smells porky, with a high overtone of shrimp if you used it. When you add the rice wine, the smell staggers a bit and opens up. Then you add the soy, and it takes on salty, definite edges. You add in a bit of stinging scallion and a bit of bracing ginger, and the smell sits up at attention. You throw in a pinch of sugar, to mollify it a bit. You put in a bit of oil to spread the word, and a little chicken broth to loosen up the attitude. And then you have that final smell that I most remember: fresh, sweet, and good.

Like life, it's a series of sequential approximations. If you trust the famous parable from Herodotus—and why wouldn't you? the old liar—you never know if you've had a good life until it's over. So it is with wontons, but thankfully, the wait's a little shorter. It's only an hour or two of sniffing and folding before you arrive at a steaming pot of certainty.

It's strange to produce something so concrete from so imprecise a sense. You can't record a smell on a hard drive; you can't upload it from a server. The exactness of the written word means nothing when you don't speak the language. But smell, however vague, is indelible. It's never turned off, and it's not erasable.

When it comes to culture, the lines of transmission are never continuous. Yet, from nothing more than a smell you can patch together broken bits and pieces of memory and common sense and find, to your shock, years later, that you have something your children recognize as their own, as if it were always whole and perfect. Like it or not, you're not just a descendant—you're a forebear too.

Today, Po Po is ninety-seven, still alert and smiling, though very deaf and certainly too frail to cook. Having had my fill of Dickens—at least for the moment—I am finally learning Chinese the Information Age way: with Rosetta Stone, while walking a treadmill. I've still not going to ask about the shrimp, though. I would say something incomprehensible, and Po Po would laugh and shake her head at me, the mutest of her granddaughters. Knowing she loves me that much is enough. I know it for a wordless fact, just as I know that the wontons I eat from this point forward will all be my own.

Best Guess Wonton Soup

I try to double the wonton part of the recipe when I feel up to it. They're so good, and you can freeze them in little quart-size ziplock bags for a later lunch. I freeze them raw, but it's also possible to blanch them—cook them in boiling water for just a couple of minutes, till half-done—drain them, and then freeze them that way. If you do this, you also have the messy but outrageously good option of deep-frying them, which everyone should try at least once.

Serves 4

For the filling:

1 pound ground pork, or pork butt/shoulder (if you have a grinder)

½ pound shrimp, peeled and deveined

2 tablespoons Shaoxing cooking wine or dry sherry

1 tablespoon soy sauce

1 teaspoon minced fresh ginger

1 teaspoon minced fresh garlic

2 fat or 4 skinny scallions, whites only (reserve the greens for later use), minced

1 ½ teaspoons cornstarch

If you have a meat grinder or a meat grinder attachment for your mixer, run the pork and shrimp through it, using a disk with medium-sized holes. If you don't, you are probably working with ground pork and whole peeled and deveined shrimp, and you'll need to mince the shrimp as finely as you can; it's easier if you freeze them for 10 minutes first. Cut the shrimp into 1/8-to 1/4-inch slices, then turn them crosswise and slice the other way. When you have minced all the shrimp in this manner, hash them a bit finer by holding the knife tip down with one hand and seesawing the blade through the shrimp mass against the cutting board. Precision isn't as important as thoroughness here.

1 tablespoon chicken broth or homemade chicken stock
1 ½ teaspoons vegetable oil, canola oil, or corn oil
½ teaspoon sesame oil
Pinch of sugar

1 package wonton wrappers (about 45–50)

For the soup:
½ head Chinese (napa) cabbage
6 cups chicken broth or homemade stock
Greens reserved from 4 scallions (see above)
1-inch piece fresh ginger, unpeeled and crushed

1. Place the pork and shrimp in a large mixing bowl and add the rest of the filling ingredients. Toss gently but thoroughly with a fork or chopsticks; the mixture should remain loose and smell fresh, briny, and gingery.

2. To fill the wontons: Set the filling and a small bowl of water next to your work area. Take out a wonton wrapper and set 1 teaspoon (more if you dare, and as you get better at it) of filling in the center. Dip your finger in the water and trace along the top edge and halfway down the sides of the wrapper. Fold the wrapper in half so that the dry edges meet the wet edges. You should have a rectangle with a big lump of filling in the middle. Moisten one corner of the folded edge.

Draw the other corner of the folded edge over it—not face to face as if you were closing a book, but front to back—and press them together firmly. Set your finished wonton aside and repeat until you've exhausted the filling.

3. Chop the cabbage roughly into pieces about 1 inch square.

4. For the soup: Bring the broth, scallion greens, and crushed ginger to a simmer. Add the wontons. If the broth doesn't quite cover them, add a bit of water. Salt to taste. Add the cabbage, and any extra wrappers if you have them, atop the broth and return to a simmer. As it simmers, tuck the thickest bits of cabbage into the broth with a wooden spoon to help cook them through. The wontons should be cooked through, with the wrapper puckering around the filling, and the cabbage tender within about 8 or 9 minutes at a steady simmer (if you had more broth, you would see the wonton float to the surface, but I prefer a less brothy soup). Serve immediately, with Special Sauce.

Special Sauce
1 tablespoon finely minced ginger
1 clove garlic, finely minced
1 tablespoon finely minced scallions
½ teaspoon white sugar
½ teaspoon black vinegar (Chinkiang vinegar)
A few drops white vinegar (rice vinegar)
1 teaspoon dark sesame oil
⅓–½ cup dark soy sauce (e.g., Kikkoman)

1. In a small bowl combine the ginger, garlic, and scallions. Add the sugar, vinegars, and sesame oil. Crush the mixture lightly with a fork or chopsticks to help release the flavors. Let it rest for at least 5–10 minutes.

2. Add the soy sauce gradually to taste. Less soy makes for a thick, pungent sauce; more for a milder dressing.

Curious Cookies

By Eagranie Yuh

From *Edible Vancouver*

⚬⚬

Vancouver-based Eagranie Yuh teaches classes about chocolate—a logical focus for a pastry chef with a master's degree in chemistry. As a copywriter, blogger, and freelancer, she is a frequent contributor to *Northwest Palate* and *Edible Vancouver* and edits IACP's newsletter *Words*.

Here's how most chocolate-chip cookie recipes go: in a mixing bowl, cream sugar and butter until light and fluffy. Dribble in eggs and vanilla. In a separate bowl, combine flour, baking powder, baking soda, and salt. Fold the dry ingredients into the wet ingredients, then sprinkle in chocolate chips and stir just to combine. Drop identical dollops of cookie dough onto a baking sheet, leaving gaps between neighbours. Bake into perfectly golden-brown cookies, evenly studded with chocolate chips.

Here's my mom's method for making cookies: In a saucepan, melt margarine and sugar. Crack in an egg, and stir furiously to minimize scrambling. Dump in a mixture of whole-wheat flour, baking powder, baking soda, and salt. Toss in a few handfuls of miniature carob chips, then mix roughly until the batter comes together. Slap the batter onto an ungreased cookie sheet, glossing over instructions like "place the cookies two inches apart" and bake one enormous frankencookie that covers the entire pan. Snap off the blackened edges, and divide it into rough squares.

I was the only kid at school with square cookies, but it didn't bother me. I didn't know the difference between creaming and melting the fat, that butter and margarine have different properties, or that whole-wheat flour can make baked goods dense and heavy. And I certainly didn't know that carob is a legume masquerading as chocolate.

For every recipe that begins, "cream the butter and sugar," there's someone who looks confused. It simply means to mix the butter and sugar vigorously until light and fluffy, but it might as well be secret code, because there's no way for you to figure that out. By creaming, you incorporate air, thereby creating a lighter, fluffier cookie.

When my mom melted, rather than creamed, the margarine and sugar, she set things up for flat, dense cookies. Even worse, the melted margarine resulted in a warm, fluid batter that gave the cookies no choice but to smoosh into each other as they baked into a crisp carob-chip pancake.

Hydrogenated vegetable fats—like margarine and shortening—lead to crisper, crumblier cookies with little flavour. When it comes to chocolate chip, I prefer butter. Aside from being tasty, it results in a cookie that spreads slightly when it bakes, leading to crispy edges and soft centres. So why did she use margarine?

In the '80s there was a backlash against saturated fats. Consumption of red meat plummeted, prompting pork to advertise itself as "the other white meat." Sales of skinless, boneless chicken breast shot through the roof. And well-meaning people, like my mom, eschewed butter in favour of margarine. And not just any margarine—hard margarine, sold in bricks, full of trans-fatty acids that have since been linked to heart disease. Whoops.

While she was substituting margarine for butter, my mom also swapped out all-purpose flour for whole wheat. Whole-wheat flour, as the name suggests, is milled from the entire wheat grain and so contains the bran, germ, and endosperm. All that added stuff can throw off the balance of dry and wet ingredients in a recipe, so simply substituting whole-wheat for all-purpose flour can be risky. Dry, crumbly cookies weren't the only result; I also ate my share of hockey puck muffins.

Finally, let's be clear: carob is not chocolate. It's a legume. In some countries, carob is a legitimate food, used as a sweetener and in hot drinks. When I was growing up, carob was faux chocolate, synonymous with health-conscious hippies. It came from a bulk food store that smelled like stale spices, and it tasted like dirt—with a hint of cumin and coriander, common carob neighbours in the bulk food section.

To this day, my mom hates to cook and baking mystifies her. Still, my childhood memories are punctuated with a steady stream of square chocolate-chip cookies. When I was small, my mom sat me on the kitchen counter while she made them. From my perch, I stared intently at the kitchen floor, lost in the kaleidoscope of orange, brown, and avocado blotches on the linoleum.

One day, I was old enough to unwrap the pre-portioned bricks of margarine from their waxed paper. And when I could see above the counter, we made square cookies together. I remember scraping a spoon across the bottom of the saucepan, the crunch of the sugar, the smell of the margarine. Those cookies may have broken all the rules, but to me, they were perfect.

Sneaky Whole-Wheat Chocolate Chip Cookies

These handsome cookies are crispy on the outside, chewy on the inside, and full of melty chocolate goodness. You'd never guess that they contain whole-wheat flour, which lends a pleasant chewiness and nuttiness without being heavy or dense.

Patience is a virtue, especially where these cookies are involved. First, to avoid scrambled eggs, make sure your butter-sugar mixture has cooled to room temperature before you add the eggs. Second, chill the cookie batter for at least two hours before baking, to give the butter enough time to re-solidify. And if you are saintly enough to wait for the dough to rest overnight, the cookies are even better.

Makes 24 cookies.

½ cup (114g) butter
¾ cup (150g) brown sugar

¼ cup (55g) granulated sugar
¾ cup (95g) all-purpose flour
½ cup (80g) whole-wheat flour
¾ teaspoon (4g or 3mL) baking powder
½ teaspoon (2g or 2mL) baking soda
½ teaspoon (2g or 2mL) salt
1 egg
¾ teaspoon (3g or 3mL) vanilla
3 oz (81g) dark chocolate (70–80% cocoa solids), coarsely
    chopped

In a medium saucepan, heat butter, brown sugar, and sugar over low-medium heat. Stir occasionally until the butter melts. Remove from the heat and set aside for 15 minutes or until it cools to room temperature.

In a medium bowl, combine all-purpose flour, whole-wheat flour, baking powder, baking soda, salt, and chocolate. Set aside.

When the butter-sugar mixture is room temperature, add the egg and vanilla to the saucepan. (CAUTION: If the butter-sugar mixture is still warm, you will cook your eggs.) Using a spatula, stir to incorporate. Add the flour mixture and stir just until there are no flecks of flour remaining. Transfer the batter to a sheet of plastic wrap, wrap tightly, and chill in the refrigerator for at least 2 hours until firm, and preferably overnight.

Preheat the oven to 350°F. Lightly grease two cookie sheets, or line them with parchment.

Break off teaspoon-sized balls of dough and roll them into balls, allowing at least 10cm between nearest neighbours. Flatten each ball to a thickness of 1.5 cm. Bake for 12–14 minutes until golden brown on top. Let the cookies cool for one minute on the cookie sheet, then transfer to a cooling rack.

Note: Refrigerated cookie dough will keep for three days. Alternately, you can bake and cool all the cookies, then freeze the extras.

CHICKEN BRICK

By Henrietta Clancy

From *Fire & Knives*

∞

South Londoner Henrietta Clancy writes on food, drink, and
travel for various publications such as *Imbibe*, *Square Meal*,
Fresh Escapes and DrinkBritain.com. A sometime beekeeper
and hard cider fanatic, she trained at the Ballymaloe Cookery
School in Ireland.

Before Dad married Mum, he lived in what he now refers
to as his "bachelor pad" in Ealing; a place that I've
painted a vague picture of from the small snippets I've gathered
about his premarital existence. In the living room there was a
moleskin sofa and a dark wooden bowl of walnuts with a nut-
cracker; in the bedroom he'd done a bit of late 70s man cave decoration and fashioned himself a waist-high mustard-brown border.
This last piece of info is a fact that's often volunteered by my
mother—I gather she was quite impressed at the time, what with
being 20 and still living in the parental home in Enfield, amid fake
flowers and floral carpets.

In the kitchen, among some obligatory kitchen paraphernalia of
the era—most of it orange, brown or cream—there was a chicken
brick, not hidden behind the doors of a Formica cabinet, but
proudly sitting on a Formica surface. This chicken brick got so
much use that storing it in a cupboard out of arm's length would
have been plain silly; however, that's not why it was on the surface.

No, it lived perpetually beside the oven because it was always cooling down having perfectly cooked one tender chicken—presumably a hormone-munching monster of a thing, because being kind to edible livelihood hadn't been invented yet—and awaiting the raw carcass of the next one. That's how much use it got: it literally never stopped. He fed moist chicken to the masses, and they were all impressed. The more he used it the better it, and consequently he, became. As that layer of chicken fat coating the brown clay interior of the brick developed and mollified, so he, by doing nothing more than staying faithful to his brick, became a better cook. Armed with the brick, there was nothing my father couldn't do.

That was until my mother moved in, and everything changed. She was a graduate of Leith's School of Food and Wine, and a maker of directors' lunches. Naturally she brought her tools with her. I can see her now, whirling around the kitchen brandishing a piping bag—she had at least seven different nozzles—whipping up all manner of decorative toppings for pâtés and pavlovas. Anyone could use a brick, you see—she had qualifications. Prue was lapping up the ways of her contemporaries and showing my mother the ways of the International Kitchen; there was duck *à l'orange, bœuf bourguignon*, steak *au poivre*. When they ate chicken it was in goujons, or as Kiev; perhaps the occasional *coq au vin*.

No doubt there were some roast chickens in there too, but by that point, Dad had handed over the reins, relinquished his kitchen power. Roast chicken was cooked the way mum wanted it—on a tray, basted with lard, cavity filled with mushroom stuffing, sitting on the shelf above some courgettes, also stuffed. The chicken was separate from the veg, not inappropriately nuzzling them, and most importantly it was exposed to the crispifying roof of the oven.

The brick lay dormant for many years, in the back of a never-used utility room cupboard, sharing space with Tupperware lids who'd lost their better halves and things that looked like they might belong to a piece of kitchen equipment, but in reality didn't. Not that I ever saw it, nor seemingly ever did my father, but one post-millennial day its absence was noticed.

I was but a fresh-faced fresher at the time, not long flown the nest, when I missed a phone call from my father, and beheld a voicemail that contained a roaring accusation: "You have stolen my chicken brick!"

I listened to it several times. Breathless, outraged, desperate and confused, he was indeed talking about a chicken brick.

I had done no such thing, of course; the brick was, to me, a mythical piece of kitchenware that was only referenced once every three years when, on the rare occasion that the subject of my father's cooking skills came up, it was put forward as evidence. I had never clapped eyes on the thing.

I'm the eldest of five children and the pattern repeated itself: child left home, child received out-of-the-blue chicken brick accusation, Mum located brick in never-used cupboard, cupboard door was closed again.

The situation became farcical, but it did give me time to consider dad's perplexing relationship with the chicken brick. My mother's prowess in the kitchen had rendered the brick comatose, yes, but where did the brick burglary accusations stem from? I began to brew theories. Was this a flirting tool—something he could fall back on if he was left alone? Was it sitting in our cupboard to keep Mum on her toes, silently reminding her that it had seduced many a fine lady before she came along, and if she misbehaved it was quite capable of doing it again? Or was it simpler than that: the brick represented independence for him, so maybe he assumed that in order to properly grasp ours, we'd need a tool?

Or was it more of a practical thing: maybe on a subconscious level he assumed that, without our mummy around to fill our belly, we would need a brick to take care of us. He viewed it as the provider, the caretaker, the other.

I theorized, but perhaps I overtheorized. Essentially he could have bought us all brand new bricks as "off to uni" presents. No, it was this specific brick to which he had a personal attachment.

I paid an unannounced midweek visit to my parents' house not too long ago. I had hopes of being fed, but there was no car in the drive when I arrived and only a single kitchen light on. As I put my key in the door I half expected an alarm to go off, but no, I could hear the hubbub of sports noise coming from the TV room and the sound—comforting and infuriating in equal measure—of a happy dog's tail slapping kitchen cabinets.

In the kitchen, dinner had been started, just—there was a whole chicken still hugged by plastic wrap, an unnecessarily large and perpetually blunt Sabatier, and a mess of onion and carrot—but the cook was missing. And there it was, the brick, sat on the central unit. I don't think I'd ever actually seen it before, and it looked smaller, less able than the legacy that rested upon its shoulders. Almost like a sleeping woodlouse. I stopped suddenly: no car, no mum, a forlorn brick. . . .

Oh right, I thought, she's left him, and he's coping with it just how he always knew he would; he's following his well-made plan and he's dealing with it. Just as I began to seriously envision the painful and uncomfortable chicken dinner I was going to have to chew my way through, staring at a man who'd sadly and swiftly replaced the woman he'd loved for 36 years with a piece of insect-like terracotta, my apron-clad mother trotted in—she never walks—and amidst her salutations resumed chopping.

"So you're actually using the chicken brick?" I said, unable to mask my intrigue.

She looked confused.

"The brick," I said.

Nothing.

"The chicken brick!" I wailed, pointing.

"This!" I slapped my hand on its lid.

She registered it, and promptly reeled with the sheer absurdity of the idea. "NO! No, no, no, no, no. . . . No, I'm doing this new recipe from my, you know that book you bought me with all of the nice, different recipes in it, I've used it loads . . . the one with the caramelized garlic and goa. . . ."

"Ottolenghi."

"That's it. It's a roast chicken dish from there. It's with honey, saffron and hazelnuts. . . . I just really fancied it. So, anyway, let me tell you, I was teaching that lovely little boy today. . . ."

"Hold on, back to the brick—why is it out?"

"Erm. . . . Daddy was looking for it so I just left it out for him. What was I saying before?"

Of course, how silly of me. My youngest brother had recently left for university and the coming-of-age accusation had been hot on his heels.

Televised match over, dad sailed in and registered me *en route* to a wine bottle, poured three glasses and handed them out, then started searching for a music video on YouTube (a fairly recent and incredibly odd phase my parents have found themselves in, eating dinner to a backdrop of pop ballads), settled for Adele and spotted the brick.

"Ah, great, you found it."

The time had come to ask him the question that had been perplexing me and my siblings for over a decade.

"Dad, why is it that you always think we're after your chicken brick?"

He smiled, wiggled his eyebrows up and down on his face for a while, picked up the brick and did a little Irish jig or sorts (cue some silly laughter from mum) and just before placing it back in the cupboard—presumably forevermore, the nest is now empty— he said, "It doesn't matter. It's mine."

ANGRY BREAKFAST EGGS

By Elissa Altman

From PoorMansFeast.com

Award-winning blogger Elissa Altman does a lot of things well: She's a humorist, political commentator, cookbook editor, and food columnist whose work has appeared everywhere from the Huffington Post to GiltTaste to *Saveur*. Her book *Poor Man's Feast: A Love Story* will appear in 2013.

She has never slept, for as long as I can remember.

First, there was the hair, which, when I was very small, was very tall; these were the days of teasing, and to keep her updo in place, she climbed into bed every night next to my father with three feet of toilet paper wrapped around her head, a six inch tail of Charmin hanging off the pillow, blowing in the air-conditioned breeze like a Coppertone banner dragged behind a beach plane. She lay there stiffly all night, immobile and exhausted, and sat up the next morning, her hair perfect.

Eventually, it was just plain pique that kept her awake—the constant working of herself into a lather over imaginary transgressions, while my father and I and the world around her, ever the transgressors, slept soundly. When the black and white numbers on her bedside clock flipped over to 6:30 a.m. and the alarm went off, she swung her legs off the side of the bed and stood up, already furious and seething.

And then she made eggs.

A lot of eggs.

At first, when things were still good and happy, they were soft boiled, and sat in the broad end of our porcelain egg cups, their tips sliced away so that my father and I—perched side by side at the breakfast counter half an hour before he dropped me off at the school bus stop on his way to the subway—could dunk untoasted fingers of Pepperidge Farm Diet White into the runny yolk. As my parents' marriage wore on and she grew angrier, the eggs were medium boiled, their firm yolks like thick golden velvet, with spots of remaining tenderness just barely discernible.

When I turned fourteen, my mother began hard boiling our eggs; she'd put them in a small pot filled with a shallow inch or two of water, set them on the stove, crank up the flame, and walk away. Eventually, they'd explode, their snow white glair erupting like Vesuvius through the fissures of her discontent. I'd refuse to eat them at that point, and when she came back into the kitchen, she'd grab the black plastic handle of the pot and dump its contents—the water had long since evaporated—directly into the trash.

My parents divorced the following year.

My mother still doesn't sleep, and she still cooks eggs every single morning, even with cholesterol that hovers near the 400s if she's forgotten her to take her Lipitor. She's been through a passel of saucepans—the brown and white Dansk pan that followed her into the city after her divorce, and that she burned until its white enameled interior melted away into a noxious cloud; two Revere-Ware pans that we brought to her apartment from our basement stash—they'd belonged to Susan's mother who had them for fifty years. My mother burned them until their insides turned black as coal. Now she uses a tiny butter warmer, big enough to hold exactly one jumbo egg.

Eggs are my mother's mood barometer: when she's happy, she'll deftly separate yolk from albumen, throw out the former, dump the whites into the one tiny stick-proof pan she owns, and while they bubble and spread, she'll lay a piece of Diet White bread right down in the middle of it, and top it off with a dollop of honey. This, she says, is her version of French toast, and she loves it. If Susan and I are staying there and she's feeling glad, she'll insist on scrambling some whites for us because, she says, they're low fat and good diet food, and together we'll sit at her dining room table, having breakfast, while the traffic rumbles down West End Avenue twenty-one stories below. Not overcooked and not runny, the eggs bear no evidence of seasoning; it's just them and us, a piece of bread, and my mother's favorite morning cup of hot water. If we're staying there and she's furious, she'll boil the eggs until a sulfuric haze wafts out into the living room; we'll leave while the pan is still rattling over the flame.

"I *had to throw them OUT*," she'll tell me later.

The correlation between cooking and scorn is a fraught, famous one; food created by angry people seems, somehow, to be bitter, and so attuned to their off flavors and textures am I because of my mother's eggs that once, when a conversation with a well-known cookbook author took a sudden and surprising turn south, I had to get rid of her book, because every one of the dishes I cooked from it after our argument tasted of her rage; no matter what I did, none of the recipes worked anymore. Food cooked in anger becomes collateral damage; meat is carbonized, pasta becomes starchy mush, vegetables go limp and sad, and it's not like you can—or even want to—revive them, to coddle or comfort them, or to save them for another meal. You simply can't do it. If the optimum way to cook and live and run a kitchen is, as Tamar Adler says, with economy and grace—use everything, every shard and peeling and drop of fat with care, kindness, and thoughtfulness—scornful cooking results in the opposite: profligate waste and clumsy distraction.

It was six in the morning last Sunday; I lay in bed, listening to the ticking of the ignition on my Viking's pilot light. There was the sound of running water, the clank of a pan on a burner. When my mother came to visit us last weekend and awoke in the throes of pre-dawn Bad Mood, she rifled through our refrigerator, pulled out four eggs, set them in shallow water, turned the burner on high, and cooked them until they burst with fury.

"I couldn't sleep," she barked from the guest bed where she'd laid back down after preparing the breakfast she decided I needed to eat, "so I made you eggs. THIS is what you should be eating for breakfast—not the *heel of a baguette* and a piece of cheese."

She had been watching me *that* closely the previous morning; to my mother, a piece of bread—no matter how small—spells o-b-e-s-i-t-y. She was in a rage.

"But I don't have any eggs," I answered, suddenly remembering the half-crate of six local duck eggs that were hovering in the back of the fridge, waiting for a recipe test.

"They're in the SINK—" she shouted from the guest room.

I walked into the kitchen and there they were, in a now-dry All-Clad saucepan, the shells cracked and broken, their whites extruding like Elizabethan collars. Susan broke one into a cup to see if the yolk was hard-cooked, and somehow salvageable; it was raw and cold. The eggs had been sitting out at room temperature for over two hours.

My mother marched into the kitchen behind me and watched Susan put on the tea kettle; I stepped on the pedal of the trashcan and tossed each duck egg out, one by one, like small grenades.

Sweet Southern Dreams

By Ben Mims

From *Saveur*

❦

It's been a long journey from Koskiusko, Mississippi, to his current home in New York City for associate food editor Ben Mims, along a sweets-paved road passing through the French Culinary Institute, the Saveur test kitchen, and an Ice Cream Takedown victory in Brooklyn.

Prior to October 7, 2010, my mother and I were the best of friends. A consummate Southern lady, Judy Mims is a fantastic cook, gossiper, and mom—and in her relationship with me she had always drawn on all those talents. But on that October day, I flew from New York City to my childhood home in Kosciusko, Mississippi, to come out, at 25 years old, as a gay man to my parents. As anyone who grew up in the Bible Belt can imagine, the outcome was heartbreaking. My mother and I used to talk at least weekly; now months go by without a call. I miss her. And I can't help feeling like I've lost touch with not only my mother, but also my lifeline to the world I grew up in. Thank goodness I still have the cakes.

Layer cakes originated in the South, and with their over-the-top grandeur and unapologetic sweetness, they're inextricably linked to the culture I grew up in. The drama, excitement, and praise—they all speak to the South.

My childhood in rural Mississippi was filled with fantastic bakers: my mother, of course; her sister, Barbara Jane; my paternal grandmother, Carol; and Mom's friends, those church ladies decked out in hats who produced a never-ending procession of astounding cakes. My grandmother's neighbor Louise Hodges made a cake three yellow layers tall, draped in warm caramel fudge icing, which exuded a fragrance of vanilla and browned butter that could knock you over. Carol, who bought those cakes from Mrs. Hodges, served one to our family virtually every Sunday after church. We would sometimes have two slices each, and when I'd tease my grandmother, asking her who made the cake, she would primp her curly blonde hair, give me a wink, and reply, "Why, who do you think?"

My mother, for her part, turned out mammoth sour cream Bundt cakes, domed lemon and cream cheese pound cakes, and a ludicrously rich cheesecake that was my staple birthday cake. I spent my childhood at her elbow, watching her pour glaze down the grooved sides of a Bundt cake, mirroring her smile as she passed me a beater with batter barely clinging to it. Unlike Mrs. Hodges, Mom was never big on making layer cakes. Maybe she didn't have the patience to stack and frost all those layers, though she liked them just fine as an effortless treat baked by someone else. The only layer cake in her repertoire was red velvet, for just as most Southern women have a subscription to *Southern Living* magazine and at least one gilded holiday wreath in their attic, most also have a red velvet cake up their sleeve. The deep crimson cake against the luminous white frosting is pure Southern drama. It's Shirley MacLaine in *Steel Magnolias* hacking into the blood-colored tail of an armadillo-shaped groom's cake. It's my mother's ceramic white skin contrasted by her lips, always burnished with brick-red lipstick.

My mother stacked her red velvet only two layers deep and almost always made it with cream cheese frosting. One Christmas during my teen years, though, she got adventurous with a whipped cream frosting consisting of cooked flour, sugar, and milk beaten into butter. When executed correctly, a frosting like this holds up like a dream and provides just the right balance—not too sweet or rich—for the slightly acidic, chocolate-flavored red velvet layers. She labored over that cake all day, and we carried it in our car two hours away to my grandfather's house in Holly Springs. After dinner, once the coffee was perking, the cake dome was lifted, and my mom sliced into the scarlet layers and snow-white frosting. Everyone took bites, and then spit them out. The frosting was as chalky and tacky as wallpaper paste; my mom was nearly in tears.

She never tried her hand at it again, but that whipped cream icing had a profound effect on me. Motivated by my mother's failure, I made it my mission to learn how to make the cake she had envisioned. Schooled at her apron strings, I was already an avid baker, and nailing that recipe helped direct my life's path. In my current job, I'm able to hone my skills every day to produce the platonic ideals of the cakes my mother raised me to love.

Some of my best recipes were passed down from my mother's own mother, Jane Newson, who died the year before my birth. The very morning following the red velvet cake disaster, my mother sat with Barbara Jane and me on my grandfather's living room floor and sorted through hundreds of her mother's recipe cards. By all accounts, Jane was a fantastic maker of layer cakes: prune and fig in a cinnamon meringue; Lane cake filled with boozy nut and raisin custard; walnut spice laden with cinnamon, allspice, and cloves. It was the coconut cake recipe, though, that the sisters agreed was the one to save if ever the house caught on fire. The first time I tried the recipe, it exceeded all my expectations. The cake was filled with freshly grated coconut, the sweet water seeping into the yellow layers surrounded by fluffy Italian meringue. Left for a day to "mature" in the refrigerator, every inch of it was suffused with rich coconut flavor.

Still, of all the Southern layer cakes I have known, the one that sticks with me the most these days is lemon. It goes back to the summer before my senior year of college, when I moved to Vicksburg, home of the Miss Mississippi Pageant, to work as a reporter for *The Vicksburg Post*. Toward the end of my stay, just before the beauty queen pomp began, my mom came to visit, and we took a walk along the riverfront. When we ducked into a little café for coffee, we noticed a case full of beautiful layer cakes. We ordered a pastel-yellow slice of lemon cake to share. It was a stunner: four layers of citrusy butter cake drenched in lemon syrup and enrobed in a lemon buttercream frosting. We sat and chatted, and every bite of cake tingled our cheeks with delicious tartness. Now, whenever

I get nostalgic for the South, I break out my cake pans, butter, and sugar, and whip up a lemon cake like the one we shared; it buoys my hope for a future in which my mother and I are as close as we once were. The result—bittersweet and beautiful—reminds me of that afternoon, four years before our lives changed, when we sat together in that café without a care in the world and just talked about cake.

Coconut Cake

Serves 10–12

For the Cake:
16 tbsp. unsalted butter, softened, plus more for pans
2 ½ cups cake flour, plus more for pans, sifted
1 tsp. baking soda
1 tsp. kosher salt
1 cup buttermilk
1 tbsp. vanilla extract
2 cups sugar
5 eggs

For the Frosting:
4 egg whites
½ tsp. cream of tartar
2 ¼ cups sugar
¼ cup light corn syrup
1 tsp. kosher salt
2 tsp. vanilla extract
¾ cup fresh coconut water
3 cups freshly grated coconut

Instructions
1. Make the cake: Heat oven to 350°. Butter and flour two 9" cake pans, and set aside. Whisk together flour, baking soda, and salt in a bowl; set aside. Whisk together buttermilk and vanilla in a bowl; set aside. In the bowl of a stand mixer fitted with a paddle, cream butter and sugar on medium-high speed until pale and fluffy, about 3 minutes. Add eggs one at a

time, beating well after each addition. On low speed, alternately add dry ingredients in 3 batches and wet ingredients in 2 batches. Increase speed to high, and beat until batter is smooth, about 5 seconds. Divide batter between prepared pans, and smooth top with a rubber spatula; drop pans lightly on a counter to expel large air bubbles. Bake cakes until a toothpick inserted in middle comes out clean, about 35 minutes. Let cakes cool for 20 minutes in pans; invert onto wire racks, and let cool. Using a serrated knife, halve each cake horizontally, producing four layers; set aside.

2. Make the frosting: Place egg whites and cream of tartar in the bowl of a stand mixer fitted with a whisk, and beat on medium-high speed until soft peaks form; turn mixer off. Bring sugar, syrup, salt, and 1/2 cup tap water to a boil in a 2-qt. saucepan over high heat, stirring to dissolve sugar; attach a candy thermometer to side of pan, and cook, without stirring, until thermometer reads 250°, 4–5 minutes. Turn mixer to medium speed, and very slowly drizzle hot syrup into beating egg whites. Add vanilla, and increase speed to high; beat until meringue forms stiff peaks and is slightly warm to the touch, about 3 minutes.

3. To assemble, place one layer on a cake stand, drizzle with 3 tbsp. coconut water, spread with 1 1/2 cups frosting, and sprinkle with 1/2 cup grated coconut; top with another cake, drizzle with 3 tbsp. coconut water, spread with 1 1/2 cups frosting, and sprinkle with 1/2 cup coconut. Place another cake over frosting, drizzle with 3 tbsp. coconut water, spread with 1 1/2 cups frosting, and sprinkle with 12 cup coconut; top with remaining cake and drizzle with remaining coconut water. Cover top and sides with remaining frosting, and cover outside of cake with remaining coconut, pressing it lightly to adhere; chill cake to firm frosting. Serve chilled or at room temperature.

Lemon Layer Cake

Serves 10–12

For the Cake and Syrup:

16 tbsp. unsalted butter, softened, plus more for pans

2 ½ cups cake flour, plus more for pans, sifted

2 ½ tsp. baking powder

1 tsp. kosher salt

½ cup milk

1 tsp. vanilla extract

1 ¾ cups sugar

1 tbsp. lemon zest

4 eggs

⅓ cup fresh lemon juice

For the Frosting:

1 ½ cups sugar

¼ cup cornstarch

¼ cup lemon zest

1 tsp. kosher salt

10 egg yolks

1 cup fresh lemon juice

1 ½ cups unsalted butter, softened

1 tsp. vanilla extract

Instructions

1. Make the cake: Heat oven to 350°. Butter and flour two 9" cake pans, and set aside. Whisk together flour, baking powder, and salt in a bowl; set aside. Whisk together milk and vanilla in a bowl; set aside. In the bowl of a stand mixer fitted with a paddle, cream butter, 1 1/2 cups sugar, and zest on medium-high speed until pale and fluffy, about 3 minutes. Add eggs, one at a time, beating well after each addition. On low speed, alternately add dry ingredients in 3 batches and wet ingredients in 2 batches. Increase speed to high and beat until batter is smooth, about 5 seconds. Divide batter between prepared pans, and smooth top with a rubber spatula; drop pans lightly on a counter to expel any large air bubbles. Bake cakes until a toothpick inserted in middle comes out

clean, about 30 minutes. Let cakes cool for 20 minutes in pans; invert onto wire racks, and let cool. Using a serrated knife, halve each cake horizontally to produce four layers; set aside. Bring remaining sugar and juice to a boil in a small saucepan over high heat. Remove from heat, and set syrup aside.

2. Make the frosting: Whisk together sugar, cornstarch, zest, and salt in a 4-qt. saucepan. Add yolks, and whisk until smooth; stir in juice. Stirring often, bring to a boil over medium heat; cook, stirring constantly, until very thick, about 3 minutes. Remove from heat, let cool, and transfer to a bowl; chill the lemon curd. In the bowl of a stand mixer fitted with a paddle, beat butter and ¼ of the curd on medium-high speed until fluffy and smooth, about 1 minute. Add half the remaining curd, beating until smooth, and then add remaining curd and vanilla. Increase speed to high; beat frosting until pale and fluffy, about 3 minutes.

3. To assemble, place one cake layer on a cake stand, drizzle with 2 tbsp. syrup, and spread with ¾ cup frosting; top with another cake, drizzle with 2 tbsp. syrup, and spread with ¾ cup frosting. Place another cake over the frosting, drizzle with 2 tbsp. syrup, and spread with ¾ cup frosting; top with remaining cake, and drizzle with remaining syrup. Cover top and sides with remaining frosting; chill cake to firm frosting. Serve at room temperature.

Someone's in the Kitchen

THE KING OF POP-UP

By Brett Martin

From *GQ*

Brett Martin's profiles, food and travel pieces, and essays appear regularly in *GQ*, as well as *Vanity Fair*, *The New Yorker*, *Bon Appétit*, *Food & Wine*, and public radio's *This American Life*. Connoisseur of the edgy and trendy, here he parses a modern dining scene phenomenon: The pop-up restaurant.

There is, naturally, a truck. Just as surely as there are the tattoos, the facial hair, the coif, the Twitter feed, the reality-TV show, the silent *pop pop pop* of the bloggers' cell-phone cameras. He who has these—all the signs and signifiers that have replaced whisk and toque as emblems of modern chefdom—is 40-year-old Ludovic Lefebvre, a classically trained, preternaturally handsome Burgundian who's become Los Angeles's most talked-about cook. What he doesn't have is a restaurant. Instead, Lefebvre and his wife, partner, and brand manager, Krissy, run a series of wildly popular pop-ups called LudoBites, which occupy, hermit-crab-like, the off-hour shells of other eateries—first in obscure corners of L.A. and, more recently, across the United States for the Sundance Channel's *Ludo Bites America*, debuting July 18. Lefebvre is a kind of walking, talking, preening manifestation of all the blessings and damnations, transcendence and silliness, that mark this moment in American dining.

In any other context, Gram & Papa's, a soup-and-sandwich spot in L.A.'s Garment District, would hardly suggest culinary adven-

ture. Nevertheless, that's where the Lefebvres staged the fifth iteration of LudoBites—LudoBites 5.0—for six weeks last summer. By
day, this area downtown was crowded with shoppers at rows of
fabric stores and zipper distributors; after dark, it was all but
deserted—save, in those weeks, for questing foodies dubiously
checking their GPS units.

The production of high-end food in low-end and otherwise
improbable settings is, of course, part of the pop-up phenomenon.
But that doesn't mean a chef raised in the great kitchens of Paris
won't grumble. On this morning, the Lefebvres arrived with Ludo
in full temperamental-artist mode. The immediate object of his
pique: the state of the walk-in fridge.

"It's like fucking Baghdad in there," he muttered to Mike Ilic,
Gram & Papa's owner.

Behind the register, Ilic raised his eyebrows. He had invited the
Lefebvres to assume weeknight squatter rights in exchange for a
fee, a cut of the profits, and the publicity; it was obviously a suffi-
cient trade-off to make him tolerant of his tenant's moods.

"They cleaned up Baghdad, Ludo," he said. "It's gonna have to
be like Afghanistan."

"Every morning, the same routine," said Krissy, rolling her eyes.
She was sitting at a nearby table, looking over that night's reservation list.

Upstairs, in a tiny storage area, it wasn't difficult to tell which
shelves belonged to Gram & Papa's and which to LudoBites: On
one side, ketchup and La Choy Chinese noodles; on the other,
kombu seaweed, industrial-grade gelatin, star anise. Nearby was a
pile of Lefebvre's niftier gadgets: an immersion circulator, which
looks like the mating of a heating coil and a medical device, and a
Gastrovac, which first cooks ingredients in a vacuum and then
reimpregnates them with flavor the moment the seal is broken.

In the kitchen, Lefebvre's skeleton staff was assembling. One
sous-chef was cutting perfect rectangles of pork belly, uniform and
creamy as frosted sheet cake. Lefebvre runs his kitchen in a manner
in keeping with his French education. That is, he yells. And the
staff is expected to yell back. "I want the kitchen clean before I
start!" he hollered now. "Use your fucking heads!"

"Yes, Chef!" came the chorus.

Lefebvre's eye fell on a young cook named Joon Sung.

"Joon!"

"Yes, Chef!"

"Do we have dashi made?"

"No, Chef!"

Lefebvre made a face that suggested it might be easier simply to end it all via Gastrovac right there. The dashi broth, infused with kombu, was for a dish he had woken up intent on adding to that night's menu. It would act as a poaching liquid for oysters that would then be served with a froth of butter infused with the briny taste of their own smashed shells. All this he patiently explained to Sung.

"You understand, Joon?"

"Yes, Chef!" Sung thought it over for a moment.

"Chef!"

"What, Joon?"

"The oysters. They'll be poached *à la minute*?"—meaning "to order."

"Of course!" said Lefebvre. "Or else it's no fun!"

He came out front, where Krissy was still at work, and wiped his forehead with a kitchen towel.

"This is my last LudoBites," said Ludo.

"Nice try," said Krissy.

They are a pretty couple, in an easily alliterative way: he Gallically goateed, she classically Californian (or blonde and buxom, if you prefer). With his pierced ears and arms covered in ink, Ludo could be an instructional diagram for the Metrosexual Pirate look that has dominated kitchens for the past decade. Both Lefebvres are camera-ready, and even before the Sundance show, both did time on reality TV: Ludo as a contestant, and designated villain, on *Top Chef Masters*, Krissy on a season of *The Apprentice*. (She subsequently posed for a *Playboy* cover.) They met, in an oft-told story, when Krissy, at the time an intellectual-property attorney, was dining at L'Orangerie, the late old-guard French restaurant that was Ludo's first stop in Los Angeles; she thought the amuse-bouche was a flirtatious gift just for her. In addition to running the front of the house, she anticipates his moods, minds his malapropisms ("I cook through instant." "Instinct, honey"), and acts as adoring PR agent. That the adoration is obviously genuine and reciprocated isn't inconsistent with a parallel impression she gives: that of a business-savvy cat with a particularly telegenic bird in its teeth.

Not that star looks are necessarily good for a man's culinary cred—just as a *Playboy* spread doesn't result in instant respect for one's litigation skills. This is especially true in Los Angeles, where the local eatocracy has an uneasy relationship with the rules of celebrity that dominate the rest of town. Woe to the big-name chef who arrives from somewhere else and is perceived to worship at the altar of Scene over that of Food. Take San Francisco's Michael Mina, whose L.A. outpost, XIV, a barn on the Sunset Strip, might as well be Olive Garden for all its reputation among local foodies. Likewise, Rick Bayless's Red O, which has been pummeled with unequaled ferocity since opening last year. Bayless's crime, in part, was daring to offer "authentic" Mexican food to a town that thinks it pretty well knows its Mexican. But one got the feeling that the bigger sin was the fedora-wearing valets.

Angelenos are, of course, susceptible to the status-seeking inanity that infects eaters everywhere. But the logic of the moment demands that their culinary heroes—Jon Shook and Vinny Dotolo of Animal and Son of a Gun; Sang Yoon of Father's Office and Lukshon—be immune to the usual course of Hollywood power, that they be in some sense of the People.

Lefebvre walks this line closely. A crucial element of LudoBites is its reservations system—a characteristically savvy confluence of idealism and show business. There is no phone number, just a Web site that opens at a random hour posted on Twitter. When Ludo-Bites 5.0 was announced, 3,000 hopeful diners crashed the page within six minutes.

There have been missteps on the path to fame and credibility. The most egregious is Lefebvre's cookbook, *Crave: The Feast of the Five Senses*, published by Judith Regan in 2005. On the cover, Ludo stares intensely into the camera, holding forth a split pomegranate and a spoon. He looks like nothing so much as Chris Gaines, Garth Brooks's short-lived Goth alter ego. Most infamously, there is the

Fish Photo, in which a bare-chested Lefebvre, dressed in tight jeans, stands shin-deep in the surf, a large, glittering striped bass in each hand.

Among other things, the image presented logical problems: Were we to believe he'd *caught* the fish with his bare hands? If so: Both simultaneously? Or was he so used to catching fish in this manner that it was hardly worth heading in with just one? If not: Had he brought the fish with him? Or had he found them floating there already dead?—a notion that detracts substantially from the overall sexiness of the picture.

More to the point: It made him look like a world-class douche.

Both Lefebvres now express appropriate embarrassment at the Fish Photo. Krissy recalls that it could have been worse; Regan, she says, had already demanded three new photo shoots, each "sexier" than the last.

"She wanted him to be rolling around in the sand with the fish," Krissy says.

These are the kinds of semiotic negotiations that have become de rigueur in the era of the celebrity chef. It helps that Ludo's path has taken him to both extremes. He arrived in L.A. in 1996 as starstruck as any would-be actor getting off the bus. "I had never tasted sushi! I discovered jalapeños! Green tea! It was crazy," he says. Paradoxically, he had a more difficult time exploring such wonders at conservative L'Orangerie than he would have back in Paris, where he had worked under acclaimed and innovative chefs including Alain Passard and Pierre Gagnaire. "I was a very typical French chef. No tattoos. Short hair. Perfect for the army," he says.

That changed when Joe Pytka, the mercurial commercial director and impresario, decided to fire the beloved chef at his restaurant Bastide and installed Lefebvre in his place. Up went the sleeves, revealing a chiaroscuro of Hawaiian girls, dragons, and Sanskrit he had secretly accumulated, and out came the liquid nitrogen, gelatins, and other accoutrements of molecular gastronomy. Some critics were smitten by dishes like chicken crusted with popcorn and foie gras piña colada, others less so—*L.A. Times* restaurant critic S. Irene Virbila wrote, "I feel as if I've been mugged," and busted Bastide down from four stars to one. (She now says that two stars may have been more appropriate, but stands by the rest of the review: "He was trying interesting things, but it just wasn't very good.")

"She was so mean," Ludo says, clearly still angry. "I decided I won't cook for critics anymore."

That decision was one half of the epiphany that led to Ludo-Bites; the other—not to cook for investors, either—came soon after. That's when Lefebvre was lured to Las Vegas to open a 300-seat restaurant at the Palazzo casino. Named Lavo, it came with a "Mediterranean" menu (which, oddly, included a Reuben-stuffed knish "slider") already set in stone; Lefebvre wasn't even allowed to add nightly specials.

"'Money,'" he says sadly, when asked what the investors could possibly have said to lure him into such a creative disaster. "They said, 'Money.' I used to go home at night and cry."

So what's a tortured-artist chef to do? Why, throw off the yoke of the restaurant altogether! LudoBites 1.0 and 2.0 took place in 2007 and 2009 at BreadBar, a bakery on the border of Beverly Hills, and were immediate sensations. Iteration 3.0 was staged at a cavernous Culver City gallery-café called Royal/T. Krissy set up a professional light box at one end of the room, the better for the stream of bloggers to photograph each dish. "If they were taking pictures anyway, why not make them as beautiful as possible?" she says.

Next came the LudoTruck, a thirty-foot-long beauty wrapped in lurid red, decorated with roosters and called the Big Red Coq. In keeping with the lowbrow obsession of the moment, it serves fried chicken—albeit fried chicken whose recipe begins, "Day One." (There are three in all.) When the LudoTruck debuted at the L.A. Street Food Fest, a three-hour line developed, surprising even the Lefebvres. "There's nothing three-hours-and-$5 good," Krissy says.

Since, the couple set up shop for six weeks in an Italian restaurant in Sherman Oaks, and LudoBites 7.0 is expected to happen this summer. The Lefebvres spent the intervening time filming *Ludo Bites America*, for which Ludo took on barbecue in North Carolina, chilies in Santa Fe, and, quite literally, buffalo outside Denver: Krissy tweeted a photo of the chef sinking his teeth into a freshly killed bison's heart.

The pop-up life has its drawbacks. Lefebvre never gets to work in a kitchen he's designed for his own needs. He has trouble keeping quality staff at either the front or the back of the house. He can't build lasting relationships with butchers, fishmongers, and the like.

In return? No permit issues. No dishwasher and refrigerator maintenance. No electric bills, oil-disposal problems, breakage costs, laundry bills, venting-regulation compliance—all the bullshit that comes along with running a permanent restaurant. And of course, there's the freedom to cook whatever his heart desires, to treat each night as a piece of harrowing theater, a magnificent fire that only he can extinguish.

"J o o n !"

"Yes, Chef!"

"The dashi!"

"Done, Chef!"

With service approaching, the kitchen was in full swing. An intern scooped whole steaming octopi from a bubbling pot. Another was monitoring the circulator; the eggs inside would be used in one of the evening's less obviously pyrotechnic but most sublime offerings— a dish of feathery-smooth potato mousseline capping, shepherd's-pie style, the barely poached egg and a warm bed of chorizo. As with most of Lefebvre's food these days, it made use of technology and imagination without seeming to do so for its own sake. The stuntiest item on the LudoBites 5.0 menu—a cheese "cupcake" frosted with chicken-liver mousse—was also the least successful.

"It's a miracle what we do every day, working in these conditions. You see that?" he said, pointing to the beat-up four burner stove. "That's magical."

It *is* magical. It could also, one worries, become a dodge—a perpetual deflection of the question of what someone with this much talent might do with the kitchen and staff of his dreams. Krissy says as much, remembering the thinking that went into LudoBites 1.0: "Just using 'Bites' diminished expectations. It could never be a failure, because it had a beginning and an end."

Jonathan Gold, the Pulitzer-winning dean of L.A. food writing and one of Lefebvre's earliest and most consistent champions, likens LudoBites to a series of first records, with all the excitement, energy, and rough edges first records entail . Eventually, though, you want your favorite band to risk it all with a double-length theme album.

Put another way, the question is this: Is it possible to be a great chef without a great restaurant? The kind of place, as Animal's Jon Shook memorably puts it, where "you go back after it's been open ten years and it's still fuck-your-mouth good"? The question matters, because at the very heart of celebrity chefdom there lies a problem that may prove irreconcilably hostile to the future of the restaurant: the boredom of chefs.

Remember that the stars of the dining world used to be in the front of the house. They were the great maitre d's, wizards of the seating plan, social impresarios who got their names above the door. That made sense, since every night in the dining room was like a freewheeling improvisational concert, complete with an ever shifting lineup and the ever present potential for disaster. The kitchen was more of a stellar rhythm section: steady, reliable, above all consistent.

Nowadays, chefs have completed the radical shift from anonymous laborers to celebrated artists. For some, that's meant leaving the kitchen altogether, traveling the world, expanding their brands. But for those who can't give up the particular adrenaline rush of being behind the stove, there's no getting around the fact that the essence of the job—turning out the same dish over and over again, night after night—is deeply, profoundly dull. And that means we may soon be living in a pop-up world.

At Gram & Papa's, it was almost curtain time. French rap played over the sound system as Krissy's team of young waitresses set tables. Taking his position in the open kitchen, Lefebvre carefully laid out his tools: a silver quenelle spoon, a tiny grater with bamboo brush, a Sharpie. At the head of this little shrine, he lit a Mexican prayer candle.

The doors opened, and the first seating poured in. At one table, each of five diners held cameras or camera phones. One customer presented Lefebvre with a bundle of locally picked Spanish garlic. "Tomorrow we have garlic soup," the chef announced. "With escargots."

Orders came in. Dishes flowed out: a cheese "cupcake" frosted with chicken liver and foie gras; a feathery-smooth potato mousseline capping, shepherd's-pie style, a barely poached egg and a warm bed of chorizo; a version of a classic French *frisée aux lardons* reimagined as a tower of greens teetering in a bowl of smooth, rich goat-cheese soup. (When I tried the dish at dinner with Gold, I nervously approached it with knife and fork. "It's hard to cut soup," the critic deadpanned.) All but the oyster dish, which nobody had yet plated or tasted—leaving no assurance that Lefebvre's morning inspiration would even work.

One by one, the tickets for oysters piled up. Lefebvre hovered over the simmering dashi, watching as a test run poached. Krissy looked on in a state of bemused panic. Finally, Lefebvre lifted two of the oysters from the water and pried them open, revealing the pair of perfectly swollen iridescent bubbles within. He swiveled toward the counter where Joon Sung was supposed to be assembling the dishes.

"Joon!"

"Yes, Chef!"

"Why haven't you fucking prepped for the oysters?"

Something in Sung snapped: "Because I don't know what the fuck I'm supposed to do, Chef!"

The kitchen came to a halt. The chef spun slowly in his clogs. Sung waited, blinking. Then Lefebvre grinned, clapped his cook on the shoulder, and screamed right back:

"Well, neither do I!"

HOT PLATE

By Rachel Hutton

From *Minnesota Monthly*

⟨⟨⟩

One index of a regional restaurant culture's vitality is the
number of talented food writers it supports. Among the leading lights of the Twin Cities' lively dining scene is Rachel Hutton, formerly of *CityPages* and newly named food editor of
Minnesota Monthly.

7:00 a.m.

It's going to be another big night at The Bachelor Farmer and
Marvel Bar.

The cooler is stocked. The reservation book is full. And the
overnight cleaning crew just eradicated the last trace of yesterday's
service. On this chilly morning, 50 North Second Avenue looks
much as it must have a century ago, when the brick-and-timber
warehouse was new to Minneapolis's North Loop. The streets are
deserted and the sky is dark except for the florescent lights streaming from the building's kitchen—a beacon for the hottest thing
going in the neighborhood.

The former Northwestern Hide and Fur Building wasn't at-
tracting much attention until Eric Dayton, son of Minnesota Governor Mark Dayton, purchased it in 2008. Its most recent occupant
was an industrial wire-cutting business called Marvel Rack, so architect James Dayton (yes, he's a relative) faced no small task in
converting the space into a modern restaurant, bar, and retail shop,
while preserving its historic character.

When Eric and his brother, Andrew, conceived of their contemporary Scandinavian restaurant and subterranean speakeasy, they imagined an intimate neighborhood hangout. But as soon as the kitchen served its first plate of Swedish meatballs, patrons flocked from near and far, packing the place night after night. How were a couple of hospitality greenhorns able to pull off such a feat?

The Bachelor Farmer's baker and pastry chef are the first to arrive, as always. Their first stop: the storage room. The restaurant makes almost everything from scratch using premium ingredients—even growing some produce on the building's roof, which is buried in snow. The pastry chef bypasses a tub labeled "Top Secret Pickle Project" and half a hog carcass to collect dozens of Larry Schultz eggs, pounds of Hope butter, and gallons of Organic Valley cream. She has less than six hours to create a dessert that will earn a spot on tonight's menu.

Back up in the kitchen, the two feed bread starter, melt chocolate, heat milk for fresh cheese, and roll dough into long sheets of flatbread. It's too early for conversation, so they work in near silence, save for the hum of the ovens, vents, and refrigeration units.

8:58 a.m.

Chef Paul Berglund enters looking rather like a lanky graduate student with his narrow glasses and day's worth of beard growth. Rather than rely on Eric's experience with line cooking at Goodfellows restaurant back in high school, the Dayton brothers called upon Paul, an alumnus of Oliveto, a highly respected restaurant in Oakland, California, to lead The Bachelor Farmer's kitchen. Paul starts his day with a clipboard in hand, reading through the to-do list: ducks, lentil base, paté; render pork fat. His first task is to fillet last night's shipment of rockfish—beautiful specimens, with red-and-white skins, clear eyes, and resilient flesh.

9:35 a.m.

Eric and Andrew arrive. Although they're both already clutching Dunn Brothers cups, Andrew starts the coffee maker. Their preppy outfits look as if they might have come from the same closet. The brothers' similar taste in clothes has become something of a running joke. If they accidentally dress alike, Andrew says, "We do rock-paper-scissors to see who has to go home and change."

As if the brothers didn't have enough to do between overseeing the bar and restaurant, they followed in their forefathers' retail footsteps and opened a men's shop in the building's storefront. It's called Askov Finlayson, a name that should sound familiar to anyone who's driven I-35 between the Twin Cities and Duluth and paid attention to the exit signs.

The restaurant and the store often share clients: fans of farm-to-table cuisine seem to appreciate the classic clothing and accessories. One night, the Daytons sold two handcrafted leather iPad cases when a Bachelor Farmer guest showed the one she'd just purchased to her dining companion, who promptly went down and did the same.

While they wait for customers, Eric and Andrew meet with the retail manager to plan their itinerary for the menswear shows in New York and time an order of British umbrellas. The shop is minimally furnished with leather chairs and an area rug pulled from Andrew's emptying apartment. Eric, too, has sacrificed home décor for the business, having lent the restaurant several of his photographs by local-boy-made-good Alec Soth. "My apartment looks like it's been robbed," Eric explains. "There are bare hooks where art used to be." The brothers spend far more time at work than home these days, so at least here they can enjoy their possessions.

Askov Finlayson's merchandise tends toward timeless pieces: dress shirts, slacks, Danish wool sweaters, sailcloth duffel bags. The common denominator, Andrew explains, is quality, partial justification for the $125 price tag on the store's most casual item: sweatpants with their brand name, "Warriors of Radness," spelled out down the leg in rainbow-colored cursive script.

11:14 a.m.

In the office upstairs, the general manager sits at his computer and scans the evening's reservation list, which already shows 150 diners on the books. He's going to need every last table in the dining room, including the corner booth that went out of commission last night due to an icy draft, so he heads downstairs armed with a caulk gun.

At Andrew's computer, the brothers update the Marvel Bar's Facebook page. Today's post describes a new drink called the Strong-water, which the Marvel Bar's head bartender, Pip Hanson, recently invented. Bourbon, cognac, thyme liqueur, and lemon zest are mixed together and then highly diluted. It's a surprisingly pleasurable technique: the water smooths out any harshness and highlights the spirits' subtleties. Pip developed a reputation for precise, innovative bartending at his previous position at Café Maude, where the brothers recruited him after he poured the best Manhattans they'd ever sipped.

Naïveté more than confidence may have spurred the Daytons to tackle their ambitious project, but what the brothers lack in entrepreneurial experience, they seem to make up for in diligent management. (Presumably they have picked up a few tips from their father's overseeing of the entire state of Minnesota.)

The brothers plan to add brunch service to the restaurant as well as private events, but they have prioritized fine-tuning their current operation versus expanding—don't expect to see The Bachelor Farmer franchises out in Bloomington and Maple Grove. Building wealth would seem less of a motivator to the Daytons than creating a restaurant experience that proud locals show off to out-of-towners. Considering the Dayton family's legacy in retail and political leadership, thinking small would be uncharacteristic. And who better to understand the collective consciousness of Minnesotans than the Daytons? They practically invented our aspirations of what it means to be one.

1:02 p.m.

The kitchen staff gathers in the dining room for their daily meeting. Paul instructs one of his cooks on how to prepare an appetizer made with small fish called sand dabs. "You're going to need capers, white wine, olive oil, and mullet roe," he says in confident rapid-fire, like Brad Pitt trading baseball players in *Moneyball*.

"You need a shaver for that," he adds, talking the cook through the steps. "Microplane. Same one you're using for the Bibb."

"Large flake?" the cook asks, furiously scribbling in a notebook.

"I don't want a microplane-microplane," Paul clarifies, in language only cooks can understand. "But a microplane is preferable to really large flakes."

1:43 p.m.

Paul and his sous chef have just finished testing a new shrimp appetizer and roast-chicken entrée. It's now the moment of truth for the pastry chef's dessert: a flourless chocolate cake with salted-caramel semifreddo, lingonberry pâtes de fruit jellies, and a dollop of cream. Paul takes a bite and says he loves the flavor combination, but he's concerned about the pâtes de fruit sticking to the plate. The two discuss a few options before deciding to simply plop the gummies into the cream.

After they've finished, Paul sets forth on one of the kitchen's lowliest tasks: dicing an array of onions with mechanical precision. The former naval officer isn't exactly *Food Network* material—he's too calm, too disciplined.

2:35 p.m.

A deliveryman wheels a 300-pound block of sculptor's ice into the Marvel Bar. When even the world's purest ice cubes can't give the Marvel bartenders the drink-cooling control they desire, they chip their own ice from large blocks. Two bartenders help the deliveryman heft the thing onto the counter and immediately start attacking it. One scores the block into eighths with what looks like a large putty knife, while the other splits it with a hammer and chisel. The first bartender breaks the block down further by aggressively stabbing it with a metal pick, like he's a human sewing-machine needle. The smaller blocks are neatly stacked in the freezer within a matter of minutes. "It reminds me of a cave man taking down a mammoth," Pip remarks.

3:59 p.m.

After a staff meal—a substantial spread that includes the roast-chicken tester, two types of potatoes, popovers, salad, and a hearty split-pea soup—the front-of-the-house staff gathers upstairs for their pre-shift meeting, which takes place in one of the restaurant's private dining rooms. The walls are covered with a funky collage of crocheted afghans, which lends the otherwise modern space a warm familiarity.

First on the agenda: the sous chef explains the new dishes. After subjecting the servers to a beer-list pop quiz, the general manager issues a warning: "Do not cap the stack." More than one blank look results. "When stacking similar dishes for the dishwashing crew," he explains, "you should never add a different dish to the top of the pile"—not only is it inefficient, but the whole thing could topple.

Andrew previews some exclusive new Alec Soth merchandise for the store, including coloring books from Soth's publishing company that may be the first in the genre to feature Bronko Nagurski and the Coen brothers. The general manager then pours the staff samples of a hard-to-find new wine he's acquired. "I buy wine like they buy Soth," he says of the Daytons. "Take it all so no-body else can get it."

4:45 p.m.

Seated in the Norsten Bar, next to the dining room, the assistant general manager undergoes her daily ritual of reviewing the comment books that the servers drop off with the check. She initials each remark, incorporating the feedback in her mental databank. "Coming from a bachelor farmer, we love this place." "Uffdah! Very good." "It's not Manhattan, but it's surprisingly hip, delicious, and cool." Minnesotans always seem to find the need to make coastal comparisons, don't they?

The books contain poems, a fake mustache, a lipstick kiss, and, inexplicably, what appears to be someone's senior-class photo-graph. One of the servers has received multiple marriage proposals from anonymous guests. Books that have recently received "edgier" messages—"I f—-ing love you guys," for example—cir-culate in the bar. Only a few book pages with "inappropriate" sketches (a group of the Dayton brothers' friends are prime sus-pects) had to be removed.

5:20 p.m.

Guests with 5:30 p.m. reservations are already peeking through the windows and the assistant general manager doesn't want them to wait in the cold. "We're opening the doors," she announces to the kitchen. A cook makes shots of espresso for the entire line. "Double? Or triple?" she asks.

5:24 p.m.

A server cuts butter pats for the restaurant's complimentary appetizer of flatbread and radishes and ferries the first plates to the dining room. Restocking the butter pats is among the hundreds of details that front-of-the-house staff has to track. Dozens more tips are posted on a list called "Service 101" near the servers' order terminal. No. 1 is a no-brainer: "Acknowledge all guests with eye contact and a smile immediately." But others are more obscure, like "12. Level the art." Several deal with appropriate guest interaction: "18. Do not react to the amount of the tip; 30. Do not ask a question while a guest's mouth is full; 31. Do not enter a guest's conversation unless clearly invited."

6:00 p.m.

The sous chef stands at the pass, a counter that divides the kitchen from the dining room, lining up tickets and calling out orders to the various cooks. She's essentially playing air-traffic controller so each table's orders will be ready at the same time. "Fire Camembert, no shallots," she hollers. Two old tickets are taped to the wall with messages scrawled on top, "10-top in 23 minutes," and, "9-top in 20 minutes": house records in putting together big orders, the kitchen equivalent of scalps.

Paul runs his kitchen like the Daytons run their business: hire people you trust and let them do their thing. He lets his staff handle tonight's dinner service as he scores the fat on dozens of duck breasts and makes other preparations for the upcoming days. From the back of the kitchen, he can watch the orders flow and anticipate any problems—demonstrating strong "field awareness," as they say in team sports.

7:04 p.m.

Much like The Bachelor Farmer's dining room, the accompanying Norsten Bar has a mellow vibe despite being nearly full. No matter the guest's dress—lumberjack plaid and sequins inhabit adjacent barstools—they seem to appreciate the food and beverage. A man approaches the bartender and gruffly asks her what's in one of the drinks. She shows him the bottles: aquavit, gin, orange bitters, and Cocchi Americano, an aperitif wine. "Is that your favorite cocktail?" she asks. "It's delicious," he says. "In fact, I should probably tip you." He pulls a stack of folded bills from his pocket and tosses $5 on the counter.

8:32 p.m.

The kitchen is running full tilt. Eggshells pile up. A stove burner flares. The cooks fill the pass with plates and servers rush to distribute them. Meanwhile, in the relative serenity of the basement cooler, Paul deconstructs the pig carcass with a hacksaw.

In the dining room, guests appear rapt in conversation, enjoying the evening and blissfully unaware of all these activities. The lights are low, the music is soft, and wine glasses cover nearly every table. Diners may never make a conscious note of all the tiny details that made their meal great versus simply good—the house-butchered pork, the hand-chipped ice, the plating of the pâte de fruit, the minute difference between a "microplane-microplane" and a "large flake." When they next recall this meal, all they will remember is that they ate well and enjoyed themselves.

In fact, The Bachelor Farmer's secret to success may be that its food isn't necessarily the star: the cooking is novel enough to discuss, but not at the expense of other topics. It's the restaurant's vibe—its contemporary spin on nostalgic comforts and Volvo-like sense of understated luxury—that accounts for its enduring appeal. Sure, a few guests may have been hoping to rub shoulders with politicians and scions, but mostly they are drawn in by the way the place reflects their own sophisticated populist sensibilities. And besides, who doesn't love the idea of hopping from shop to restaurant to bar without the hassle of re-parking the car?

10:49 p.m.

Eric and Andrew finally sit down to eat dinner in the Norsten Bar. Paul comes in to say goodbye, sporting a new Band-aid on his finger—he pricked himself with the giant syringe he was using to pump brine into cuts of pork. Trying to brine himself, it seems.

11:26 p.m.

Eric stops in the kitchen and says goodnight. Andrew will leave a few minutes later and both will be back tomorrow morning by 10 a.m. to open Askov Finlayson. The cooks clean up as the servers start to cash out, counting their tips and dispensing a few appreciative bills to the hostesses and food runner.

12:05 a.m. Sunday

A guest is upset that his party can't get into the packed Marvel Bar and a couple staffers gracefully smooth his ruffled feathers. Restaurant diners are given priority access, but walk-ups must take their place in the queue—no VIPs, no favorites. Supposedly, even Governor Dayton doesn't get to cut the line, but that scenario has yet to arise.

1:52 a.m.

The Marvel Bar's last patrons head out the door and someone flips on the lights. A bartender pours a round of beers and passes out a loaf of homemade banana bread. (The only food the bar serves is Cheetos, and often the bar staff doesn't stop to eat during their shift.) After nearly 12 hours spent thinking about booze, two devoted bartenders discuss the merits of 110-proof gin as they clean up.

2:56 a.m.

The last of the crew bundles up—one bartender pulls on an Askov Finlayson sweater—and spills out into the cold, dark night. The kitchen emits the same florescent light it did 20 hours earlier, a reminder that in roughly four hours, the cycle will start all over again.

Austria's Culinary Ambassador

By St. John Frizell

From *Edible Manhattan*

St. John Frizell has an insider's perspective on the restaurant
biz, as the proprietor of Brooklyn's popular bar-café Fort
Defiance. Meanwhile, he plies his trade as a food-and-drink
writer in such publications as *Bon Appétit*, *Saveur*, *Islands*, *The
Oxford American*, *Edible Brooklyn* and *Edible Manhattan*.

High above the Austrian village of Ratsch, on a hilltop
overlooking a sun-soaked valley planted with rows of
grapevines, I'm all set to tuck into the biggest plate of fried
chicken that I've ever seen. Walnut trees shade the deck of Wein-
lokal Maitz, a restaurant on the Southern Styrian wine route,
where I sit with Kurt Gutenbrunner, the Austrian-born chef-
owner of five restaurants in Manhattan, and Michael Gross, the
charming young scion of a local wine family. The chicken, served
with lemon wedges and a salad made with purple-specked käfer-
bohnen—"beetle beans," what we know as "scarlet runners"—is a
local specialty called backhenderl, and a dream come true. Just under a crust that has the airy crispness of a perfect Wiener schnitzel,
the meat bursts with gamy juice that makes me want to find the
chicken farmer and shake his hand. And I could, without much
trouble; at this point in my travels in Austria, I know the country is
a locavore's fantasy—and that the chicken I'm about to eat was
clucking in someone's yard the day before yesterday. (The English

menu reinforces my belief in plain language: "Needless to say, we know all of our distributors personally.")

The wine we're drinking is local, too—on the hillside across the valley is the Gross winery and vineyards, where Michael lives and makes wine with his brother, Johannes, and their father, Alois. From here we can see the terraced slopes where they grow grüner veltliner. Down in the valley, we can make out the roof of the buschenschank that Michael's grandparents still run. The buschenschank is a glorious Austrian tradition—a little tavern where winemakers, with special governmental permission, serve their own vintages and a small selection of hot and cold dishes to tourists and locals alike. "In the fall, we live to go to the buschenschanks," Michael says. "People come for the leaves—every tree you can see in this valley turns a different shade of green, gold and red. And they come for the sturm." That's the newest wine of the year's harvest, the grape juice that's just started to ferment. The men at the table smile and let out a collective groan, as if they've all gotten into plenty of trouble drinking sturm, and can't wait to do it again. "I think it continues to ferment in your stomach," Kurt says.

Just then, the server brings Michael a plate of schafkase im mantel—sheep's milk cheese wrapped in speck. What, no backhenderl? "It's delicious, but no. I had it for lunch yesterday," Michael says, sheepishly. "And the day before."

Since he opened Wallse, his Michelin-starred homage to Viennese cuisine, in the West Village in 2000, Kurt Gutenbrunner has been turning Manhattanites on to schnitzel, spaetzle and gruner veltliner. He's the primary advocate and most recognized representative of Austrian food culture in America, and in Austria, a country with a population about the same size as New York City's, he's something of a local hero. For six days, Kurt and I scoured the country in search of new ingredients, producers and dishes that will inspire his menus in the year to come at Wallse and his other restaurants: Blaue Gans, the Austrian bistro in TriBeCa; Café Sabarsky, the Viennese café at the Neue Gallerie; Café Kristall, at the Swarovski Building; and his wine bar, the Upholstery Shop. To kick off the week, we meet at Plachutta, one of Vienna's most respected traditional restaurants, for a crash course in Austrian Cuisine 101.

Looking at the menu, Kurt explains how Austria has always been a crossroads, a place in the middle. Once the seat of power of the Austro-Hungarian Empire, Vienna was also the easternmost city in Western Europe during the Cold War. Centuries of trade, diplomacy and conquest have left their mark on the city's cuisine. "Gulasch? From the Hungarians," explains Kurt. "Schnitzel, that's essentially a Milanese, from Italy. A lot of these pastries are Czech. And the coffee in our famous cafés? From the Turks."

But since the end of the Empire, the major influence on Austrian cuisine has come from within. In the early 20th century, Austrian thinker Rudolf Steiner provided the philosophical underpinnings for what would become the organic farming movement.

Naturally, Austria has become one of the world's leaders in organic farming; it was one of the first countries to set official organic guidelines, and its government continues to subsidize ecological farming practices. As a result, close to 20 percent of its farms are organic, more that in any other European country (except tiny Liechtenstein).

From the hippest Viennese nightspot to the most rustic small-town gasthaus, we see these two forces working in harmony, and they define contemporary Austrian cuisine—traditional dishes, like Wiener schnitzel and krautsalat, are thoughtfully prepared so that the flavors of the fresh, local meat and produce shine through. Kurt is tickled by the recent rise of Austrian cuisine in New York's dining scene, where Midtown's Seasonal now has a Michelin star, and dozens of beer gardens have sprouted up over the past 10 years.

"When I put tafelspitz on the menu in New York, people said, 'You're serving us boiled beef?' It wasn't very cool," Kurt says. Plachutta is famous for this quintessential Austrian dish, which is essentially a simple boiled dinner; the name refers to the cut of beef, which comes from the round. Other cuts—kavalierspitz, tafelstück and so forth—are commonly used, but "tafelspitz in particular is accompanied by a myriad of legends, and no other dish has a comparable historic significance," according to the Plachutta cookbook. The service is warm and formal; the food, simple and hearty as corned beef and cabbage. Kurt serves kavalierspitz at Blaue Gans, his casual Austrian bistro in TriBeCa. Does he lighten it up a bit for his downtown Manhattan crowd? "No, of course not," he says, between forkfuls of beef. "Does the Viennese Philharmonic play Mozart any differently when they come to New York?"

After getting through almost a pound of beef, I put my fork down, while Kurt continues to eat. He is a man of voracious appetites and seemingly boundless energy—it's no wonder at all that his little hometown of Wallsee, a little village in Upper Austria, couldn't hold him.

In 1988, after a two-year stint at Munich's then-Michelin-Three-Star restaurant Tantris, he was introduced to Hermann Reiner, chef of Windows on the World in New York, who hired his 26-year-old fellow Austrian as sous chef. Gutenbrunner fell in love with New York, but found the experience of cooking at the top of the World Trade Center disconcerting. "I was used to buying produce off a truck in back of the restaurant; now, we were buying produce 110 floors below. It was like working on a submarine," Kurt says.

In the meantime, an American chef with ties to Austria and impeccable French training was earning rave reviews in TriBeCa; before opening his eponymous restaurant, David Bouley had worked at the then four-star restaurant Vienna 79 with chef Peter Grunauer. In 1990, Gutenbrunner found his first real home in the States in the kitchen at Bouley, and started a working relationship with chef David Bouley that would last, off and on, for 10 years. The restaurant Bouley has become a proving ground for American chefs—Eric Ripert, Dan Barber and César Ramirez all passed through in the 1990s, to name a few. Gutenbrunner was suitably challenged and invigorated by the other chefs in the kitchen. "We were a great team. No one could beat us. It was a shitload of work, and there was a lot of pressure, but when people push each other like that, a lot of extreme things can happen," Kurt says, before turning wistful. "I think if things happened on schedule, David and I would still be working together."

"What are you doing, Johnny?" Kurt asks, gesturing at my half-full plate as he scoops the last bites of kavalierspitz from his own. At our first meeting, Kurt started calling me Johnny, and after a couple of days, I stopped correcting him. I told Kurt I was stuffed; I probably should have passed on the chanterelle omelet that we had as an appetizer. "What's the matter? You only ate half a cow," he says. "Let's get dessert."

When we meet early the next morning, we have dessert again. "I love cake," Kurt tells me as he quickly demolishes a slice of Landtmann torte, with its decadent layers of walnut cream and marzipan. Vienna's cafés are justly famous for their extravagant cakes—like sachertorte, linzertorte and apfelstrudel, to name a few—and during our week in Austria, Kurt never misses a dessert. His trim silhouette can only be explained by his inexhaustible energy and outright speed; I often have to jog to keep up with him as he navigates the twisting streets of Vienna like he's being chased. He only stops to eat, as he is now, at Café Landtmann, a fabled Viennese café a stone's throw from Vienna's University, the City Hall and the monumental Burgtheater.

An hour later, we stumble onto a frozen yogurt shop called "Kurt" on a cobblestone street; Kurt warmly greets the owners ("You're Kurt? I'm Kurt!"), drops business cards on all of the shop's patrons and orders a blueberry-acai yogurt, in the "Classic Kurt" size. "Once, I went to Café Sabarsky for a business meeting, and I ate four apricot cakes before it was over," he says. Kurt opened Café Sabarsky in the Neue Gallerie, Manhattan's museum of Austrian and German art and design, in 2001. Kurt had met the museum's founder, Ronald Lauder, when they both ordered Thonet chairs from the same Austrian company. After visiting Vienna, the likeness of Café Sabarsky to its Viennese cousins is almost eerie— from the waiters' uniforms to the Thonet hat racks to the menu, with its Staud's jams and sachertortes and grosser brauner (coffee with steamed milk), it's all the same.

Gutenbrunner comes to Austria several times a year, in part to see old friends and family, and in part to source new ingredients for his New York kitchens. This is what has brought us to Heimschuh, a sleepy town in the southern state of Styria, near the Slovenian border. It's home to the Hartlieb mill, where some of the world's best pumpkinseed oil is pressed. "This was once oil of the poor," says Thomas Hartlieb, whose great-grandfather opened the Hartlieb mill in 1896, when they used river power to mill lumber as well as grain. "People thought it was low quality, because of its dark color." In the bottle, pumpkinseed oil is a dark, almost purplish green; when Hartlieb holds a bottle high and pours it so that the afternoon sun shines through the oil, it's a vivid crimson. Now, it is to Austria what EVOO is to Italy; in a week, I think I had it at every meal, dressing greens, tomatoes, cheese and fish with its distinctive nutty flavor.

Hartlieb keeps a collection of antique pumpkinseed presses in a makeshift museum on the mill's second floor, but on the ground floor, high-tech presses and grinders do the work today. Local farmers grow special Styrian "oil pumpkins," whose seeds grow without hulls. This squash's harvest is the inversion of its American cousins: they keep the seeds and discard the flesh. At Hartlieb, those prized seeds are ground and roasted, which causes the proteins in the seed puree to separate from the oil. That mixture is pressed, the oil collected, and what's left behind—a protein-rich puck of pressed pumpkinseeds—becomes livestock feed on nearby farms.

Over a seidel of Puntigamer, the go-to lager in Styria, at the café across the street, Gutenbrunner and Hartlieb talk about pumpkin-seed oil's appearance on the gourmet food scene; until about 20 years ago, it wasn't even common in upper Austria, though it's been used in Styria for centuries. "It wasn't that we didn't want it; you Styrian guys just didn't want to give it to us," says Kurt. It's an ingredient Kurt has always showcased to great effect. Ruth Reichl, in typical for-mature-audiences-only prose, reviewed Gutenbrunner's food when he was chef at the Monkey Bar, a clubbish Midtown restaurant then owned by steakhouse czar Peter Glazier, in the New York Times in 1998: "Just take a spoonful of his butternut squash soup. Hold it in your mouth, rejoicing in the deep richness of the pumpkinseed oil on top. . . . It is irresistible."

Eight years earlier, when his first son was born, Kurt had left Bouley and moved to Germany—he thought Europe would be a better place to raise a family—but returned to New York to work with his old boss whenever time allowed. In 1996, he moved to New York for good and hatched plans with Bouley to open the Austrian restaurant that would become Danube. But plans stalled, Kurt became impatient and steakhouse czar Glazier made Kurt an offer he couldn't refuse—his first executive chef gig, at Monkey Bar. "He gave me everything and beyond. I didn't want to do it at first, but it's hard to see everyone else moving ahead when you're standing still," Kurt says. After two years there, he met the investors who would help him fund Wallse—parents of a kid on his son's soccer team—and a restaurant empire was born.

From the roof of the Gegenbauer vinegar factory, we can see the broken roof tiles of the surrounding apartment blocks in this unglamorous neighborhood of Vienna's 10th district. We've come to check in on an old friend of Kurt's, Erwin Gegenbauer, whose grandfather Ignaz started making sauerkraut and pickled vegetables in this building in 1929. In the 1990s, Erwin sold off most of the company's assets to focus on his true aspiration: to make the world's best fruit vinegars. Gegenbauer makes vinegars from every kind of foodstuff imaginable: apples and grapes, but also honey, figs, cucumbers and asparagus. These are not the vinegars on your typical grocery shelf, flavored with raspberries or other fruit. "Those vinegars are made by adding fruit flavors to wine vinegar. That is chemistry, and I don't do that," Gegenbauer says, in near-perfect English. "My raspberry vinegar is all raspberries, no other ingredients. You could say it's more simple this way. But the simplest products can be the most complicated."

Gegenbauer starts his process by working with local farmers, selecting fruit with the careful attention of a winemaker. "How many leaves per branch is optimal? When do we harvest? How do we press the fruit to get the juice? These are the questions we ask," he says. The fruit juice is allowed to ferment, creating a wine; Gegenbauer then introduces specific strains of bacteria—he keeps several hundred on hand—which will, over several weeks, convert the alcohol in the wine to acid, creating vinegar. Some vinegars are then aged in oak wine barrels, either in his cellar or on his roof, exposed to the elements. I ask why there's no tradition of making this kind of vinegar in Austria, or anywhere else. "There's a popular perception that vinegar must be cheap, that vinegar is wine that's gone bad," Gegenbauer says. "That's changing."

Gegenbauer brings out his newest project to show Kurt, an oil made from pressed raspberry seeds—a by-product of his vinegar process. "I love working with Kurt," Gegenbauer says. "I give him vinegar, we taste it and discuss. Sometimes I work with him in the kitchen, and together we create a new dish. I'm the craftsman; he's the creative, pushing me to experiment with new flavors."

He places a few drops on the back of Kurt's hand and mine; Kurt licks it off and stares at Gegenbauer as he rolls it around in his mouth. The flavor is subtle and woody at first, then slowly blossoms into something like raspberry jam on toast. "The berry flavor comes late," Kurt says.

"But it stays a long time," Gegenbauer says. "That's amazing! Can I take this with me?" Kurt says. Our hands will smell, pleasantly, like raspberry bushes for the rest of the day.

A photographer from an Austrian society magazine arrives; she asks the two men to pose between the batteries of casks on the roof. Gutenbrunner is totally relaxed in front of a camera, posing for pictures like an aging rock star, to which he sometimes compares himself ("You know what they say about British rock and rollers? They don't fucking die! Keith Richards. Robert Plant. I'm like that. You can't kill me."). His body totally relaxed, Kurt looks directly into the camera, eyelids heavy, his lips slightly curled in the suggestion of a smile.

"Let's go see Claus, Johnny," Kurt says. The open fields of Burgenland, planted with chest-high cornstalks and sunflowers, whip past the windows of our Mini Countryman, as Kurt drops gears to pass another ambling truck. "You'll like this guy. He's a little crazy."

Claus Preisinger's winery is a strikingly modern poured-concrete bunker filled with strikingly low-tech equipment—just a bunch of stainless steel tanks and wooden barrels. There's not even a pump in sight—when Preisinger needs to move his wine from tank to barrel, he uses a length of tubing to siphon it, concerned that mechanical pumping will disturb his wines. In the corner, there's a stack of crates of mineral water ("Good for breakfast," Preisinger says.) and Budweiser Budvar ("Very important after a day in the vineyards: cold beer.") and, off to the side, the winery's most advanced piece of machinery: a 500-liter teapot, where he makes chamomile tea to feed his vines during times of stress. He hasn't used pesticides or herbicides in years and cites Rudolf Steiner as a direct influence.

Kurt includes a wide swath of Austrian winemakers on the lists at his New York restaurants, from the most traditional old houses to the newest, most cutting-edge vintners, like Preisinger. With the tousled good looks of an emo rocker, Preisinger is, at 31, the youngest member of Pannobile, a group of nine local winemakers who have banded together to form their own appellation—like a French AOC, which controls what grapes can be used in what wines, but without the government. Each year, the winemakers in the group submit their wines to a tasting panel of their peers; to be considered a Pannobile wine, all nine winemakers must unanimously approve.

He pours his 2008 Pannobile, a blend of zweigelt, blaufränkisch and a little bit of St. Laurent, a rare, highly aromatic grape. "It's tricky to grow," says Preisinger, "but sometimes the trickiest grapes make the best wines." It's lovely stuff, light-bodied and subtle, with flavors of black currant and earth. As we drink, watching the sun set over Lake Neuseidl into a bank of clouds, a burly farmer with mud-spattered boots walks in—it's Paul Achs, another Pannobile winemaker, carrying a bottle of his 2000 blaufränkisch, and the glasses are filled again. The two winemakers are eager to take him out to dinner, to a restaurant called Blaue Gans—the same as Kurt's TriBeCa bistro. But Kurt begs off, and we get back on the road. "I know these guys," says Kurt. "We go out with them to dinner and it'll be sunrise before we get to our hotel."

Erich Stekovics, with his round red cheeks, deep-set eyes and red polo shirt covering a round belly, fits his nickname: Kaiser der Paradeiser (the emperor of tomatoes). In the fertile plains of Burgenland, he raises more than 800 varieties of tomatoes every year; in his stores, he keeps the seeds for 2,000 more. "I think he named one of his daughters Tomato," Kurt whispers, as we follow Stekovics into his greenhouses.

As we stalk quickly through rows of six-foot plants heavy with fruit, he pulls tomatoes off the vines for us to taste. With his knife, he splits a small, dark tomato and shows us the purplish flesh. "Black cherry," he says, before popping half in his mouth and motioning for me to do the same. The flesh is lush and flavorful; the juice is thick and heady, like a swig of Achs's blaufränkisch. The tomatoes follow in quick succession, and Stekovics rattles off the names; he can identify hundreds of varieties by sight. There's de Barao, yellow and plum-shaped; Russian pear, sweet and smooth, as fragrant as a ripe peach; vibrant red Schlessian raspberry—each more flavorful and succulent than the one before.

His secret? He doesn't water his plants. Ever. Bred for hardiness, they're forced to sink their roots ever deeper into the earth, giving them greater access to resources and, he believes, producing the world's most flavorful tomatoes. His methods buck conventional wisdom, which dictates that tomatoes need plenty of water, and baffle experts; a research team from the University of Innsbruck took three days to excavate the root-ball of one of his plants. Home gardeners from all over Europe visit to see Stekovics's plants and hear his gospel—but their hearts are not strong enough to follow him. "They're afraid," he says, obviously a little hurt. "They go home and water their plants."

As Kurt tries to convince Stekovics to visit the U.S. ("I want to introduce you to some of my farmers," he says), Stekovics brings us to one of his favorite plants: the Firework tomato, a Russian variety that's 450 years old, its carmine flesh streaked with the yellow and gold flecks that give it its name. As he cuts into it, red juice drips down his hand; the flesh is dark red to its core. It's just delicious, fruity and aromatic, like summer savory and wildflowers, the Platonic ideal of a tomato. "You want a restaurant?" Stekovics shouts, flourishing the knife in his seed-stained hand. "Bring your table in here. I'll make you a feast you won't forget. Seven courses of tomatoes." He leans in close, and fixes his hound-dog eyes on mine. "If you write about this, no one will believe you."

Within minutes of arriving in the town of Axberg in northern Austria, Hans Reisetbauer, perhaps Austria's most respected distiller, is making us coffee, and after hours on the road, we need it. We started the day just past dawn in the farmers market of Graz, where Kurt loaded my arms with sunflowers, tiny raspberries, dry pork sausage studded with pumpkinseeds, a huge bag of ripe apricots, and some slices of poppy-seed cake as he flitted from stall to stall, chatting with the vendors. "It's good to talk to these old ladies," he told me, as he handed me a squash. "They know best. This pumpkin? She told me you can cook the whole thing, leave the skin on. Makes good soup."

It's the start of Reisetbauer's busy season—he makes his living turning Austria's best fruit into award-winning eaux-de-vie, or schnapps, and as we saw in the market this morning, the first fruit of the summer was already ripe. He distilled his first batch of raspberries the week before our visit; through the porthole in one of his copper stills, I see his first batch of apricots cooking away, bubbling like a pot of jam.

Reisetbauer grows all of his own apples and pears on his estate, just outside the distillery; other fruit, like these apricots, he sources from farmers who grow fruit especially for him. "I have to find farmers who are as crazy as I am," Reisetbauer tells me. He doesn't look crazy, he looks like fun—like a retired actor, with an easy smile, graying hair pushed back, and shoulders as big as a bear's. "Most customers want to see the perfect color of an apricot. Me, I want the perfect taste. I need the best fruit to make the best schnapps."

"It's the same in the kitchen," Kurt says. "You have to work with the farmers to get what you want. See, Johnny? It's always the same."

"Once we have the perfect fruit, it's up to us not to make any mistakes," Reisetbauer says.

Schnapps are not always pretty spirits—some are just fiery moonshine, roughly distilled by farmers and drunk by same to fend off cold, fatigue and boredom (and forget the cinnamon-and-watermelon-flavored liqueurs called schnapps in the U.S.—they're completely unknown in Austria). But schnapps can be magical; clear, high-proof spirits, enjoyed after dinner, that somehow evoke through taste and smell the sensation of biting into a ripe fruit, at the peak of its season, right off the vine—or better.

Reisetbauer's pear schnapps is better than any French poire Williams I'd ever had—as the flavors spread across my tongue and waft up through my sinuses, I have the illusion of tasting a pear with the backs of my eyes. His elsbeere ("serviceberry") schnapps is the most expensive in the world; he needs more than 35 kilos of the rare fruit to make one liter of spirit. Last year, the only three bottles exported to the U.S. went to Wallse. It tastes like blueberry marzipan, in between layers of God's own wedding cake.

After an amble through his orchards, it's time for lunch; we head to his kitchen in time to see his entire staff—farmhands, still operators and marketers alike—sitting down to eat with his young children. His wife plates slabs of the pork neck she's been roasting all morning with hunks of browned cabbage, herb dumplings and a good ladleful of dark brown jus. Everything is perfectly cooked, and the gemütlichkeit, that sense of warm hospitality in which all Austrians take pride, has never been stronger. We all help ourselves to glasses of apple juice from the orchards outside.

"Here's where I fished for semling, that fish you had the other day," Kurt says, standing on the grassy banks of the Danube in Wallsee, his hometown, a quiet village of about 3,000. "Up there, by those reeds, I caught eel and catfish." While fishing as a child, Kurt would watch the river cruise ships pass by, some on their way to Vienna. He didn't know much about them, but he knew they had cooks, and they seemed as good a way as any out of Wallsee. In the 1970s, aspiring Austrian chefs didn't aim too high; if he paid attention and worked hard in culinary school, he might even make it to the kitchen of a hotel in Switzerland. Before Kurt, Wallsee's only claim to fame was a castle that was once home to Archduchess Marie Valerie, daughter of Emperor Franz Joseph. Now it can claim a famous American chef, too. This fall, Kurt's cookbook *Neue Cuisine* will be published by Rizzoli, and this fall he'll return to Austria to receive the Decoration of Honor for Services to the Republic of Austria, a prestigious award given by the Austrian president to citizens who promote Austrian culture abroad.

His parents still live in town; so do his brother and sister. When we stop by his old family homestead, his mother, as hospitable and charming as her son, brings out a homemade plum cake and some coffee. I grill her for embarrassing stories from her son's youth, but she comes up short. "When he was about 10, he made me a cake for Mother's Day. After dinner, his brother said, 'Kurt, where's the cake?' but Kurt just shushed him. It turns out he had hidden the cake under his bed."

"It didn't come out right! I had high-quality standards, even then," Kurt says.

Our stay isn't long; we have dinner reservations in Vienna that night. Before we leave, Kurt carries in bags bursting with the bounty of Austria's fields, orchards, cellars and shops, and starts to unload them onto the kitchen table, despite his mother's protestations: the market sunflowers; sausage studded with pumpkin seeds; bottles of Gegenbauer's vinegar and Hartlieb's pumpkinseed oil; fresh apple juice from Reisetbauer's orchard; tomatoes from

Stekovics's miraculous vines; and from the farmers market in Graz, a small mountain of apricots. "We love it when Kurt comes to visit," his mother says. She beams with pride for her son, the chef, who has made good in New York and is the reason Americans have heard of Wallsee. Then she looks distractedly back at the kitchen table. "But now I have to do something with all of these apricots."

REMEMBERING SAVOY

By Rachel Wharton

From *Edible Manhattan*

∽≫∾

North Carolina native Rachel Wharton has become immersed
in New York City food culture since earning a master's in food
studies from New York University. A former food reporter for
the *New York Daily News*, she is now deputy editor of *Edible
Manhattan* and *Edible Brooklyn* and a contributor to GiltTaste.

When Peter Hoffman announced that on June 18 he
would shutter Savoy—the SoHo restaurant he has run
for 21 years at the cobblestoned corner of Prince and Crosby—
Manhattan learned it would lose more than just a fine dining land-
mark, a longstanding icon of its culinary landscape. Hoffman, you
may have heard, promises to open a more casual, up-to-date place
in the space by September. But when Savoy's golden glow goes
dark, with it goes the urban version of our very own hearth, our
collective spiritual home—the kind of place where people gather
around the fire not just to eat, but to commune with kin and take
the long view of life.

The hearth, after all, is a literal one: Until the end of next
month, at least, the restaurant boasts two fireplaces, both used for
cooking. The restaurant's many regulars will long mourn the loss
of Savoy's cassoulet suppers simmering away inside the fire each
fall in embertopped cast-iron Dutch ovens, and the shad feasts celebrating the return of that fish to the Hudson River each spring.
For this year's shad dinner, Hoffman and his executive chef, Ryan

Tate, nailed the boned and bacon-larded fish to planks inserted right into the flames the way the Colonists did. In true Savoy style, they served those fillets with smoked shad fritters and a charred spring onion aioli; a briny-sweet bite of house-pickled fish tucked between a buttery crisp of bread and a layer of green garlicky omelet; and a wedge of its creamy roe with brown butter cream in a lemony sorrel broth.

If you'd been paying attention at Union Square Greenmarket just a few days before, you'd have seen Hoffman tuck the sorrel into the back basket of his trademark giant tricycle, emblazoned with a sticker reading "The revolution will not be motorized." That line is exactly the kind of idea those family-style, special-occasion dinners are meant to highlight. Savoy has long been Manhattan's place not just to share in one season's harvest and plan the next, but to critically evaluate what we eat, how we live and the American state of home economics, in the Wendell Berry sense of those words. (Berry, for decades regarded as the back-to-the-land poet laureate, has personally spoken during one such Savoy dinner, as have Michael Pollan, Alice Waters, Mark Kurlansky and just about every other living luminary in the farm-to-table world.)

Savoy has always been a Greenmarket-showcasing pioneer, starting in 1990 when Hoffman and his wife, Susan Rosenfeld, opened its doors in what had been a shiny luncheonette. (And before that, a barber shop: The old painted pole still stands guard in the downstairs dining room.) Savoy has since steadied city souls with its über-sustainable sustenance: A crusty wedge of real bread redolent with rustic local grains and slathered with cultured Vermont butter; a snarl of saber-toothed dandelion greens slicked with anchovy dressing and crowned with a slow-poached egg laid by a hen Hoffman may have even met.

True, if farm-to-table awards were given out by how much product a chef buys from local farmers, Hoffman wouldn't win. Even combined, the volume at his two restaurants (Back Forty, his more casual spot, opened on Avenue B in 2007) couldn't come close to a place like Gramercy Tavern, which could serve a hundred hungry locavores at lunch alone. He wasn't Manhattan's first cook to obsess over Union Square, nor would he score first-place for flat-out farm-driven deliciousness, either. Which is understandable: Many of the best city chefs regard ingredients with integrity as a win-win, but their main goal is taste; for Hoffman, one gets the feeling it's the other way around.

But Savoy never sought to be a Fine Dining Experience, as Blue Hill or Del Posto or Gramercy Tavern all are. It's the kind of place to order a pint of local suds and a few fat slices of housemade mortadella at one of the city's loveliest little bars, or where your Eileen Fisher–wearing aunt can come after her environmental book club for a wedge of silky, oil-poached wild-caught striped bass, perhaps paired with house-pickled ramps and spring's first spinach with walnut-mustard dressing. And Back Forty is decidedly down home, an Alphabet City outpost serving outstanding burgers, berry crisps and beer milkshakes—dishes that Dan Barber, who long ago supplanted Hoffman as the locavore spokesmodel, would never offer on his extraordinary—and extraordinarily refined—menus.

But while Hoffman's fare may be more rustic than rarified, it's often wonderful—and if you're hungry for a heaping helping of meaning, he serves up multiple kinds of satisfaction. That's because for him, farm-to-table is not a cooking style or a purchasing preference: It's a belief system that's just one piece of his progressive worldview. Ask him what he ate for lunch, and he'll likely connect the answer to healthcare reform or congestion pricing or this morning's op-ed about fracking in our foodshed.

This is a man who would never willingly miss a single day at Union Square Greenmarket, and not just for the grub. Other chefs may drop in for a frenetic Saturday spree before hailing a cab (or simply send their sous-chefs), but Hoffman's approach is to savor the experience. He'll park that giant trike and lean against box trucks and benches for hours, discussing pests, peapods and parenting, what the Japanese nuclear crisis means for Obama's energy agenda and whether it's possible to taste the difference between maple sap collected in metal buckets and sap that ran through plastic tubing. (Hoffman claims he can.)

There are hellos to the grad student working Flying Pigs' stand (ever the mensch's mensch, he asks after her dating life); a chat with the president of Abrams publishing company ("your bar was the best thing about working at Scholastic," he says wistfully of his time in that SoHo office); and a stop to score ricotta at Dancing

Ewe, a sheep dairy whose owners, like so many farmers here, credit Hoffman with their success. Hours later, the chef has still not bought the sorrel he originally came for.

"That's part of the whole point," says Hoffman of all these exchanges, "there's a conversation that doesn't happen at Whole Foods." Here you don't just read a sign that tells you how much sea scallops cost; you spend 20 minutes talking with the fisher about the social-political-ecological meaning behind their place in history.

These are all ideas he's been pondering since adolescence. As a 16-year-old in Tenafly, New Jersey, in the early 1970s, he knew he wanted to do something "intellectually stimulating but still physical," he says: "I didn't want a desk job." Seeking work connected to the natural world, he considered forestry and biology, but was set on a culinary path by an unlikely friendship with a retired commercial fisherman and a shot of a chef clutching vegetables to his chest on the cover of *Time*.

The fisherman was Chris Letts, now a Hudson River Foundation frontman in his 70s who long ago introduced the teenage Hoffman to his lifelong love of the sea and to the concept of foraging via Euell Gibbons' *Stalking the Wild Asparagus*.

The chef was Paul Bocuse, the Frenchman famous for his farm-forward food. "I think the title was *Cuisine du Marché*," recalls Hoffman of the *Time* cover. "I was like, 'that's it.' I don't think I even read the article." (Skimming is not standard practice for Hoffman, who's celebrated Proust with a four-course meal and counts *New Yorker* writer Adam Gopnik as a friend.)

Hoffman decided to fast-track high school and took an entry-level job at a resort restaurant in Stowe, Vermont. The continental cuisine didn't thrill him but the kitchen energy did. "I loved the theater of it, the community, the performance and the climax of Saturday night at 8:30."

When the weather warmed, Letts landed him a fishing gig back home, plucking writhing shad from nets off 138th Street, when the waters were still alive with the herring cousin heading up the Hudson River to spawn. (Hoffman chronicled the experience in this magazine in 2009.) But before he could go back to cooking, there was college to attend, as per parental demands. So Hoffman enrolled at UC Santa Cruz, where he counted gray seals for a professor and learned about the perils of the green revolution before dropping out to cook at a local restaurant. He again loved the line but, ready to come home, ignored a friend's advice that he should go work at this place in Berkeley called Chez Panisse.

Instead, back in Manhattan, he cooked at La Colombe d'Or, one of the first French restaurants in New York to serve rustic Provençal cooking rather than haute cuisine. That sensibility appealed to Hoffman—simpler food that wasn't "Frenchie La French," as he puts it. So did John McPhee's 1979 *New Yorker* piece Brigade de Cuisine, about a European-trained chef in a tiny town in Pennsylvania raising his own trout and cooking what grew nearby.

When the opportunity to master that kind of cooking arose, Hoffman jumped at the chance. He had wanted to study in Paris with chef Madeline Kamman after reading her book *The Making of a Cook* but her classes were full. "I got a phone call on the pay phone at [La Colombe d'Or]," he recounts: "'There's been a cancellation,' a voice informed him. 'If you can be in France in two weeks, you can be in Madeleine's class.'" He made it, and spent the last of his college money on three months cooking with Kamman, whose core concepts have formed the framework of his cooking since: that regional foods were rooted in geography and social history, and that the true way to cook was using, he recalls, "what was in the moment and what was in the market."

Those seem like no-brainers now that everyone has turnip tattoos, but at the time, the approach was just taking root stateside, coalescing as something called New American cuisine. Back home, Hoffman immersed himself in it, reveling in the food of trailblazing restaurants like An American Place, originally opened on the Upper East Side by chef Larry Forgione—"I ate my first morel in his restaurant," Hoffman dreamily recalls—and the Quilted Giraffe, the quirky French farmhouse-y spot in Turtle Bay where Hoffman cooked alongside Ray Bradley, who would go on to be one of the Greenmarket's most beloved farmers. He moved to the kitchens of Hubert's on 22nd, a townhouse turned New American bistro where he met Susan Rosenfeld, who would eventually become his wife.

They knew they wanted to open a restaurant, but first he would complete two more stints abroad—one in Provence with Richard

Olney, the Iowa-born author of cookbooks on French country fare, the second at a restaurant in Japan. ("I saw an aesthetic that would bring the natural world to the plate," says Hoffman of the latter trip, counterbalancing the French penchant for what he calls "manipulation of the natural world: dots and cubes and brunoise.")

Hoffman married Rosenfeld in 1988, and they set out in search of a space to open the restaurant they'd been imagining together. When they stumbled on that shuttered SoHo luncheonette, Hoffman looked up the lease in the city's records. It was coming up for grabs, and thus Savoy was born in a fledgling artists' outpost in the wasteland east of Broadway, a lifetime before direct trade macchiatos proliferated and shoppers' stilettos provided the sidewalk soundtrack. Susan worked the simple, 40-seat dining room, behind which guests could glimpse Peter in the tiny kitchen. He made connections with local farmers and fishers and foragers, cooking their harvests into dishes like marinated halibut with cucumber salad and braised duck with Concord grape puree. In 1995 they annexed the upstairs apartment, got a liquor license, and put in a bar and a working fireplace. The Times noticed, and critic Ruth Reichl awarded the restaurant two stars.

Hoffman was still Savoy's sole chef, and his handiwork would go on to become signatures of a scene: He has an "instinctive understanding of vegetables," Reichl wrote, a way with salads ("you will instantly be seduced"), plus a penchant for breaking rules: "Who would expect that rosy slices of grilled peppered tuna in a vinaigrette based on the classic Catalan romesco sauce (ground nuts, peppers and tomatoes), would be served with good old American onion rings? Fabulous onion rings, I might add, made of sweet red onions." Reichl nailed the feel of the place itself: "The small restaurant is so casual, so comfortable and so unpretentious," she wrote, "that it is hard to believe it is in Manhattan."

Many restaurateurs have taken the same approach, and several have done it better, but Hoffman's serious study of farm and food issues remains a rarity. Which makes it easy to see why, when Frank Bruni gave Savoy its second glowing two-star *Times* review in 2009, he called the restaurant New York's Chez Panisse, an East Coast answer to Alice Waters's Berkeley-based birthplace of the good food revolution.

Both Waters and Hoffman drew inspiration from youthful tours of France and Italy, but both ultimately formed consistent allegiance to Americana—from half-wild cress foraged on a Hudson Valley riverbank to wild salmon caught by Native Americans off the Alaskan coast. ("It's a delicious fish, and it's supporting indigenous fishing communities," says Hoffman, for whom the latter is as important a trait as the former.) Both kitchens have served as springboards, their line-cook lineage traced like one big family tree across the country's locavore landscape. Hoffman's culinary offspring all but created what *New York* magazine dubbed "New Brooklyn Cuisine:" Minds behind RoseWater, Diner, the Grocery and Franny's were all sparked at his stoves.

But moreover, like Waters, Hoffman has long been happy to leave the stoves to hired hands like Ryan Tate at Savoy and Shanna Pacifico at Back Forty, freeing him up to save the world. While others pursue television spots and lucrative advertising sponsorships—Hoffman has turned down both—this guy is after another kind of action, the kind whose payoff is a different kind of change.

He's always been much more than a chef, even back when he was still the one cooking. The man spent 10 years as the only chef on the Greenmarket's advisory board, helping guide and grow the city's market system to the marvel and model it is today. He is a founding member of Chefs Collaborative, the national network of professional cooks working to teach their colleagues where, how and why to find sustainably sourced products. And when he's not considering the concept and a name for his new restaurant—it will balance his philosophy with a price point and feel that fits Soho's touristy clientele, he says—he's hard at work on a marketdriven memoir (with recipes) that we can't wait to read.

Those projects are only possible when you delegate the day-to-day: Having traded his whites for brown cords and button-downs, he still shows up at both restaurants nearly every day with new product and new ideas, but insists on changes only when something's really wrong. (Missteps, like a basil cocktail from a new bartender in February, are pretty rare.) "I'm not the chef anymore," Hoffman freely admits, "but I'm still the culinary director. I hold out a set of guidelines by which the restaurants operate."

Those go beyond sourcing to stuff like caring about your staff: "One good thing about Peter," says Tate, "is he wants his employees to have a life." For the most part, he lets Tate and Pacifico do what they want if they follow his heart. "It doesn't have to be his food," says Tate, "it just has to be his philosophy."

This summer he'll focus that philosophy at Back Forty, which he named after the hidden quarter of land on the Midwestern parcels doled out by the Homestead Act of 1862. The government gave away 120-acre blocks, Hoffman explains, sketching rectangles on a scrap of paper, and the quarter farthest from the road was most likely to be left wild and wooded. It was also the place, he adds with a smile, "where you would go to make out."

That's maybe true of his own Back Forty, too, thanks to its sweet backyard, communal tables and that laid-back menu—"great ingredients in casual delicious ways," as Hoffman puts it—that will likely inspire what happens at the space where Savoy now stands.

Back Forty's menu is largely driven by the butchery skills Pacifico mastered in order to break down whole carcasses from Fleisher's Grass-Fed Meats upstate. While her vegetables shine— roasted roots and tangles of the sweetest spring greens—Back Forty is a carnivore's delight: fried pork jowl nuggets with pepper jelly; fat housemade sausages that change nearly every week; a terrine with stoneground mustard; grilled flatbread made with lard and topped with a mouthful of pig's trotters, bacon, melted onions and thyme. Yet Back Forty is best known for Pacifico's contender for best-in-city patty, transformed from trimmings of her two weekly deliveries of a half steer, served on a buttered sesame bun with spicy ketchup and a housemade pickle. (Tomatoes, too, says Pacifico, but only in season).

Despite the handiwork of his chefs, Hoffman is still master of ceremonies, especially during those idea-centric fireside feasts held for 18 years at Savoy. At those family-style nights of dinner and discussion, all manner of tastemaker—from Betty Fussell to Joel Salatin to Stephen Jay Gould—have held forth in front of the upstairs fireplace and, between each course, discussed the fate of local fisheries, the flavors of the Riviera, the follies of the Farm Bill or the forestry skills of Umbrian truffle hunters. Way back in 1995, Michael Pollan spoke about the history of apples in America—a decade before his Omnivore's Dilemma would hit nearly every nightstand in the nation.

As much about philosophy as they are about food, those communal hearth-side chats are what we'll miss most about Savoy, those nights when the place transcended typecast and become nothing less than a salon. Savoy's final shad dinner this March featured a lecture on the species (and a recipe for the pickled fish) by none other than Chris Letts, who took Hoffman fishing for shad back in 1974 and put him on the path to Prince Street. When he and Hoffman took the floor that night it became a pulpit, as they re-inspired eaters that when it comes to voting with your fork, hell yes you can, and hell yes you should.

Still, while Hoffman is often called the ur-locavore, he doesn't identify himself as such: "It's a simplistic look at an extremely complex topic," he says of the term. Citrus, olives, chocolate and countless other foods from afar share pride of place on both his menus, just as long as his sustainable sensibilities—that those foods come from independent groves or eco-enlightened fishers—stay true. Moreover, Hoffman claims the question of what to call his culinary philosophy isn't what matters. "You don't think Jackson Pollock called himself an experimentalist, do you? He was too busy painting. I could talk about it," he says of his life's work, "but mostly I was just doing it."

As it happens, for once we disagree. It's not so much Hoffman's cuisine that draws us back time after time, or Savoy's menu that we will miss most, but his fireside wisdom, and his longstanding role in illuminating our place in the world. "Savoy has been my life for the past 21 years," he says wistfully, "that place, that style and all the rest . . . but now I am getting excited about what it will become." If that includes conversation by the hearth, then we are, too.

APPETITE FOR PERFECTION

By Ed Leibowitz

From *Los Angeles Magazine*

Writer-at-large Ed Leibowitz has profiled everyone from
actor Charlton Heston to controversial defense attorney
Gloria Allred for *Los Angeles Magazine*. He has also written
about culture and politics for *The Atlantic*, *Smithsonian*,
Men's Journal, *Money*, *BusinessWeek*, and the *New York Times*.

R obyn Sewitz is almost done flipping through the latest
Bon Appétit this Sunday afternoon when she makes a
discovery she just has to share with her son. Brushing back a lock
of her auburn hair, she calls to him across her spacious kitchen.
"Jon," she says, "here's boar hunting for beginners!"

"Oh yeah?" he says, halting his knife's progress. Several weeks
shy of his 16th birthday, Jon is tall and lean, his full cheeks not yet
ready for their first serious shave, but after all those months he's
spent studying cookbooks, mastering culinary modernism, and ap-
prenticing in professional kitchens, he's a more capable cook than
either of his parents will ever be. Jon's a sophomore at the Oakwood School, a private progressive academy in North Hollywood.
His mother is a psychotherapist, while his father, David, designs
furniture and window treatments for clients of enormous net
worth.

Like many Oakwood parents, the Sewitzes regard their child's
artistic ambitions not as some passing teenage fancy but as a creative flowering that could lead to great things. When Jon thought

he wanted to be a musician, they signed him up for lessons and invested in a Bellafina double bass. He plays in the school orchestra and jazz band, but much of the time now his instrument sits on its side in the deserted music parlor of their Encino home, like a dejected mastiff.

Jon's food epiphany came during a family trip to Spain a couple of years ago. Robyn wasn't trying to make a chef out of him when she booked dinner reservations at El Celler de Can Roca, which earned three stars in the 2011 Michelin Guide. She wanted to expose him to something that would pique his interest more than the art museums were. Jon's palate still carries the sensations of that meal: oysters served in the bottom half of a wine bottle with carbonated *cava* sauce; eggplant soufflé wrapped in white sardines; a lineup of mussels, one bathed in bergamot foam, another in nectarine jelly and caramelized rose petal, and another in "distilled earth jelly," a clear sauce derived from a dab of mud that was boiled for hours at low temperatures in an evaporator. "It tasted like dirt you'd try when you were a kid," he says, "when it didn't taste bad." Dessert was even more spectacular. "It had apple in it, cinnamon, and vanilla crème," he says. "They brought out a DKNY perfume bottle and had us taste the dessert as we smelled the perfume, and the dessert tasted exactly like the perfume's aroma." In nine courses Jon was transformed. "I would always go back to that experience in my mind," he says, "how food could be so amazing you could remember it forever."

As Jon continues with his knife at the marble-topped kitchen island, he's joined by 17-year-old Sam Yehros and 18-year-old Macklin Casnoff, both seniors at Oakwood. They dice and pulverize, clarify and puree, strain and scour. For almost two years the friends have been collaborating on original multicourse dinners, charging only for ingredients, that they prepare for special occasions—a brother pushing off to college or a mom celebrating a birthday along with a tableful of relatives and friends.

If there were any single event that brought these three together as a cooking collective, it would be the Oakwood winter immersion program of 2009. While other students headed out with teachers to roam China or photograph Death Valley, Macklin found himself with 15 classmates in a cabin in Utah contemplating

Euclid's Golden Ratio. They cross-country skied and discussed whether the ancient Greek concept of beauty and proportion could apply to their world. Macklin's world had been sharks, then skateboards, but lately he had rekindled an old passion for food. Back home, when he wasn't watching *Iron Chef*, Macklin and his friend Henry Kwapis would explore how to apply the Golden Ratio to fine cuisine. They tried cold-calling some of the best chefs in L.A. to see if they could come in and ask them about their craft. José Andrés, meeting them at his Beverly Hills restaurant the Bazaar, was so impressed by the philosophical sweep of their questions that he answered in a 45-minute stream of consciousness, punctuating his thoughts with a liquid olive and molecular *caprese* in a pipette. "Look at the light above your head," he commanded, loud and jolly. "Now try to eat it. This is how I look at food."

When Jon heard about what Macklin and Henry had been doing, he asked to tag along for their talks with Michael Cimarusti at Providence and David Myers at his now-defunct dining room, Sona. Before long Jon was an unpaid apprentice in Sona's kitchen, and Macklin was learning by Cimarusti's side. As the two boys began cooking meals for friends and family, Macklin started experimenting in the kitchen with Sam, his Hancock Park neighbor, who had his own apprenticeship with Neal Fraser of Grace. Within a few months the two operations merged.

"See, look how cool," says Jon's mother, holding up the magazine article, which has shots of the hunter and roasted pork, but no dead pigs. "This is a vacation you should take. You can get in touch with your inner Michael Pollan."

"What?" says Jon, distracted.

"You haven't read *The Omnivore's Dilemma*?" asks Sam, referring to Pollan's book, a James Beard award winner that ends with the author trying his luck at hunting and gathering.

"I did," Jon says.

"You didn't read all of it," Macklin says with a smile.

"Yeah, I did."

"You admitted to me you hadn't read all of it."

"Well," Jon says, "I read a *lot* of it."

"Jon is dying to kill an animal, which I don't approve of," Robyn tells me. "I don't like the idea of holding a gun and killing anything, to be honest. It goes against my whole belief system, but it's better than suffering on one of those terrible farms."

Often Sam, Macklin, and Jon seem more like they're members of a teen rock group than three exceedingly capable cooks. One moment they'll be chomping blueberry Airheads or playing basketball on the Xbox or downloading Toto's "Africa" from iTunes just to goof on it. The next they'll be transfixed by a YouTube video of Chicago chef Grant Achatz demonstrating his solid-sauce technique or discussing the radical foraging philosophy of René Redzepi, the chef at Noma restaurant in Copenhagen. Like a band, the boys have given themselves a name: Samacon (Sam, Macklin, and Jon squished together). For their gigs they even bring in backup players—Henry, who's 17, and another Oakwood friend, Brendan Garrett, who's 16, to help out as sous-chefs.

Unlike teen rockers, though, the Samacon chefs have taken up an art form thoroughly rooted in the adult world and have mastered it with an idealism and fellowship that usually disappears with age. They aren't cocky about their work or egomaniacal—they are constantly challenging each other but never competing for supremacy. I could tell they knew they were good, but they had no way to measure *how* good. The friends and relatives at their dinners were cheering for them regardless of what came out on the plate, and the chefs they've worked for hadn't tried the boys' creations.

So one afternoon over burgers I asked them if they'd like to put together one of their nine-course meals for the chefs they admire most. "It would be nerve-racking," Jon told me, "probably the most nerve-racking thing we've ever done. But it would be amazing if we could cook for great chefs."

After wresting a blank check from my editor to pay for ingredients, I asked the boys for their ultimate guest list and began making calls. Five agreed to attend: Nancy Silverton of La Brea Bakery and Osteria Mozza; Vinny Dotolo and Jon Shook of Animal and the recently launched Son of a Gun; Fraser, of Grace; and Ludo Lefebvre, creator of LudoBites pop-up restaurants, an occasional judge on *Top Chef*, and starting next month, the star of his own reality show on the Sundance Channel. Now all the boys needed to do was pull off the best meal of their young lives.

A La Carte

A week and a day before their big dinner, the Samacon chefs gather at Jon's kitchen table to hammer out their menu. They agree on the squid kimchi *amuse-bouche*; the scallop with radish and black sesame; the hay-roasted, kale-wrapped pork medallions; and a whiskey-tangerine-nutmeg palate cleanser. Consulting the list in Macklin's disintegrating Moleskine notebook, they even agree on the raw oyster with bittersweet chocolate—admittedly a risk. They only have to settle on one more entrée. To Macklin, what their meal lacks is a strong narrative, and he has a solution: "Chefs, I think, are less concerned about being served the type of food they might be doing in their own restaurants," he says. "I feel like a chef's favorite thing to eat is, like, a roasted chicken or a fatty piece of pork."

"That would be *so* good," says Sam, his brown eyes almost moistening behind his horn-rimmed glasses. It's as if he's just turned 70, not 17, and has bitten into Proust's madeleine. "My mom makes roast chicken, and then you add quartered sweet potatoes and then potatoes and carrots, and the fat from the chicken soaks them as you're roasting."

"We roast a chicken and bring it to the table," Macklin says, "and they pull it apart. It's not like we're serving people who want everything to be done for them. Chefs love to get involved."

Jon is aghast. "We'd have to carve it for them," he says with the crumpled brow of somebody whose universe is near collapse.

"No, we don't," Macklin says. "I see one of the chefs cutting it. It can be a communal thing, and we can even be out there talking because that's sort of where there's a little bit of a break in the meal."

"Yeah," says Jon, "but they're not coming to this dinner for that. They're expecting teen chefs who've worked at some of the best restaurants. I know it's cool, but there's no restaurant that has beautiful, sophisticated plating, and suddenly it goes family style and back to beautiful plating. The menu *is* all about a story, and it has to flow. If it doesn't flow, the diners are not happy, and they just leave confused."

Like many Macklin concepts—the seemingly impossible wheat grass puree he executed for their last dinner, the rosemary soda company that hasn't gotten off the ground—his homey chicken interlude could lead to counterintuitive triumph or the abyss. Jon brings to the enterprise his expertise in modernism and molecular gastronomy, and Sam, his more traditional approach. But Samacon wouldn't be what it is without their combined talent for managing Macklin.

"I believe," Macklin says, "that doing a dish that's family style and the most simple, perfect thing in the world would show our reverence for what food is. What food means. The fact that it brings people together."

Eventually Macklin loses his ally. "If we're trying to make the whole meal communal," Sam says, "then we have to change the entire menu." Instead they opt for *loup de mer*, which will evoke the simplicity of country French cuisine, though Macklin has trouble letting go. "I don't want to argue about roast chicken anymore," he says. "Because I have very strong feelings about roast chicken. OK?"

Locally Grown

His generation of L.A. teenagers has taken to food like no other before it. They've grown up in a messy, polyglot city where often only the shared experience of eating Vietnamese *pho* and Salvadoran *pupusas* and Ethiopian lamb cakes can seem capable of holding everything together. They've spent countless hours watching the culinary blood sport of *Top Chef* and *Iron Chef* and (for those whose parents can swing it) learned their way around the menus of high-end restaurants. They'll opine authoritatively on Yelp about tripe soup just as quickly as they'll wince when Grandpa asks the waiter what the hell a *pappardelle* is.

But Sam, Macklin, and Jon are a category unto themselves. Of the five guests at their chefs' dinner, only Ludo Lefebvre hasn't met at least one of them before. Shook and Dotolo got to know Jon, Macklin, and Henry the way many other L.A. chefs did: a series of phone calls and e-mails, unanswered in this case, followed by a teenage siege on their restaurant. "We kind of blew it off at first," says Shook. "Then we saw a couple of bicycles parked outside. 'Like, it's so cool that somebody stopped in on a bike ride here,' we thought, and the manager was like, 'Oh, it's those kids.'"

Shook and Dotolo invited them into the kitchen to observe and help out. By closing time there was a steady rain. "And I was like, 'Put the bikes in the back of the Jeep, and I'll drive you home,' " Shook recalls.

Jon and Brendan, the Samacon sous-chef, met Nancy Silverton through Oakwood. They're close friends with her son, who also attends the school. In fact, they're all spending time together with Silverton at her house in Umbria this summer as soon as Jon and Brendan finish the two-week apprenticeship she's arranged with Dario Cecchini, Italy's most famous butcher. "Jonathan Gold is going to be in town working on a *Saveur* article they're doing about Umbria," she says of the food critic. "So it will be fun for those guys to eat with Jonathan."

Macklin may meet them there, too. The Silverton influence reaches far back into his past, when he carpooled with her son to kindergarten. At the time Silverton and Mark Peel were married, running Campanile and La Brea Bakery together. Picking up Macklin in the morning, they were already well into their work-day. "They would come from the fish market or the vegetable market," he says. "I was always interested in their double life." When Macklin was 13, he bumped into Peel at school. "I was like, 'Hey, I've been thinking about it,' " he remembers, " 'and I'd love to come in and work.' "

"He spent one day peeling garbanzo beans," says Macklin's father, Philip Casnoff, an actor who had his breakthrough playing Patrick Swayze's nemesis in the 1985 miniseries *North and South*. "I never saw him look so exhausted in his life. His second day he cut his finger badly, and after the third day he was gone."

"I was too young to appreciate it," Macklin tells me, "and I didn't force myself to stay there long enough to really get it. I thought, 'This isn't for me—it's too much.' I really loved it, though."

He's had an easier time working on Sundays with Cimarusti at Providence. "Coming out of cooking school, three or four years into a career, people can be making great progress, but they may also have developed bad habits," says Cimarusti, who will be in France the night of the chefs' dinner. "They believe what they've learned so far is gospel. But Macklin came here to be programmed, and whether it's the sous-chefs teaching him or myself, we've molded him to be exactly what we wanted. Also, he realizes quality—what are good ingredients, what are great ingredients, and what are bad ingredients—and that's something that doesn't come naturally to most people."

Neal Fraser says much the same thing about Sam. "I've had people who've come in from culinary school who were very game, then they'd get their Gucci loafers dirty," he says. "With Sam, he'd burn or cut himself, and all you would see was him in the corner taping himself up." From that first conversation, when Sam cold-called Fraser, they hit it off. "I rode my bike down to Grace," he says. "Neal had told me to ask for Jason, the sous-chef. I got there at about two o'clock and started chopping carrots." He began as a prep cook, then graduated to garnishing salads before Fraser let him work the fish station and the grill.

Sam's success in landing a job at Grace shocked his father. "When he said, 'I'm going to call these restaurants and ask for an internship,' and mentioned some highbrow ones in Los Angeles, I just rolled my eyes," says Ilan Yehros, who waited tables and worked in the kitchens at several restaurants in Toronto. "There's no way in hell that somebody would let a 15-year-old in with all the knives and equipment around. Kitchens are busy places. No one has the patience."

Ilan still liked to cook after he became a banker. He would wake up at four in the morning and pad into the kitchen to check his beef stock for some bravura French meal weeks in the making. Back then Sam and his siblings would occasionally serve their parents breakfast in bed and cook simple dinners. Without cable TV, Sam didn't have the Food Network for inspiration, so he turned to his father's copy of *Larousse Gastronomique*, the classic-French culinary encyclopedia.

During the Yehroses' vacation in Provence last summer, Sam and his dad took a seven-and-a-half-hour excursion to chef Edouard Loubet's two-star Michelin restaurant at the hotel La Bastide de Capelongue. "I wanted Sam to be enlightened about food," says Ilan, "to understand it as a chef clearly at the top of his profession understands it." They got there early, and Loubet gave them a tour of the kitchen. Sam worked his way through 14 courses on a hilltop patio, awestruck. "The first course was a really light vinegary soup and escargots," he tells me. "It was amazing, with this beautiful bouquet of tiny flowers on the edge of the bowl." He loved the snails and the frogs' legs but not the veal kidneys. "I could only eat one and a half of them," he tells me. "It's an acquired taste."

Garnishing

One more day until dinner is served. The Lakers are fighting hard against the Celtics and their own lethargy, which isn't good for sautéing vegetables. "Henry," Jon yells. "You haven't been watching your oil, and now it's burnt." Henry springs from his seat in the den and sprints to the Thermidor range in his skinny jeans and distressed leather shoes. The damage turns out to be minimal. They all watch part of the game during lunchtime, when Brendan, gentle faced and built like a linebacker, refuels everybody with helpings of his home-cooked stew.

Earlier this morning the chefs went shopping at the Hollywood Farmers' Market. They knew right where to find the vendors with the plumpest Kumamoto oysters, the most recently harvested pea tendrils, and were gone within an hour. From there they visited McCall's Meat and Fish Shop in Silver Lake, whose owner had cooked in several highly regarded restaurants before becoming a butcher.

"I swear," Macklin told me earlier, "McCall's is like the best butcher shop in the world, probably." At which point Sam offered a little perspective. "They are not the best butcher shop in the world. There are so many instances where Macklin says, 'This is the *best* thing I've ever had.'"

"I was just excited," Macklin explained.

"You just haven't had a lot of life experience," Sam said.

All week, with lesser ingredients, the chefs had rehearsed almost every dish. Today they work the kitchen with practiced efficiency and no trace of nerves. They don't use measuring spoons or timers, and aside from Henry's incident with the oil, they don't lose any ingredients to mishaps or crossed signals. Jon, Samacon's youngest and most focused chef, assigns Henry and Brendan tasks that send them scurrying across the bamboo floor. Sam tosses two scorched eggplants into Jon's Vitamix 5200 and grinds them to a sweet, smoky paste. He tries a teaspoonful, letting it settle on his palate. "Needs sherry," he says.

"Don't put too much sherry in it because of the red pepper," Jon warns.

Macklin drops a slotted spoon into a tall, steaming pot and captures a sweetbread. He gives it a jab with his finger and then throws it back in.

"They're being poached," Henry tells me, his blond bangs wilting in the steam. Then turning to Macklin, "Did I use the right terminology?"

"Poached in lime and lemon juice and chicken stock," says Macklin. He's dressed in a vintage short-sleeved shirt with thick red and white stripes—standard issue for selling saltwater taffy on the Atlantic City boardwalk in 1952. "This is how they do sweetbreads at Animal," he explains. "They said that when you're preblanching sweetbreads, you have to cook them to the consistency of . . . " he trails off.

Of what? I ask him.

"Silicone breast implants."

"Macklin, Jesus," Jon says.

"I had visions of lots of things other than that, when he was so circumspect about talking about it," says Jon's mother, Robyn, at her usual post in the kitchen. The boys have slept at her house for the past couple of nights. Twice they've tried to watch the Disney movie *Ratatouille* on Jon's flat screen, and both times they've fallen asleep before Remy the Rat becomes the greatest chef in all of France.

Table for Five

7 p.m. The table has been set in the Sewitz dining room, with its polished limestone floor, antique Chinese doors, and high-backed seats designed by Jon's dad. To psych themselves up, Sam, Macklin, and Jon are sporting white headbands, the kind favored by Ginsu-wielding chefs at those rock-and-roll sushi palaces of the '90s. The look clashes with the Zen-like tranquillity they've maintained as they've prepped the dinner. They might be more anxious if they were able to read the thoughts of the guests now trickling in for the meal.

Nancy Silverton is the first to arrive, in chunky eyeglasses and a dark coat, her hair a mass of curls gathered tightly on top of her head. She plants a big kiss on Robyn's cheek and gives the boys a maternal hug. All the while she's puzzling over how she's going to give the boys honest feedback about a meal she doesn't expect to be spectacular.

A few minutes later come Vinny Dotolo and Jon Shook, hirsute and stocky in respectable dark sweaters. Dotolo has been worrying about the food as well. On the ride over he'd asked Shook what they should do if the meal bombs. "I think it's going to be pretty good," Shook assured him. "They didn't do that bad when they were in the kitchen at Animal."

Then Ludo Lefebvre strides in, the rolled-up sleeves of his plaid shirt revealing a riot of tattoos, his hair thick and stylishly cut. As the boys awkwardly shake his hand, he's not sure what to make of them. He just knows that he wouldn't have felt comfortable cooking for a bunch of chefs when he was their age. In fact, Neal Fraser is the only chef who comes to the dinner table with high expectations.

The guests don't have much time to settle into their seats before Sam, Jon, and Henry swoop down in dive-bomber formation with the amuse-bouche. Brendan follows, filling the glasses halfway. Sly and the Family Stone play on hidden speakers. "So this is sort of an amuse," Macklin says with an adrenaline grin. "It's squid marinated in kimchi, and there's a little bit of kimchi at the bottom. There is lime zest and parsley, and then we have unfiltered sake. I don't know much about pairing, but we went to a wine place, and they told us that this would go well with it."

The chefs wait until the boys are safely back in the kitchen before anyone gives the dish a try. Silverton scoops up the squid, finishes it in a bite, and scans the table for reactions. "*All right*," she says. "I'm impressed."

"As an amuse," Lefebvre says, "it's good."

The mood dampens with the arrival of the second course, which Jon introduces as a Kumamoto oyster with buttermilk sauce, a disk of dark chocolate, radish, and fennel fronds on top. The guests spend a few moments contemplating the glistening bulk on their plates with the gallowslike expression of that Dr. Seuss character compelled to try a mouthful of green eggs and ham. "The first time I cooked an oyster for my family," Lefebvre says, "I was 14 years old. I didn't prepare the oysters very well. I kept them out all day."

"And everyone got sick?" Silverton says, laughing. Lefebvre gives her a sheepish nod.

"Are you trying to warn me?" Fraser asks Lefebvre, looking up from his dish. "Is that what you're telling me?"

When they finally put it in their mouths, most seem astonished to find that the combination isn't awful. Fraser is almost enthusiastic. "The fattiness of the chocolate is completely different from the fattiness of the oysters, you know what I mean?" he says. "Usually you just swallow oysters. Because of the texture of the chocolate, though, you can almost chew them together."

"You know what I appreciate?" says Silverton. "That the chocolate is so thin."

"I don't taste the chocolate," says Lefebvre. "I don't know about the dish, but I like the risk. I love risk in cooking. And it's not bad."

The third course—cubed scallop, radish, and black sesame—is a hit. "It's cool that they have that edge, to think of that combination at this age," Lefebvre says. By the time she's tried the sweetbreads with burnt eggplant puree, almond marshmallow, and two-toned parsley bread crumbs, Silverton is verging on exuberance. "These bread crumbs are beautiful," she says. "And their technique from start to finish is spot-on."

"It's a solid dish," Lefebvre says. "I have some cooks working for me for a long time—I don't know if they could do a dish like this. And the sweetbread is cooked perfectly. It's very pink inside and crispy. Perfect! To see this technique at this age . . ."

"You know what I think we need? We need a photo of our plates," Silverton says. She waves over the photographer who's shooting the meal for this story. Turning to me, she says, "We're not being polite."

"I am from France," Lefebvre says. "I'm *not* polite."

In the kitchen there's no clattering, no commotion, no voices raised in panic or frustration, no rushing feet or bodies bumping into each other. Macklin rests his knuckles against the loup de mer on the cooling rack. "The fish is done," he says. "The skin could be a bit crispier." He gently lowers each fillet back into the frying pan. The seasonal vegetables in their butter glaze are bright as protoplasm beneath the lights. Sam, Jon, Brendan, and Henry plate them in a tight circle. The loup de mer is placed atop, slightly cantilevered, skin side up.

It's fallen to Jon again to introduce the dish. "On the bottom is our attempt to have a traditional French sauce, and it's a sauce *bercy*," he says, pronouncing it "ber-*say*."

"It's what?" Lefebvre asks.

"Ber-*say*," Jon says.

"Ah, ber-*see*," Lefebvre says. Then, like a schoolteacher: "Remember it the next time when you speak French."

"*Oui, oui*," says Jon, backing out of the room.

"So why do you think he said 'attempted' to do a sauce?" Silverton asks after the boys have gone.

"'Cause Ludo's sitting here," Fraser says.

"It's cool that they do a classic like this," says Lefebvre. "It's well balanced. You have molecular dishes and then a little classic. And what I'm impressed with is really their technique, and the fish is cooked perfectly. The skin is crispy."

"The vegetables are cooked really nice," says Dotolo.

"I like this even better than the sweetbreads," says Shook. "I wish I could get a dish this caliber at most restaurants in the city."

"This city?" says Silverton. "*Any* city."

The dishes the boys had cooked during their practice sessions looked beautiful, and what I'd tried tasted pretty amazing. But just as Silverton came to this meal worrying about the euphemisms she'd have to come up with, I was concerned about having to hear praise that would betray itself as little more than a pat on the head. Nonetheless this is getting ridiculous—five of the city's leading chefs cleaning their plates, raving about the food, and as best as I can tell, meaning every word. Seeking shelter from the hosannas, I return to the kitchen. Sam asks how they like the meal. After I repeat some choice quotes, the boys are hugging each other and high-fiving.

"We should all stick together," Sam says. "I don't really want to graduate anymore."

"I just want to cook for chefs," Jon says.

"I just don't want to go to school tomorrow," Macklin says. "Let's just open a restaurant."

"Yeah," Sam says. "Can we open a restaurant now?"

"Hey," says Henry, "we're getting way ahead of ourselves."

Tonight will be the culmination of their work together. Jon, though he'll have two more years to decide, is thinking of skipping higher education, since it would be too big a detour from his goal of becoming a professional chef. This fall Macklin is bound for Bard College, in the Catskills, and Sam might take a year off to travel before beginning at Reed College, in Oregon. They may still end up opening restaurants, or they'll be pulled away by fresh possibilities. Jon will be getting his driver's license soon, able to transport himself to a new restaurant job—wherever it may be—on weekends. But it seems certain that none of the chefs they've worked under or might work under, and none of the other friends they've made or will make, are likely to have nearly the same impact on their creative growth as they've had on each other.

The next dish—hay-roasted pork medallions with coleslaw, minimalist barbecue sauce, and mahogany-tinged roasted potatoes on a cat-eye-shaped plate—seems to flow right out of them. So too the whiskey-tangerine-nutmeg palate cleanser and the hazelnut streusel with coffee soil, hay ice cream, and caramel broth. In the dining room Fraser admires the spare Scandinavian beauty of the final course: pear sorbet, sponge cake, apricot puree, lemongrass, lemon rind, and chamomile gel. "This," he says, "is the essence of winter. It's kind of stoic. Like if Ingmar Bergman made a dessert, this is what it would taste like, right?"

"I'm glad that there is one smart person at this table," says Shook.

Tentatively the teen chefs peek in, then pull up a few chairs.

"You're the calmest cooks I've ever seen," Silverton says. "We think you did . . . "

"An amazing job," says Shook.

"To cook a fish perfectly," says Lefebvre, "or do a sweetbread perfectly, or cook pork perfectly—that's not easy."

"Everyone at this table was so blown away by the technique that you guys put into the dishes," says Dotolo, "and the thoughtfulness of them all—even though we all taste the food differently. If you stay in this business, it will constantly happen where some people taste something and they might love it, and some people might hate it, especially if you guys are taking risks, which you're obviously doing, which is cool. Definitely don't stop doing that."

"We all said that we could have been eating at anyone's restaurant as a contemporary," says Silverton. "Anywhere, easily ... "

"Now we're going to do one of the most embarrassing things," says Shook. "The applause."

Slumped in their chairs or over the table, the Samacon chefs absorb it all, exhilarated but beyond exhaustion, their faces still flushed after the clapping dies down. "So," says Macklin, grinning at the dinner party. "Now are you guys going to cook for us?"

SUPPER CLUBS IN DENVER

By John Broening

From the *Denver Post*

Having worked in various big-name kitchens in New York, San Francisco, and Paris, John Broening is now the executive chef of three Denver restaurants, Duo, Olivea, and Spuntino. An ex-English major and son of a foreign correspondent, he keeps his writing skills honed with a weekly column for the *Denver Post*.

"**I**f Paul Prudhomme were dead, he'd be rolling in his grave," says Chris MacGillivray as he seasons his gumbo with a few decidedly nontraditional ingredients: sherry vinegar, agave syrup, and butter.

The gumbo is a sauce for what MacGillivray calls an "Asian-Cajun dish"—Andouille sausage and shrimp-filled shumai dumplings garnished with a cross-section of fried okra.

It is the third course of Noble Swine Supper Club's August dinner, hosted by the owners of Crema, a scruffy luncheonette/coffee shop in the heart of Denver's warehouse district north of Coors field.

The Noble Swine Supper Club, a loose collective of line cooks, chefs, managers, servers and sommeliers, has been around since 2010. Liz Batkin, a front-of-the-house manager who calls herself the Club's "cat herder," describes Noble Swine as a "floating dinner party." Batkin prefers to limit the events to about 30 people and mix half regulars with half newcomers.

Noble Swine events feature place cards with assigned seating ("we aim to inspire unexpected community" the website declares). Democratic, informal, inexpensive to mount, spontaneous, and often wildly varying in quality, supper clubs are the perfect culinary vehicle for the Internet age—they are the culinary equivalent of blogs. Unlike pop-up restaurants, which usually offer an a la carte menu and can run as long as several months, a supper club offers one fixed menu and a single seating. But both formats give otherwise unheralded cooks the opportunity to flex and shine.

Batkin's husband, Andrew Van Stee, a slender, bearded wood-oven cook at Potager who helped found Noble Swine, enjoys the freedom to experiment and the freedom from having to run Noble Swine as a for-profit business.

Traditional restaurant kitchens are usually the expression of the vision and personality of one person and value consistency and obedience to that vision. In a supper club, mistakes, experimentation, involved group discussion, and last-minute, improvisations are not frowned upon but actively encouraged. The menus are, more or less, conceived and executed collectively.

A group e-mail about the event goes out about two weeks beforehand, listing the date and the site. Previous sites have included warehouses, empty apartments, and backyards. The menu is unknown to the guests until they sit down, but most of the regulars like that just fine. "You're going out on a limb, but it's a controlled limb," says Carl Nixon, a regular who describes himself as an Internet abuse analyst.

An hour before a recent 7 o'clock dinner, the dining room at Crema is empty of people and furniture. But by 6:30, two folding tables and a few dozen mismatched chairs have been set up, a few rumpled tablecloths have been smoothed out and decorated with clumps of dried lavender, flowering dill and eucalyptus branches. Red-and-white wine glasses are set on the table, flanked by Mason jars for water.

It's been a hot day, and by the time the guests start to trickle in, the dining room thermostat reads a sweltering 83 degrees. Andrew Burch, the Supper Club's sommelier, has toweled off his glistening shaved head and changed his sweat-soaked T-shirt for a marginally dressier plaid button-down.

Noble Swine does "concept" dinners: a Mexican dinner, a vegetarian dinner, an all-tomato dinner; and the Breakfast for Dinner menu, which featured a now-notorious take on chicken and waffles made with a huge slab of guinea hen. Tonight's dinner is a market menu, eight courses plus a cocktail, five wines, and coffee for $50. The menu features late-summer fruits and vegetables from the farmers market.

The vibe in the kitchen is chatty and casual. The food simmers away on makeshift equipment, camping stoves balanced on narrow counters, a three-tiered plastic steamer from Bed Bath & Beyond that looks like something you'd find at a yard sale. Stubby bottles of beer appear on workspaces after the second course goes out. A call for fresh herbs on a chicken liver dish demands a quick foray through a tenant's apartment to reach herb boxes behind the restaurant.

Most of the cooks wear street clothes and sneakers. The best-groomed Swiner is the dishwasher, a barista at Crema who works in two-tone wingtips and sports a complicated hairstyle. ("We pay him in high fives and beer," Van Stee says.)

The first course is a chilled soup made with Rocky Ford melons, garnished with slivers of yellow Peach tomatoes and shavings of pinkish Coppa salami from Il Mondo Vecchio. The dish pulses with color in the bowl, and on the palate, it tingles with farm-freshness. The soup brings out, surprisingly, the melonlike notes in the tomato. (MacGillivray admits that the combination of melons and tomatoes came from California chef David Kinch.)

If I've had a better restaurant dish in Denver, I can't remember what it was.

The chef in me wonders if a few dishes could have been improved by the intercession of a single, authoritative guiding hand. But the batting average is high. Crispy, pungent buttermilk-battered chicken livers with a deeply flavored jam made of heirloom peppers are followed by a moist grilled quail with pickled tomatoes and a sauce made from charred peaches.

In the long wait between the livers and the quail, BlackBerrys, cellphones, and digital cameras are taken out at the dinner tables. A few of the guests wander over to Crema's coffee nook, which doubles as the plating area, and chat easily with the cooks.

Dessert courses appear. A simple, vibrant dish of Red Heart plums marinated in Meyer lemon juice and sweet basil. A rectangle of zucchini cake garnished with pecan praline and brown butter ice cream. The zucchini cake is super-moist and more deeply flavored than most quick breads: Van Stee has replaced the traditional neutral oil in the recipe with cold-pressed hazelnut oil.

For the Noble Swine Supper Club, this is success—cachet in a small corner of the food world and an opportunity to do the food they want without shortcuts. And enough money to buy equipment and beer and, occasionally, to pay themselves.

Why Chefs Sell Out

By Richie Nakano

From Chow.com

∽⊗∾

After several years as a line cook at San Francisco dining
hotspot NOPA—a high-octane existence chronicled in pod-
casts, tweets, and his entertaining blog LineCook415—Richie
Nakano launched his own trendsetting noodle shop, Hapa
Ramen, a pop-up based at the Ferry Plaza Farmer's Market.

I used to think I was a real cook, legit: burnt arms, late
nights, and an unusually high tolerance for whiskey. I believed I was part of something, a generational stance on cooking
that was a strange mix of punk ethos and military discipline—a
savage precision. It felt like the food I cooked was real food. Honest food.

On any given night you could find me spouting off over a shift
drink about all the food world's bullshit. I would rant about cooking shows I hated, restaurants that were corny, and above all which
chefs were sellouts. Guys who pandered to critics made me crazy.
And whenever I found myself at another glossy event plating bites
of yellowtail crudo, I would scowl and mumble disdain for all the
elite foodies I was serving.

In my days as a line cook there was no degree of compromise I
found acceptable. I had come up reading *White Heat* by Marco
Pierre White. Anthony Bourdain's *Kitchen Confidential* informed
and usually validated my behavior. Rick Bayless was the crazy guy
talking Mexican food in his bathrobe on PBS.

CHEFS, INC.

Then came *Top Chef* and the rise of foodie blogger-ism, Bayless endorsing a shitty chicken sandwich for Burger King, White bending over to do a reality show, and suddenly it was all Bourdain, all the time. Tom Colicchio was hawking Diet Coke, and chefs who'd won James Beard Awards were taking jobs at Chipotle. Just a few weeks ago I saw Thomas Keller (the brand, not the man) in an American Express commercial.

What does it mean to sell out when you're a chef? Consulting for a chain restaurant on the side? Sellout. Being slathered in makeup for a TV appearance? Sellout. Pebble Beach/Aspen/South Beach food festivals for the elites? YOU ARE A SELLOUT. And it got worse. Guys I knew who became personal chefs, caterers—they were all compromised. I was righteously purist even with my own kind.

That is, until I sold out.

The Fame Racket

Kitchen lifers are notoriously underpaid. It's part of the game, what you signed up for. In the beginning, this is fine: You get hooked up at friends' restaurants, live in a rough neighborhood that compensates with good banh mi. You scrape by. Then you get older. And when a child enters your life, all of a sudden things look very different.

So when some ad agency for a housewares manufacturer contacted me to appear in a new "edgy" magazine campaign, I listened. They said: Here's the equivalent of a few months of line-cook wages; all you have to do is fly to New York and have your picture taken for the ads. That's how I found myself with an endorsement contract in hand, getting caked in makeup for the photos, and plotting out monthly cooking demos I'm legally obligated to do for the next year.

Back in San Francisco, I ran into a chef I know at a market one day and told him what I'd done. His judgment was quick: "Sellout!" But other chefs—guys who are also dads—they understood. Corporate chefs get to spend evenings home with their kids, make a better life for their families. Shit, with that money I was going to be able to pay off my Diapers.com bill and put some away for the restaurant I'm planning to open. Selling out is always a calculation, a weighing of benefit against cost.

I have limits. I won't do any endorsement for food corporations, especially for industrial or fast foods. I refuse to appear at those mega-exclusive events in Aspen and Pebble Beach—I have no idea who those festivals are for, or why they exist.

But I do know that selling out comes with new responsibilities. Will I totally lose any credibility I've built to this point? It's one thing for an ad executive to look at my tattoos and think I'm edgy; it's another thing for my food to live up to the hype. The result: I'm under new pressure to be a better chef. The truth is, I took the cash for my kid, but money's never free. Sometimes the sellout is the realest guy in the room.

A Chef's Painful Road to Rehab

By Kevin Pang

From *Chicago Tribune*

As the *Tribune*'s feature writer and Cheap Eats columnist, the prolific Kevin Pang works a dual beat: food and popular culture. Though his approach is usually snappy and humorous, this cautionary tale of a chef's self-destructive downward spiral reveals the darker aspects of life on the line.

Here the man falls, all gruff and bravado, falling like a rocket that exploded midflight. One week he's poised to be the wunderkind chef of a big-time downtown restaurant; the next, he's slipping away from the success he'd hoped to achieve, falling from the grace he's yet to taste.

Brandon Baltzley slides into the middle seat of a taxi. Sitting by the door might give him second thoughts about what he's about to do. The cab swings out the driveway of the Gold Coast high-rise where his girlfriend lives and onto southbound State Street.

It is 8:35 a.m. His belly feels scorched from the bottle of Jim Beam and the nearly entire deep-dish pizza consumed the night before, when the thought of the cab ride and where he was heading filled him with such anxiety that he stayed up all night. Arriving at rehab exhausted and hung over isn't the best idea, but Baltzley has been through this before and is keenly aware of what he is about to face.

"I definitely don't want to go," Baltzley says to his girlfriend, Emily Belden, 24. He exhales loudly, clears his throat. "These 30 days are going to be f——— rough."

A week earlier, Baltzley, 26, was the head chef at Tribute, an ambitious, 170-seat restaurant set to open in the Essex Inn in the South Loop. He spent months developing his menu, crafting a document to tell the world: This is who I am. Instead, on this morning in late May, he will check himself into a drug rehabilitation program on the Southwest Side.

The night before, he paid $100 he owed his dealer. He gave his apartment keys to a friend with instructions on locating his cocaine paraphernalia. Throw it all away, he told him.

In his duffel bag are clothes, two cooking books, toiletries and paper for letters he promised to write Belden every day.

The pressures of the kitchen drive an untold number of chefs into substance abuse. "Aside from officers and firefighters that put their lives on the line, there's no other profession that puts demands on an individual and sets (its workers up) so well to fall into substance abuse and failed marriages," said chef Phillip Foss of the forthcoming El restaurant. "And the vast majority of substance abusers just let it slide." But Baltzley sought treatment voluntarily, and in the process let go of a high-profile position many cooks would kill for.

The cab will arrive at the rehab center in eight miles, 26 minutes.

In the mid-1990s, years before he frittered away what he called his dream job, 9-year-old Brandon needed a stepping stool to reach the kitchen counter. He'd cut corn from the cob, mom would slice cabbage.

It was the two of them—always the two of them in life—working in The Whistlestop, the cafe Amber Baltzley owned in Jacksonville, Fla., where Baltzley made his first bowl of white corn turkey chowder. His mother sought ways to spend time with her only child and cooking held his attention like no other.

He was less devoted to his studies, and he dropped out two weeks into high school. Amber Baltzley knew forcing her son to return was a waste of energy, so she cut him a deal: If you don't go to school, you work full time. By 16, Baltzley was cooking at one of the toniest restaurants in Jacksonville, Stella's Piano Cafe.

Baltzley found parallels with cooking and his other love, playing drums. Both provided immediate and intense tactile gratification. For two years he toured with the metal band Kylesa, and he submitted to all the rock star vices—booze, girls, weed, his first line of cocaine. Amber Baltzley first realized her son was dabbling while watching a show. He looked as if he'd been awake for a week, she recalled. After the last song, Baltzley collapsed onto his drums.

Tired of traveling and eager to cook again, he landed at an Italian restaurant in Savannah, Ga., at 21, but the drug habit lurked. He said he stayed clean in Georgia but lapsed when he moved to Washington, D.C.

Moving to New York only made things worse. Getting cocaine was as easy as pizza, Baltzley said—you called and they'd deliver in 30 minutes. He was making good money at restaurants like Allen & Delancy and Bouley Upstairs. But the jobs were more pit stops: six months here, nine months there. On days off, he'd disappear from the world, snorting cocaine alone in his apartment, always fearing the crash that followed the high. In a single four-day binge, he recalled going through $2,000 of product.

Baltzley was, however, lucid enough to check himself into a rehab facility early last year. He called it the worst 30 days of his life. The withdrawals were hell. His three roommates were legally obligated to be there, he said, and offered no support. And for a chef— the indignity of hospital food! Square slabs of fish served on compartmentalized trays, well, that just put it over the top.

He emerged a shaken man, with a result that would not hold.

Three miles, 14 minutes in, the cab turns onto the Eisenhower Expressway on-ramp. He stares down at nothing in particular; Belden is looking out the window. Their arms are hooked at the elbow.

As Baltzley describes what he's feeling, the conversation turns to vaccinations, and the feeling of knowing a needle's coming. How the nurse removes the plastic cap and you catch a glimpse of metal, and every muscle tenses up, and you know the needle's coming, and your heart's pounding, and you're rubbing the tops of your knees for distraction, *and still you know the needle's coming* . . .

"That's exactly what it's like," Baltzley says.

He sent his resume to Alinea on a whim. Not a chance, Baltzley thought. So when he was hired in September, Baltzley was over the moon. He moved to Chicago, and his trajectory was headed in one direction: to the skies.

But two weeks after he started at Alinea, his mom's Jacksonville home was hit by bullets. She lived in a part of town plagued by gang violence. Baltzley flew down to comfort his mother, knowing fully well that if he went home, his old friends would come around, and the urge . . .

When he returned to Chicago a week later, Baltzley was in bad shape. He'd taken up drinking again. He wrote chef Grant Achatz, and, in one of his most humiliating moments, apologized and said he wasn't in any state to continue.

A month after Alinea, Baltzley took over the head job at Mado in Bucktown. He didn't realize the mess he was in for: He was told he had 48 hours to open, so he scrambled and assembled a kitchen crew mostly of culinary school students. When squabbles with the owner over finances began to boil over, he and his staff walked out right before Thanksgiving.

Around this time, restaurateur Simon Lamb was looking to open a restaurant at the Essex Inn on Michigan Avenue. (Lamb oversaw daily operations at Gioco and Redlight.) Lamb called Baltzley and suggested he apply, and, from 100-plus applicants, Baltzley made it to the round of a dozen finalists. Then came the cooking tryout.

"Brandon blew everybody away," Lamb said. "He cooked food where I was later dreaming about the dish." Baltzley wowed him with a modern take on Carolina barbecue: pork belly confit with Brussels sprouts coleslaw, sweet potato panna cotta and mustard barbecue sauce. "He was driven, entertaining, nontraditional, very relaxed and very funny. I thought, I gotta give this guy a shot."

Baltzley landed the highest-profile job of his career—a tattooed dropout heading a restaurant on Chicago's most famous avenue. But his newly steady paycheck also enabled his drug habit. Gaps of time appeared in the otherwise constant chatter on his Twitter feed; phone calls went unanswered.

It is difficult to quantify substance abuse among chefs, or, when it comes to drinking, at least, even to define it. Television would have you believe that cooking is a glamorous industry when a reality of 14-hour days and $350 a week is closer to the norm.

Before Rick Gresh became executive chef at David Burke's Primehouse, he witnessed friends strung out during service. At one restaurant, Gresh recalled asking a line cook working next to him, "Dude, are you alive?" The cook collapsed moments later.

Anecdotes suggest a combination of factors that make work in the kitchen conducive to substance abuse after hours: a high-pressure environment, the type of people the job attracts and a social hour that begins after midnight.

"We're in a business where you can get anything you want, any time of day, any day of the week," Gresh said. "It's just how it is."

Seven miles, 23 minutes in. The cab turns off the Eisenhower and onto Independence Boulevard.

"Cooking gives me a gratification that nothing else gives me," Baltzley says. "It's the fact that I'm so f———-up and I do all these horrible things in my life, but when I can cook for someone they don't think about those things. Cooking is my mask."

Silence inside the cab.

"I'm secretly wishing they'd turn me away . . . "

Nervous laughter.

Baltzley is asked if he's done his last line of cocaine. Seven seconds tick by.

"Yeah. I think I'm done."

Why the long pause?

"It's been in my life for seven years."

On the right, a three-story brick building appears.

"Oh God, we're here," he says. *"Oh my God."*

Emily Belden doesn't know why she fell for him. She was the product of a stable, drug-free household in the suburbs and dated clean-cut men with steady careers. An hour into their first meeting, three months ago, Baltzley gave his full disclosure—"I'm self-destructive. I'm an addict. I pretty much would ruin everything."—and yet it developed into romance.

Belden first saw him use on their second date. They spent a perfect Sunday together, but that night Baltzley said he needed to get high, and, being naive about cocaine's effects, she didn't protest. In hindsight, she said, it was a mistake.

The first sign of trouble came in late April. Baltzley, between apartments and staying at the Essex Inn, left work one night and started doing lines in his hotel room. It was a few days until anyone reached him, and by then, Baltzley was in cocaine's full grip.

His kitchen staff found him shaking, sweating, vomiting, suffering from chest pains. Belden walked into his room and found empty wine bottles, cigarette butts and drug bags strewn about. She was massaging out fist-size bumps of lactic acid built up on Baltzley's back.

Lamb entered and saw shame in Baltzley's eyes. They read, "I let you down." Lamb was more concerned than angry—by that time the two had become friends first and colleagues second. Still, Lamb had a lot of investors' money riding on Tribute. He made Baltzley sign an agreement saying he'd find help.

But it happened again in mid-May. He called Belden: "I'm doing drugs tonight. You don't want to be around me."

The next five days were a blur for him. Baltzley simply vanished. Lamb said he left 20 messages for him and called around to all the hospitals. Thursday, Friday, Saturday, Sunday, Monday—nothing.

Tuesday morning, May 17, Lamb got a text from Baltzley. It read: "We have to talk."

The cab meter stops at $23. Baltzley arrives at the Gateway Foundation Alcohol & Drug Treatment center at 9:01 a.m. One week has passed since he and Tribute agreed to end their relationship. He and Lamb remain amicable. (On May 18, Tribute announced Lawrence Letrero, who worked under Baltzley, as its new chef.)

Baltzley says he doesn't know which is more frightening: the next 30 days, or the first day he re-enters the world. He doesn't know if people will ever take him seriously again. But he says he's sorry for the people he has let down.

Said Belden: "Seeing him do drugs has changed my opinion of what a drug addict is. Brandon does this alone on a Sunday night. Yes, he decides to take the first hit . . . but once he does that, he loses all control over it. I feel like he's trapped in a body that's convincing him that he needs it."

A patient stares out the window, as if sizing him up. Then, he waves a friendly wave. Baltzley lights up one last cigarette.

"I don't want to be here for the next month, but I have to if I want to . . . if I want to be hirable. If I want the opportunity again for someone to put their trust in me."

He takes one final puff and extinguishes the cigarette. He rubs the back of Belden's neck with his hand. She drapes her arm across his back. Brandon Baltzley walks inside.

BITTER START TO A LIFE OF SWEETS

By Chris Macias

From *Sacramento Bee*

⬥

Then there's the other side of the coin: A chef whose life was
turned around by the opportunity to perform in a high-end
kitchen. *Sacramento Bee* food reporter and wine columnist
Chris Macias profiles an unlikely pastry chef and his against-
all-odds success.

Edward Martinez gently places a chocolate orb in the
center of a white bowl. To the touch, this confection is
hard and impeccably smooth, like a small eight ball.

His right hand, emblazoned with a skull tattoo, holds a small ladle of warmed chocolate-infused milk. He drizzles the liquid over
the orb, accompanied by chocolate streusel and toasted hazelnuts.
It soon breaks open, revealing a sumptuous filling of hazelnut and
milk chocolate pudding, mixed with more crispy bits of chocolate
and hazelnut.

"I like making pretty food," Martinez said. "The first thing you
do is eat with your eyes. You want it to be beautiful. If the flavors
work, it brings that whole dish together."

Martinez serves as executive pastry chef of Hawks in Granite
Bay, which specializes in seasonal ingredients and is among the region's finest restaurants. Even in a chocolate-stained apron, Martinez doesn't look like a guy you'd want to mess with. He stands
over 6 feet tall with a shaved head and a black widow spider on the
back of his neck. His body is an evolving canvas of tattoos, some of

which hark back to a past that he's since left behind: membership in one of California's most notorious street gangs.

Learning to make pastries may have saved Martinez's life, or at least spared him a stretch in the state penitentiary. In 2005, facing three felony charges, Martinez promised to enroll in a pastry-making program, leading to a reduced sentence—and perhaps a last chance at an honest life.

Martinez's Facebook photos show a collage of the sweet and a bitter taste of his past. There's a shot of his moelloux of white chocolate, compressed mandarins, pistachio macaron and mandarin sorbet; an "I heart foie gras" T-shirt sported by his baby son; and the casket of one of Martinez's homeboys from his Fresno gang days being lowered into the earth.

"I never expected to get this far," said Martinez, who recently turned 27. "I expected . . . (to be) in jail, or dead."

Now, Martinez surrounds himself with sugars, ripe seasonal fruits and delicate desserts. He's devouring "Modernist Cuisine," the six-volume book of cutting-edge cooking techniques. His repertoire at Hawks includes nitrogen-frozen chocolate mousse with gianduja crémeux and hazelnut pudding.

"He's the best working pastry chef I've seen," said Pajo Bruich, midtown's Lounge ON20 executive chef, known for his complex cooking techniques. "Hands down, nobody in the Sacramento market is doing the creative elements he's doing."

The Rise of Baby Gangster

Baby Gangster was always ready to fight.

That's what the Bulldogs gang members called Martinez, after he was "jumped into" the gang at age 13.

"I was at the homeboy's house, in the backyard," Martinez recalled, between sips of coffee at a midtown Sacramento cafe. "I'm telling them, 'I want to be in. This is what I want. I want to be a Bulldog.' And they said, 'OK, let's do it.' They beat me up for about 30 seconds. It's weird. You're beating up your friend so they can hang out with you. I got "FRESNO" tattooed across my chest about six months after that."

The Bulldogs have few friends, except for those also inked with the dog paws and "BD" tattoos. Bulldogs are recognized as a violent

California gang, based primarily in Fresno. Law enforcement esti-
mates the gang has more than 6,000 members. The Bulldogs, who
take the name and logo from the mascot at California State University, Fresno, have no allies and no leadership structure. Crips,
Bloods, Norteño and Sureño gangs are all sworn Bulldogs enemies.

Both of Martinez's older brothers were Bulldogs; so were other
close family members. One cousin was nicknamed "Big Gangster,"
while an older brother was "Lil Gangster." Baby Gangster Martinez
was "Baby G" for short—and had it tattooed into his left forearm.

He said his turf was on the east side of Fresno, where he claimed
"Mariposa Street Gangsters"— or "MSG" for short. He'd moved
there from San Jose at the age of 9, about two years after his mother,
Theodora, died in a car accident. He said he still thinks of her baking in the kitchen, surrounded by the smells of sugar and frosting.

His father, Joe Martinez, said his son didn't cope well after her
death. The elder Martinez, who earned an economics degree from
Stanford University, had hoped his four children would get educa-
tions, but his wife's death fractured the family spirit.

"With Edward, he kept a lot inside and started getting into
trouble at school," said Joe Martinez. "Prior to that, he was doing
excellent in school."

Baby Gangster developed a taste for stealing. He was charged
and later convicted in 2001 with grand theft for stealing $2,000
worth of DVD players and other merchandise from a Blockbuster
Video.

In April 2005, while at a Fresno fast food restaurant, Baby
Gangster thought someone looked at his girlfriend the wrong way.
He attacked, punched the victim and fled. According to docu-
ments in Fresno Superior Court, the victim identified his attacker
as a gang member because of his tattoos.

The victim and two witnesses picked Edward Martinez out of a
photo lineup. Martinez was already on parole for the second-
degree burglary at Blockbuster. Baby Gangster went on the run for
more than three weeks.

He knew he couldn't hide forever.

"I finally got tired of running and went to my dad's house," said
Martinez. "I knew they were going to get me there. When they
came to the door, there were cops everywhere. I was going to jail."

Sweet Salvation

Martinez's dad had heard all the talk before about changing for good. So had judges. Martinez was 20 and had served stints in county jail.

Now he faced felony charges of assault and battery, both with gang enhancements, and street terrorism. Facing eight years in state prison, he said he wanted to enroll in a local baking program.

"I pretty much begged," Martinez said. "I knew if I was going to prison that I would do the whole eight years. It would be me gang-banging harder than ever before, trying to fight with everybody."

Martinez pleaded no contest to misdemeanor battery. The other charges were dropped, but he'd have to honor his parole and enroll in the pastry program as promised.

By this time, Martinez had spent nine months in county jail. He was ready to bid his Baby Gangster persona goodbye.

"I needed to prove I wasn't a (screw) up," said Martinez. "I just had to prove to my dad that this is what I was going to do. Baking and pastries was something I could have fun doing. I remembered being happy doing that."

In the Fresno suburb of Clovis, Martinez enrolled at the Institute of Technology's baking and pastry specialist program. He felt self-conscious at first, still sporting a nearly bald head with a "BD" tattoo he had inked in county jail.

"When he came into my class he wasn't very talkative, but when he did talk he had a lot of questions," said Thomas Mendoza, a culinary mentor and instructor there. "He was very inquisitive on things that were new, and when he got a basic technique down, he wanted to take it above and beyond, and make it his own."

His older brothers were still in the gang. In many cases, leaving a gang means "blood in, blood out"—you can only leave with your life.

"There were times when I had a friend come over and tell me some stuff happened in the 'hood and we needed to go handle it," said Martinez. "I'm like, 'I can't.' I'd never told anyone that. He kind of gave me a look like, 'Are you serious?' I said, 'I just can't.'"

Martinez dug into his textbooks and other reading, including "The French Laundry Cookbook." He learned a new vocabulary:

crème anglaise, mignardises, crème de farine and velouté of bitter-sweet chocolate.

"I was loving it," said Martinez. "When I was making breads for the first time, they would look exactly like the stuff in the book. I started showing my dad, 'Look what I made!'"

For his final exam, after the nine-month program, Martinez presented a complex tuile cookie cone with garnishes and the point side down in the center of the plate. His attendance had been perfect, and Martinez made the dean's list.

"He had all the awards you could receive," said Mendoza. "He was one of the leaders in the class. He's one of those students that just gets it."

Martinez applied for a job at Slate's, one of Fresno's finest restaurants. The interview was the first time he'd ever stepped into a fancy restaurant.

"I took him on because no one would probably hire the kid," said Roy Harland, former executive chef of Slate's. "A lot of the ultraconservative Fresno clientele would not be comfortable with a former Bulldog gang member walking through the dining room. I immediately knew this guy has talent and could create."

His New Persona

Like the chocolate orb, Martinez's "Baby Gangster" persona has melted away. When he's not working at Hawks, Martinez raises four children in Antelope with his wife of seven years, Michelle.

Martinez moved his family to the Sacramento area two years ago from Napa, where he worked at the Michelin-starred Bistro Jeanty. He's had other job opportunities, but lost some after potential employers checked his background. Either way, Martinez says, Hawks and Sacramento are happy homes for him.

"My kids are happy and they're going to a good school," said Martinez. "It's about my wife and my kids now. That's why I do everything I do. If it wasn't for them, I wouldn't be working 14 to 15 hours a day."

Past the restaurant's houndstooth chairs and blue walls, Martinez towers over the kitchen's pastry station. He keeps a tank of liquid nitrogen close to whip up new pastries. One looks like something from a mad scientist's laboratory: frozen coconut mousse with coconut sorbet and cilantro oil drizzle.

The infusion of liquid nitrogen to the coconut mousse adds a theatrical kind of fog as the dessert freezes, with the final product looking like delicate cauliflower. The dish's coconut flavors are perfectly pronounced, with Martinez's cilantro oil adding a pleasing herbal accompaniment.

"I like to do modern stuff, but with classic techniques," said Martinez. "I can put some liquid nitrogen into a mousse, but I can also knock out some perfect crepes for you. People will say, 'Oh, this is so beautiful, can we speak to the pastry chef? Where is she?' They'll look at me like, 'You made these plates?'"

He visits other restaurants for inspiration. In February, he and his wife traveled to New York City, dining at wd-50, Eleven Madison Park and Per Se. Over 14 courses at Per Se, dressed in a suit with his collar barely concealing his neck tattoos, he thought of how far he'd come.

"When I walked in, they were all, 'Hi, how are you, Mr. Martinez?'" said Martinez. "I'm pretty sure I'm the only one from my neighborhood that's ever going to do anything like this."

Sometimes he feels the shadow of his past. Before St. Patrick's Day this year, Martinez and others in the Hawks crew shaved their heads for charity. Everyone could see the "BD" tattoo. Two days later, he covered it with a giant skull tattoo.

His goal is to ink over all of his gang tattoos.

"I don't want to be somewhere, like at the beach with my wife, and all of a sudden someone's like, 'What's that FRESNO for?'" said Martinez. "I don't give off the same vibe that I used to."

Still, in the rush of a packed night at Hawks, and especially if someone botches one of Martinez's desserts, he can snap. The difference now, Martinez said, is that he'll apologize.

"To some degree, I think he still has some issues there," said Joe Martinez. "But, he's managed to control it quite a bit. . . . He's done pretty good, and I'm very proud."

Martinez said that both his older brothers have also left the Bulldogs gang. A younger brother, Matt, lives in Sacramento now and works as a line cook at Lounge ON20.

Martinez dreams of opening his own dessert bar, hoping to be known around the country for his pastries.

"I'm Edward now," said Martinez. "I'm not a gangster. He's gone. He's no longer there. I don't look back."

Personal Tastes

KITCHEN CONFESSIONAL: BURNIN' DOWN DA HOUSE

By David Leite

From Leite's Culinaria

This award-winning website's title says it all: It centers on food and cooking, and its founder and editor-in-chief is David Leite, author of *The New Portuguese Table* (among many other publishing credits). Leite's hallmark self-deprecating humor sparkles through an all-too familiar scenario of kitchen disaster.

Now that the turkey leftovers are gone, the tryptophan torpor has receded, and we've physically and emotionally pushed away from the Thanksgiving table, I need to get something off my chest. A kitchen confessional, if you will: On the Holiest of Holy Days for culinistas all over the country, I failed miserably at the stove. Twice.

It was far and away the worst hatchet job I've ever committed—and it was at baking, my bailiwick. In the 20-something years that I've been cooking Thanksgiving dinner, yes, I've forgotten to take the giblets packet out of the bird; yes, I've both under- and overcooked the turkey; and, yes, I've neglected to heat the stuffing to the ideal (read: salmonella-free) temperature. But I've never, ever failed to whip up gasp-inducing desserts. But I can't take full responsibility for my fumble: I mostly blame Twitter and Instagram, because if it weren't for me snapping pictures of my marvelosity in the kitchen for public consumption, I would've had a relaxing holiday, and the members of the Roxbury volunteer fire department would've been able to finish their meal undisturbed.

Let me backtrack. Please.

The Tuesday night before Thanksgiving I was planning to make my pumpkin cake with maple-cream cheese frosting and Melissa Clark's spiced maple pecan pie for dessert. The One is a pumpkin freak and demands the cake every year. The pie was a concession, a peace offering to those poor friends of ours who've been politely eating the same dessert for nearly a decade. I thought they might need a change.

Knowing that some of my blogging brethren, among them Ree Drummond, Shauna James Ahern, David Lebovitz, Gail Dosik, Sara Kate Gillingham-Ryan, are quite adept at snapping cell phone pics of their kitchen hijinks and tweeting them while cooking, I decided I could, too. So with iPhone in hand, and iPad in its kitchen condom, I began clicking away. But instead of waiting until the cake was safely in the oven to upload the shots and check Twitter for the inevitable onslaught of kudos from you all, I decided to reply to every single response while baking.

Basking in your immediate adulation and unconditional love with one hand while meticulously dividing, weighing, and smoothing the batter with the other, I noticed something odd. As in the batter spreading as thick as spackle. I had to work it into the edges of the pan, where the sides meet the bottom. *No big deal,* I thought. *I've made this a million times, and it **always** comes out perfectly. Must be the dry weather.* With that, I slid all three pans into the oven and returned to my 4G iNeedConstantLoveMachine.

Forty minutes later, I pulled the cake layers from the oven to discover they hadn't risen much. *No big deal,* I told myself again. *I'm using three nine-inch pans instead of the usual two eight-inchers.* They're bound to be a little thinner.

I tipped the cakes out of the pans, and instead of steaming circles of spicy pumpkin loveliness, I was affronted by what can only be described as mutants. Each layer was riddled with worm holes. Entire sections were curdled and dry, with huge gaps in them. *No big deal, that's why God made frosting.* It was while reaching for my iPhone, to see who else liked my photos on Instagram, that I spotted them sitting on the counter, mocking me: a chorus line of three cans of unopened solid-packed pumpkin. I'D FORGOTTEN TO ADD PUMPKIN TO THE PUMPKIN CAKE.

For a brief, dark moment, I contemplated passing off this castrato of a cake as the real thing. Chances are my guests wouldn't know, and, most important, neither would you. I imagined millions of you sitting at your computers or holding your cellphones while watching "Body of Proof" just waiting for the final shot of my towering creation. Guilt, my constant sniggering companion, won out. I dumped the damn thing into a plastic trash bag like so many dead bodies on TV.

The next morning, refreshed but hours behind, I turned out what The One later called the best pumpkin cake ever. I tweeted its headshot, of course.

The cake redo slapped me all the way into the middle of Wednesday afternoon. If I worked quickly and efficiently, I could knock out the spiced maple pecan pie and prep my three side dishes: Virginia Willis's bourbon sweet potatoes, roasted carrots with an agresto sauce (a to-die-for mix of chopped nuts, lemon juice, vinegar, wine, parsley, and spices), and homemade green-bean salad.

Melissa's recipe calls for maple syrup and demerara sugar to be simmered until reduced by about a third. Being in a hurry, I calculated I could save almost 20 minutes if I let it *boil* down—and who the hell has demerara sugar in the middle of rural Connecticut? So I used granulated sugar instead. It was then that I walked out of the kitchen into the family room to get a recipe. I'm talking all of 60 feet, people. I was flipping through a cookbook when what sounded liked a nuclear-disaster siren went off.

I ran to the kitchen and from the pot billowed the blackest, foulest-smelling smoke I ever had the misfortune to encounter. Now, I'm good in emergencies. The One and I were like hopped-up Eagle Scouts on 9/11, filling bathtubs and sinks with water; withdrawing huge sums of cash from all of our accounts; and shopping for food, flashlights, batteries, and the current issue of *People* magazine. But on this day, as I ping-ponged between four fire alarms and three French doors, shooing out the smoke with my apron and a spatula (*spatula?*), what's the one thing I forgot to do? Turn off the stove. So as soon as I got the air raid under control, it started again. And again. And again. Finally, I tossed the pan in the sink then thought better of it and flung it out into the yard.

With the bleating now over, the phone rang. *Holy go to war, the alarm company.* I smoothed my sooty apron and cleared my throat. "Hello?" I said, as if I were the top earner at a phone sex company.

"Sir, we have a report of an alarm trigger at this residence. Who am I speaking with?"

"David Leite." My voice was all warm caramel and Cognac.

"Who else is on this account?"

"_____," I replied, using The One's real name.

"What's the passcode, sir?" *Passcode? **What** passcode?*

And as if reading a roll call, I listed every single password I could remember. (Note: None of these are real. What do you think? I'm crazy?) "Ginger, Gilligan, Miss Piggy, Marcia Brady, Julia Child, Tom and Jerry, Mr. Spock."

"Sir . . ."

"Murphy Brown . . ."

"Sir!"

"I DON'T KNOW THE FREAKING PASSCODE, ALL RIGHT? BUT IT'S ME, DAVID LE—"

Dial tone. He'd hung up on me. Then the most sickening sound pierced the air: the wail of the town's fire alarm. "Noooooooooooo!" *The One is going to kill me.* I could see the headlines in the *Litchfield County Times*: "Lauded Food Writer Almost Burns Down the House." Frantic, I called 411 and asked for the Roxbury Fire Department.

"Sir," said the operator, "you don't need to call the fire department. You just need to dial 911."

"No, I don't need to report a fire—"

"Then why are you calling the fire department?"

"Because . . ."

"Sir, I'm required to connect you to 911—"

I pressed "End Call" and dropped my iPhone on the couch as if I were letting go of a putrid piece of pork. Lying there, it chimed an alert: "Instagram: Talon245 liked your photo." *Oh, how sweet of him.* I instinctively reached out to see what he'd written. "No!," I shouted, shaking my head trying to gain perspective.

After a few minutes, The One and our friend Caroline, who was spending the holiday with us, came home. He looked around the kitchen and out into the backyard at the tar-colored pot, slack jawed. "Don't ask," I said before he could say anything. "Please, don't ask." As we stared at each other the whine of another siren grew louder.

"Don't tell me . . . ," he said pointing over his shoulder to the sound, realizing it had my name on it. I nodded my head. "Oh, David" was all he could get out before flashing red lights splashed across the family room walls. I rose to go to the door. "Sit," he said. "SIT!" I obeyed.

"Think this will end up in the newspaper's police blotter?" I asked Caroline, looking for some sympathy.

Ever immune to subtle interpersonal cues, she said flatly, "Probably."

I ran through the kitchen cutting off The One before he got to the door and opened it. A man in a flannel jacket and a bruised fire helmet poked his head in. "Um, is there a fire here?" he asked, unsure he got the right address.

Suddenly self-conscious about what I looked like—after all I was in my Warner Bros. pajamas and a sooty apron—I smoothed my hair.

"Hi, officer," I said, smiling. Behind him was a fire truck and several men putting on gear. "Um, is it *officer*," I continued trying to sound nonchalant, "or *fire marshall?*"

"John. It's John."

"John," I replied, emphasizing his name, "this is rather embarrassing, but I kind of messed up my Thanksgiving dessert. Just a bunch of smoke and drama, but no fire." He looked at The One who was behind me for some kind of assurance. The One nodded.

"I hope I didn't pull you all away from anything important."

"Well, some of the guys were just having an early Thanksgiving at the firehouse." It's amazing how small a 295-pound man can feel.

"Stay away from the stove, will ya?" he said as he jumped back on the truck. "And happy Thanksgiving."

"You, too." I waved off my own personal fire brigade parade.

Exhausted, I curled up on the couch and fell asleep for the rest of the afternoon. I awoke after dark, shivering. The windows were still open; the kitchen still smelled acrid. I avoided The One's gaze as I quietly made my fallback chocolate pecan pie. When I pulled it

from the oven, it was a picture of baking mastery. Forgetting myself, I held it out for him. "Look!" He just nodded. Realizing that
the coolness in the room wasn't coming from just the windows, I
slid the pie on a rack, and then I couldn't help myself.

I took a picture and posted it.

Do I Dare to Eat a Peach?

By John Spong

From *Texas Monthly*

SM senior editor and Texas native son John Spong covers
everything from dance halls and outlaw country to Texas
Longhorns football and *Friday Night Lights*. Mulling over his
childhood as a card-carrying Picky Eater, Spong ponders how
his own children might escape a similar fate.

I've never eaten a pickle, at least not on purpose. It's not a
claim I make with pride, though it comes up somewhat
often, especially in the summer months. Backyard-beer-and-
burger-flip season. For much of my life, such occasions were actually harrowing affairs, hardly conducive to the relaxation for which
they were purposed. The stress typically kicked in at the end of
hour one, just as the congregants moved to the fixings table. The
sun might shine and the birds might sing. A piñata might even
hang in the yard. But the spread would stretch out like a minefield.
Plates stacked with onions, tomatoes, and lettuce, items that, to my
mind, had no more business on a burger than peanut butter. Bowls
filled with potato salad and coleslaw, two concoctions whose very
names I preferred not to let pass my lips. For dessert, the dreaded
watermelon. My only solace would come when the chef called,
"Who wants cheese on their burger?" at which point, if I was
lucky, I'd spot a five-year-old wearing my same look of disgust. A
compatriot. We'd get our burgers first—less time was spent in their

construction—then go eat at the swing set. "You know," I'd explain, "I've never eaten a pickle, at least not on purpose."

On one such occasion a friend's son got curious. "Does that mean you've had one on accident?" he asked.

"Actually, your father once snuck four pickle slices and some mustard on a hamburger he fixed for me. It was at a cookout shortly after we got out of college, an engagement party for him and your mother."

"What did you do?"

"I took one bite and spit it all over the table. I think your grandmother was pretty grossed out."

He looked up at me skeptically, causing me to worry for a moment that he might be pro-pickle. But as he turned to examine the burger on the paper plate in his lap, I knew it didn't matter. I could make him understand by likening the pickle to the beet. Or to broccoli. For that is the essence of the picky eater's dilemma: Whatever that foodstuff is that he finds most objectionable, nothing will be as terrifying as the thought of having it in his mouth.

I say that with intimate authority. I grew up the worst eater I'd ever heard of, the kid that my friends' parents always sent home at suppertime, a sufferer of bizarre food phobias that were absolutely nonnegotiable. I'd refuse to eat cheese, except on pizza, and then only with pepperoni. Mac and cheese and grilled cheese sandwiches were out. By a similar logic, french fries were in but mashed potatoes were out. Condiments were unthinkable, and so too soup, fruit, and any vegetable that wasn't corn. Those few foods I did eat could never be allowed to touch on the plate; "casserole" was the dirtiest word I could think of. I would eat a peanut butter sandwich but had no use for jelly and would refuse to take a bite within an inch of the crust. Chicken was fine, turkey was not, and fish was just weird. Essentially, all I ate willingly was plain-and-dry hot dogs and burgers, breakfast cereal with "sugar" in bold letters on the box, and anything with Chef Boyardee's picture on the label. Or, rather, almost anything. I didn't fully trust the shape of his ravioli; something told me cheese might be lurking within.

Such proclivities came at a cost. In elementary school, I was regularly disciplined for not eating enough of my lunch, sequestered to

the "baby table," where talking was forbidden and cafeteria moni-
tors would loom overhead, pushing me to eat. When summer came,
my parents would no doubt have loved to ship me off to camp but
didn't out of a legitimate fear that I'd starve. That was fine by me. I
was similarly terrified that some camp counselor would force me to
drink iced tea.

At home, my parents did what they could but never had much
heart for the battle. According to my dad, the opening skirmish
was over a sweet potato, when I was two. Though I remember
nothing of the encounter, my guess is—given that my parents were
children of the Depression and were neither adventuresome eaters
nor particularly adept in the kitchen—that the sweet potato had
been boiled, probably for longer than it needed to be. I looked at it
and told him that I didn't eat those. He responded that this was the
first sweet potato I'd seen. At his strong insistence I took a bite,
then airmailed it onto his chin.

Meals became a combination of accommodation and sub-
terfuge. My mom served dinner on steel cafeteria trays purchased
at an Army surplus store. That allowed her to segregate my food.
She'd sprinkle Jell-O mix on banana slices to make them seem
closer to candy. She'd even turn a blind eye—occasionally—when
I'd slide objectionable items to my two younger brothers, neither
of whom suffered from finickiness. One of them actually ate
crayons and cigarettes.

My palate did broaden as I got older, though none of these victories were won at my parents' table. And so ingrained were the
food phobias that I can clearly remember each time I branched out.
I first tried ketchup as a tenth grader, at the old Holiday House on
Austin's Ben White Boulevard, in an effort to look sophisticated in
front of two much cooler upperclassmen. I was a University of
Texas sophomore standing on the corner of Speedway and what is
now Dean Keeton when I became an acknowledged fan of
caramelized onions. A friend argued that they were the primary at-
traction in the $1.50 fajitas we'd just bought from a campus vendor,
then opened one up to prove it. I was shocked. At that point I'd
been enjoying them unwittingly for more than a year.

And then there were tomatoes. I'd long heard that garden-fresh
tomatoes were nothing like the canned ones I'd picked out of my

mom's spaghetti. I could even recite the lyrics to Guy Clark's celebratory hymn "Homegrown Tomatoes." But I'd never been willing
to try one until an afternoon twelve years ago at the home of the
writer Jan Reid. The occasion was a reunion of sorts. Four months
earlier some friends and I had been with Jan in Mexico City. Our
cab had been hijacked by two pistoleros, and Jan had fought back,
ending up with a gunshot wound in his belly and a bullet near his
spine. While rehabbing in Houston, he had asked me to water his
cherished tomato plants. When he finally got home, the Gang of
Four, as he called us, met at his house for dinner.

As we sat down, he announced he was serving BLTs, casually
mentioning how good it had felt to have been able to pick the
tomatoes that afternoon. He thanked me for keeping them alive
while he'd been in the hospital. It didn't seem an appropriate time
to say, "I don't eat those." They tasted as great as food served by
someone who's saved your life should. And the affinity held up; the
next time I encountered a homegrown tomato I bit into it as if it
were an apple.

By then I was 33 years old. And though nowadays I'll eat just
about anything—and have never really wondered what my life
would have been like if only I'd met tomatoes sooner—a new
concern has arisen. At 44, I've finally gotten married, and my wife
and I are talking about starting a family. We've seen enough friends
have children to know that wearing regurgitated yams will be part
of the bargain. But we'd like to find a way to make that stop sometime before the kids go to college. Since my genes will get the
credit for any picky eaters produced, the burden of learning why
they happen and how best to deal with them has fallen to me. So I
started doing some research.

Imagine a caveman is eyeballing a hamburger. His reaction will be
as instinctual as going to the bathroom or looking for love. The
sight and smell will alert his brain that proteins and calories are
available. With the first bite, chemical reactions between the
burger's ingredients and taste receptors in his tongue will send
messages through his nervous system, primarily the chorda tympani nerve, which stretches around his eardrum to the stem of his
brain. If there's a tomato on it, or maybe some ketchup, he'll get a

sweet taste, which upon arrival upstairs will trigger a small dopamine release. His body will read that as good news. The same will happen with the salty fat in the meat and cheese. But if by chance there's some arugula onboard, a bitter taste will register, signifier of potential poison. He'll likely spit that out and pick it off the rest of the burger. As he continues, chewing and swallowing each bite, a second, internal smelling process will take place every time he exhales. This information will be more detailed than that from the tongue, which can read only the five basic tastes: salty, sweet, sour, bitter, and the newly discovered, ever-nebulous umami. The news will combine in the brain and be read as distinct flavors. He'll go about the rest of his day with a good supply of energy and remember that meal as a fine thing.

Now picture the caveman eating at Austin's Counter Cafe, rightfully considered home to the city's best burger. Sitting next to him and regarding an identical lunch is a member of that class of Austinite that considers itself the town's most evolved: the trendy hipster. (Though they share the same bedhead and beard, the hipster will be identifiable by the pair of Ray-Bans folded next to his plate.) His relationship with the burger will be much more complicated. Assuming his parents were middle- to upper-class, he's at least one generation removed from foods of necessity, so he's known only the luxury of choice. If he grew up in the seventies or eighties, his earliest exposure to vegetables was probably via Del Monte and Green Giant, black-magic alchemists who, through canning and freezing, confused an entire nation on the meaning of "garden fresh." If he suffered from chronic ear infections as a kid, his chorda tympani may have been damaged and his sense of taste permanently altered. Or he may even be a supertaster, one of that quarter of the populace whose tongues can have twice as many taste receptors as the average eater's. In that case, every taste will be magnified, particularly the bitter ones. Given all the variables, if the hipster chooses to leave everything off his meat patty but the bun, there'd be plenty of potential reasons why.

"When we talk about picky eating, we are talking about pleasure and people who don't get the same hit from eating that others do," instructs Linda Bartoshuk, the director of human research at the University of Florida's Center for Smell and Taste. She was one

of the first experts I called, a legend in the tight circle of neuroscientists, psychologists, and nutritionists who study the way people
eat. She's researched taste for 45 years, and among her discoveries is
the supertasting phenomenon. "There are major categories of
things that affect how much pleasure we take from food. One is
sensory, and that's where the supertasters fit in. We don't all taste
things the same way. That's hardwired. The other is experience, the
pathologies you have encountered. That is all learned."

Those lessons come early. When Bartoshuk explained the fundamental nature of conditioned food preferences and aversions, she
pointed to baby rats, who sniff their mother's breath to learn what
is safe to eat. In finicky humans, the primary pathology is gastroin-
testinal problems. If a person of any age throws up shortly after
eating, he'll automatically develop an aversion to whatever he just
ate, regardless of any causal connection between it and getting sick.
"When I see a picky kid, the first thing I try to find out is his medical history. If the parents say he threw up a lot when he was
young, I've got a pretty good idea why he finds many foods dis-
gusting. It's a brain mechanism he can't help."

The neuroscientists I consulted stressed the same kinds of physical problems as Bartoshuk. Psychiatrists and psychologists, on the
other hand, steered the conversation to the behavioral side of the
equation. They said that many kids between the ages of two and
four will experience some measure of pickiness. It's as natural as
learning to say no. Timid children may have an ingrained distrust
of things that are new. Tactilely sensitive kids, like the ones who
need the tags cut out of their T-shirts, may have trouble with food
textures. Others may live in the neon food world of a supertaster.
In these instances, the key is the parents' reactions. If the parent
forces the kid to eat food he doesn't like, meals will turn into
power plays. With a strong-willed child, that's the kind of problem
that can stretch well into adolescence. (The chefs I talked to, by the
way, piled on the parents even harder. The problem, they said, is
that most moms and dads can't cook.)

As the experts ticked off the things that typically go wrong, they
sounded as if they had had access to my childhood scrapbooks. My
first extended hospital stay came shortly before I turned three, during a frightful bout with epiglottitis. Because of a virus, my throat

was closing shut, producing the kind of prolonged, painful eating trauma that the shrinks and neuroscientists said could lead a kid to reject a whole host of foods. But the sole connection my parents ever made to that event and my diet was of a different sort: They cited it as an example of how obstinate I could be. The hospital stay had been cut short because I wouldn't eat the food. My folks got tired of bringing me Spaghetti-O's.

As my teen years approached, every meal became a battle of wills. My parents would tell me to eat, I would refuse, and they'd wait me out. My brothers would finish dinner and be excused to their rooms before I could sneak them my green beans. The family dog, a supremely overfed basset hound named Bobo who was my greatest ally in such matters, would be shooed to the garage. While Mom cleaned the kitchen, I'd remain at the table. Eventually she'd sit and watch me, sometimes for as long as an hour. She never turned cruel. One doctor I talked to described parents who tell their children, "If you don't want it for dinner, you'll have it for breakfast," then put the plate in the fridge to serve it again in the morning. That sounds like torture, and that didn't happen. Instead, I'd ultimately give in, choke down my two green beans, and wash off my plate.

But those wars were fought just once a week. My dad worked days and my mom worked nights; Thursdays were the only time we assembled for what we called "sit-down family meals." Only years later did I recognize another dynamic at work. My folks split at the start of my senior year at UT, after 29 years of marriage. Suddenly it dawned on me that they'd never exactly been crazy about each other. That explained their work schedules and the tension around mealtime and the fact that my dad moved into my room when I left for college. It also provided a new name for the suppers he had cooked solo: Dysfunctional-Family Recipes. We ate a lot of fried bologna sandwiches and pancakes made with Bisquick and water when there was no milk in the house. A favorite among us three boys was something my dad called "barbecued hot dog casserole," which consisted of butterflied foot-long wieners spread out in a glass dish, bathed in a full jar of hickory sauce, and baked. I'd always thought that eating a condiment and a casserole represented growth.

On weekends we'd occasionally hit the McDonald's drive-through as a full unit. I was, of course, unwilling to eat any of the already prepared items that give fast food its name. The burgers under the heat lamp sported mustard, pickles, and onions, and I wouldn't touch one, even with everything scraped off. Instead I'd insist on one specially made.

The cashier at the window would direct us to a corner of the parking lot, where we would sit in the station wagon and wait. My mom didn't believe in air-conditioning, and my dad didn't believe in bickering, so the interludes were quiet and uncomfortable. He might fiddle with the radio; she might comment that the car needed washing. My brothers and I would turn around to stare out the back window at the McDonald's front door.

Eventually an employee would emerge and bring out our order, then wait by the car while I inspected my burger. If so much as a hint of yellow mustard showed up on the outside of the wrapper, I'd send it back.

Chef Andrew Zimmern is the co-creator and star of a program on the Travel Channel called *Bizarre Foods with Andrew Zimmern*. For six seasons, he's played the part of the cheerfully daring food tourist, landing each week in a new spot on the globe to sample local staples, always something that would shock any eater back at his Minneapolis home. He's become a devotee, for instance, of spoiled foods. "Whether it's fermented skate wing in Japan, or hákarl [fermented shark] in Iceland, or stinkhead in Alaska, fermented and rancid foods are eaten all over the world," he told me. He's had bat meat on three continents. "Fruit bats are actually really clean. You can even eat all the innards because they have a very small diet in a very-small-ranging area." He once stood with members of the Masai tribe in a corral inside the Ngorongoro Crater, in Tanzania, drinking cow's blood directly from the source. "That was a big jump," he admitted.

The segments are essentially snuff films for picky eaters, the kind of TV that would have once given me nightmares. "It's been amazing to watch my gag reflex get less responsive," he said over the phone after a weekend exploring Montreal's finest seal meat dishes. "I was certainly more trepidatious about food when I started. But when you taste something that at first scares you, that you don't understand or just don't want to eat—maybe you've had a bad version of it before—if it's good you learn to stop practicing contempt before investigation."

Zimmern the world traveler blames limited diets on cultural forces. "I've been running a kind of experiment with my son, who's six. I've tried to get to him before the cultural guardians can. He had a book called *Yummy Yucky*, and it associated worms with yucky. So he won't eat worms, which is very interesting to me. Because he loves crickets and june bugs and all of the other funky little things that are edible in our garden in the summertime. Sometimes we just sit and eat them off the ground."

Zimmern makes meals in his household sound uncomfortably close to meals on his show. But assuming he's not telling his son that he can't go inside until he finishes his bugs, his experiment isn't far from the fix suggested by every expert I consulted on getting past picky eating: Kids learn to enjoy food from parents who model—not demand—healthy eating habits. There's no way to predict how a child will react to a food; identical twins can have completely different diets. But as soon as a parent tells a kid that his preference is something that needs correcting, the discussion stops being about food. Nutritionists say most children need to be exposed to an objectionable food twelve to fifteen times to develop a taste for it. Psychiatrists insist that every plate at the table should have the same foods on it, but in portions that reflect what each person wants. Chefs suggest giving the kid authorship of his meals. Let him pick an item or two, then encourage him to help cook. If possible, plant a garden together. But above all, don't create a problem where none exists. The key is to provide regular, stress-free family meals.

It's worth noting, however, that none of the experts said those family meals had to be with people you were actually related to. Shortly after my parents divorced, I started law school at UT, and a new economic reality set in. With nothing but a student loan to fund my first year, I had to make adjustments in every aspect of living, and particularly in eating. Most meals came from boxes of frozen chicken breasts that my mom bought at Sam's Club. But each Sunday night I had dinner at the table of Marisol Vidal-Ribas Brown.

An elegant, aging daughter of upper crust Catalonia, Mrs. Brown had moved to Washington, D.C., in the mid-sixties and gone to work for the CIA, where she fell madly in love with a spy named Glenn. They married almost instantly, then raised two sons at various Pan-American locales where he was stationed before settling down in Austin in 1979. But Mr. Brown died in 1990, while their older son, Carlos, a college roommate of mine, was off at medical school. I started stopping in Sunday evenings to tutor Glenn the younger and get a free meal.

Her dinners were different from anything I'd ever known. The dining room walls were covered with black and white photos of her parents and twelve siblings from before she left Barcelona, the women in gowns and the men in morning coats, some with a hand tucked inside their lapel. They each had Mrs. Brown's same long, somber Spanish face and seemed to be watching to make sure she held to her Old World upbringing. She did. There was always a crisp white tablecloth and polished chargers, along with the rest of Mr. Brown's family silver. We said grace. We drank wine, but never to excess. And we never stacked plates when clearing the dishes.

She would hold court at the table's head, fingering her pearls and Mr. Brown's wedding band, which she wore on a long chain around her neck. Her stories were incredible, often summoned by the meal she was serving. If she had been lazy that day and only managed to fix chicken, it might be good, but never as good as the chicken roasted by her governess, Tata, on a beach in Genoa when her family fled Barcelona during the Spanish Civil War. If she made Spanish rice, she'd point out that it wasn't Spanish at all but a variant of something she'd first tasted in Honduras, when Mr. Brown was keeping an eye on the Cubans.

The great lesson from her wasn't just to try food but to experience it. Well-mannered as she was, she wasn't above dropping her fork at a satisfying bite and grunting loudly, "Oh, wow!" And though she took an immigrant's pride in her American citizenship, she never let go of an ounce of her Spanishness. "In Spain," she explained, in an accent that grew thicker as she got older, "food is as big a part of who we are as Picasso or Gaudí." Gradually, because Carlos had been a picky eater too—he and I didn't fully bond until he introduced me to the magic of late-night ketchup-only Whoppers at UT—she started bringing out her native dishes. Paella made with saffron sent by one of her sisters. White almond gazpacho with frozen green grapes sunken in and topped with a dollop of aioli. She cleaned out the fridge like her mother had, by making what she called a "tortilla apartment building": four egg omelets, each with a different "room-mate," like potatoes, mushrooms, spinach, and shallots. She'd stack them one on top of the other, cover them with a simple red sauce, then cut slices, like a cake.

I ate there once a week for the next ten years, continuing after Glenn left for law school, with a regular group of his friends that she called her "stray dogs." As I started to experience adult life's little victories and defeats, she coaxed me through career changes and romantic entanglements, and our relationship became about more than meals. But food was how we expressed it. Before she moved away in 2001 to join Carlos's family in Los Angeles, we determined that our last outing together should be a trip to Central Market, where she would teach me how to "buy Spanish."

On the day after Christmas 2006, I joined her and Glenn in Barcelona for a week of meeting her family and seeing her country. All I remember are the meals. Each day a three-hour afternoon feast was scheduled at someone's apartment, every one a rerun of our Sunday nights. But we decided to skip out on the final day's invite. Mrs. Brown wanted to take me to a famous restaurant near the harbor called Les Set Portes, which is Catalan—not Spanish—for the Seven Doors. "I know it is touristy now," she said, "but this is where my family came when I was a little girl."

In a huge formal dining hall with two attendants at our table, Glenn made the boring order, a simple seafood paella. Mrs. Brown had monkfish roasted in romesco sauce, a traditional Catalan accompaniment that looked like a creamy tomato sauce but was actually made from almonds, pine nuts, olive oil, and roasted sweet peppers. But I ordered best. I had a fideuà negra, a paella variant with tiny Catalan pastas that looked like minced straw. They were soaked in squid ink and cooked with mussels, oysters, shrimp, and small, whole squid. The fish had clearly been caught that morning, and the taste was as rich as cake icing. It was the single greatest meal I've ever eaten.

Shortly before I left on that trip, my mother asked me to bring her back a gift. By that time, the nature of our food fights had changed, if not the outcome. When picking a place to eat, she would suggest something Southern fried and I'd push for sushi, just to get under her skin. She'd get as irritated at that torture as she once did the tantrums. But on this occasion she had a surprise: She asked me to return with a Spanish cookbook.

We flipped through it together when I got home, and I showed her some of the dishes I'd eaten. Most of them struck her as far too exotic. But then she saw a recipe for a lightly battered, pan-fried tilapia. We agreed that would be a meal we should prepare together.

Sweetly, she made no mention of pickles. To this day I've never tried one. Maybe I'll wait and do that with my own kids.

A Proposal for Feeding the Fat and Anxious

By Josh Ozersky

From *Gastronomica*

Columnist (*Time, Esquire*), founder of the Grub Street food blog, and star of his own web-based OzerskyTV, Josh Ozersky is the author of *Hamburger: A History* and *Colonel Sanders and the American Dream*. A man of prodigious appetite, Ozersky can be as entertaining as he is often controversial.

I want to design a restaurant for fat people. You may be thinking, "Wait, aren't all restaurants designed for fat people?" They're not, not really. For one thing, almost all good restaurants are designed by slim androgynies wearing Buddy Holly glasses. Their friends are slim, and the people who eat there are slim. The servers are slim, and frequently slim and winsome. The cooks themselves, who in happier times were the very images of portly mirth, are now sinewy whippets, the cords of their young muscles visible beneath full-sleeve tattoos. Even the very chairs and tables themselves are designed for thin people. In short, what is needed is a full, radical rethinking of restaurants from the point of view of fat people—something like what Temple Grandin did for beef cows, but further up the food chain.

I believe that I am the man for that job. The fat have a fellowship, a shared knowledge that regular people can never grasp. Once Michael White, a chef of no small bulk himself, looked at my shoes and said, "I see you have 'fat man laces.'" "Fat man laces?" I asked. "What's that?"

"They're tied on one side of your shoe. Fat guys tie their shoes with their legs crossed because they hate to bend down." The inescapable truth of this hit me; a glimpsed image in a passing mirror, and I knew he was right. I did have fat man laces! Sherlock Holmes, cadaverous though he was, might have figured out such a thing—but he would never have known the indignity of pushing and peering over his own stomach, of it getting in the way of his feet and knees like the gross, distorted imposition a fat man's stomach really is. Nor would the genius of Baker Street ever deduce the general unsteadiness that threatens a fat man on those rare occasions when he bends down, trying to hold bodies in balance when every law of physics seeks to topple him unhappily to the floor.

I know about this because I've been varying degrees of fat for most of my life. I'm at a low ebb at the moment, and this has allowed me to reflect on how to make a restaurant for fat people. We're only really happy at restaurants, you know—and then only for a few minutes. (We prefer to be at home, eating over the sink or munching away in front of a monitor of some sort; but the more gregarious of our race, when we do go out, generally head to restaurants—or would, if they were better designed.)

For example:

- Fat people have bad backs and poor posture. They don't like to sit in narrow, hard-backed chairs. What they really want most is a padded La-Z-Boy or some such contraption. But since eating requires an upright posture, a well-padded chair, with rests for bulky broad arms and plenty of lumbar support down low, is a must. Fat people live in a world with twice the gravity of Earth, after all. That's why they wheeze and waddle the way they do. We're not saying it's OK. It's not.

- The restaurant should be cold, too cold for thin people. This will have the doubly beneficial effect of driving thin people out, because, really, who wants to look at thin people? And of course fat people, their swollen, unhealthy bodies working hard just to pointlessly stay alive, are fiery furnaces deep within, churning and chewing away beneath troubled brows. We require constant refrigeration just to keep going. Thermostats should be set for a frigid 55 degrees, with all fans set on high for maximum cooling.

- The servers need to be fat themselves, but fat in a non-threatening way. The last thing a fat person wants to see in his or her server is a sweltering, shameful wretch, wincing under the stigma of her body image. On the contrary! What's needed is a cheerful vulgarian, a post-menopausal mother figure with a ready smile and a sprightly line of patter. The sort of lady who might say, "Do you want some more coffee, Hon?" were you somewhere more downscale. I say, "The last thing a fat person wants to see"—but of course, there is something a fat person wants to see less: a thin, long-limbed, care-free twenty-something, glorying in her sexual prime and regarding the customers as so many hideous zoo animals, waiting to be fed. (They don't need to actually have this attitude; just being young and attractive is enough.)

- Speaking of sexuality, there shouldn't be any. Dining here is a solitary and celibate experience, in which both sexes are protected from even a hint of having to socialize. For this reason, every table is a solo one, kidney-shaped—its full space angled to the diner's sad eyes and ravenous maw, its shape allowing advanced convex gut docking, as well as maximal hand and arm reach in every direction.

- Certain design elements are mandated for the Fat Restaurant. Obviously, there will be no mirrors, frosted or otherwise, anywhere, and the lighting will consist of a dim and melancholy twilight interrupted only by chiaroscuro spotlights not on the table, indeed, but rather on the food itself. Always the food itself—only the food.

Speaking of which, the menu will consist of, but not be limited to, the following:

- Large joints of meat—most notably the shoulder, leg, buttock or round, saddle, baron, and ham, suitably burnished with a luminous glaze, to dazzle the weak, beady eyes of gourmands, and bring a temporary sparkle to them. The imposing size of large cuts dignifies the act of eating, and the fact of having one entirely to yourself gives a temporary sense of value and worth to the customer. Uneaten portions can be used for subsequent courses, their fat rendered for hash browns, the exposed pink flesh seared off in saucepans with olive oil or brown butter, the more difficult pieces ground up for hash, the bones split and seared for marrow (to then be used as a dressing on the hash).

- High-piled platters of fried foods, including chicken, cutlets, country-fried steak with cream gravy, crusty onion rings breaded with panko, matzo, fine flour, coarse flour, and/or pork cracklings; non-vegetable tempura items; semi-boned chicken wings; untrimmed shoulder pork chops in joyously shatterable beer batter; cod filets; shoestring French fries; slow braised short ribs; tender melting lamb breast; long-simmered veal stew chunks; and other softened meats, pressed and refrigerated and bound with their own collagen, and then plunged into cauldrons of the appropriate boiling animal fat; and tater tots, lots of them, dressed with fried garlic and Maldon salt. (These should also be available as bar snacks, petit fours, and bathroom mints.)

- Grilled cheese prepared on the airiest conceivable bread, thin and diaphanous to the point of abstraction, orgiastically slathered with oleomargarine, and containing nourishing viscous, mild and rich slices of bright-orange American cheese, such as gluttons remember from the faint mists of their childhood, when a future entombed in necrotic, immobilizing tallow still lay unimagined.

- Heavy stews, civets, porridges, congee, risotto, lush plovs, and pilafs, and other starchy, melting media for fat and flavor. Each bite is prized by the portly for their soporific effect and the brief periods of torpid slumber that result.

- All variations of the hamburger, including meat loaf sandwiches, sliders, meatball subs, leftover Salisbury steak served on slices of untoasted potato bread, massive steakhouse burgers with carbonized char marks and red bleeding interiors redolent of zinc and Roquefort; flattened coffee-shop discs, served on large toasted white buns, on each half of which a slice of tangerine-colored cheese (see above) has been melted; maid-rites; Jucy Lucys; sloppy joes; steak tartare on toast points; and Manwiches.

- High-piled layer cakes with copious amounts of lemon frosting, chocolate fudge, or coconut, depending on age and region of the diner, with or without heavy dollops of fresh whipped cream, and who's kidding who, it's obviously going to be "with." (And let's have another dollop over here, too, thank you.)

Once the diner has finished eating, no further presence on his or her part is required: no labored shifting in the chair to accommodate a burdened body, no polite excuses to go out and take an "air bath," no endless wait for the server to return. Fat diners, at the moment of having eaten a big meal, are at the absolute nadir of their day-to-day existence: their best and only pleasure and goal has been sated, leaving in its wake an aching, angry nausea and a self-hatred almost as deep as the pleasure they've just taken at table. They no longer wish to sit alone with their thoughts. They don't want to face the far side of the meal now working its way through the bilious labyrinth of their innards. All they really want is to get out, and quick. So an EZ Pass-type device, perhaps implanted in an earlobe or neck fold, will debit their bank account as they pass through the gate of the Fat Restaurant back out into the world, until they are ready to return.

BONE GATHERER

By Mei Chin

From *Saveur*

Essayist and fiction writer Mei Chin often stretches the
bounds of food writing, mixing in elements of memoir and
magical realism. Besides award-winning *Saveur* articles, her
writing has appeared in *Gourmet*, *Vogue*, the *New York Times*,
and on her website bastethebook.com.

I've always loved meat on the bone—spicy, messy chicken
wings; pan-fried pork chops; the beef ribs my mom used to
bake, coated in bread crumbs and mustard butter—but I never really
thought about bones until a recent trip to South America forced me
to take them seriously. I had signed on as a camp cook for a birding
expedition to a remote part of Central Suriname. We were heli-
coptered onto a patch of bare rock several thousand feet above sea
level, a place where, we were told, no human had been before. We
were surrounded by jungle filled not only with birds, but venomous
snakes. I was assured by my companions that any resident jaguars
would mistake me for a small mammal and, hence, lunch. Torrential
rains flooded camp every night, and our waterlogged satellite phone
died, leaving us with no contact to the outside world.

It was a feral life. I hacked through bamboo with a machete,
washed my hair in a stream. I cooked with peanut butter, rice, and
from time to time, the roasted carcasses of the birds that we had
collected. I had learned the weird but beautiful art of preparing
specimens, a painstaking process in which you separate the bird's

skin from its flesh while leaving much of the skeleton intact. We had set up bird-checking nets a bit higher on the mountain, and I would check these while my mates were out exploring. The rocks above camp were slippery with moss and rain. I have been clumsy since I was a child, but in the mountains, I got very good at falling—indeed, I became kind of addicted to it.

It wasn't until a couple of weeks after my return to the States, when I took a spectacular spill on some hotel stairs, that my falls on the mountain came back to me with a vengeance. I found myself in excruciating pain, with a broken hip, and doctors were telling me that my left femur—the leg bone between the pelvis and knee—was so messed up, it would have to be replaced. I'd be off my feet for months. According to the older Chinese women in my life, I was supposed to eat a lot of bones, in keeping with the traditional Far Eastern belief that you should eat whatever body part is ailing—owl eyes for myopia, pig lungs for emphysema. Condemned as I was to crutches and virtual house arrest, the old beliefs started to make sense.

Besides, despite my own fragility, bones are powerful things. In ancient China, they were used to make prophecies. In the Gabriel García Márquez novel *One Hundred Years of Solitude*, a girl carries her parents' bones around in a sack, where they clank and groan until a spot is located for their burial. In my favorite fairy tale, the bone of a murdered man is carved into a flute, which plays a song that reveals the killer. There is a restlessness in bones, a personality that endures long after the owner has passed on.

I began my convalescence by making a stock from beef necks and veal knuckles the color of old lace. When I saw them—beautiful, haunting—I was reminded of the animals from which they came. When you look at a steak you don't necessarily think of a steer, but the neck bones, shaped like giant jacks, conjured the massiveness of the animal and how it moved.

Nothing demonstrates the elemental magic of bones more aptly than a stock. Any Chinese child with the flu will know the taste of pork bone and ginger stock, hot, heady, and healing. Korean babies are weaned on *sullongtang*, the milk-white soup made from beef bones simmered for anywhere from 12 hours to days on end. The French chef Auguste Escoffier claimed that a great kitchen is founded on great stock; serious cooks approach their stocks with shamanic intensity. It's a matter of extraction. Protein, sugar, and fat break down during cooking and are released from the meat and bones into the water in which they steep. And while the meat contributes to flavor, the bones, loaded with collagen, impart body and a velvety mouth-feel.

Home from the hospital, staring at the stove in my apartment's small kitchen, revisiting old volumes on my shelves—the fairy-tale collections and cookbooks and photo albums—I began to entertain a romantic notion of the perfect broth, based on the memory of a *brodo* I had when I was 11 years old on a chilly March evening in Venice. Limpid, sweet, and nuanced, it was as fortifying as wine or tea—a rich yet balanced infusion of meat, bone, and aromatics. Broth has always been part of my cooking repertoire, but I've frequently allowed mine to boil because I could not be bothered to watch the pot. If there's one thing all the cookbooks I now pored over agreed on, it's that should your broth ever so much as begin to boil, you should throw it away. During boiling, particles of fat and protein are agitated and become suspended in the liquid; a boiled broth is murky and greasy.

In pajamas and slightly stoned from daytime television and Percocet, I had plenty of time on my hands—time enough, finally, to heed the experts. I set my stove to its lowest heat and prepared to wait a very long time: By all accounts, the water—and beef bones and turkey wings, carrots, onion, garlic, celery, and bay leaf—would take more than an hour just to come up to temperature. I left the pot on the stove overnight and all the next day. A *brodo* should barely simmer; several seconds should pass between bubbles. At a very low and constant heat, unwanted impurities released from the meat and bones will coagulate and rise to the top or cling to the sides of the pot, and they can be easily skimmed off.

When at last I strained the broth, the result was pure alchemy: a clear, golden liquid with a perfume much greater than the sum of its parts—there were notes of caramel and nutmeg, butter and clove. It was one of the most thrilling moments I've experienced as a cook. How often do we manage to duplicate perfectly a romantic notion? I garnished my first bowl with curls of Parmesan and sipped it slowly, inhaling the sweet steam.

Of course, these days it's trendy to be into bones, not only wings and ribs, but chicken necks and ham hocks and shanks. Much as many chefs can now be found flaunting their affinity for bones, they're still a fantastic bargain: At my local butcher, marrow bones go for $2.99 a pound. This is true of all sorts of bones and bony cuts. Sometimes, if a customer orders a noisette—the meaty eye of the rack of lamb—my butcher will even give me the bony remainder for free.

Years ago, the same butcher had taught me how to french a rack of lamb, a technique that involves scraping some of the meat away with a long, thin knife to lay bare a fringe of elegantly curved bones. Now, laid up and armed with a boning knife, I found the taxidermy skills I'd acquired in Suriname useful. I started frenching everything in sight, and was alarmingly good at it. I turned chicken wings into chicken lollipops and frenched itty-bitty rabbit racks. I found out that the technique also worked wonderfully with shank—the length of bone and meat just below the knee—by far my favorite part of any animal.

The marrow was silk on my tongue, and yet the white bone on the plate retained an echo of the visceral and the wild.

Lamb shanks braised low and slow, until the meat is tender and the bones release their marrow to enrich the braising liquid, are always marvelous served with something starchy to soak up the sauce—polenta, mashed potatoes, risotto—but I like them best when they're set, gigantic and resplendent, on a bed of white bean purée. Frenching the shanks makes the presentation that much more spectacular, a hunk of meat beckoning at the end of a length of parchment-colored bone. When I tried it, I browned the shanks thoroughly before putting them in the oven, and I made sure to turn the meat every half hour or so for an evenly caramelized exterior. Cooking a shank in this way is virtually foolproof due to its high ratio of bone to meat; because the bone absorbs heat, the meat immediately surrounding it cooks slowly and is the most succulent. And let us again not forget the collagen that attaches the meat to the bone. Over the course of cooking it turns to gelatin—a special treat to enjoy once you've dispensed with the meat.

Then there's marrow. When the creamy, voluptuous stuff is scooped from the bone's hollow, it can be stirred into a sauce to add lushness. It is the best part of an osso buco—that's Italian for "bone with a hole"—and once you've stripped the meat from the long-braised veal shank and devoured it, inside that bone you'll find a final treat, a secret store, best coaxed out with a long, slender spoon.

To eat marrow—the tissue that produces new blood—is to indulge in an act that treads the boundary between the rude and the refined. There was, in fact, a time not too long ago when my supermarket was selling marrow only as a dog treat. But once I felt well enough to put on a dress and hail a cab, marrow was the first thing I sought. Together with my new hip—a man-made bone fashioned from enameled metal—I headed to a Manhattan restaurant called Ai Fiori.

If eating marrow is typically a messy, primal, hands-on affair, at Ai Fiori, chef Michael White has resolved the issue by halving the bone lengthwise. For the dish he calls *Mare e Monte* ("sea and mountain" in Italian, a play on surf and turf), White lines the halved bone with celery root purée, nestles in overlapping disks of steamed scallop and black truffle, lays out a layer of marrow on top, and then broils the whole thing. It was silk on my tongue, marrow I could eat with a knife and fork, a subtle balance of flavors and textures—and yet the white bone on the plate retained an echo of the visceral and the wild. It conjured what lurked in the shadows on that mountaintop where I fell so many times, and it evoked my mending body ensconced in that gleaming haute dining room, my crutch still at my side.

With bones, in other words, the possibilities for reincarnation are endless. A joint becomes a stock, which then becomes the base for *pot au feu*, or another rich, meaty stew. I've even taken to roasting cuts from animals on racks made from their bones, a roast beef on a bed of marrow bones. It's culinary id. At some point, though, my fridge started to look like a boneyard, my hair smelled like veal, and I began to long for another life, one away from the stove and skipping on both legs. Still, I am grateful for the chance that being hobbled for a while presented me: to linger in the kitchen while things cooked slowly; then to grip the bones in my fist, use my teeth to strip the meat, and quietly relish the savagery—and the delicacy—of it all.

They Don't Have Tacos in the Suck

By Katharine Shilcutt

From *Houston Press*

In June 2010, blogger and web editor Katharine Shilcutt inherited Robb Walsh's mantle as food critic for the alternative weekly *Houston Press*. Since then, Shilcutt rarely has time to update her original blog SheEats, but she makes up for that on the *Press*'s blog Eating our Words.

"Can I have the hot dog, please?" I asked the woman inside the bright green Tacos D.F. truck on Long Point at Witte.

"You're ordering a hot dog?" teased my friend Ryan with a chuckle. He'd already placed his order for a *pastor* taco and a can of Coke at the window. "I thought we were doing a taco truck crawl."

"I'm getting a taco, too!" I grinned sheepishly, before placing an additional order for a taco *de cabeza*.

"Is that what I think it is?" asked Ryan as he eyed the cabeza. Shreds of fine beef from a cow's head a la *barbacoa* filled the double corn tortilla that the woman handed through the window, topped with a handful of raw white onions and cilantro leaves. Despite his initial misgivings over its provenance, he ate his half of the taco with relish—pronouncing it "great" when he was finished—and I remembered why I'd missed him so much.

Ryan was my best friend in college, where we fancied ourselves a couple of misfits at a highly conservative university that made both of us itchy and desperate with discomfort. We met on the first day of school our freshman year, both of us shunted into an off-campus apartment complex because the dorms were overflowing in the late '90s and, somehow, releasing 17-year-olds into the wild seemed like a good idea at the time.

Ryan couldn't cook. I had roommates that I hated. We bonded over shared meals in his apartment and nights spent commiserating with each other about the limited kinds of politics and religious dogma that teenagers understand while the other kids rushed sororities or went to Bible study. Until last week, I hadn't seen him in ten years.

After a few minutes, the woman in the Tacos D.F. truck handed over my hot dog. It was a small frank inside a small bun, but the whole thing was topped with a confetti blast of ketchup, mustard, mayonnaise, diced tomatoes, raw onions and pickled jalapeños that packed remarkably little heat. While I mused over the surprisingly sweet peppers, Ryan finished his other taco with gusto.

"Where else can you get real meat that someone bought themselves for $1?" he mused rhetorically "Where else can you get real meat that someone bought and then cooked right in front of you and handed to you for $1? You can't do that at Taco Bell."

When he'd emailed me that he was coming to Houston for the day, I assumed that it was to visit some of his Texas family he'd left behind after joining the Air Force one day out of the blue during college.

Ryan had been attracted to EOD—explosives ordnance disposal—upon enlisting and quickly advanced to Tech Sergeant as he discovered within himself a serious and previously unknown talent for defusing bombs. He'd done four tours since 2002, in both Iraq and Afghanistan. He married a lovely German girl in between and finally settled in Florida when he wasn't in some far-flung region with a terp at his side, sweeping for mines in vast deserts.

But the trip to Houston was for the tacos.

"What is the planned criteria/theme of our hunt?" Ryan wrote me in an email a few weeks before he came to town. "Keep an eye out for goat tacos."

We didn't find any goat tacos on Thursday afternoon, but it didn't matter. It was as though a decade hadn't passed, and we fell into the same easy rhythms of bullshitting and storytelling that we always had.

"So, you're really a food critic?" he asked as we finished our cans of Coke outside Tacos D.F.

"Yeah," I responded, with a little elaboration after some prompting on his part. Yes, it's my full-time job. Yes, I really do get paid to eat. No, I'm not anonymous. "But I want to hear about *your* job."

"Most of my friends are dead," Ryan responded immediately, point-blank. "My boss was killed last year." His faced darkened briefly. I didn't know what to say and stammered softly until he started talking again.

"Let's go hit the next one."

We climbed back into my SUV and drove until he pointed another taco truck out, his eyes scanning both sides of the road in a practiced motion. "Tacos Arcelia. Let's try them next."

Tacos Arcelia has two things going for it: The first thing is the 99-cent tacos that it advertises in bold black letters on the side of its second thing, a school bus that's been painted bright red and silver. There was already a line forming around noon on Thursday, so Ryan and I figured it was a sure bet.

We ordered a taco each—*lengua* for me, *chicharrones* for him—and stepped back to await our orders. Even working in the larger-than-average confines of a school bus, the crew was moving at a slow clip.

"You know that part in *Black Hawk Down* where an RPG gets lodged in a guy's chest but it doesn't go off?" asked Ryan idly while we waited.

"Uh, yeah. Although I hadn't thought of that movie—or that scene in years." I didn't ask why he asked me, wary of the answer. He told me anyway.

"That really happens."

I thought back to the time when Ryan and I were making dinner at his apartment one night, both 18 years old, and I'd stupidly thrown a handful of frozen okra into a deep pan of hot grease to fry, not knowing any better. I started a minor grease fire which we quickly put out, but my face and hands were pockmarked with grease burns that took a few years to fade. The burns hurt terribly and I avoided frying anything at all for at least another five years, scared to death by such a minor injury.

"Have you considered moving out of EOD?" I asked finally. "I know there are other areas of the Air Force you could go into," I added with a little laugh, hoping he wouldn't be offended by the suggestion that he leave an area which poses clear and constant danger to his life every single day that he's on duty.

"No way," Ryan replied. "If I stick it out another 10 years, I can retire on a full pension. Retired at 42. Can you imagine?"

I chuckled. "No, I definitely can't." Just then, our orders came up.

The corn tortillas were listless and anemic-looking, a pale color that was closer in hue to flour tortillas. My pile of diced lengua was equally pallid, and a bite of the tongue confirmed that it tasted as bland as it looked.

Ryan's taco, on the other hand, was filled with more vibrant-looking pieces of chicharron. The fatty skin was puffy and thick with a spicy red sauce that made me mourn the terrible lengua even more. Ryan was clearly proud of his choice, too, grinning as he finished the rest of the tortilla off.

The grin never left his face as he told me about his EOD training, about the dozens of minute tactical decisions and assessments that have to be made before even approaching a bomb or a mine or an IED. He also told me about how he rarely wears the 90-pound bombsuit meant to protect him from the 132 explosive devices he's defused in his decade with the Air Force.

"Everyone knows the bombsuit and everyone associates it with EOD," he said. "It's like everyone knows a firefighter's jacket and helmet. But it also weighs 90 pounds. So we make the choice: Carry around 90 pounds worth of equipment all day long, or be better and faster without it."

"And if I can be better and faster," he finished, "that means a bunch of 18-year-old kids can go home safely from the war. I'd rather sacrifice one of me than a bunch of them. At least, that's the way I look at it."

We stood in silence for a few seconds after that. I contemplated the ways in which one makes a decision like this every day, and the ways in which so many of my own memories of Ryan are tied to us being 18-year-old kids ourselves. I balled up our trash to throw it away, then we walked quietly back to my SUV to continue the tour.

"What will you do when you retire then?" I asked as we headed out. Would he and his wife enjoy their home in Florida, the new boat he just bought? He was briefly contemplative before answering.

"I want to do something quiet," he said. "You know, like become a firefighter."

We both laughed, although I knew he was quite serious. And suddenly the conversation had turned back again to our old favorite subject.

"I ate at this crazy Puerto Rican buffet up in Dallas recently," Ryan began as we drove on.

"Let's get a palate cleanser," I told Ryan as we pulled into the parking lot of the New Flea Market on Long Point at Pech. On the weekends, you can't find a space to park in the asphalt lot. But today, on an overcast Thursday afternoon, it was empty except for a few trucks parked haphazardly around Refresqueria Rio Verde.

"What are we getting here?" asked Ryan as we climbed out. "Do they have tacos?"

"Sure, they have tacos," I said. "But I thought we'd get something different in between. Do you like *elotes*?"

Elote, as I explained to Ryan, is basically corn on the cob. But instead of serving it with butter and salt, as us white folks tend to do, elote is served with *crema*, chile powder, lime juice and a host of other condiments that only seem foreign until you taste them all mixed together. Elote in a cup, the shaved kernels topped with a thick dollop of cream and a rough shake of chile powder, is mystifyingly comforting even if you've never had it before.

I ordered a cup for myself and a giant glass of *tamarindo* for us to split, while Ryan went whole hog and got an elote-on-the-cob. "I have corn on a stick!" he called out to me like a little kid. And between swigs of the sweet, apple-like tamarind juice, Ryan bluntly asked: "So, what happened? You were married for, like, a second."

Ryan himself has been married for six years. As so often happens with Air Force men, he met a pretty German girl while stationed at the Rammstein Air Base in southwestern Germany on the edge of the hilly, green *Pfälzerwald* forest. They were married in a castle. She is beautiful, with expressive blue eyes and a kind face.

I gave Ryan a brief rundown of my own fumbling attempt at marriage, the millions of tiny ways in which my ex-husband and I both failed at the institution every single day until we were both relieved to finally call it quits a year and a half later. Ryan listened with a playful smirk on his face as I explained how I fell into the trap of being pursued by a good-looking athletic-type—the weak spot of too many nerdy wallflowers the world over, men and women alike—and refuted at least one point.

"You're not really a nerd," he laughed. "You're more of a pop culture dork. You're a female Chuck Klosterman."

"I don't know that being a female Chuck Klosterman is such a great thing!" I replied. The smirk was still on his face. He was waiting for his turn; I could tell. I promptly shut my mouth and let him have it.

"Well, the missus and I," he began grandly, "have been together since day one." He told me the story of their brief courtship and the mutually agreed-upon eventuality that they were destined to be together, so why spend useless years dating? It was sweeping and romantic and beautiful and everything you could want for your best friend, or for anyone with a good heart who deserves to meet another good-hearted soul in this world.

"When we got married," he told me, "I asked her: 'How much of what happens over there do you want me to tell you?'" It suddenly occurred to me that I wouldn't know the answer to that question were I married to a military man myself. But Ryan's wife knew the answer immediately: She wanted to know everything.

Those shared experiences became a bond between them, and Ryan grew even closer to her over time than he imagined possible. One day he told her: "You're my reason."

"My reason?" she wanted to know.

"You're the reason I want to come home after every deployment," he told her. "When I'm sent away on a six-month deployment, I just picture myself walking home to you. It's what gets me through. I picture myself walking over a huge mountain for six months until I see you again."

We sat and grinned goofily at the mountain Ryan had traced in the air with his hands. His corn-on-a-stick was gone, my cup was empty.

"My palate is cleansed," he announced happily. It was time to move on.

Ryan and I had been driving for a while, for many blocks since our "palate cleanser" of *elotes* at Refresqueria Rio Verde. I knew he was wondering why I passed other taco trucks and failed to pull up to them, but I had a plan.

In my mind, I knew this stop would be our last taco truck of the day. I had to pick my cousin up from the airport soon, and Ryan had to get back on the road.

I pulled into our final destination: El Ultimo, a brightly decorated taco truck near Long Point and Wirt. Its parking lot was already busy, a line had already formed outside that was composed entirely of blue collar workers off for lunch, equal parts white, black and Hispanic. I've made no secret of the fact that El Ultimo is my favorite taco truck in town, and I have followed it over the years as it moves a few blocks up and down Long Point.

"On the weekends," I told an impressed Ryan, "it has a waitress who takes your order, since the line gets so long."

"So this is your favorite, huh?" he said, eying the simple menu and wondering what exactly made this spot so special.

"Yes. You'll see."

The wait at El Ultimo was the longest of the afternoon, and Ryan and I had run out of polite conversation. He told me about the few phrases he's learned working in Afghanistan, about how Pashto and Dari only sound alike on the surface. Once you get to know them, he said, you can immediately spot the differences when you hear them spoken, intermingled, on the streets.

He tried to teach me a few phrases in Pashto. "Move it, asshole!" was one of them. I couldn't pick it up. I was too busy laughing absurdly, thinking of Ryan in a wholly foreign country, yelling out practiced Pashto phrases like these to his terp in what must now seem like a completely normal occurrence to him.

We commiserated about how rusty our Spanish had gotten over the years, useful these days only for ordering food at taco trucks. Ryan was even more out of practice, blaming it on the sad dearth of taco trucks back home in Florida. "There are only, like, two where I live," he grumbled. And he told me about how his German wife was startled one morning by the realization that she had started to dream in English.

When our tacos came out, Ryan finally saw what I did in El Ultimo: The tacos here are on soft, homemade flour tortillas—not corn, interestingly—and come with more than just the standard handful of cilantro and onions. Green slices of avocado and white crumbles of *queso fresco* fill the tacos, too, along with our chosen meats: fatty shreds of barbacoa and annatto-hued *pastor*.

Ryan gulped his taco down, pausing only briefly to admire the avocado and cheese on top. Then he ordered three more.

"This is your favorite, huh?" he asked again.

I nodded once more, pleased.

"Well, it's my favorite too." He smiled. And then: "I don't think I can eat any more tacos."

"Neither can I," I laughed back. We went back to the car with his extra tacos, and were nearly ready to go when Ryan said: "Katie, aren't you forgetting something?"

Only a few people call me Katie anymore; I thrilled to the sound of hearing the adolescent version of my name, as if time hadn't passed at all and I was still Katie, still 17-years-old and big-eyed and strong.

I was forgetting something: I hadn't taken his photo in front of the truck, as I'd done with all the others. I dug my camera back out of my purse as Ryan posed, hand out and thumb up, grinning. I snapped one final picture, and we packed it in.

The car ride back to Ryan's truck seemed to last almost as long as the crawl itself had. I listened hard to every last one of Ryan's words, even the awful ones and the cruel ones that involved horror stories of friends killed in battle. I listened as he told me about watching as weeping fathers carried their children into makeshift hospitals, limbs absent and blood reeling out of charred wounds. I listened as he told me about fathers who strapped bombs to their children's thin chests and sent them out to fight the battles their cowardly parents could not. I listened as he told me about watching a young girl's leg blown off by a crudely designed IED that he had not seen, was not able to defuse.

I listened as he told me about being blown up twice himself. He stared forward the entire time as he spoke, and I noticed for the first time what looked to be shrapnel wounds on his head. The curved wounds were barely noticeable except where the hair had stubbornly refused to grow back. I didn't ask about them. My chest burned as he spoke about being lucky enough to survive both times he was attacked. He'd never shot anyone, he assured me. But he'd shot *at* them.

I thought back to something he'd said earlier that day: "I'm happy to get bad guys and help people," he'd put it, simply and succinctly. This terrifying job makes him happy. This job that could wipe him out of existence in one trembling second makes him happy. Instead of happy thoughts, my mind was filled with horrific visions of Ryan dying in battle. I was ashamed of myself for thinking such a thing.

Before I could get a word out, we were back at his truck. Ryan was unstrapping his seat belt. Here was 10 years, gone in an afternoon.

"You know, I looked for you," he said, suddenly and without warning. Ryan had entered the Air Force on a whim between our junior and senior years of college, finally disillusioned enough with college after three years to make the leap. And although we kept in touch for a while, we never saw each other again. We finally lost contact entirely after his first deployment.

"I looked for you everywhere. I looked on Facebook and even MySpace, back in the day, and Googled you and then one day I found you. It was totally by accident. I was reading an article, and you had written it." He had sent me a message on Facebook later that day. I had been thrilled to hear from him, with no idea of how long he'd searched for me.

I had no idea what to say. Finally, all I could get out was: "I'm glad you did."

And then, because the hour was drawing so near: "I've got to get going." And I tried to follow it up with a casual, "What else are you doing to do in Houston today?"

"Nothing," Ryan said. "I'm driving back today. I really just came to see you."

So it wasn't just the tacos. And again, all I could manage was a short: "I'm glad you did." A smile. Unblinking eyes, because if I blinked, the tears would spill over and I'd be done for. I couldn't see Ryan's eyes at all; he never removed his sunglasses all day.

And just like that, his door was open. A brief hug and promises of a future visit—this time with his wife—and Ryan was gone. Here was 10 years and two hours, gone. I drove out of the parking lot, unable to look back, and drank the last of the apple-sweet tamarind juice until it was gone and I was home once again.

I Won't Have the Stomach for This

By Anna Stoessinger

From the *New York Times*

Native New Yorker, advertising writer, and self-professed
gastronome Anna Stoessinger inspired floods of blog posts
with this moving op-ed piece in the Sunday *Times*. In it, she
answers a question few of us will ever have to ask ourselves.

I am a ravenous, ungraceful eater. I have been compared to
a dog and a wolf, and have not infrequently been reminded to chew. I am always the first to finish what's on my plate,
and ever since I was a child at my mother's table, have perfected
the art of stealthily helping myself to seconds before anyone else
has even touched fork to frog leg. My husband and I have been
known to spend our rent money on the tasting menu at Jean
Georges, our savings on caviar or wagyu tartare. We plan our vaca-
tions around food—the province of China known for its chicken
feet, the village in Turkey that grows the sweetest figs, the town in
northwest France with the very best raclette.

So it was a jarring experience when, a few months ago, at 36
years old, I learned I had stomach cancer.

I had only mild symptoms at first: a slight pain below the breast-
bone when I swallowed, discomfort that felt like nerves or indiges-
tion. Two doctors told me it was nothing. "Take some Prilosec,"
they said, which made sense. We had just returned from a trip to
Italy. In Florence, we had eaten mounds of roast duck, crostini and

rich fish stews; maybe I just had heartburn. But the feeling lingered, and the hypochondriac in me went to the gastroenterologist.

It was a tumor. We got the call early on Friday morning. My husband and I were still in bed, and it took more than a moment to register. At my age, I am not supposed to have stomach cancer. In the United States, it's a disease that most commonly afflicts older, Asian men, and I am none of these. I have also parted with all my vices, save the occasional sugar binge. But after years of worrying that I might have cancer, years of, "Can you look at this? Is this a lump? What's this right here? No, here," I actually did.

I had only one thought about the possibility of death: the fear that I would have to part from my husband a half-century too soon. We had just married in October. We had just moved into a cottage in Connecticut. We had just discovered the simple pleasures of a happy routine. A calendar on the fridge. Roast chicken with leeks for dinner. Losing our life together was what death meant to me, and that, I think, is love.

Thankfully, my doctors assured me that death was a remote possibility. But I wasn't getting off easily; there were things to lose. First, with three rounds of intense chemotherapy, I lost my appetite. But that was only temporary. Then my surgeon told me that I needed a total gastrectomy—I would have part of my esophagus and all of my stomach permanently removed.

With nothing but a small intestine left to digest food, my gastronomic future would hold only small, frequent meals, consumed slowly and deliberately, without my characteristic gusto. Without abandon. Without—there would be a lot of without.

"You can live without a stomach," my doctor told me. I have often thought about what I could live without, if I had to: a savings account, an extra bedroom, the new Prada suede platform pump in burgundy. But a stomach never entered my mind. And food? It was so much more. As a little girl, sharing food with my mother was a solace, a joy, and a way of communicating. Sharing it with my husband has been as intimate as anything I've experienced. We fell in love one taste at a time: roadside cheeseburgers, bonito with ginger sauce, hazelnut gelato. After the first bite had lingered on our tongues, we'd say to each other: Wait for it. And then: Did you get that? The smoke? The spice? The texture? We always did.

And so, with just 10 days left with my trusted stomach, we set out to capture all that food meant—all the memories it conjured, all the happiness it brought. We were determined to eat as much and as well as possible. We made lists. What categories of food needed attention? Which meals did we want to recreate? We went from lowbrow to high, and everywhere in between. Peanut butter and jelly doughnuts, ginger ice cream, sashimi, grilled porterhouse, wild blueberries. We came up with a plan. Travel options were limited (health, timing), but we would go from Connecticut to Maine to New Brunswick, and finish in New York City three days before my surgery.

On the road, we ate candy in the car like kids. Then, at the White Barn Inn near Kennebunkport, Me., we ate a foie gras and fig torchon, which was velvety, buttery and dusted with pistachios; we ate butter-poached smoked lobster, the summery steam wafting up from the meat; and we tasted scallops with passion fruit coulis, thinly sliced disks of silky pleasure in a sweet, tangy sauce.

My mother made scallops like nobody else. Perfectly seared and turned in butter. Simple and divine. And she served them at her hugely popular, often impromptu, dinner parties. Watching her cook was what I imagined it was like to watch Jackson Pollock paint. She hurled salt and spices. Spun sugar like a sculptor. Emptied a bottle of rosemary onto a leg of lamb, massaged it with butter into the meat, and turned out a masterpiece. I surged with pride when the first guests arrived and remarked on the wonderful smells sailing out of the kitchen, to whose creation I alone had been witness.

My father was something of a tyrant, and every year my mother and I went to southern France to escape him. We were like war buddies on leave there, and we ate like queens. We drank tea out of giant bowls and picked lavender and stayed at wonderful old inns with names like L'Hermitage. There were cheese courses and pastries and the most delicious filet of sole I've ever encountered. There was also a deep and unwavering friendship between my mother and me, the tastes and smells of the food we shared overpowering even our worst memories of my father.

Those summers came back to me at our next stop: the Kingsbrae Arms in St. Andrews, New Brunswick, which had an exquisite dining room, gardens full of lavender and a chef who studied in the south of France. There we sat down to a wild boar terrine and Guinness vegetable soup with rosemary whipped cream. It was sublime and hinted of beef, celery, sweet carrot and earth. Finally, there was a warm apple and cinnamon tarte tartin—not too sweet, not too tart and not quite large enough. I ate mine and half of my husband's as well, and yearned for more.

It had been a long time since I had experienced such satisfying fullness. There was comfort and exuberance, a familiar feeling like a long embrace, a coming in from the cold—that I fear I will not know again. I know I will mourn my loss. Because for me, food—and eating it with abandon—is about shared experience. It's about love and memory and the capacity to conquer even the worst hours with something warm and wonderful.

But let me be clear: I am unspeakably lucky. Had my diagnosis come even three or four months later, my prognosis would have been much, much darker. I had the surgery two weeks ago, and thankfully everything went smoothly. Once I've recovered a bit more, I will be able to eat again. In the future, my meals will be little intermissions throughout the day. Overtures, not full symphonies. They will be small, but I will try to make them grand. Even if it's just a spoonful of pudding. And I would give up all of my organs for the possibility of many more years with my beloved husband.

We had our last good meal together—our last of the old meals—in Manhattan, at Le Bernardin. It's the best place in the city for a final meal with a stomach, the best place in the city, arguably, for any meal. When I called the hostess for a last-minute table, I was told that the only seating they had was at 10:45. I pulled out the big guns: "I have stomach cancer, and this is literally my last meal with a stomach."

"Well," she said, irritated, "I suppose we can seat you at 5:30."

What a town. And what a magnificent meal it was.

Recipe Index

First-Boil Syrup, (from "Sweet Spot"), 51

Minestrone (from "How to Live Well"), 88–89

Homemade Mayonnaise (from "Still Life with Mayonnaise"), 96

Lasagna Bolognese (from "Lasagne Bolognese"), 105–110

Pot-Roasted Celery Root with Olives and Buttermilk (from "The Forager at Rest"), 114–115.

Walnut Cake (from "The Forager at Rest"), 115–116

Best Guess Wonton Soup (from "The Legacy that Wasn't: Wonton Soup"), 234–236

Sneaky Whole-Wheat Chocolate Chip Cookies (from "Curious Cookies"), 239–240

Coconut Cake (from "Sweet Southern Dream"), 253–254

Lemon Layer Cake (from "Sweet Southern Dream"), 255–256

PERMISSIONS ACKNOWLEDGMENTS

About the Editor

Holly Hughes is a writer, the former executive editor of Fodor's Travel Publications, and author of *Frommer's 500 Places for Food and Wine Lovers*. She has edited the Best Food Writing series since its inception in 2000. Visit her website at hollyahughes.net.

Submissions for Best Food Writing 2013

Submissions and nominations for *Best Food Writing 2013* should be forwarded no later than May 15, 2013, to Holly Hughes at *Best Food Writing 2013*, c/o Da Capo Press, 44 Farnsworth Street, Boston MA 02210, or emailed to best.food@perseusbooks.com. We regret that, due to volume, we cannot acknowledge receipt of all submissions.